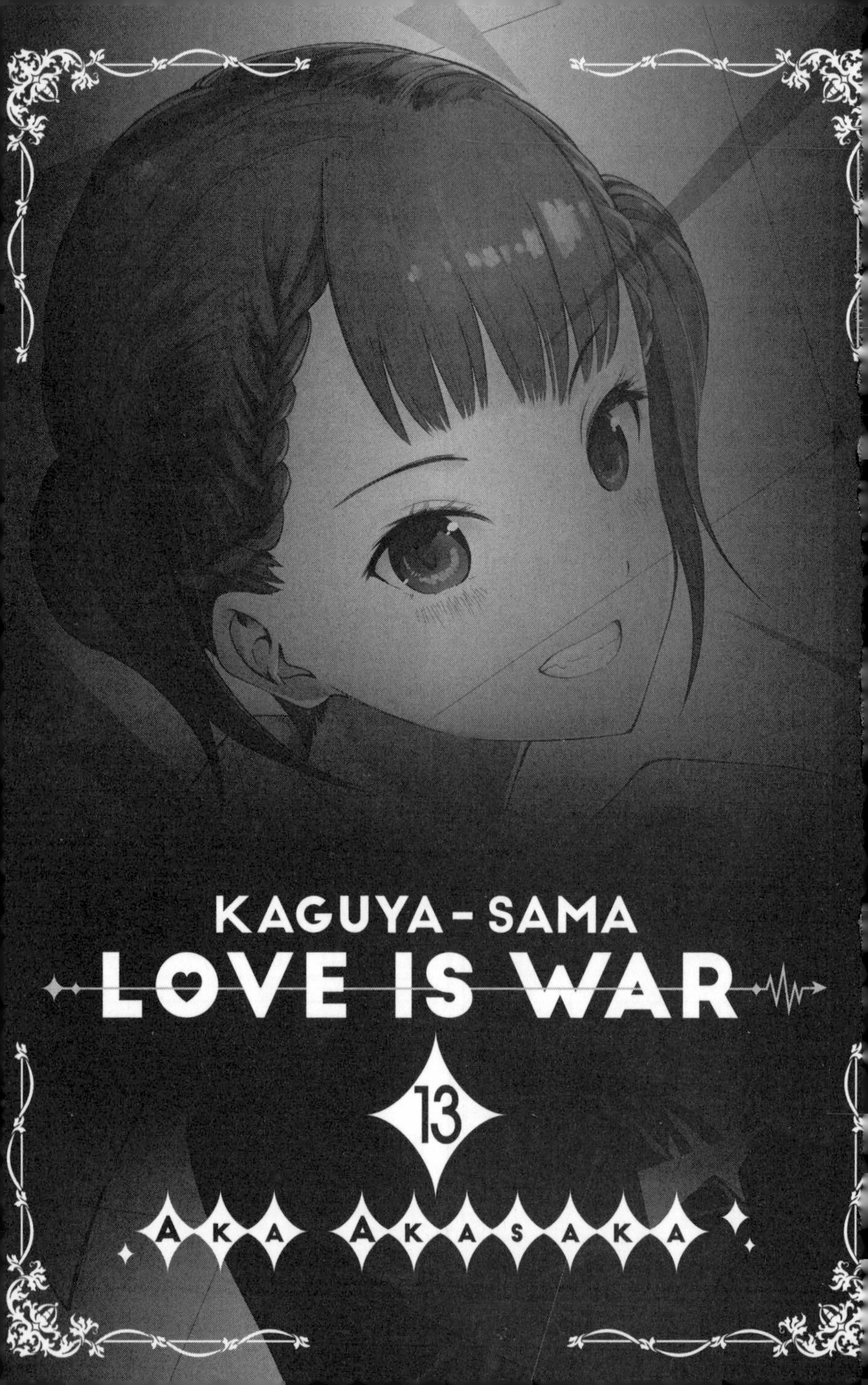
KAGUYA-SAMA
LOVE IS WAR
13
AKA AKASAKA

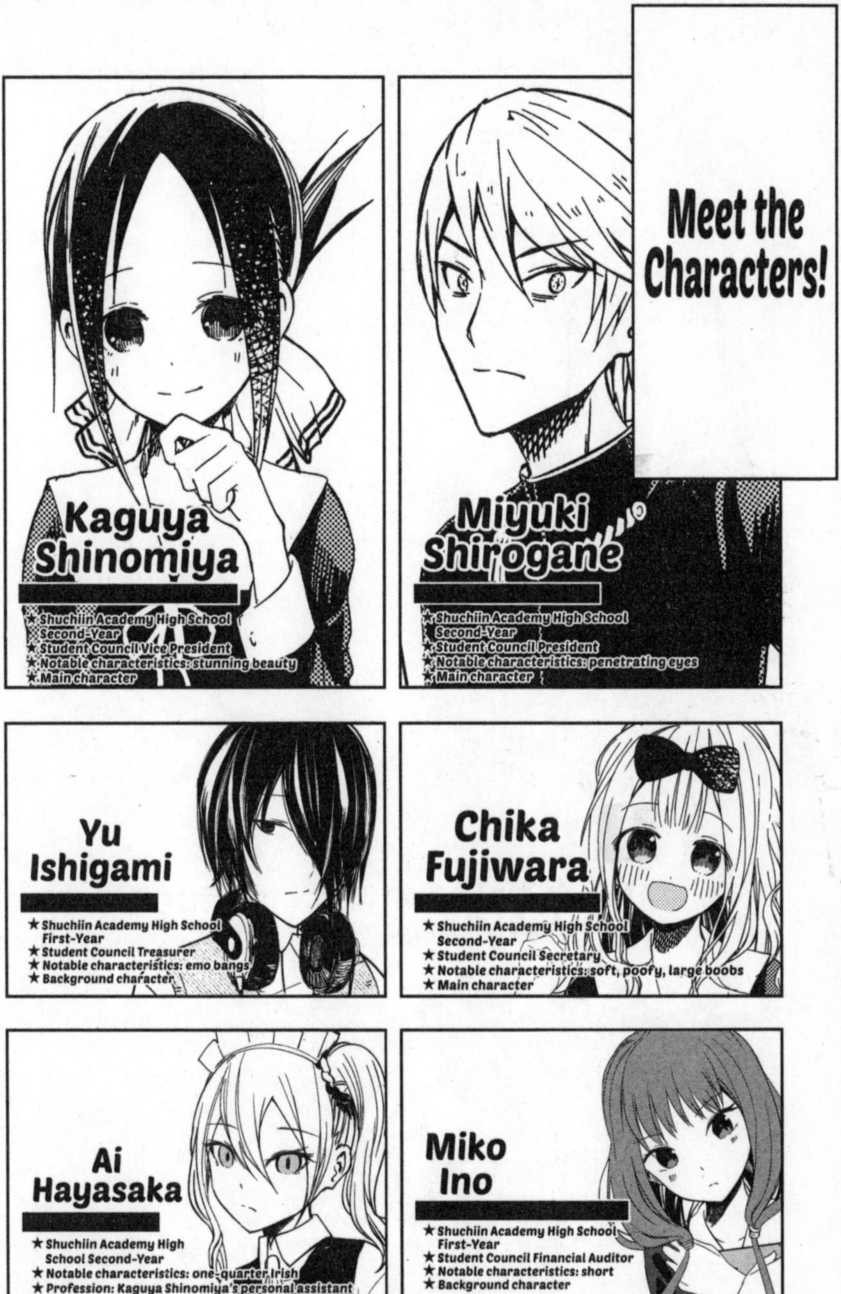
Meet the Characters!
Miyuki Shirogane
★Shuchiin Academy High School Second-Year
★Student Council President
★Notable characteristics: penetrating eyes
★Main character
Kaguya Shinomiya
★Shuchiin Academy High School Second-Year
★Student Council Vice President
★Notable characteristics: stunning beauty
★Main character
Chika Fujiwara
★Shuchiin Academy High School Second-Year
★Student Council Secretary
★Notable characteristics: soft, poofy, large boobs
★Main character
Yu Ishigami
★Shuchiin Academy High School First-Year
★Student Council Treasurer
★Notable characteristics: emo bangs
★Background character
Miko Ino
★Shuchiin Academy High School First-Year
★Student Council Financial Auditor
★Notable characteristics: short
★Background character
Ai Hayasaka
★Shuchiin Academy High School Second-Year
★Notable characteristics: one-quarter Irish
★Profession: Kaguya Shinomiya's personal assistant

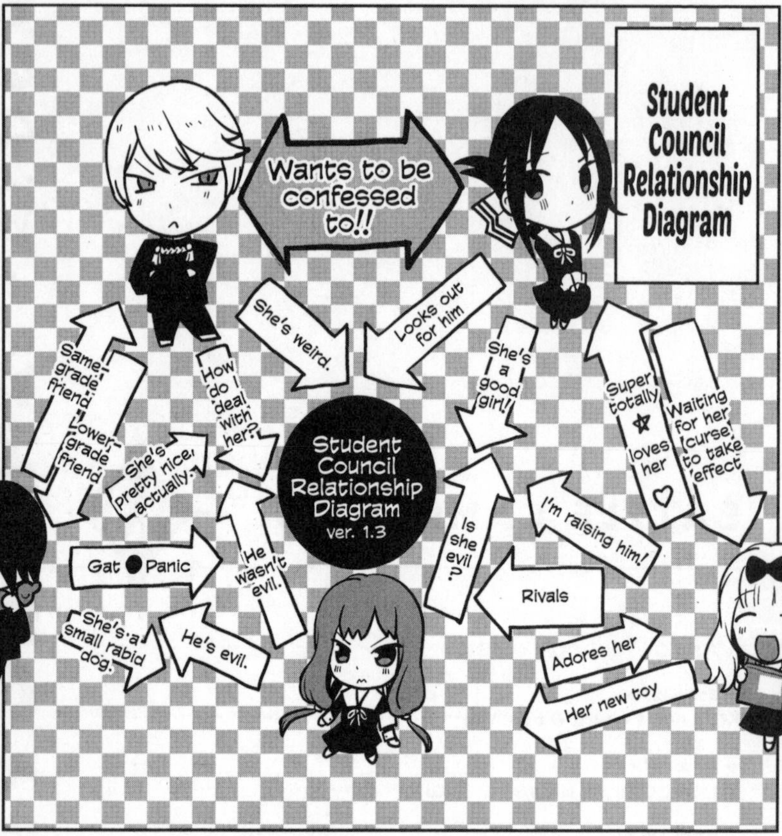
Student Council Relationship Diagram
Wants to be confessed to!!
Looks out for him
She's weird.
She's a good girl!
Super totally ☆ loves her ♡
Waiting for her curse to take effect
Same-grade friend
Lower-grade friend
How do I deal with her?
She's pretty nice, actually.
Student Council Relationship Diagram ver. 1.3
Is she evil?
I'm raising him!
Gat ● Panic
He wasn't evil.
Rivals
She's a small rabid dog.
He's evil.
Adores her
Her new toy

The battle campaigns thus far...

The two main characters hail from eminent families and are of good character. Shuchiin Academy is home to the most promising and brilliant students. It is there that, as members of the student council, Vice President Kaguya Shinomiya and President Miyuki Shirogane meet. An attraction is immediately apparent between them... But six months have passed and still nothing! The two are too proud to be honest with themselves—let alone each other. Instead, they are caught in an unending campaign to induce the other to confess their feelings first. In love, the journey is half the fun! This is a comedy about young love and a game of wits... Let the battles begin!

BATTLE CAMPAIGNS ◆13◆

◆ Battle 122 ◆
Kaguya Wants to Confess ··· 5

◆ Battle 123 ◆
Kaguya's Culture Festival ··· 25

◆ Battle 124 ◆
Yu Ishigami's Culture Festival ····································· 45

◆ Battle 125 ◆
Kozue Makihara Wants to Have Fun ··························· 65

◆ Battle 126 ◆
Chika Fujiwara Wants to Unmask ······························· 85

◆ Battle 127 ◆
Miyuki Shirogane's Culture Festival ························· 105

◆ Battle 128 ◆
Kaguya Wants to Shoot ·· 125

◆ Battle 129 ◆
Miyuki Shirogane Wants to Make Her Confess, Part 4 ···· 145

◆ Battle 130 ◆
Tsubame Koyasu Wants to Say No ······························ 165

◆ Battle 131 ◆
Miyuki Shirogane Wants to Make Her Confess, Part 5 ···· 185

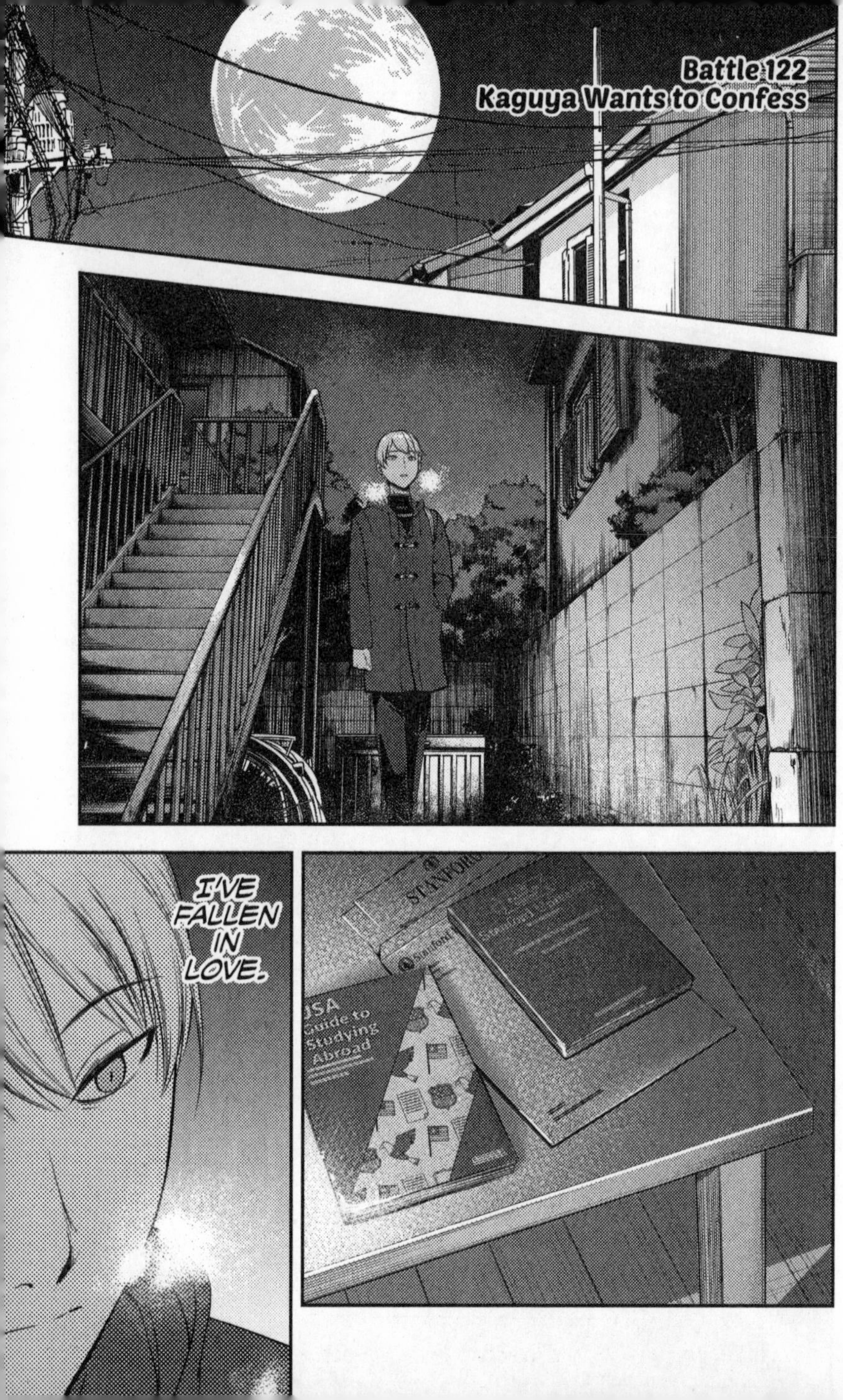
Battle 122
Kaguya Wants to Confess
STANFORD
Stanford
USA
Guide to
Studying
Abroad
I'VE FALLEN IN LOVE.

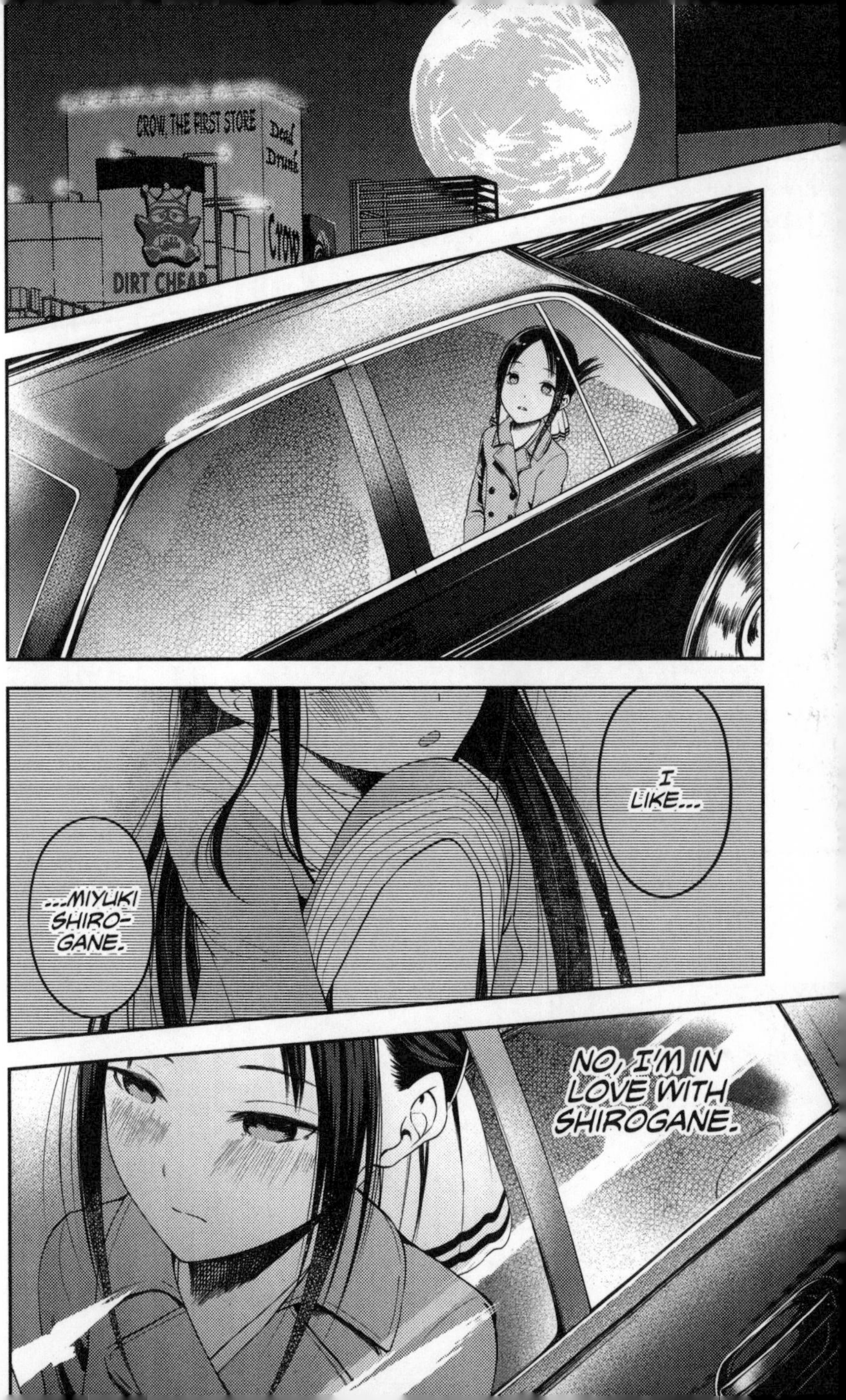

CROW, THE FIRST STORE
Dead Drunk
DIRT CHEAP
CROW
I LIKE...
...MIYUKI SHIRO-GANE.
NO, I'M IN LOVE WITH SHIROGANE.

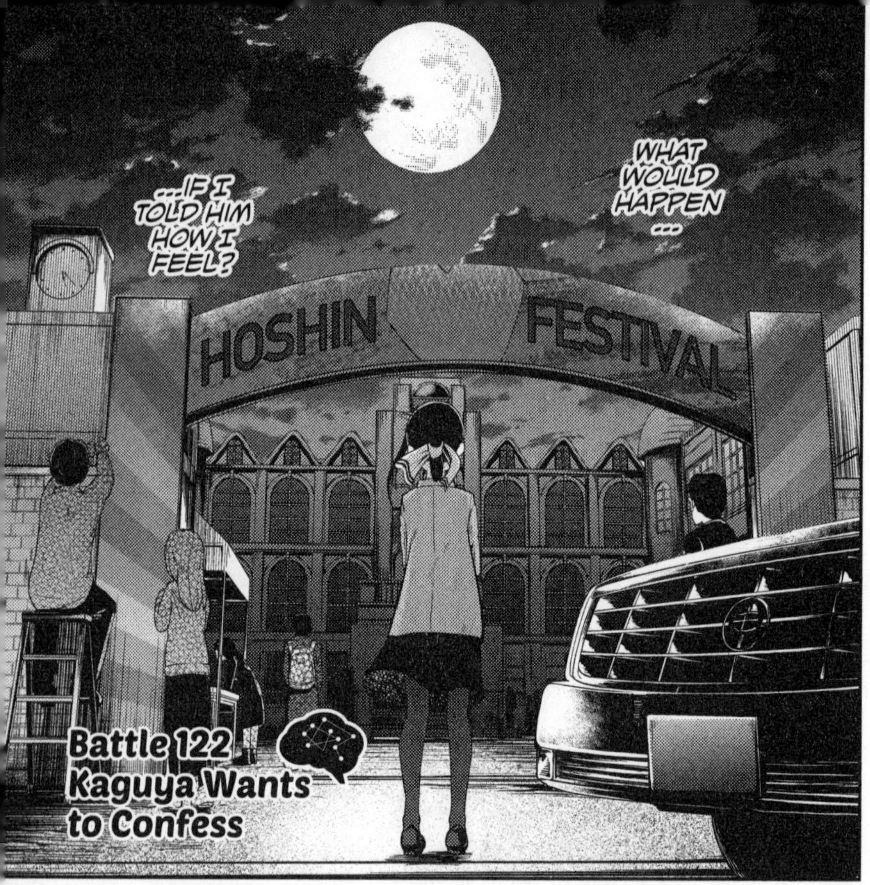
WHAT WOULD HAPPEN...
...IF I TOLD HIM HOW I FEEL?
HOSHIN FESTIVAL
Battle 122 Kaguya Wants to Confess

FIRST DAY OF THE FESTIVAL (5:23 A.M.)

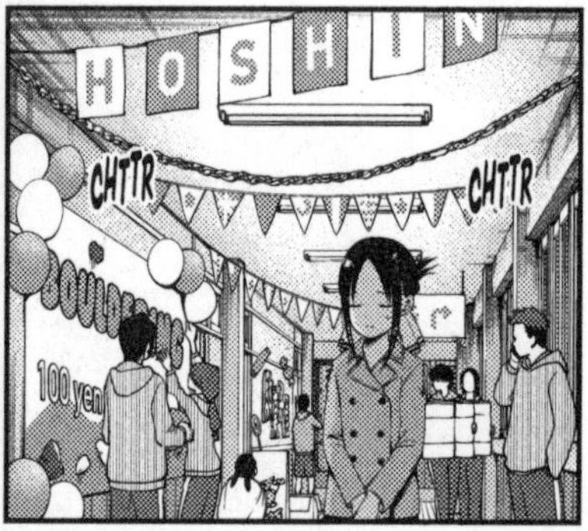
HOSHIN
CHTTR
CHTTR
100 yen

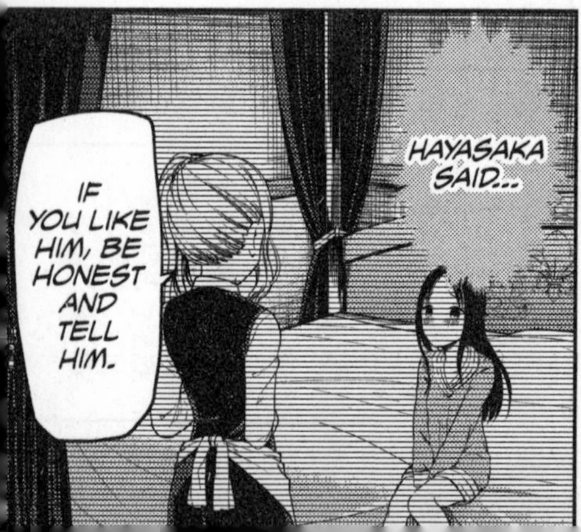
HAYASAKA SAID...
IF YOU LIKE HIM, BE HONEST AND TELL HIM.

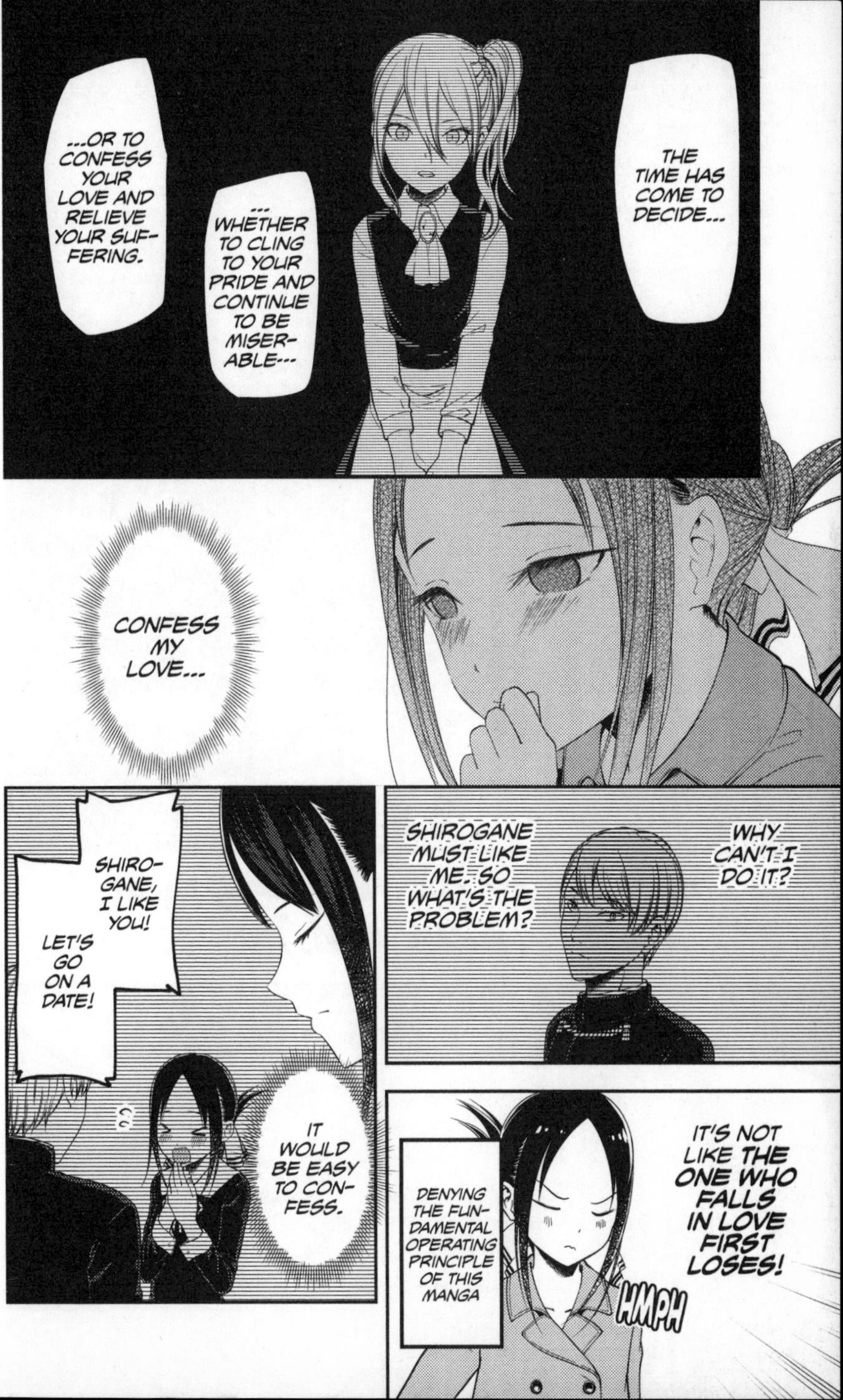
THE TIME HAS COME TO DECIDE...
...WHETHER TO CLING TO YOUR PRIDE AND CONTINUE TO BE MISERABLE...
...OR TO CONFESS YOUR LOVE AND RELIEVE YOUR SUFFERING.
CONFESS MY LOVE...
WHY CAN'T I DO IT?
SHIROGANE MUST LIKE ME. SO WHAT'S THE PROBLEM?
IT'S NOT LIKE THE ONE WHO FALLS IN LOVE FIRST LOSES!
DENYING THE FUNDAMENTAL OPERATING PRINCIPLE OF THIS MANGA
HMPH
SHIROGANE, I LIKE YOU!
LET'S GO ON A DATE!
IT WOULD BE EASY TO CONFESS.

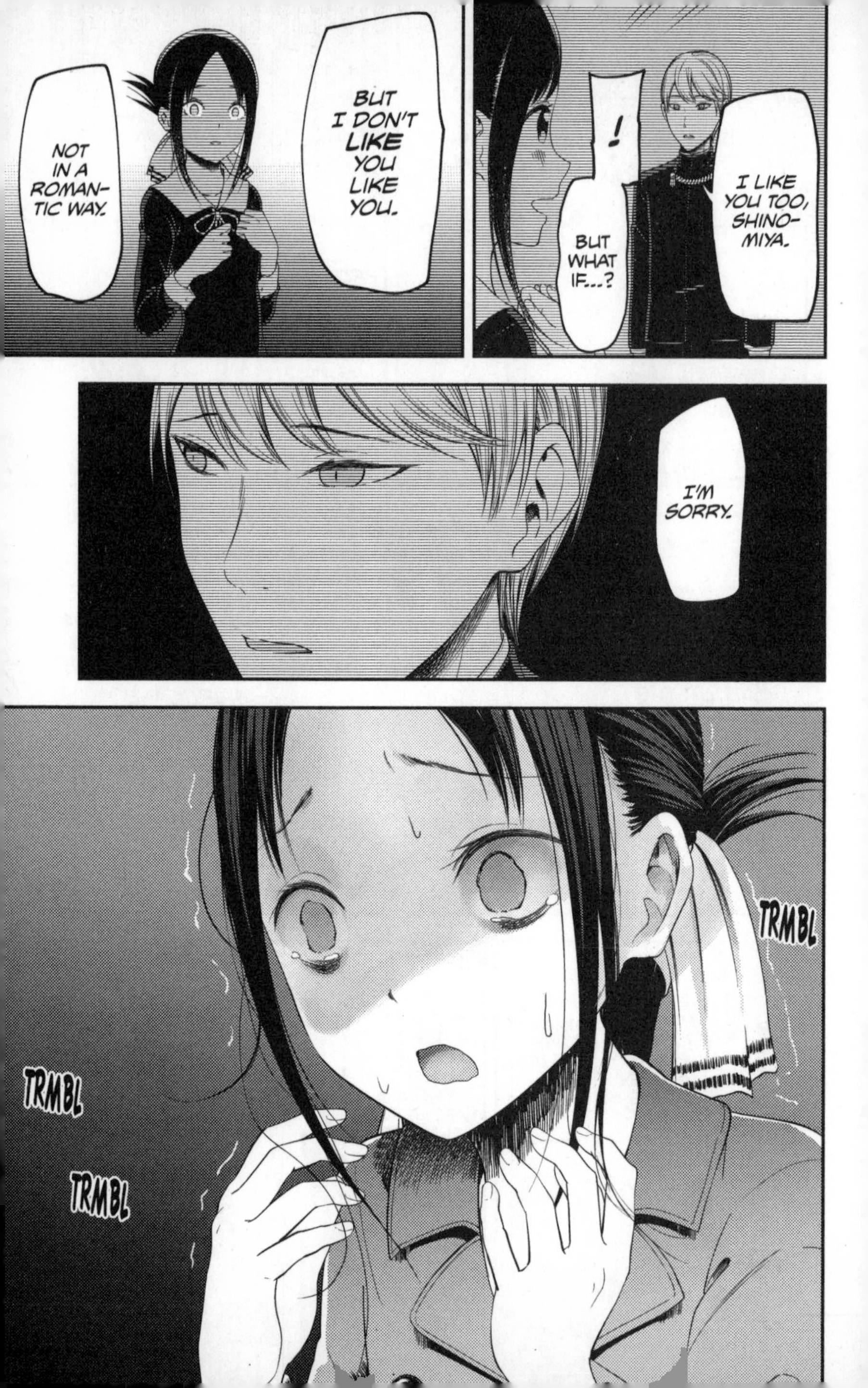
I LIKE YOU TOO, SHINOMIYA.
!
BUT WHAT IF...?
BUT I DON'T LIKE YOU LIKE YOU.
NOT IN A ROMANTIC WAY.
I'M SORRY.
TRMBL
TRMBL
TRMBL

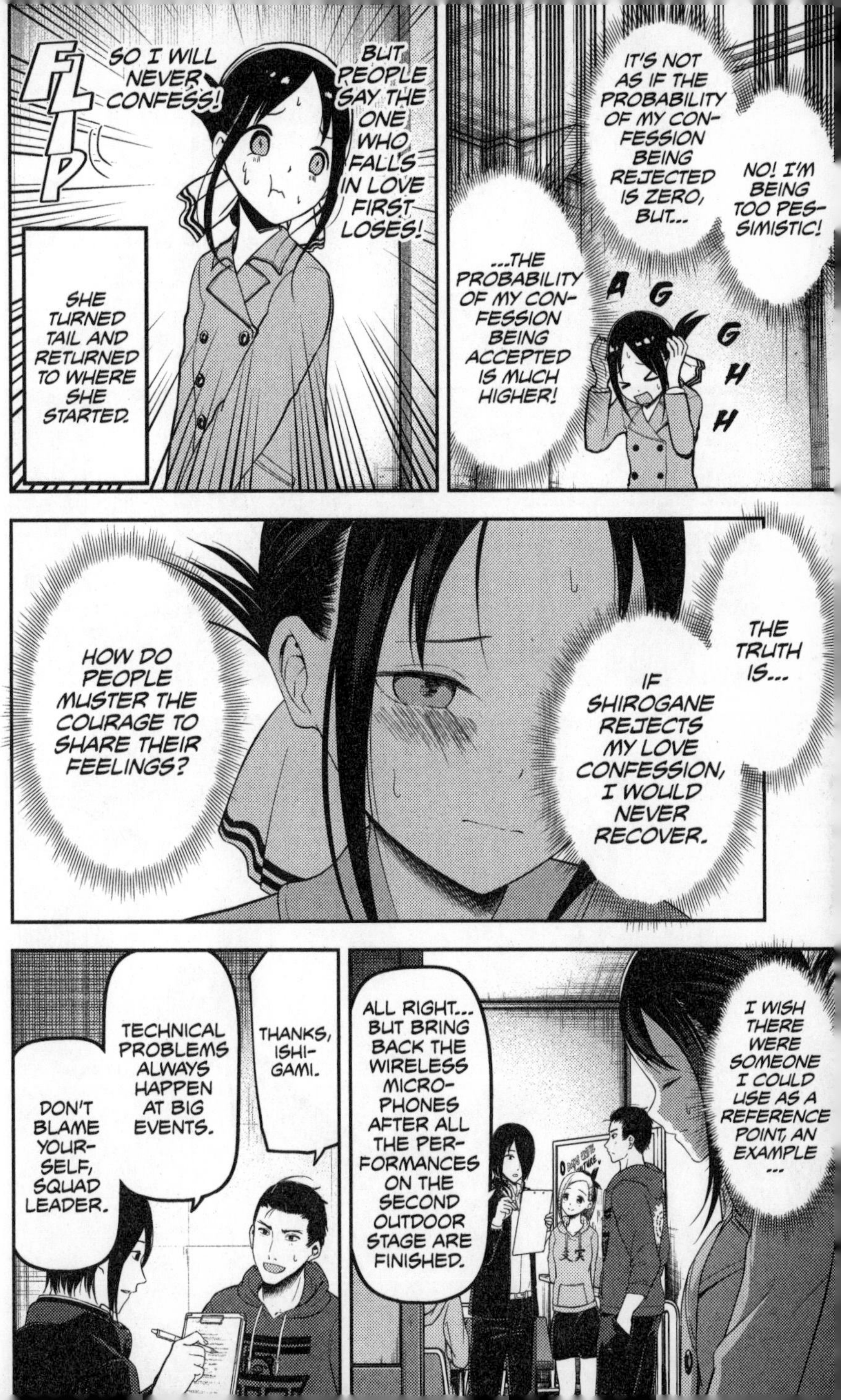
NO! I'M BEING TOO PESSIMISTIC!
IT'S NOT AS IF THE PROBABILITY OF MY CONFESSION BEING REJECTED IS ZERO, BUT...
...THE PROBABILITY OF MY CONFESSION BEING ACCEPTED IS MUCH HIGHER!
AGGHH
BUT PEOPLE SAY THE ONE WHO FALLS IN LOVE FIRST LOSES!
SO I WILL NEVER CONFESS!
FLIP
SHE TURNED TAIL AND RETURNED TO WHERE SHE STARTED.
THE TRUTH IS...
IF SHIROGANE REJECTS MY LOVE CONFESSION, I WOULD NEVER RECOVER.
HOW DO PEOPLE MUSTER THE COURAGE TO SHARE THEIR FEELINGS?
I WISH THERE WERE SOMEONE I COULD USE AS A REFERENCE POINT, AN EXAMPLE...
ALL RIGHT... BUT BRING BACK THE WIRELESS MICROPHONES AFTER ALL THE PERFORMANCES ON THE SECOND OUTDOOR STAGE ARE FINISHED.
THANKS, ISHIGAMI.
TECHNICAL PROBLEMS ALWAYS HAPPEN AT BIG EVENTS.
DON'T BLAME YOURSELF, SQUAD LEADER.

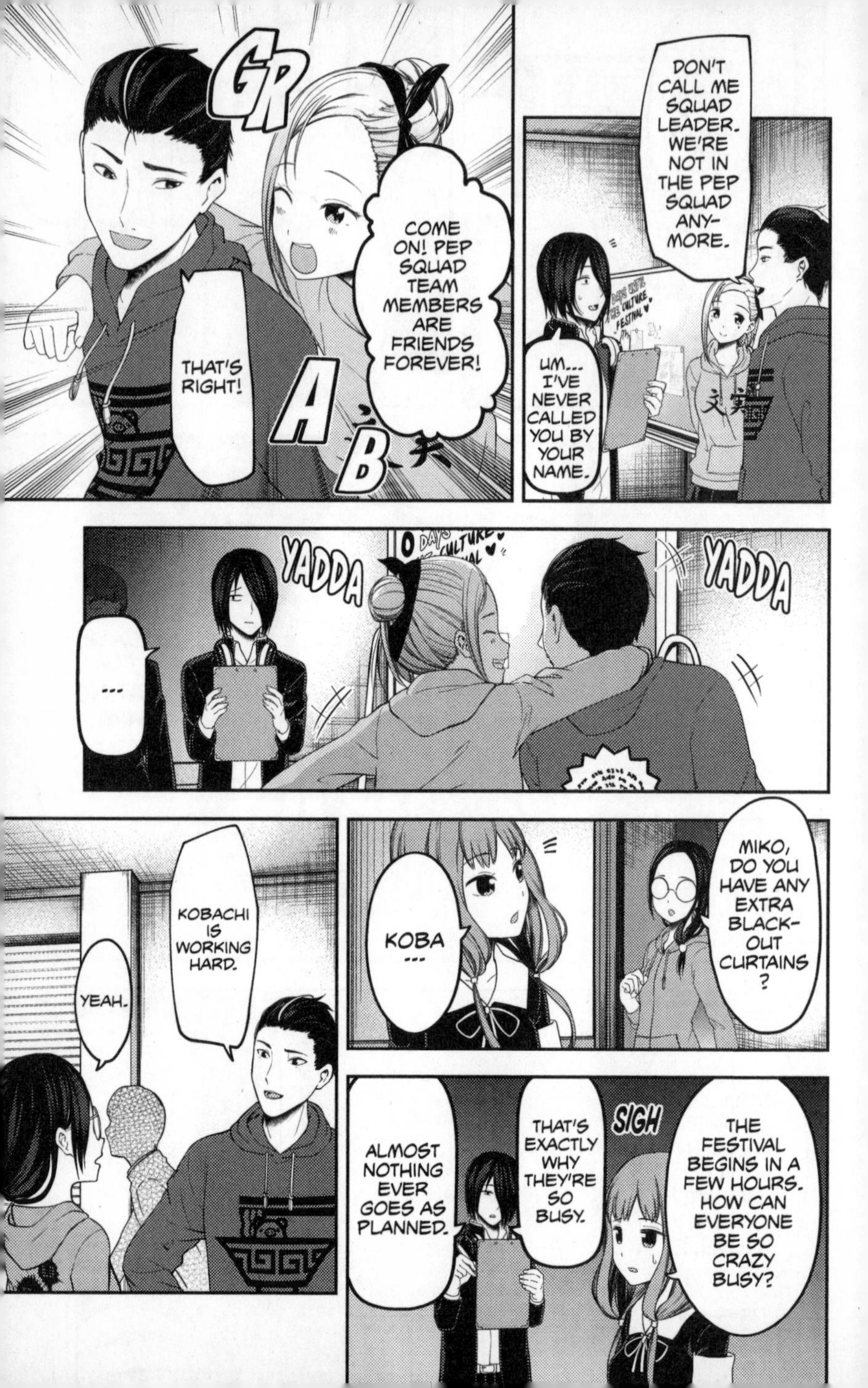
DON'T CALL ME SQUAD LEADER. WE'RE NOT IN THE PEP SQUAD ANYMORE.
UM... I'VE NEVER CALLED YOU BY YOUR NAME.
GR
COME ON! PEP SQUAD TEAM MEMBERS ARE FRIENDS FOREVER!
THAT'S RIGHT!
AB
YADDA
YADDA
...
MIKO, DO YOU HAVE ANY EXTRA BLACK-OUT CURTAINS?
KOBA...
THE FESTIVAL BEGINS IN A FEW HOURS. HOW CAN EVERYONE BE SO CRAZY BUSY?
SIGH
THAT'S EXACTLY WHY THEY'RE SO BUSY.
ALMOST NOTHING EVER GOES AS PLANNED.
KOBACHI IS WORKING HARD.
YEAH.

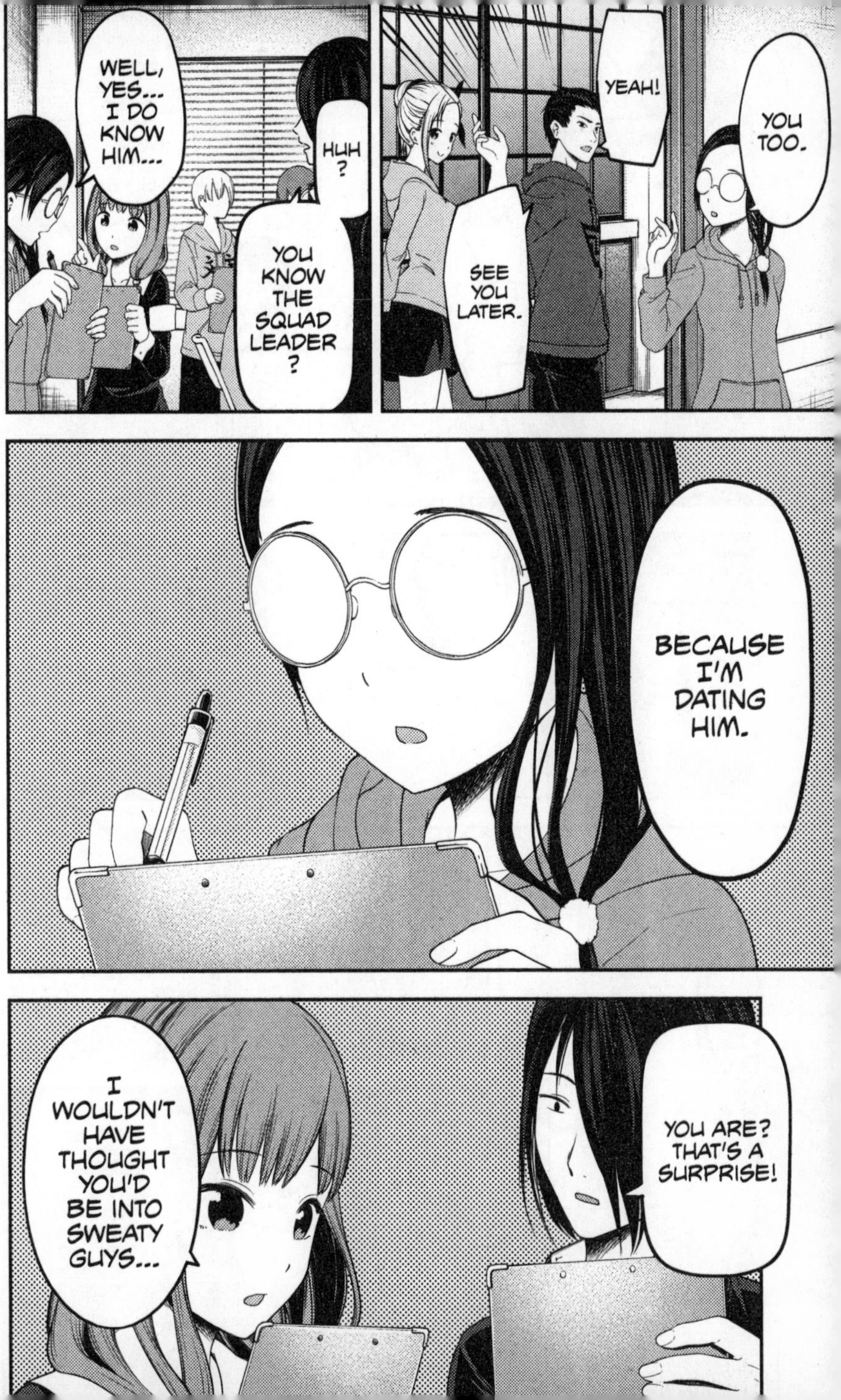
YOU TOO.
YEAH!
SEE YOU LATER.
HUH?
YOU KNOW THE SQUAD LEADER?
WELL, YES... I DO KNOW HIM...
BECAUSE I'M DATING HIM.
YOU ARE? THAT'S A SURPRISE!
I WOULDN'T HAVE THOUGHT YOU'D BE INTO SWEATY GUYS...

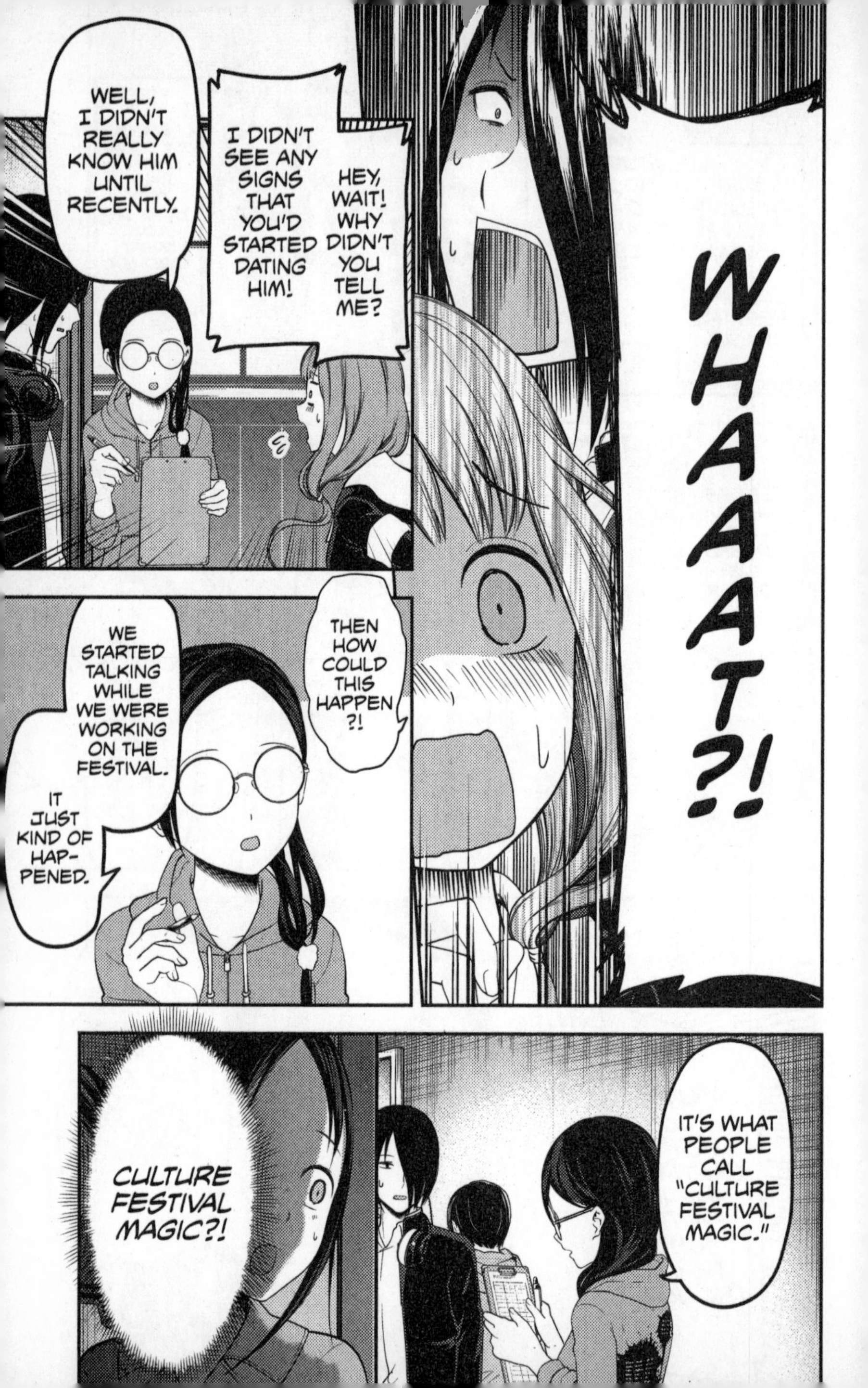
WHAAAAT?!
HEY, WAIT! WHY DIDN'T YOU TELL ME?
I DIDN'T SEE ANY SIGNS THAT YOU'D STARTED DATING HIM!
WELL, I DIDN'T REALLY KNOW HIM UNTIL RECENTLY.
THEN HOW COULD THIS HAPPEN?!
WE STARTED TALKING WHILE WE WERE WORKING ON THE FESTIVAL.
IT JUST KIND OF HAP-PENED.
IT'S WHAT PEOPLE CALL "CULTURE FESTIVAL MAGIC."
CULTURE FESTIVAL MAGIC?!

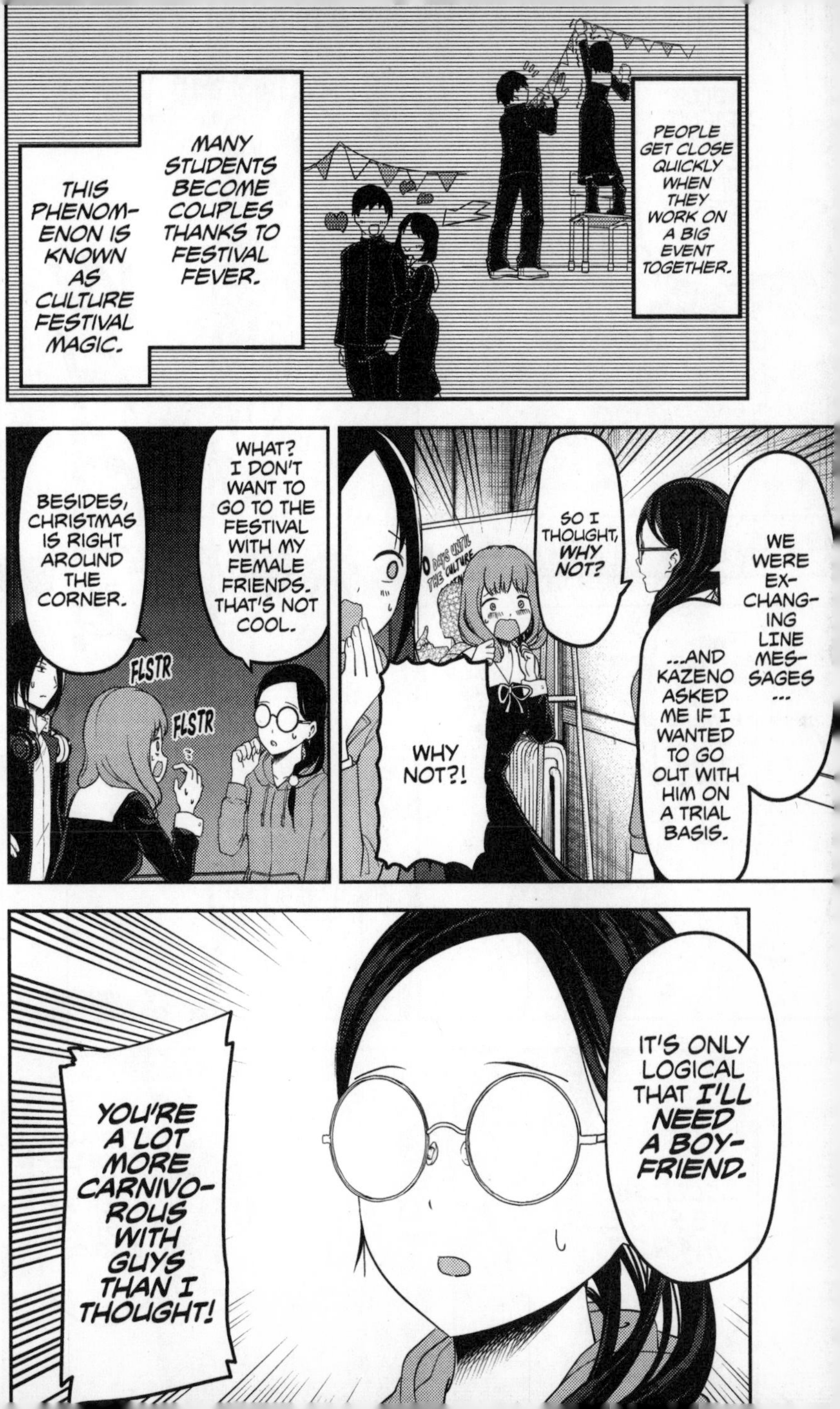
PEOPLE GET CLOSE QUICKLY WHEN THEY WORK ON A BIG EVENT TOGETHER.
MANY STUDENTS BECOME COUPLES THANKS TO FESTIVAL FEVER.
THIS PHENOMENON IS KNOWN AS CULTURE FESTIVAL MAGIC.
WE WERE EXCHANGING LINE MESSAGES...
...AND KAZENO ASKED ME IF I WANTED TO GO OUT WITH HIM ON A TRIAL BASIS.
SO I THOUGHT, WHY NOT?
WHY NOT?!
WHAT? I DON'T WANT TO GO TO THE FESTIVAL WITH MY FEMALE FRIENDS. THAT'S NOT COOL.
BESIDES, CHRISTMAS IS RIGHT AROUND THE CORNER.
FLSTR
FLSTR
IT'S ONLY LOGICAL THAT I'LL NEED A BOYFRIEND.
YOU'RE A LOT MORE CARNIVOROUS WITH GUYS THAN I THOUGHT!

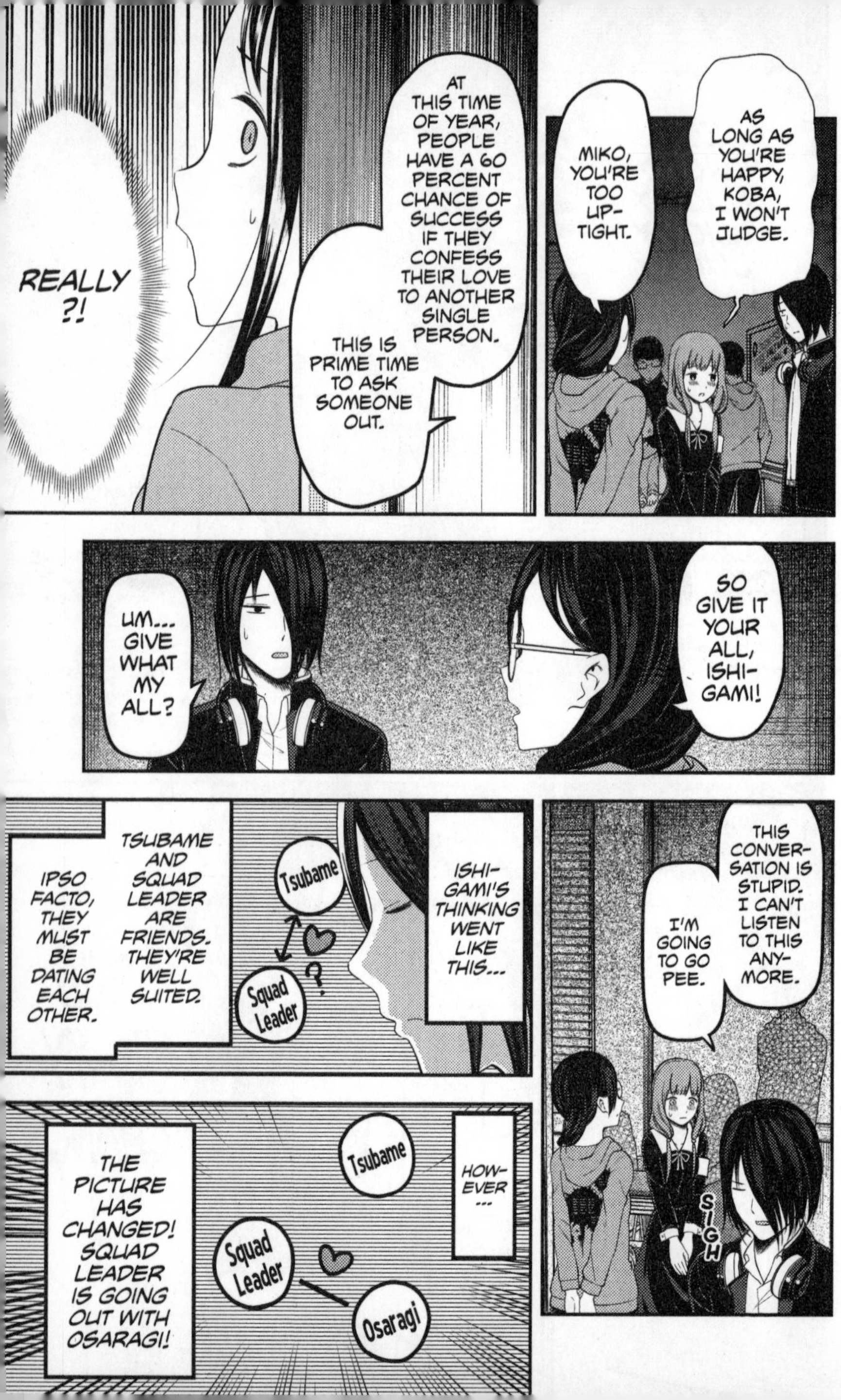
AS LONG AS YOU'RE HAPPY, KOBA, I WON'T JUDGE.
MIKO, YOU'RE TOO UPTIGHT.
AT THIS TIME OF YEAR, PEOPLE HAVE A 60 PERCENT CHANCE OF SUCCESS IF THEY CONFESS THEIR LOVE TO ANOTHER SINGLE PERSON.
THIS IS PRIME TIME TO ASK SOMEONE OUT.
REALLY?!
SO GIVE IT YOUR ALL, ISHIGAMI!
UM... GIVE WHAT MY ALL?
THIS CONVERSATION IS STUPID. I CAN'T LISTEN TO THIS ANYMORE.
I'M GOING TO GO PEE.
SIGH
ISHIGAMI'S THINKING WENT LIKE THIS...
Tsubame
Squad Leader
?
TSUBAME AND SQUAD LEADER ARE FRIENDS. THEY'RE WELL SUITED.
IPSO FACTO, THEY MUST BE DATING EACH OTHER.
HOWEVER...
Tsubame
Squad Leader
Osaragi
THE PICTURE HAS CHANGED! SQUAD LEADER IS GOING OUT WITH OSARAGI!

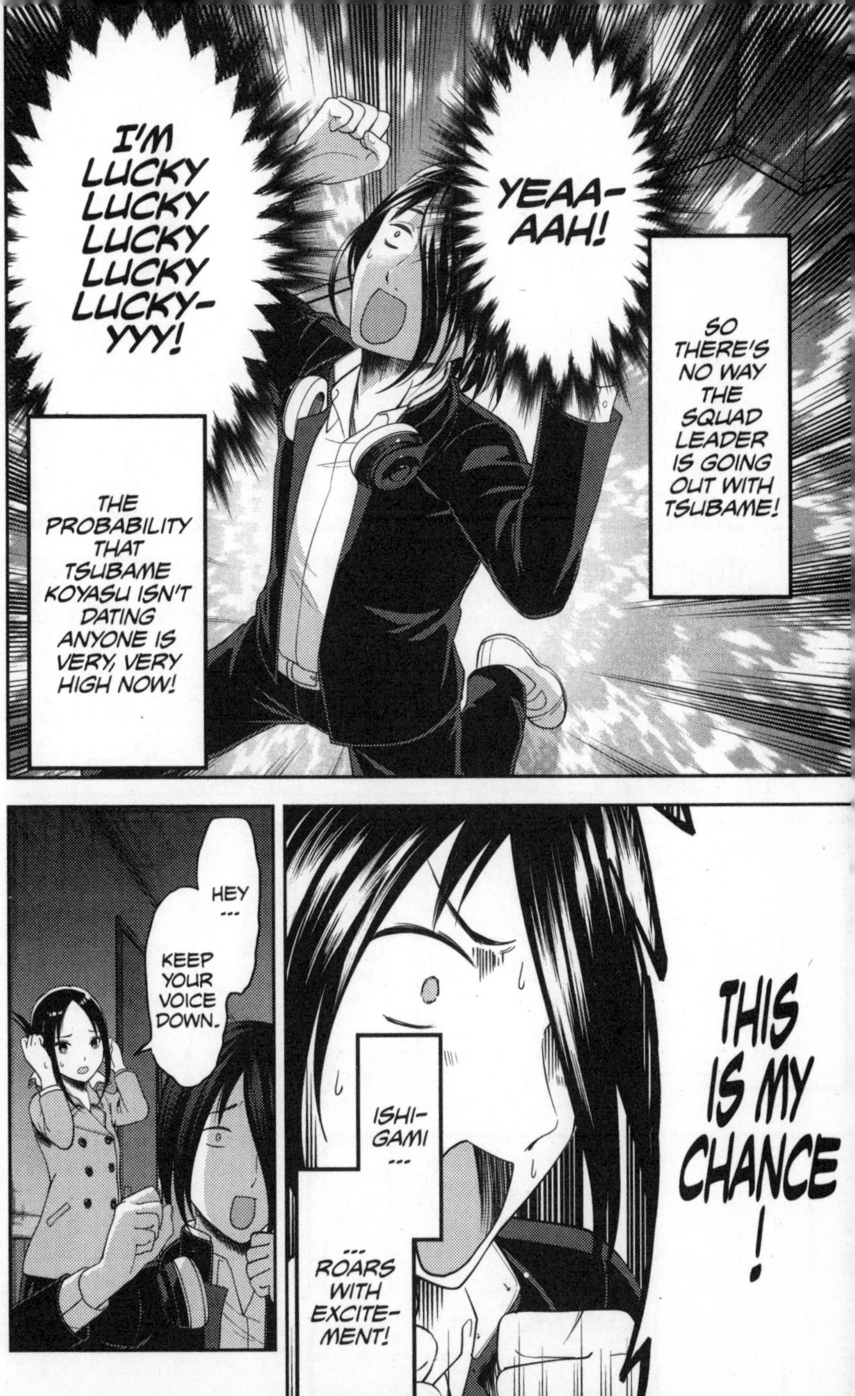

YEAAA-AAH!
SO THERE'S NO WAY THE SQUAD LEADER IS GOING OUT WITH TSUBAME!
I'M LUCKY LUCKY LUCKY LUCKY LUCKY-YYY!
THE PROBABILITY THAT TSUBAME KOYASU ISN'T DATING ANYONE IS VERY, VERY HIGH NOW!
THIS IS MY CHANCE!
ISHI-GAMI...
...ROARS WITH EXCITE-MENT!
HEY...
KEEP YOUR VOICE DOWN.

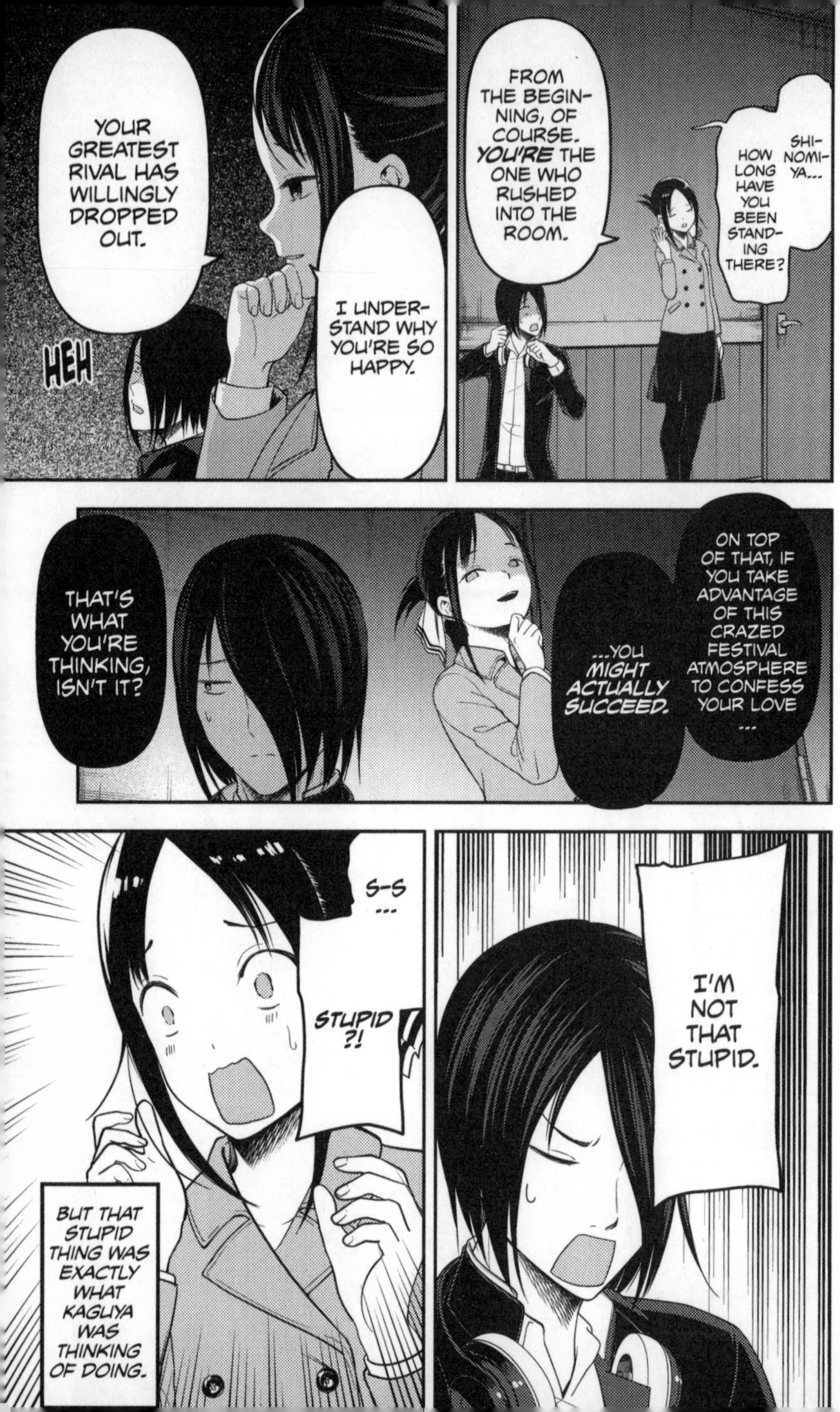
SHINOMIYA... HOW LONG HAVE YOU BEEN STANDING THERE?
FROM THE BEGINNING, OF COURSE. YOU'RE THE ONE WHO RUSHED INTO THE ROOM.
I UNDERSTAND WHY YOU'RE SO HAPPY.
YOUR GREATEST RIVAL HAS WILLINGLY DROPPED OUT.
HEH
ON TOP OF THAT, IF YOU TAKE ADVANTAGE OF THIS CRAZED FESTIVAL ATMOSPHERE TO CONFESS YOUR LOVE...
...YOU MIGHT ACTUALLY SUCCEED.
THAT'S WHAT YOU'RE THINKING, ISN'T IT?
I'M NOT THAT STUPID.
S-S...
STUPID?!
BUT THAT STUPID THING WAS EXACTLY WHAT KAGUYA WAS THINKING OF DOING.

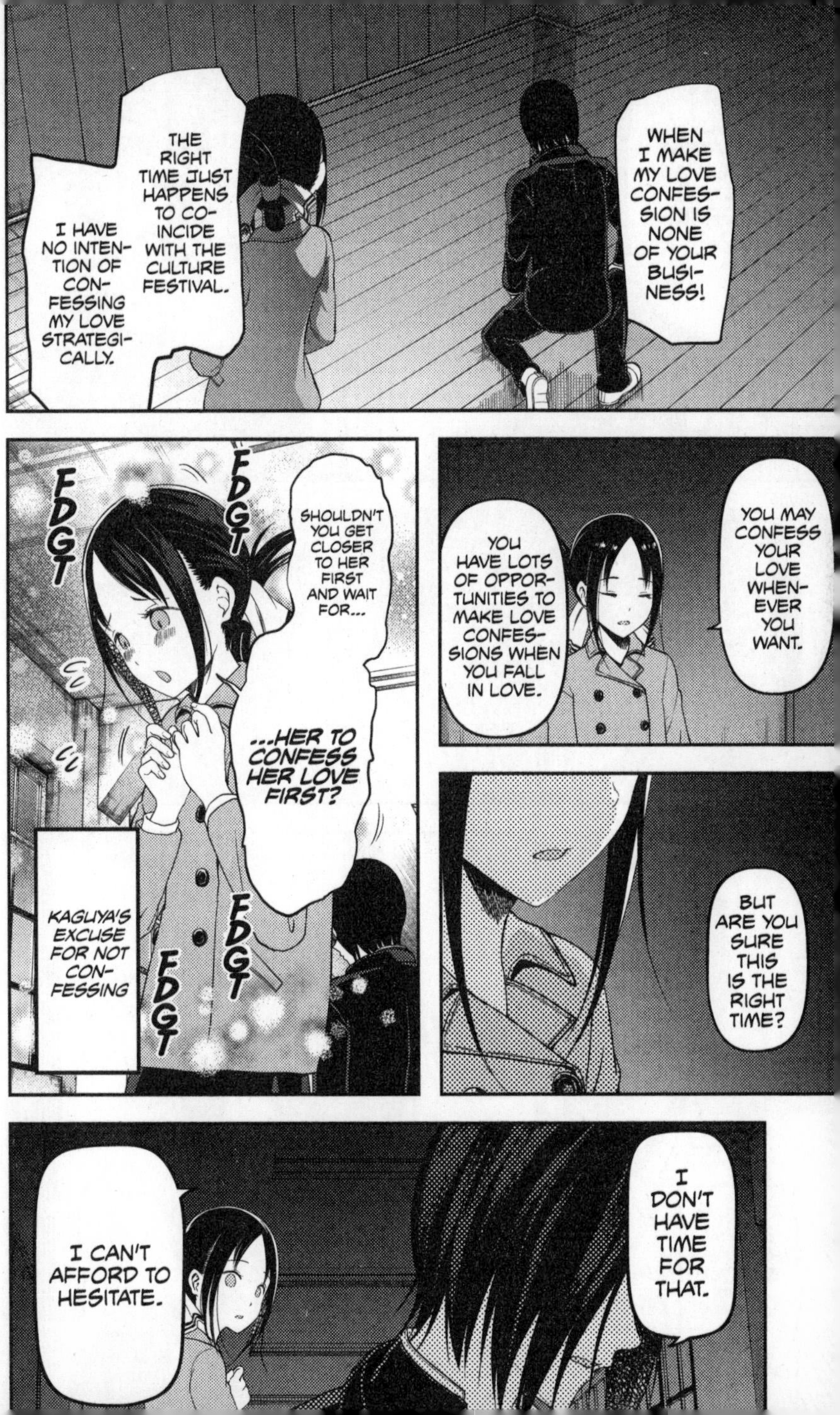
WHEN I MAKE MY LOVE CONFESSION IS NONE OF YOUR BUSINESS!
THE RIGHT TIME JUST HAPPENS TO COINCIDE WITH THE CULTURE FESTIVAL.
I HAVE NO INTENTION OF CONFESSING MY LOVE STRATEGICALLY.
YOU MAY CONFESS YOUR LOVE WHENEVER YOU WANT.
YOU HAVE LOTS OF OPPORTUNITIES TO MAKE LOVE CONFESSIONS WHEN YOU FALL IN LOVE.
BUT ARE YOU SURE THIS IS THE RIGHT TIME?
FDGT
FDGT
SHOULDN'T YOU GET CLOSER TO HER FIRST AND WAIT FOR...
...HER TO CONFESS HER LOVE FIRST?
FDGT
FDGT
KAGUYA'S EXCUSE FOR NOT CONFESSING
I DON'T HAVE TIME FOR THAT.
I CAN'T AFFORD TO HESITATE.

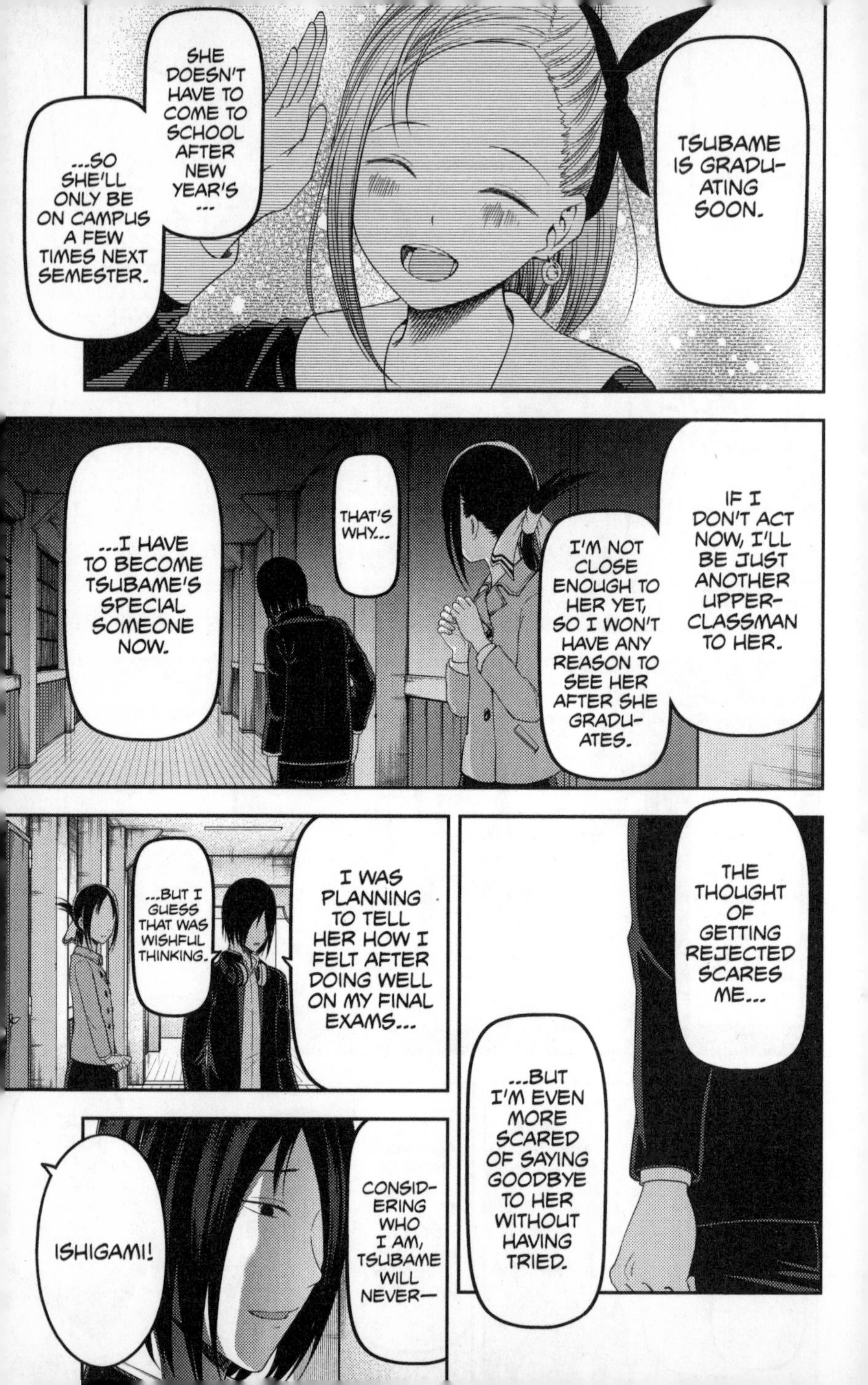
TSUBAME IS GRADUATING SOON.
SHE DOESN'T HAVE TO COME TO SCHOOL AFTER NEW YEAR'S...
...SO SHE'LL ONLY BE ON CAMPUS A FEW TIMES NEXT SEMESTER.
IF I DON'T ACT NOW, I'LL BE JUST ANOTHER UPPERCLASSMAN TO HER.
I'M NOT CLOSE ENOUGH TO HER YET, SO I WON'T HAVE ANY REASON TO SEE HER AFTER SHE GRADUATES.
THAT'S WHY...
...I HAVE TO BECOME TSUBAME'S SPECIAL SOMEONE NOW.
THE THOUGHT OF GETTING REJECTED SCARES ME...
...BUT I'M EVEN MORE SCARED OF SAYING GOODBYE TO HER WITHOUT HAVING TRIED.
I WAS PLANNING TO TELL HER HOW I FELT AFTER DOING WELL ON MY FINAL EXAMS...
...BUT I GUESS THAT WAS WISHFUL THINKING.
CONSIDERING WHO I AM, TSUBAME WILL NEVER—
ISHIGAMI!

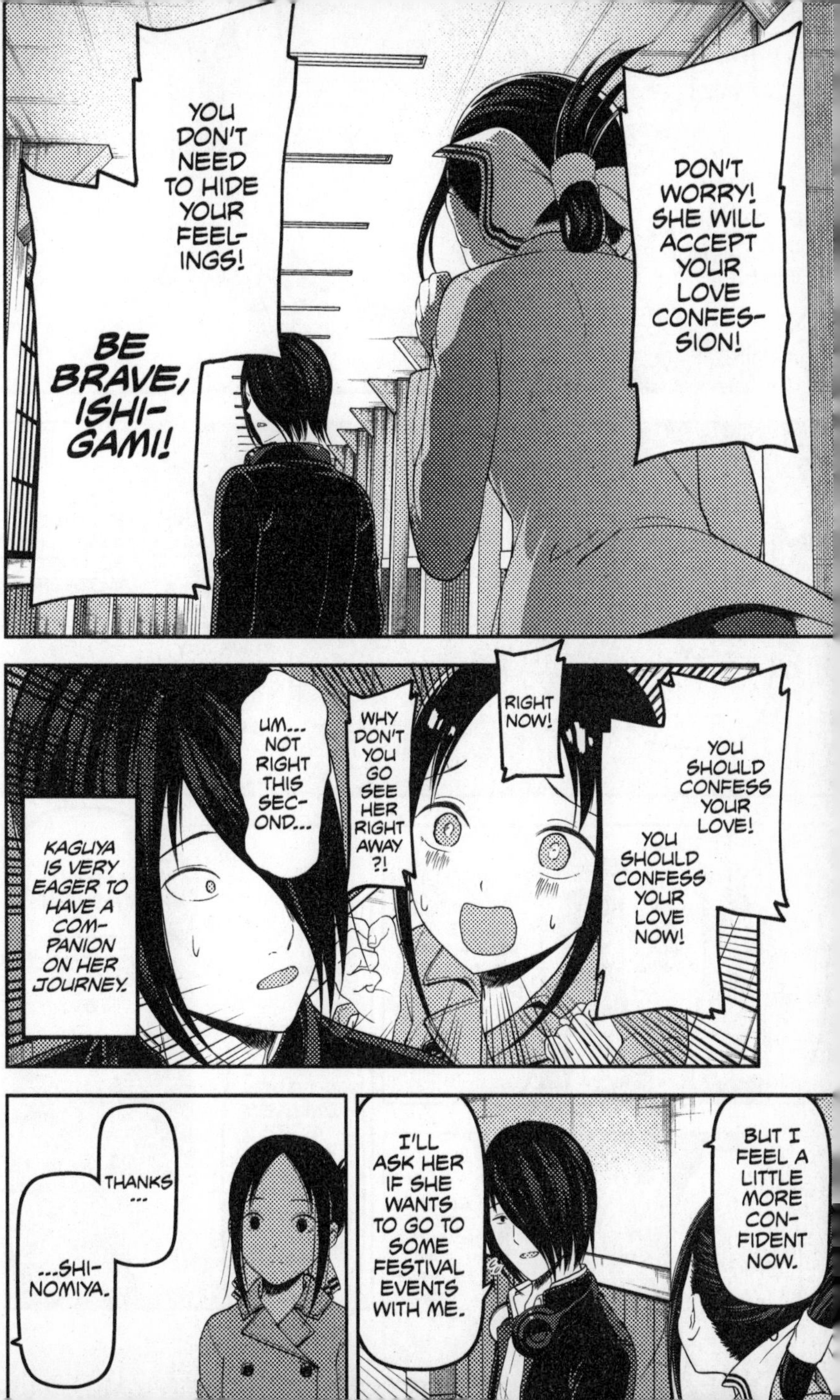
DON'T WORRY! SHE WILL ACCEPT YOUR LOVE CONFESSION!
YOU DON'T NEED TO HIDE YOUR FEELINGS!
BE BRAVE, ISHIGAMI!
YOU SHOULD CONFESS YOUR LOVE!
YOU SHOULD CONFESS YOUR LOVE NOW!
RIGHT NOW!
WHY DON'T YOU GO SEE HER RIGHT AWAY?!
UM... NOT RIGHT THIS SECOND...
KAGUYA IS VERY EAGER TO HAVE A COMPANION ON HER JOURNEY.
BUT I FEEL A LITTLE MORE CONFIDENT NOW.
I'LL ASK HER IF SHE WANTS TO GO TO SOME FESTIVAL EVENTS WITH ME.
THANKS...
...SHINOMIYA.

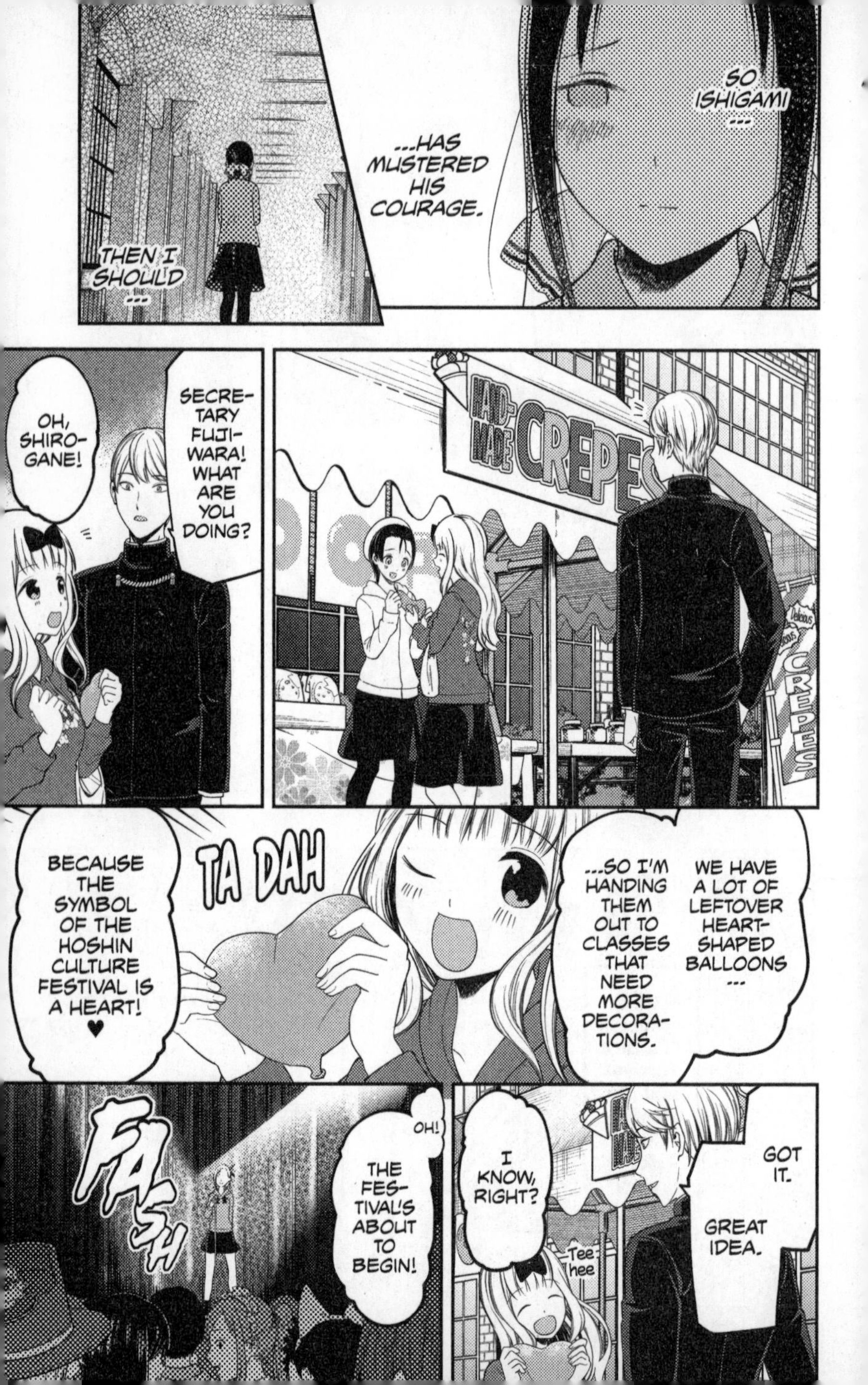
SO ISHIGAMI ---
...HAS MUSTERED HIS COURAGE.
THEN I SHOULD ---
HAND-MADE CREPES
Delicious
CREPES
SECRETARY FUJIWARA! WHAT ARE YOU DOING?
OH, SHIROGANE!
WE HAVE A LOT OF LEFTOVER HEART-SHAPED BALLOONS ---
...SO I'M HANDING THEM OUT TO CLASSES THAT NEED MORE DECORATIONS.
TA DAH
BECAUSE THE SYMBOL OF THE HOSHIN CULTURE FESTIVAL IS A HEART! ♥
GOT IT.
GREAT IDEA.
I KNOW, RIGHT?
Tee hee
OH!
THE FESTIVAL'S ABOUT TO BEGIN!
FASH

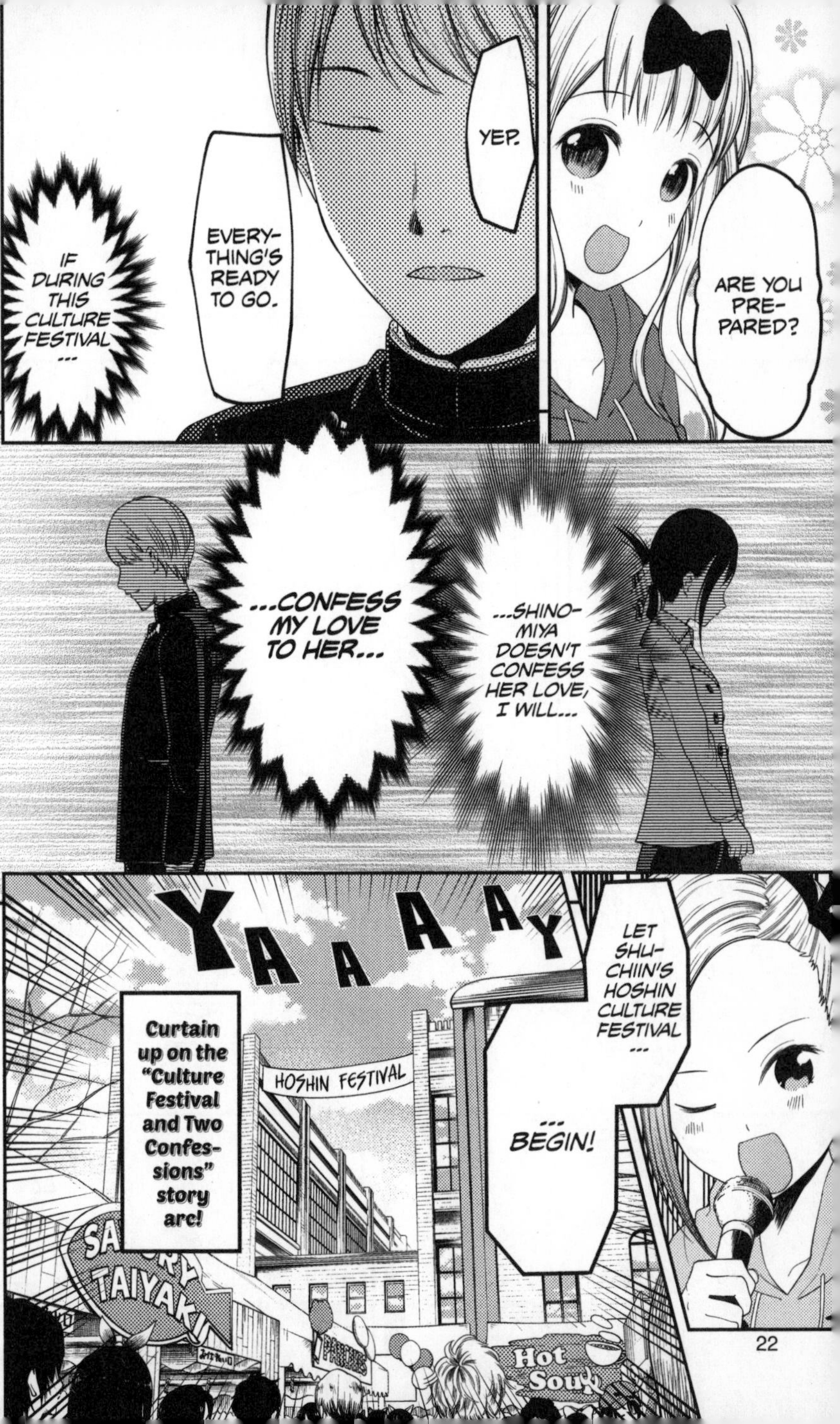
ARE YOU PRE-PARED?
YEP.
EVERY-THING'S READY TO GO.
IF DURING THIS CULTURE FESTIVAL...
...SHINO-MIYA DOESN'T CONFESS HER LOVE, I WILL...
...CONFESS MY LOVE TO HER...
LET SHU-CHIIN'S HOSHIN CULTURE FESTIVAL...
...BEGIN!
YAAAAAY
HOSHIN FESTIVAL
Curtain up on the "Culture Festival and Two Confes-sions" story arc!
SAVORY TAIYAKI
Hot Soup

STUDENT COUNCIL MEMBERS
CULTURE FESTIVAL ENTERTAINMENT

YEAR 1, CLASS A AND CLASS B
(INO, ISHIGAMI, OSARAGI, ONODERA)
HAUNTED HOUSE

YEAR 2, CLASS A (SHINOMIYA, HAYASAKA)
COSPLAY CAFE

YEAR 2, CLASS B (SHIROGANE, FUJIWARA,
KASHIWAGI, TSUBASA, SHIJO)
BALLOON ART

KAGUYA-SAMA
LOVE IS WAR

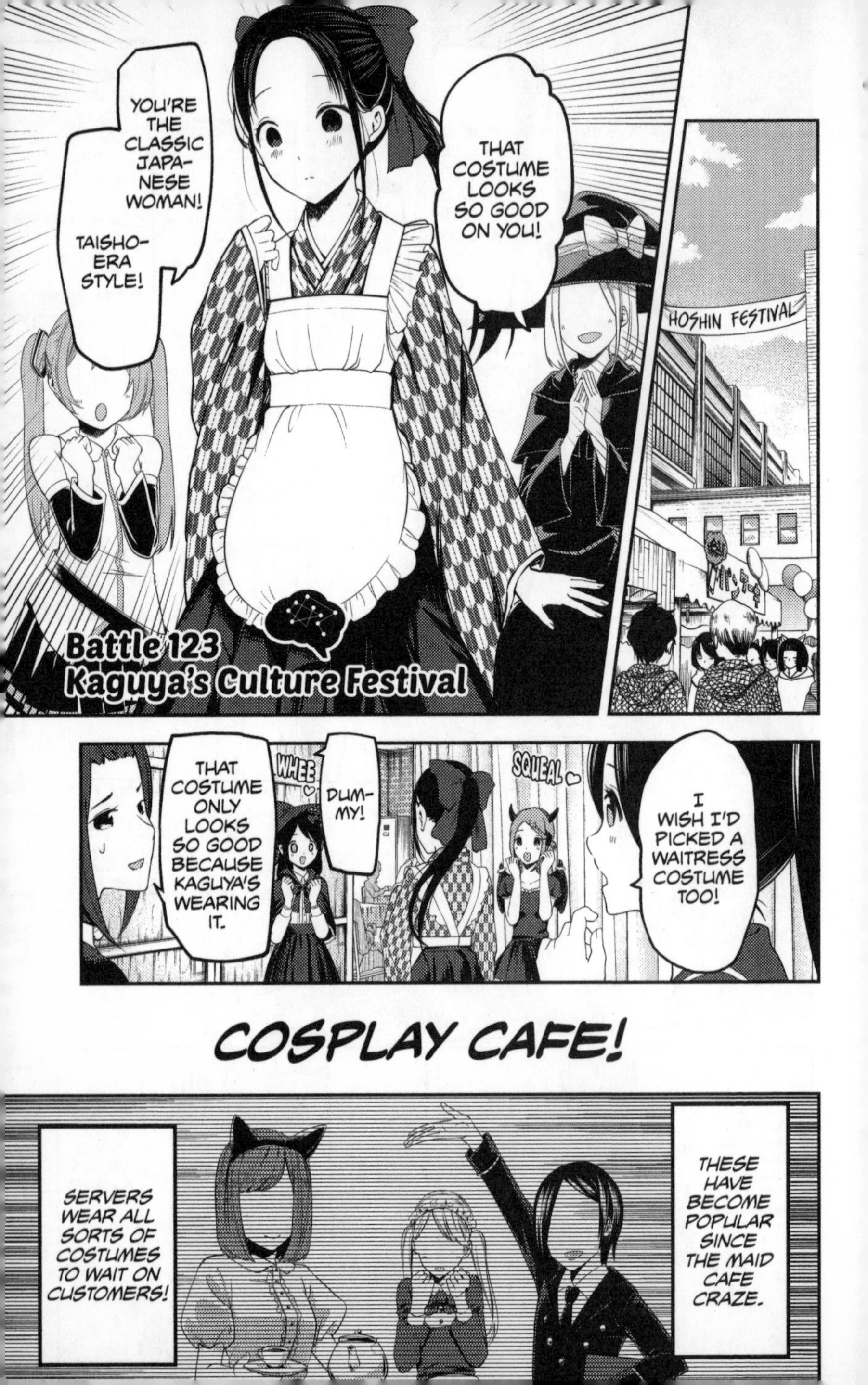
HOSHIN FESTIVAL
THAT COSTUME LOOKS SO GOOD ON YOU!
YOU'RE THE CLASSIC JAPANESE WOMAN!
TAISHO-ERA STYLE!
Battle 123 Kaguya's Culture Festival
I WISH I'D PICKED A WAITRESS COSTUME TOO!
SQUEAL
DUMMY!
WHEE
THAT COSTUME ONLY LOOKS SO GOOD BECAUSE KAGUYA'S WEARING IT.
COSPLAY CAFE!
THESE HAVE BECOME POPULAR SINCE THE MAID CAFE CRAZE.
SERVERS WEAR ALL SORTS OF COSTUMES TO WAIT ON CUSTOMERS!

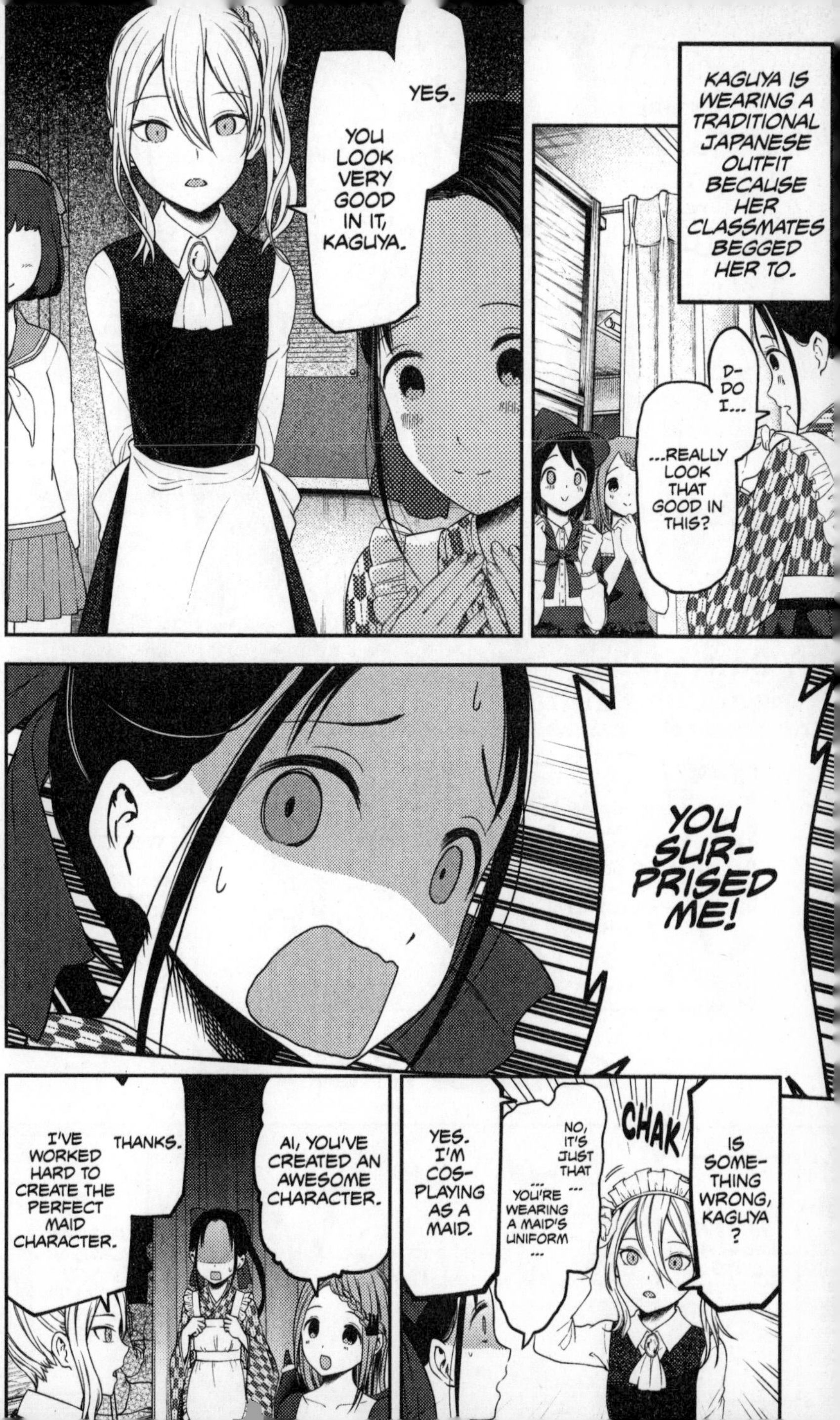
KAGUYA IS WEARING A TRADITIONAL JAPANESE OUTFIT BECAUSE HER CLASSMATES BEGGED HER TO.
D-DO I...
...REALLY LOOK THAT GOOD IN THIS?
YES.
YOU LOOK VERY GOOD IN IT, KAGUYA.
YOU SUR-PRISED ME!
IS SOME-THING WRONG, KAGUYA?
CHAK
NO, IT'S JUST THAT... ...YOU'RE WEARING A MAID'S UNIFORM...
YES. I'M COS-PLAYING AS A MAID.
AI, YOU'VE CREATED AN AWESOME CHARACTER.
THANKS.
I'VE WORKED HARD TO CREATE THE PERFECT MAID CHARACTER.

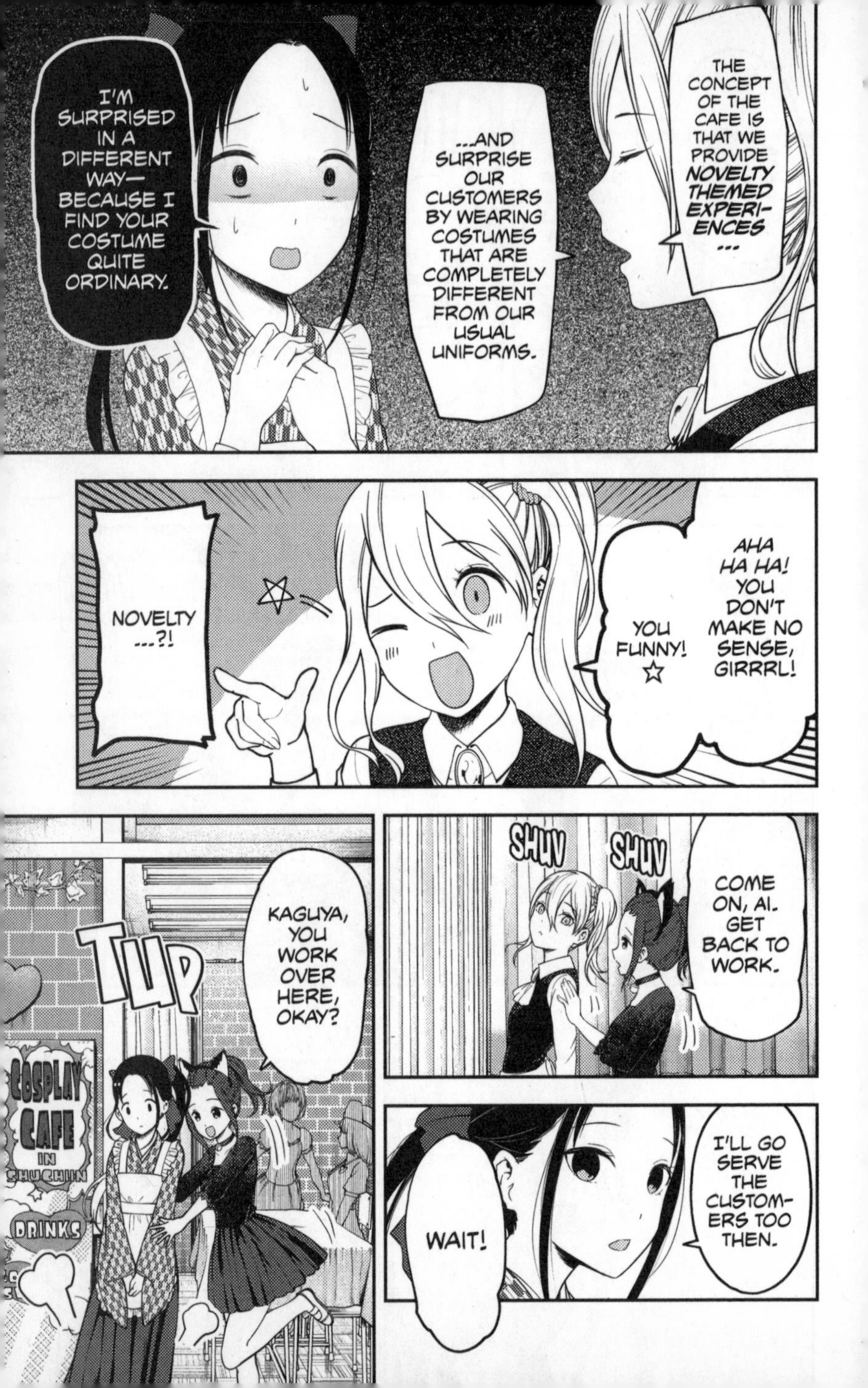

THE CONCEPT OF THE CAFE IS THAT WE PROVIDE *NOVELTY THEMED EXPERIENCES*...
...AND SURPRISE OUR CUSTOMERS BY WEARING COSTUMES THAT ARE COMPLETELY DIFFERENT FROM OUR USUAL UNIFORMS.
I'M SURPRISED IN A DIFFERENT WAY—BECAUSE I FIND YOUR COSTUME QUITE ORDINARY.
AHA HA HA! YOU DON'T MAKE NO SENSE, GIRRRL!
YOU FUNNY! ☆
NOVELTY...?!
SHUV
SHUV
COME ON, AI. GET BACK TO WORK.
I'LL GO SERVE THE CUSTOMERS TOO THEN.
WAIT!
KAGUYA, YOU WORK OVER HERE, OKAY?
TUP
COSPLAY CAFE IN SHUCHIN
DRINKS

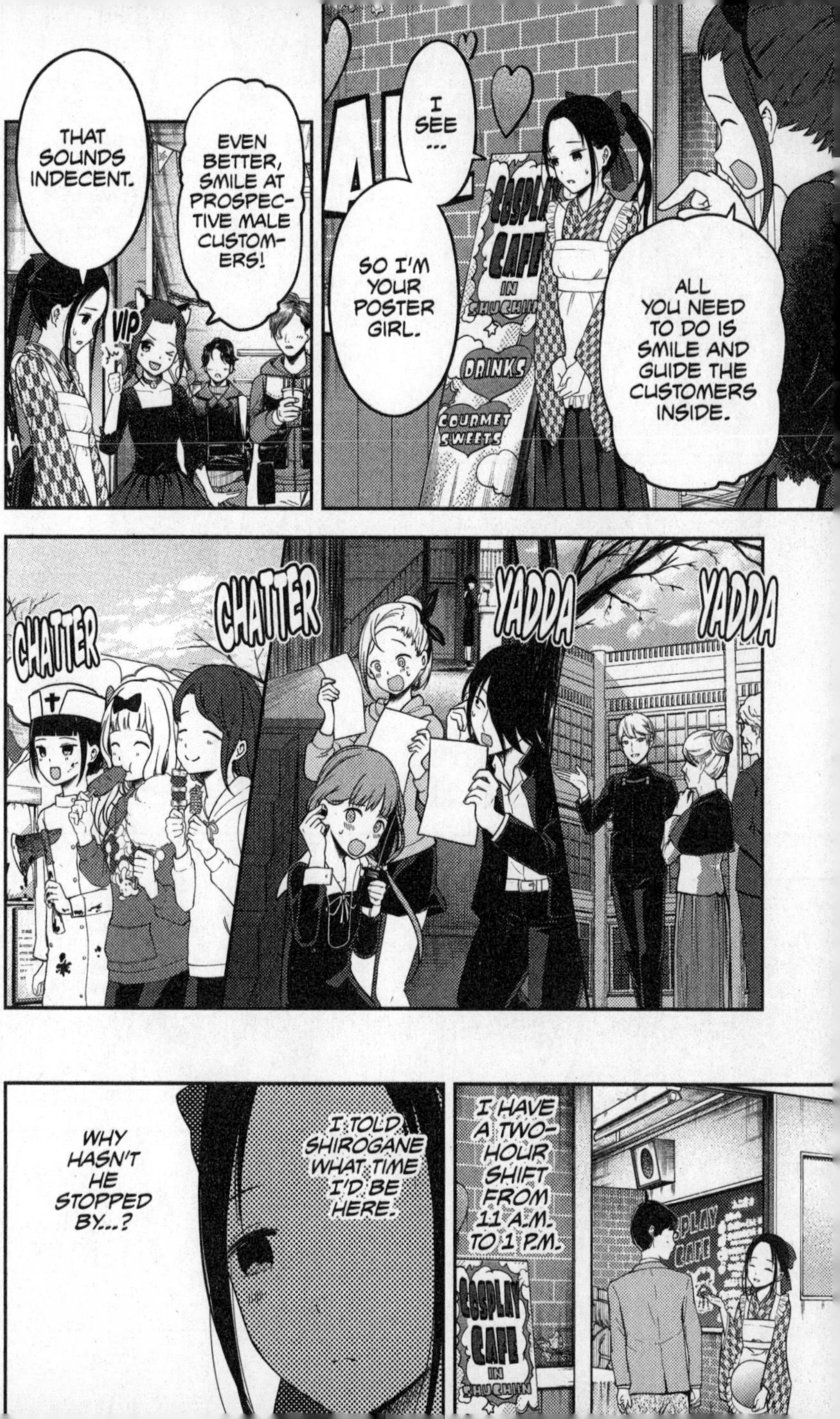
ALL YOU NEED TO DO IS SMILE AND GUIDE THE CUSTOMERS INSIDE.
I SEE...
SO I'M YOUR POSTER GIRL.
DRINKS
GOURMET SWEETS
EVEN BETTER, SMILE AT PROSPECTIVE MALE CUSTOMERS!
VIP
THAT SOUNDS INDECENT.
YADDA
YADDA
CHATTER
CHATTER
I HAVE A TWO-HOUR SHIFT FROM 11 A.M. TO 1 P.M.
COSPLAY CAFE IN SHUCHIN
I TOLD SHIROGANE WHAT TIME I'D BE HERE.
WHY HASN'T HE STOPPED BY...?

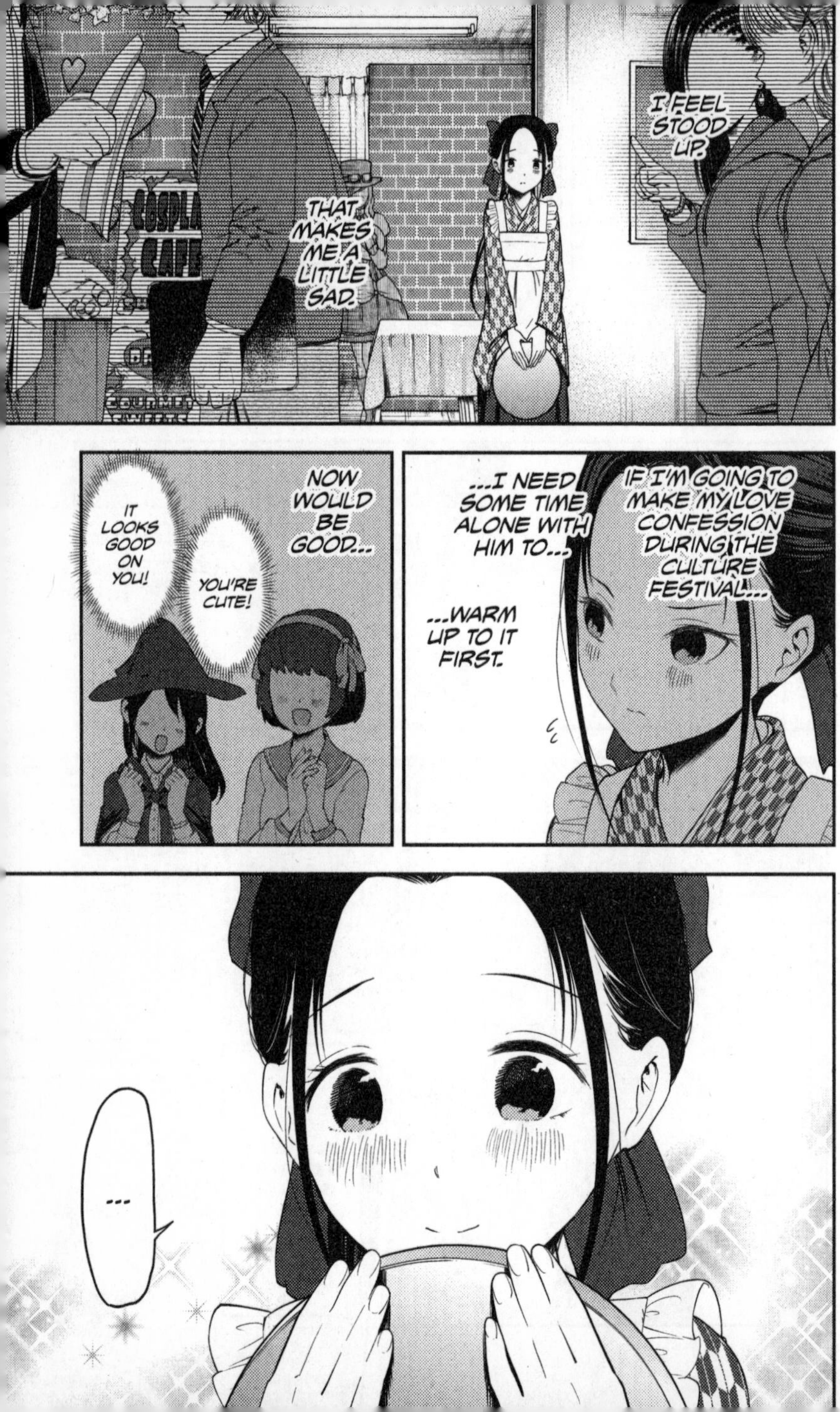
I FEEL STOOD UP.
THAT MAKES ME A LITTLE SAD.
IF I'M GOING TO MAKE MY LOVE CONFESSION DURING THE CULTURE FESTIVAL...
...I NEED SOME TIME ALONE WITH HIM TO...
...WARM UP TO IT FIRST.
NOW WOULD BE GOOD...
YOU'RE CUTE!
IT LOOKS GOOD ON YOU!
...

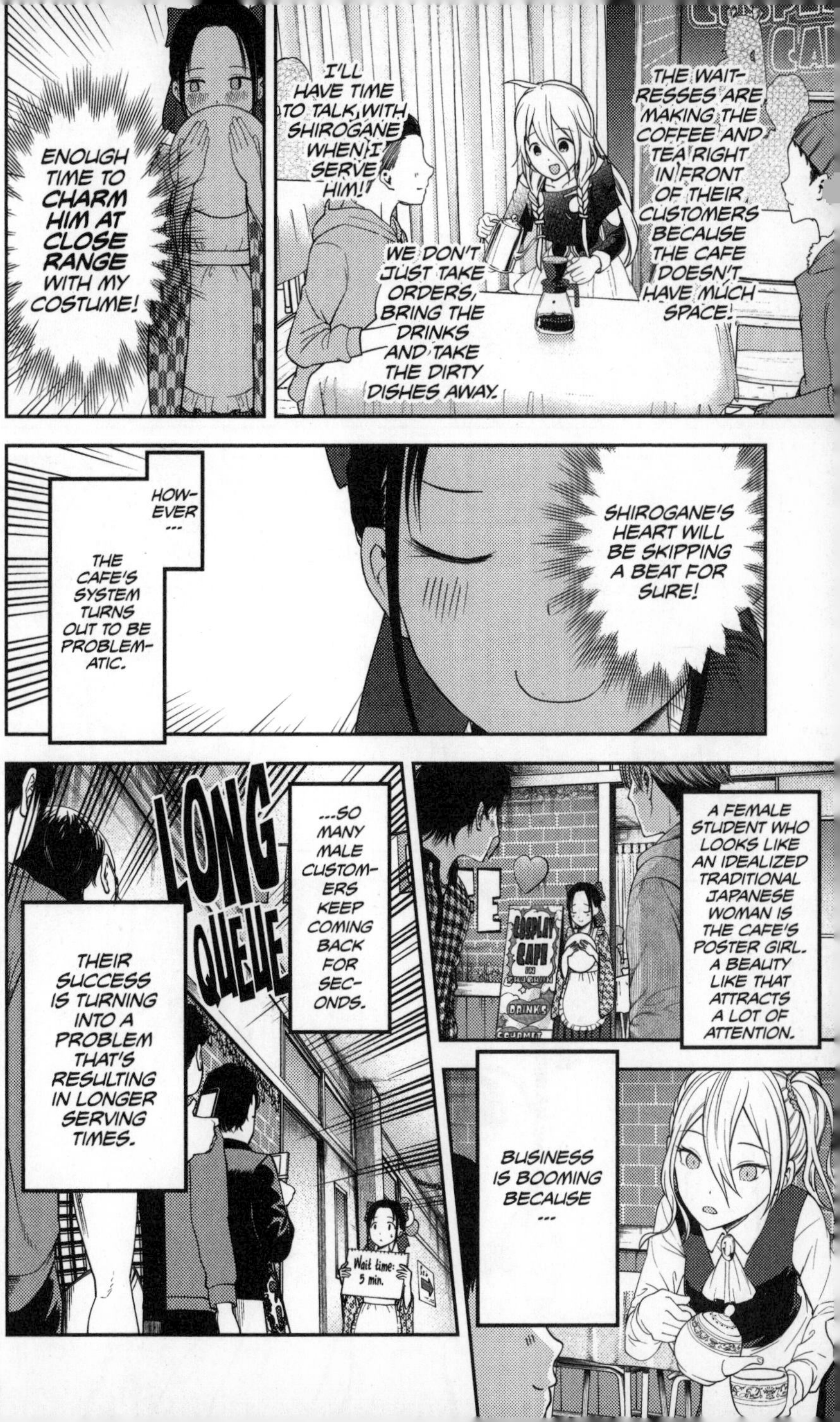
WE DON'T JUST TAKE ORDERS, BRING THE DRINKS AND TAKE THE DIRTY DISHES AWAY.
THE WAITRESSES ARE MAKING THE COFFEE AND TEA RIGHT IN FRONT OF THEIR CUSTOMERS BECAUSE THE CAFE DOESN'T HAVE MUCH SPACE.
I'LL HAVE TIME TO TALK WITH SHIROGANE WHEN I SERVE HIM!
ENOUGH TIME TO CHARM HIM AT CLOSE RANGE WITH MY COSTUME!
SHIROGANE'S HEART WILL BE SKIPPING A BEAT FOR SURE!
HOWEVER---
THE CAFE'S SYSTEM TURNS OUT TO BE PROBLEMATIC.
A FEMALE STUDENT WHO LOOKS LIKE AN IDEALIZED TRADITIONAL JAPANESE WOMAN IS THE CAFE'S POSTER GIRL. A BEAUTY LIKE THAT ATTRACTS A LOT OF ATTENTION.
COSPLAY CAFE
DRINKS
BUSINESS IS BOOMING BECAUSE---
LONG QUEUE
---SO MANY MALE CUSTOMERS KEEP COMING BACK FOR SECONDS.
THEIR SUCCESS IS TURNING INTO A PROBLEM THAT'S RESULTING IN LONGER SERVING TIMES.
Wait time: 5 min.

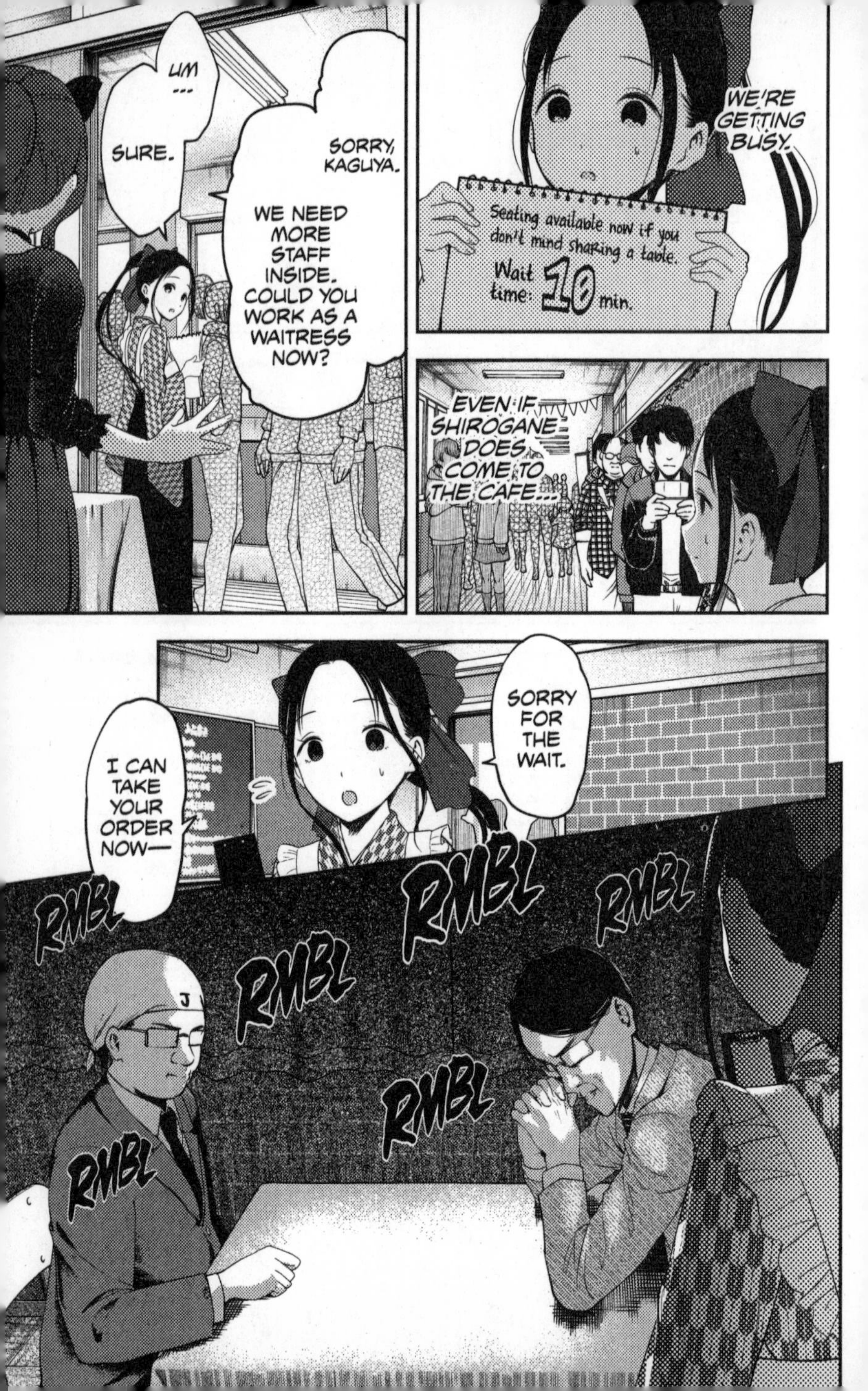
WE'RE GETTING BUSY.
Seating available now if you don't mind sharing a table.
Wait time: 10 min.
EVEN IF SHIROGANE DOES COME TO THE CAFE...
SORRY, KAGUYA.
WE NEED MORE STAFF INSIDE. COULD YOU WORK AS A WAITRESS NOW?
UM ...
SURE.
SORRY FOR THE WAIT.
I CAN TAKE YOUR ORDER NOW—
RMBL
RMBL
RMBL
RMBL
RMBL
RMBL

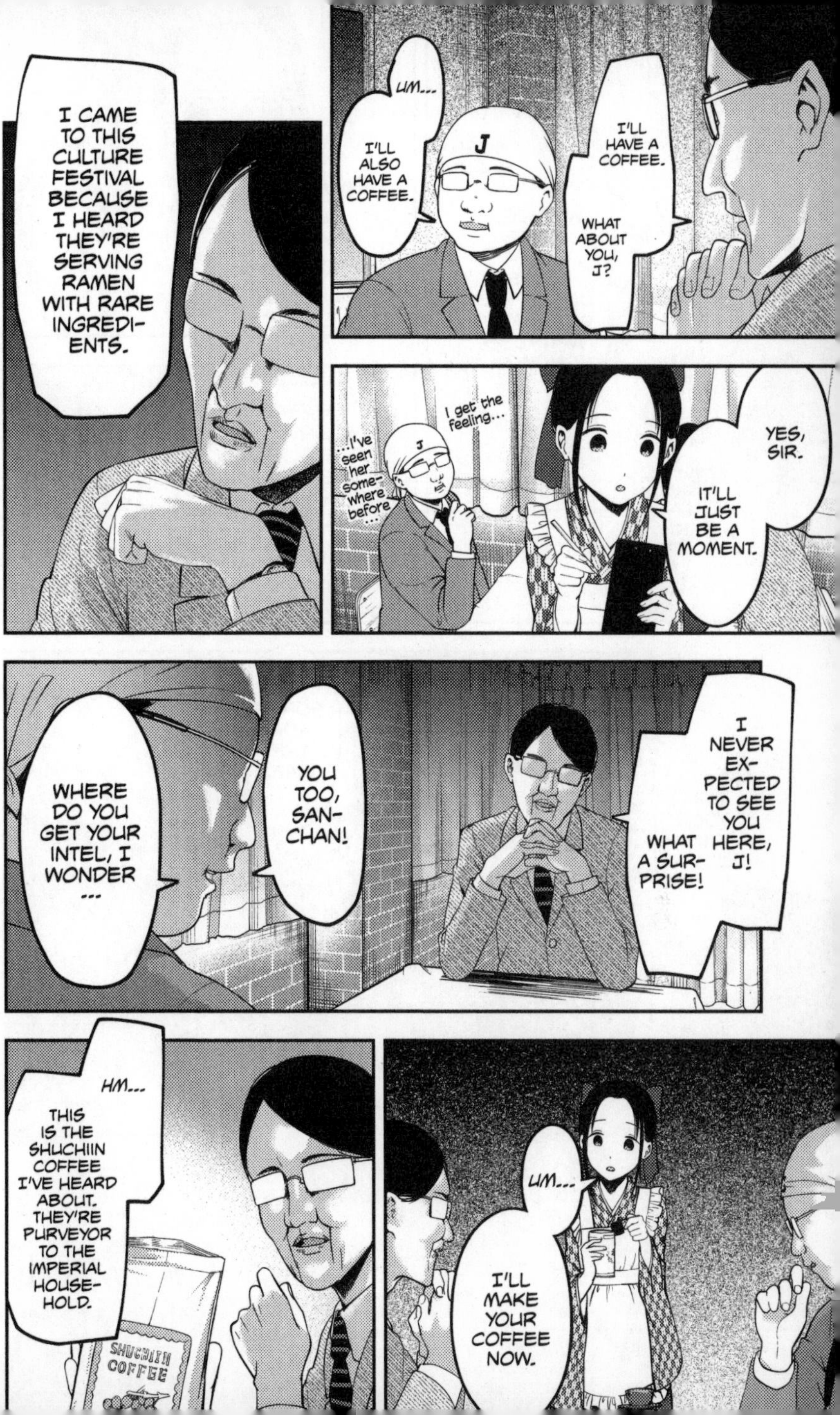
I'LL HAVE A COFFEE.
WHAT ABOUT YOU, J?
UM...
I'LL ALSO HAVE A COFFEE.
YES, SIR.
IT'LL JUST BE A MOMENT.
I get the feeling...
...I've seen her somewhere before...
I CAME TO THIS CULTURE FESTIVAL BECAUSE I HEARD THEY'RE SERVING RAMEN WITH RARE INGREDIENTS.
I NEVER EXPECTED TO SEE YOU HERE, J!
WHAT A SURPRISE!
YOU TOO, SAN-CHAN!
WHERE DO YOU GET YOUR INTEL, I WONDER...
UM...
I'LL MAKE YOUR COFFEE NOW.
HM...
THIS IS THE SHUCHIIN COFFEE I'VE HEARD ABOUT. THEY'RE PURVEYOR TO THE IMPERIAL HOUSEHOLD.
SHUCHIIN COFFEE

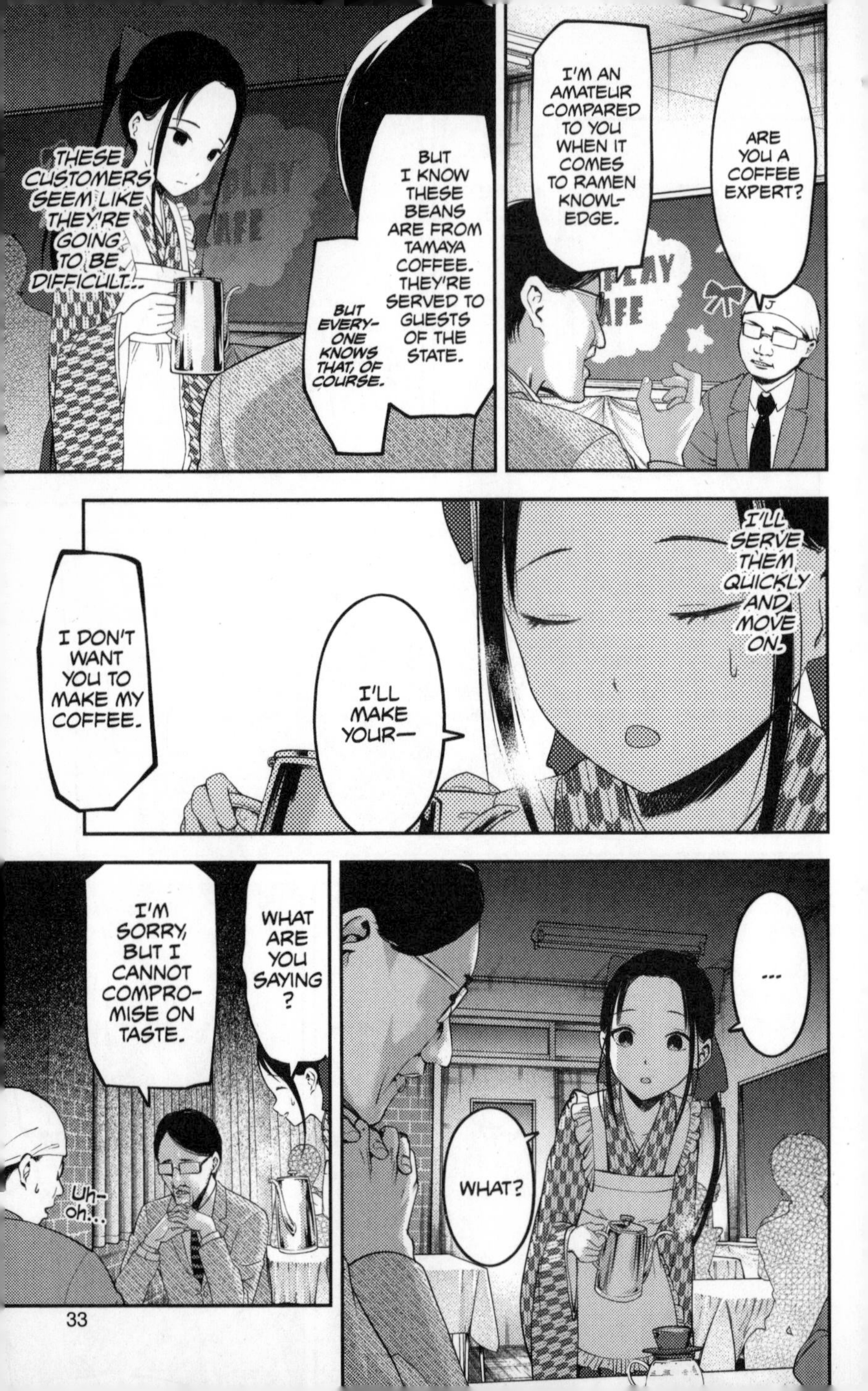

ARE YOU A COFFEE EXPERT?
I'M AN AMATEUR COMPARED TO YOU WHEN IT COMES TO RAMEN KNOWLEDGE.
BUT I KNOW THESE BEANS ARE FROM TAMAYA COFFEE. THEY'RE SERVED TO GUESTS OF THE STATE.
BUT EVERYONE KNOWS THAT, OF COURSE.
THESE CUSTOMERS SEEM LIKE THEY'RE GOING TO BE DIFFICULT...
I'LL SERVE THEM QUICKLY AND MOVE ON.
I'LL MAKE YOUR—
I DON'T WANT YOU TO MAKE MY COFFEE.
...
WHAT?
WHAT ARE YOU SAYING?
I'M SORRY, BUT I CANNOT COMPROMISE ON TASTE.
Uh-oh...

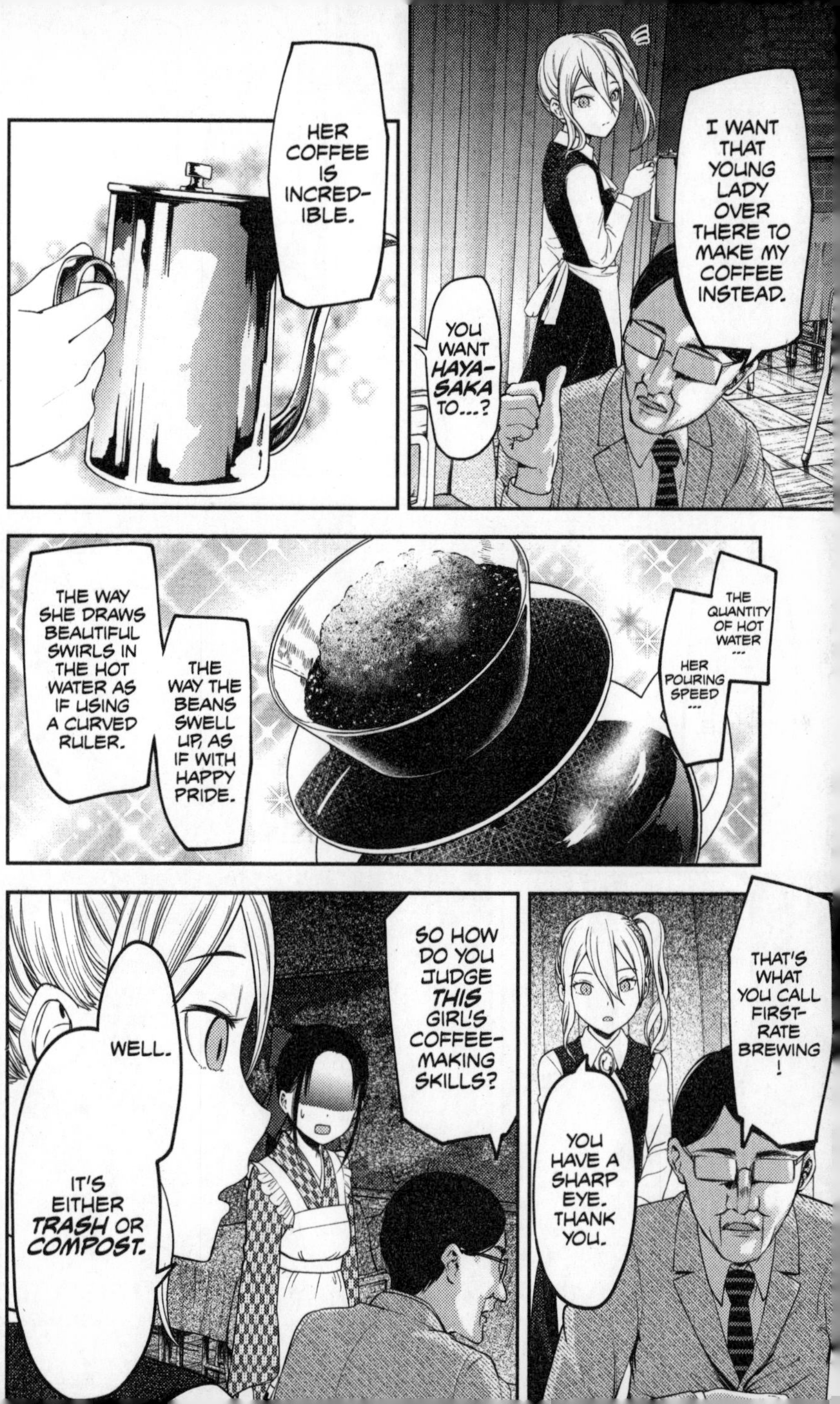
I WANT THAT YOUNG LADY OVER THERE TO MAKE MY COFFEE INSTEAD.
YOU WANT *HAYASAKA* TO...?
HER COFFEE IS INCREDIBLE.
THE QUANTITY OF HOT WATER...
HER POURING SPEED...
THE WAY THE BEANS SWELL UP, AS IF WITH HAPPY PRIDE.
THE WAY SHE DRAWS BEAUTIFUL SWIRLS IN THE HOT WATER AS IF USING A CURVED RULER.
THAT'S WHAT YOU CALL FIRST-RATE BREWING!
YOU HAVE A SHARP EYE. THANK YOU.
SO HOW DO YOU JUDGE *THIS* GIRL'S COFFEE-MAKING SKILLS?
WELL.
IT'S EITHER *TRASH* OR *COMPOST*.

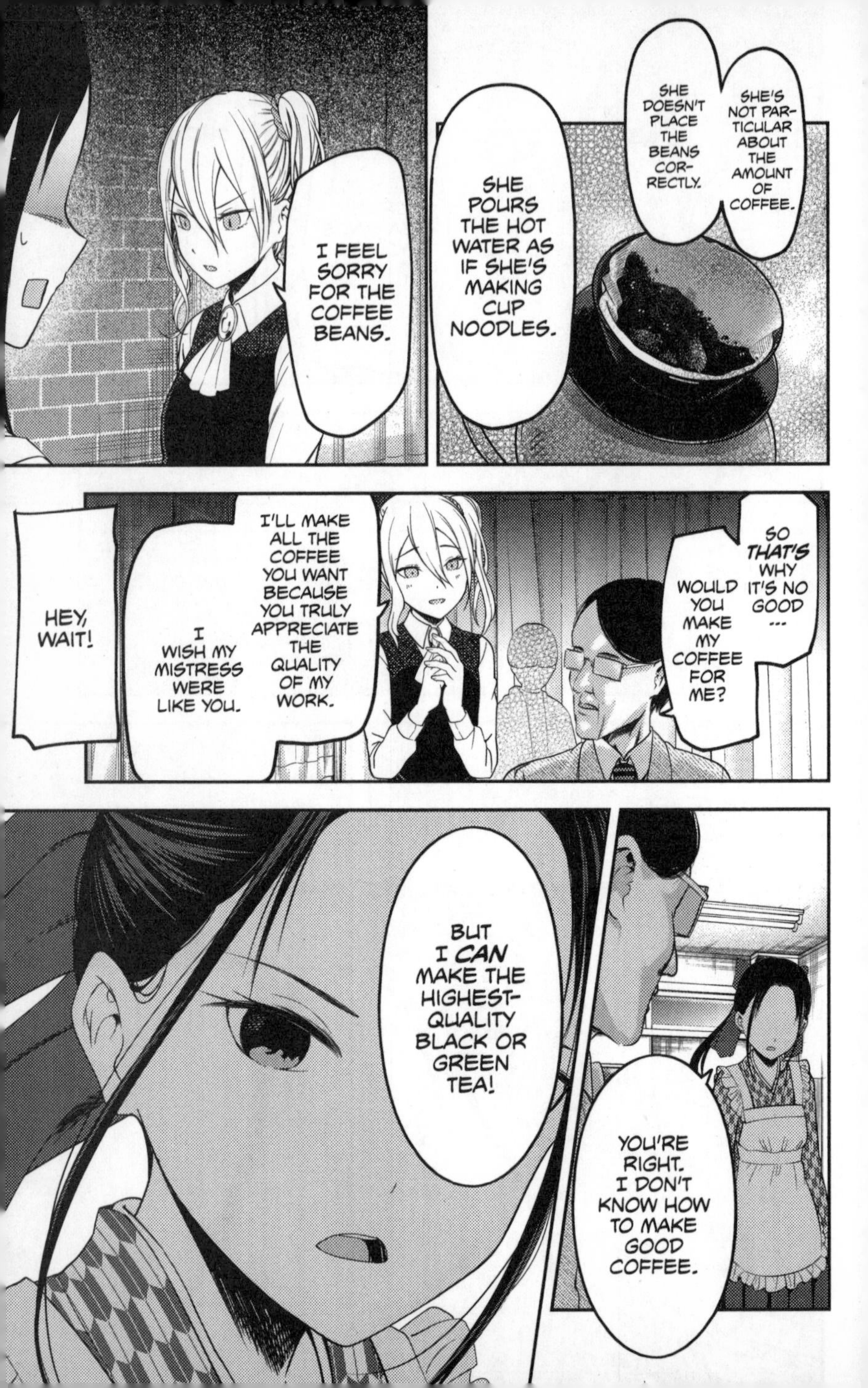
SHE'S NOT PARTICULAR ABOUT THE AMOUNT OF COFFEE.
SHE DOESN'T PLACE THE BEANS CORRECTLY.
SHE POURS THE HOT WATER AS IF SHE'S MAKING CUP NOODLES.
I FEEL SORRY FOR THE COFFEE BEANS.
SO *THAT'S* WHY IT'S NO GOOD...
WOULD YOU MAKE MY COFFEE FOR ME?
I'LL MAKE ALL THE COFFEE YOU WANT BECAUSE YOU TRULY APPRECIATE THE QUALITY OF MY WORK.
I WISH MY MISTRESS WERE LIKE YOU.
HEY, WAIT!
YOU'RE RIGHT. I DON'T KNOW HOW TO MAKE GOOD COFFEE.
BUT I *CAN* MAKE THE HIGHEST-QUALITY BLACK OR GREEN TEA!

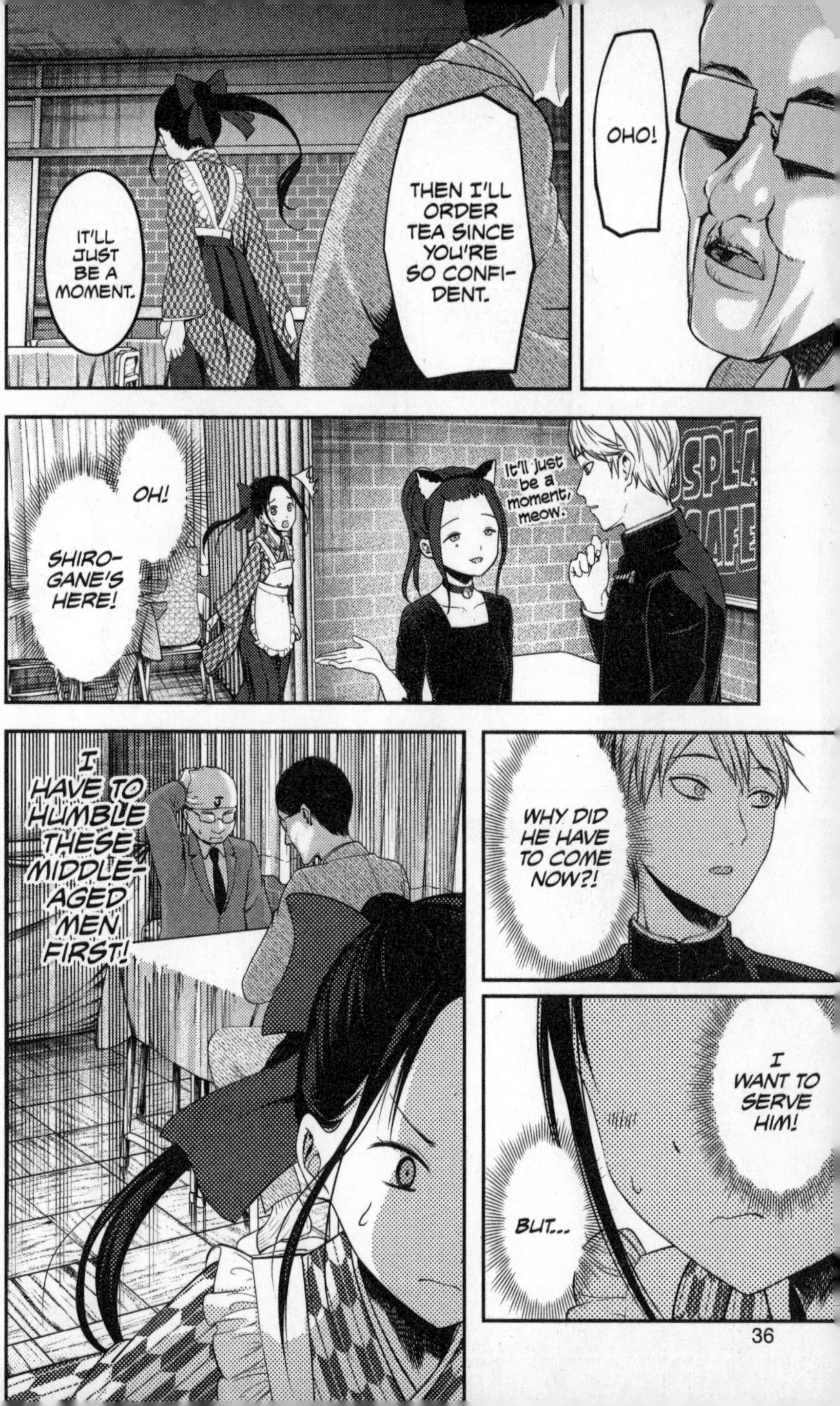
OHO!
THEN I'LL ORDER TEA SINCE YOU'RE SO CONFI-DENT.
IT'LL JUST BE A MOMENT.
It'll just be a moment, meow.
OH!
SHIRO-GANE'S HERE!
WHY DID HE HAVE TO COME NOW?!
I WANT TO SERVE HIM!
BUT...
I HAVE TO HUMBLE THESE MIDDLE-AGED MEN FIRST!

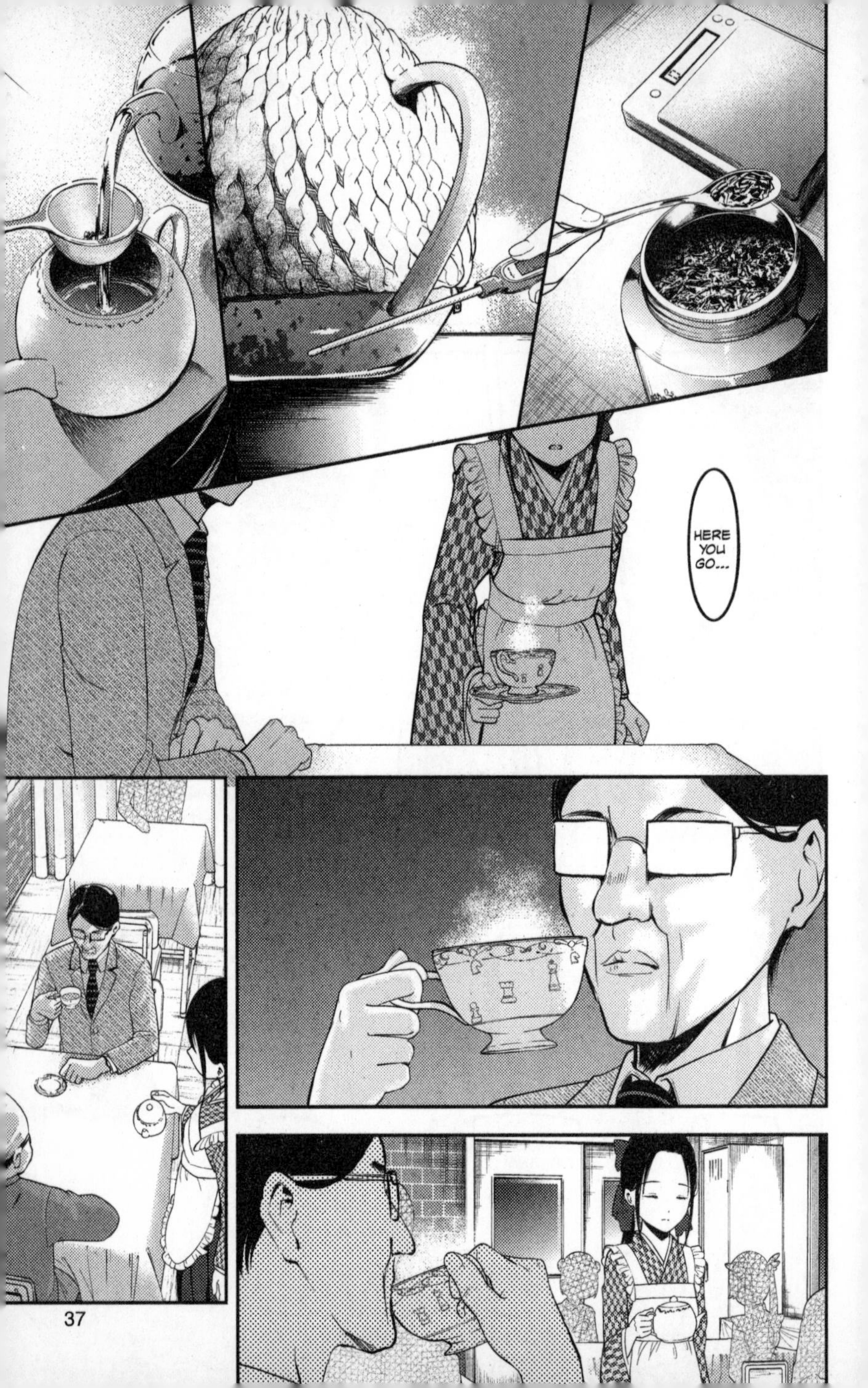
HERE YOU GO...

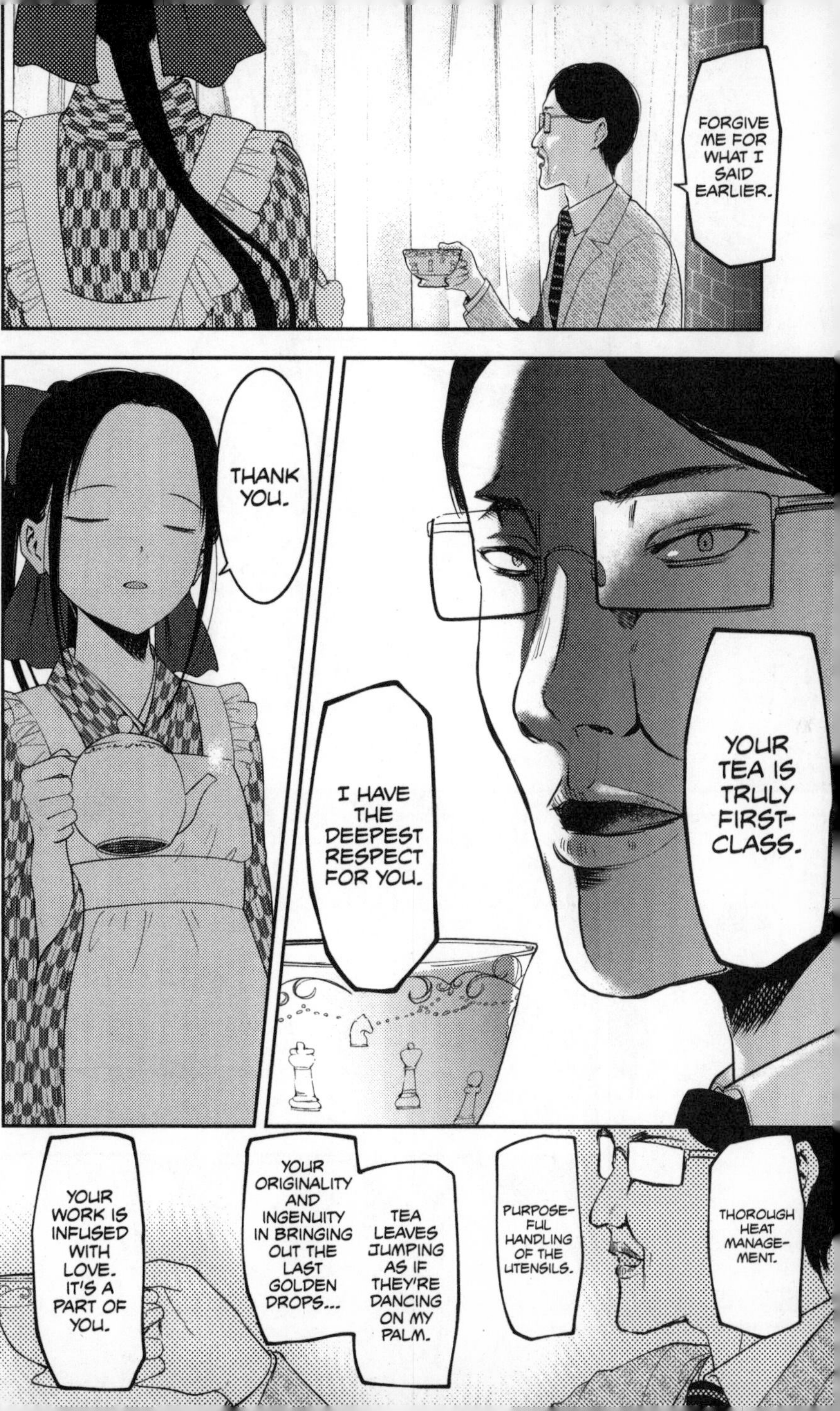
FORGIVE ME FOR WHAT I SAID EARLIER.
YOUR TEA IS TRULY FIRST-CLASS.
I HAVE THE DEEPEST RESPECT FOR YOU.
THANK YOU.
THOROUGH HEAT MANAGE-MENT.
PURPOSE-FUL HANDLING OF THE UTENSILS.
TEA LEAVES JUMPING AS IF THEY'RE DANCING ON MY PALM.
YOUR ORIGINALITY AND INGENUITY IN BRINGING OUT THE LAST GOLDEN DROPS...
YOUR WORK IS INFUSED WITH LOVE. IT'S A PART OF YOU.

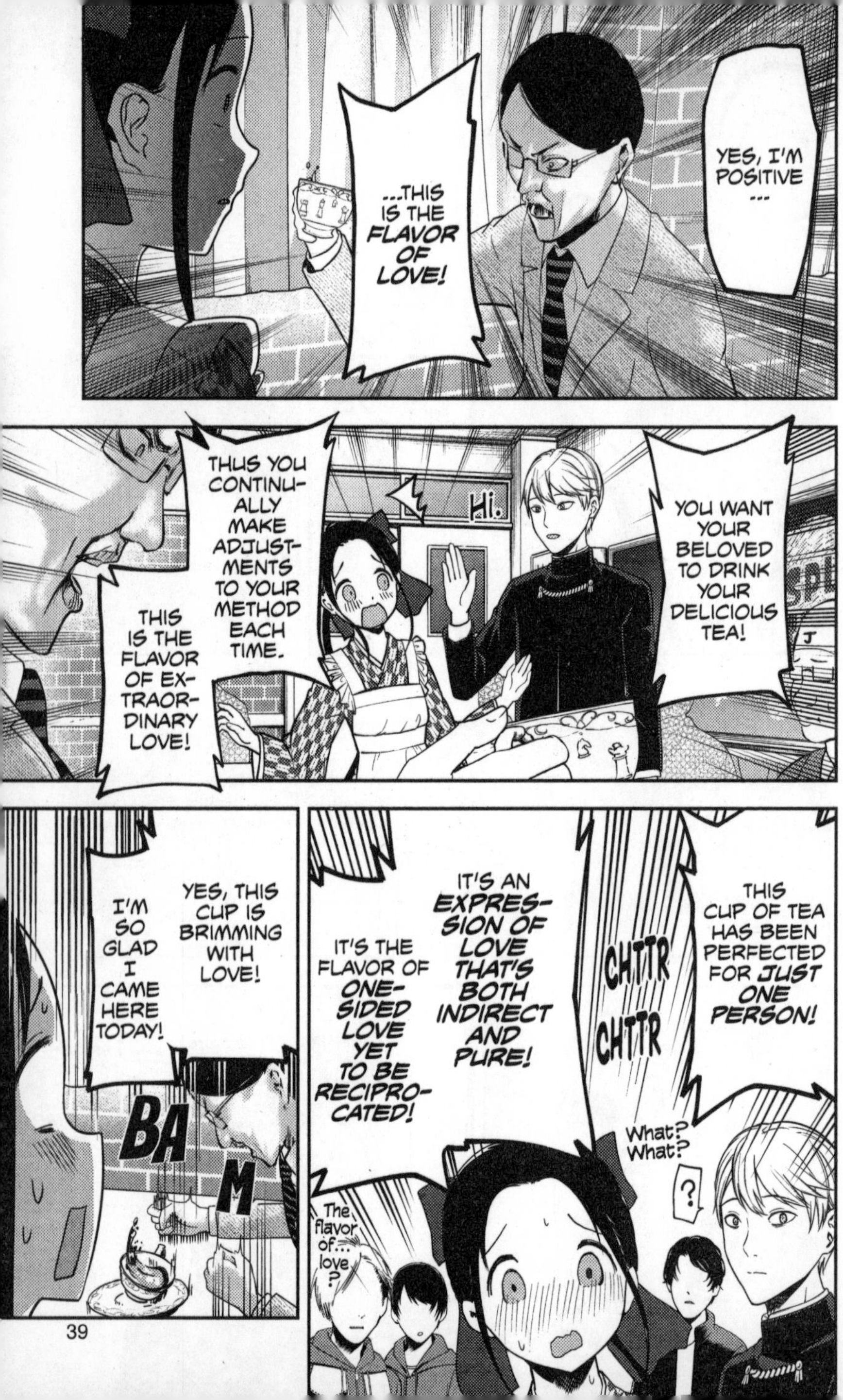
YES, I'M POSITIVE...
...THIS IS THE FLAVOR OF LOVE!
YOU WANT YOUR BELOVED TO DRINK YOUR DELICIOUS TEA!
Hi.
THUS YOU CONTINUALLY MAKE ADJUSTMENTS TO YOUR METHOD EACH TIME.
THIS IS THE FLAVOR OF EXTRAORDINARY LOVE!
THIS CUP OF TEA HAS BEEN PERFECTED FOR JUST ONE PERSON!
CHTTR CHTTR
IT'S AN EXPRESSION OF LOVE THAT'S BOTH INDIRECT AND PURE!
IT'S THE FLAVOR OF ONE-SIDED LOVE YET TO BE RECIPROCATED!
What? What?
?
The flavor of... love?
YES, THIS CUP IS BRIMMING WITH LOVE!
I'M SO GLAD I CAME HERE TODAY!
BAM

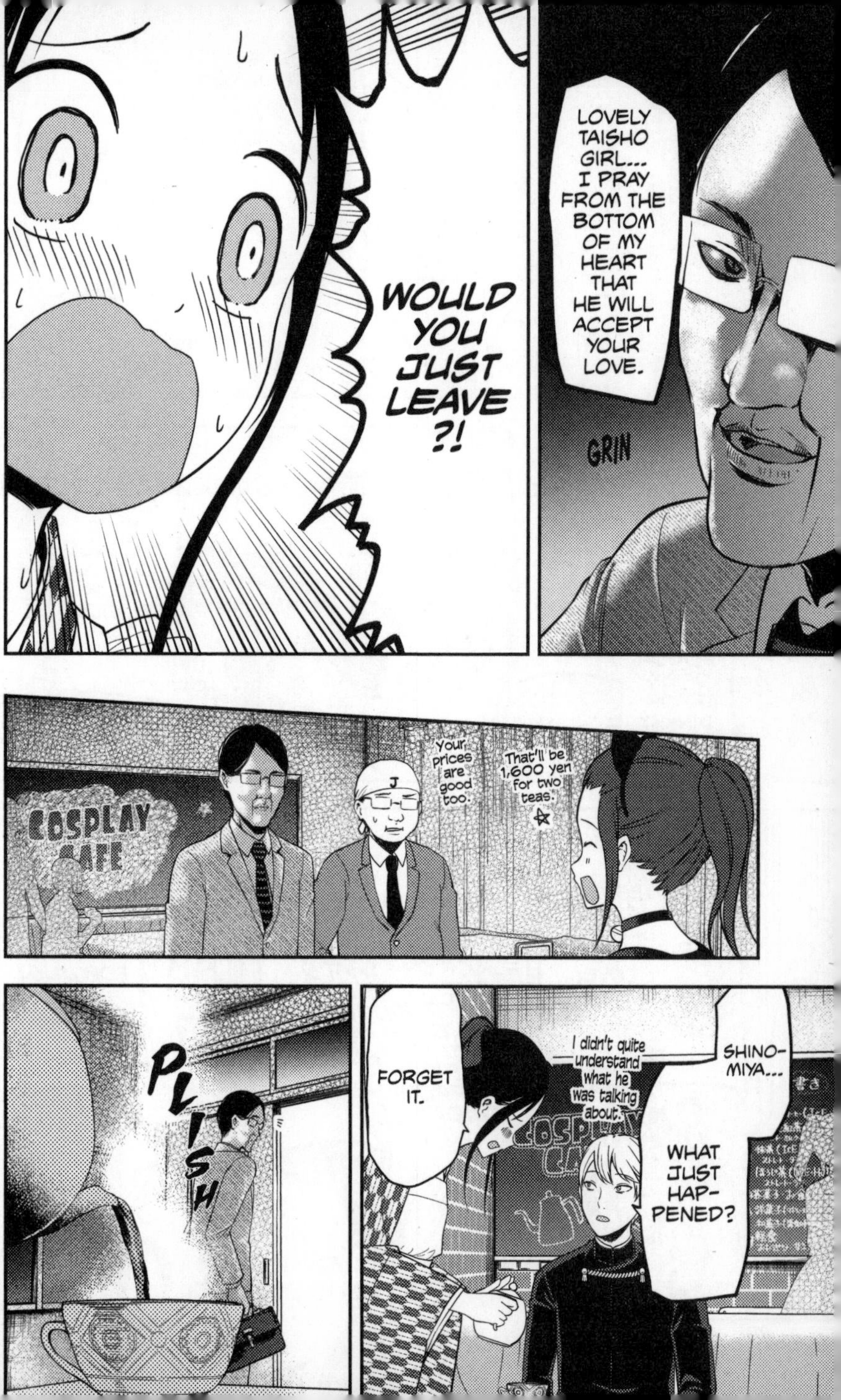
LOVELY TAISHO GIRL... I PRAY FROM THE BOTTOM OF MY HEART THAT HE WILL ACCEPT YOUR LOVE.
GRIN
WOULD YOU JUST LEAVE?!
That'll be 1,600 yen for two teas. ☆
Your prices are good too.
SHINO-MIYA...
WHAT JUST HAP-PENED?
I didn't quite understand what he was talking about.
FORGET IT.
PLISH
COSPLAY CAFE

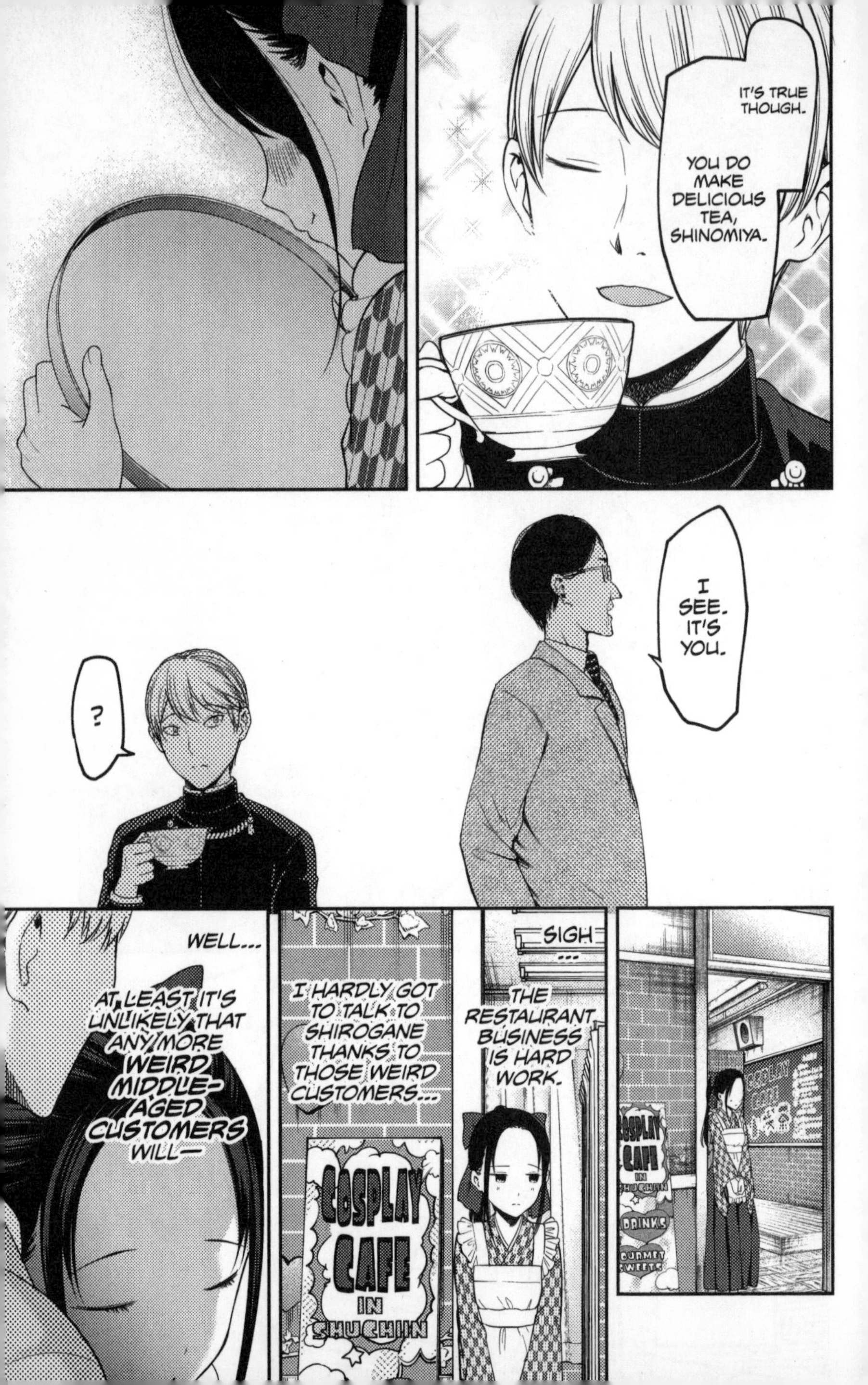
IT'S TRUE THOUGH.
YOU DO MAKE DELICIOUS TEA, SHINOMIYA.
I SEE. IT'S YOU.
?
DRINKS
SIGH...
THE RESTAURANT BUSINESS IS HARD WORK.
I HARDLY GOT TO TALK TO SHIROGANE THANKS TO THOSE WEIRD CUSTOMERS...
COSPLAY CAFE IN SHUCHIIN
WELL...
AT LEAST IT'S UNLIKELY THAT ANY MORE WEIRD MIDDLE-AGED CUSTOMERS WILL—

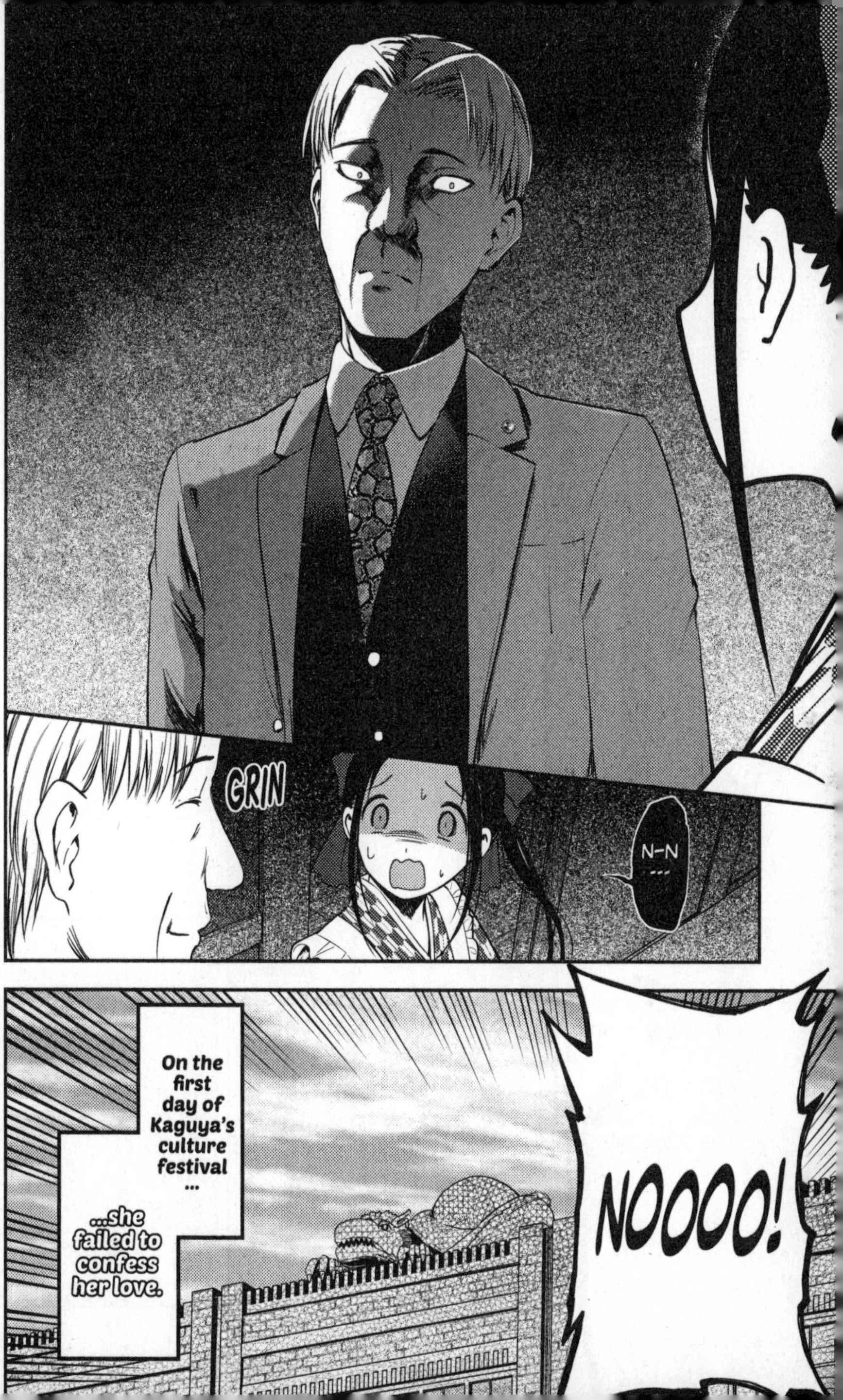
GRIN
N-N ...
NOOOO!
On the first day of Kaguya's culture festival ...
...she failed to confess her love.

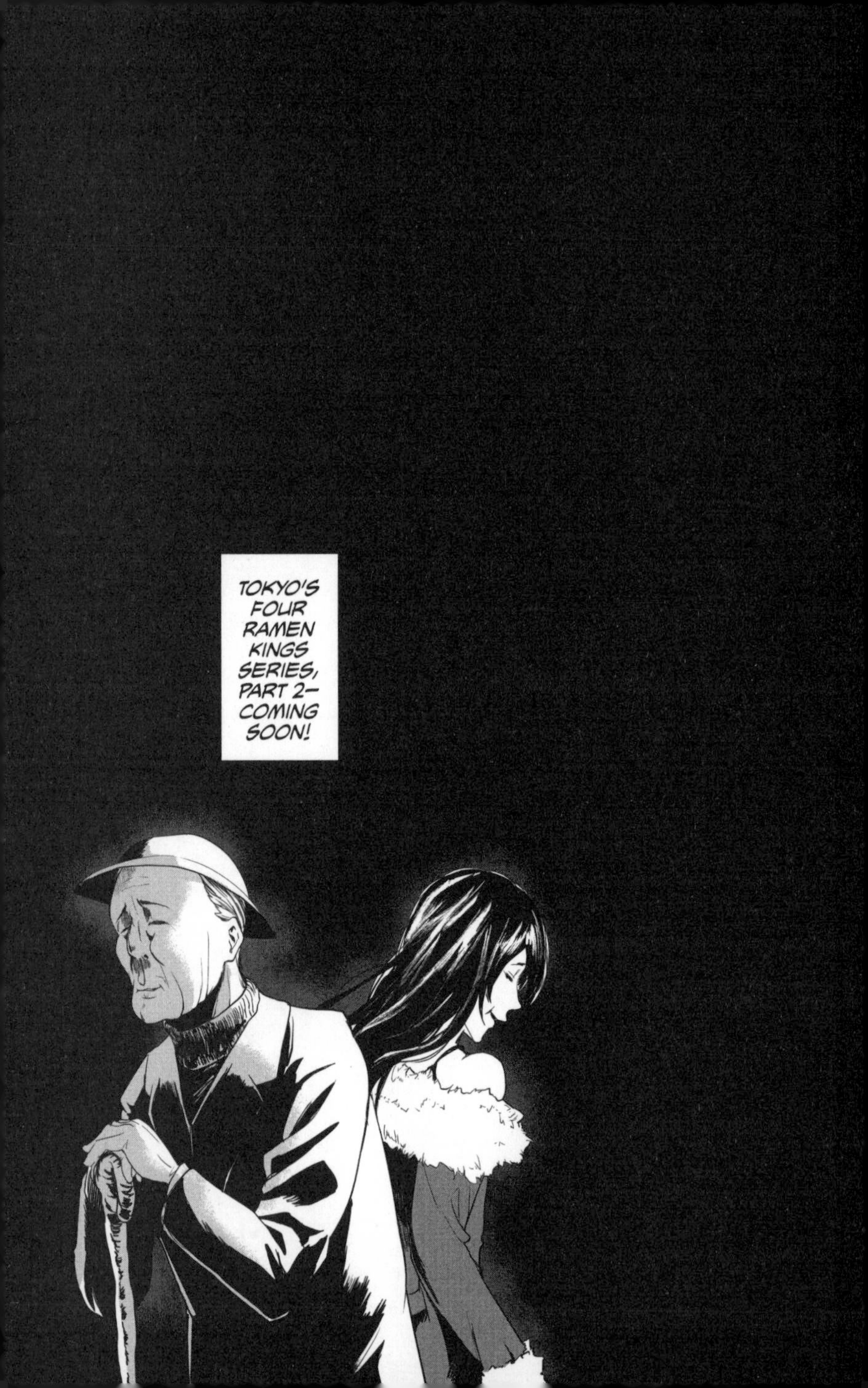
TOKYO'S FOUR RAMEN KINGS SERIES, PART 2—COMING SOON!

KAGUYA-SAMA
LOVE IS WAR

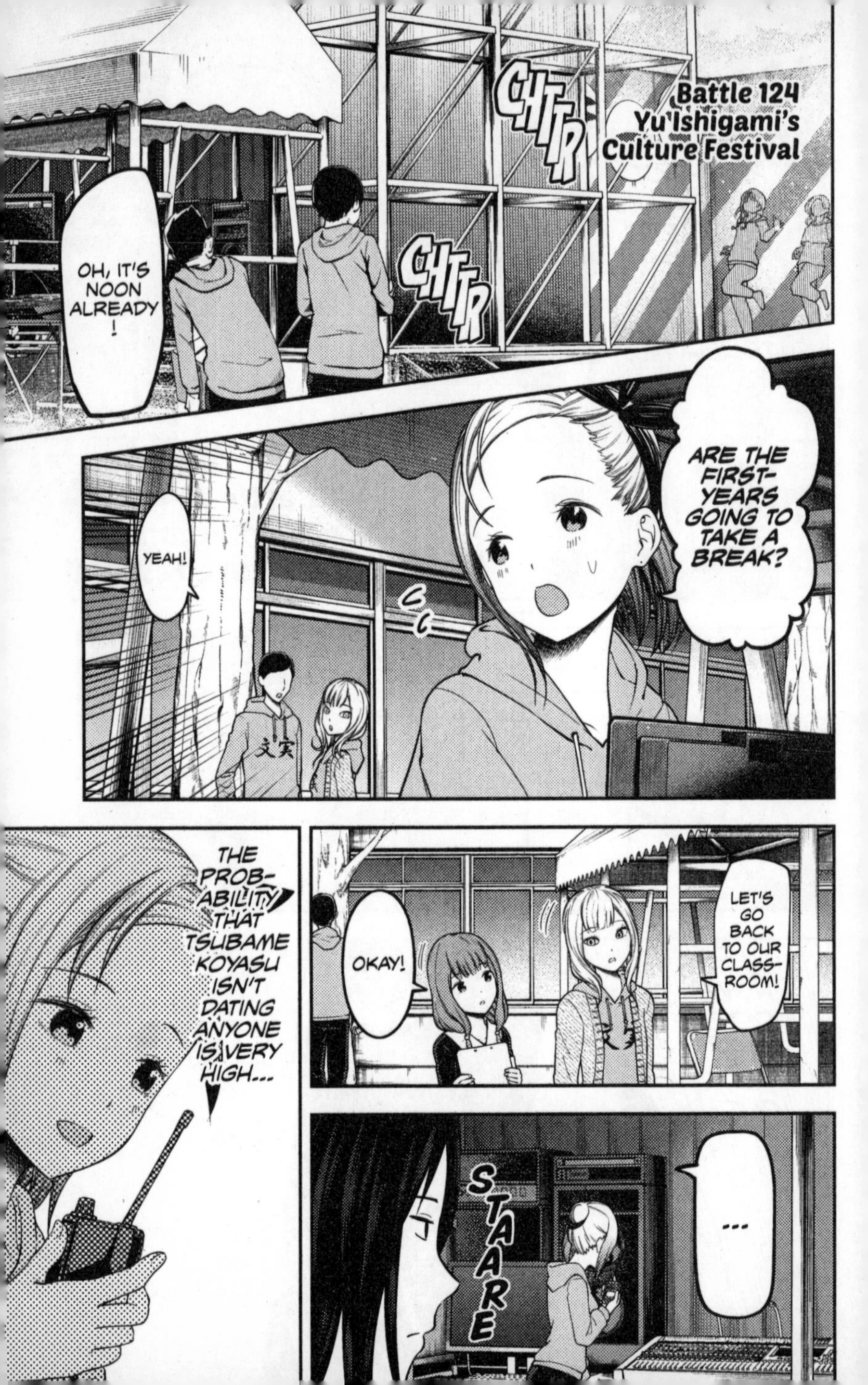
Battle 124
Yu Ishigami's Culture Festival
CHTTR
CHTTR
OH, IT'S NOON ALREADY!
ARE THE FIRST-YEARS GOING TO TAKE A BREAK?
YEAH!
LET'S GO BACK TO OUR CLASSROOM!
OKAY!
...
STAARE
THE PROBABILITY THAT TSUBAME KOYASU ISN'T DATING ANYONE IS VERY HIGH...

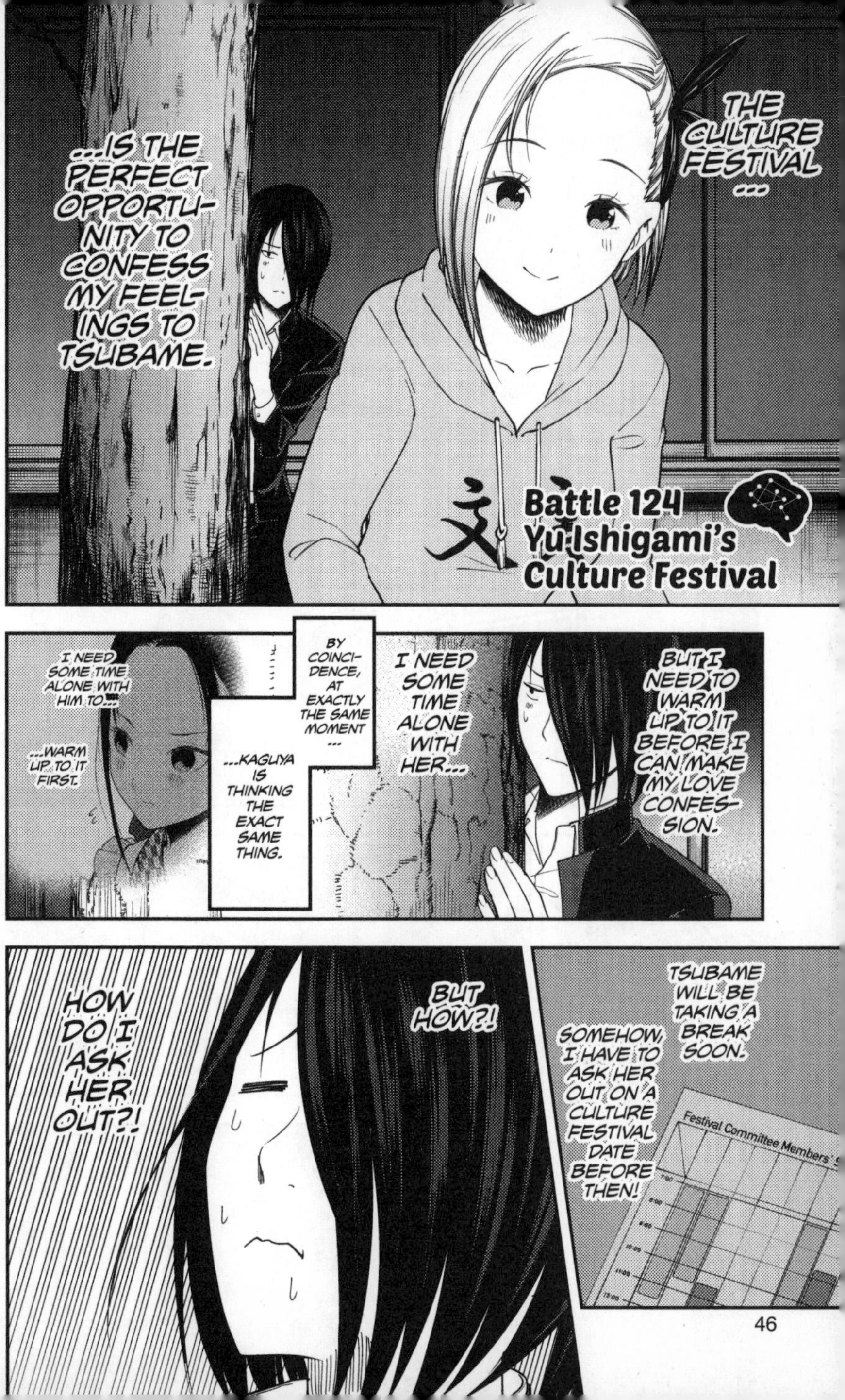
THE CULTURE FESTIVAL...
...IS THE PERFECT OPPORTUNITY TO CONFESS MY FEELINGS TO TSUBAME.
Battle 124 Yu Ishigami's Culture Festival
BUT I NEED TO WARM UP TO IT BEFORE I CAN MAKE MY LOVE CONFESSION.
I NEED SOME TIME ALONE WITH HER...
BY COINCIDENCE, AT EXACTLY THE SAME MOMENT...
...KAGUYA IS THINKING THE EXACT SAME THING.
I NEED SOME TIME ALONE WITH HIM TO...
...WARM UP TO IT FIRST.
TSUBAME WILL BE TAKING A BREAK SOON.
SOMEHOW, I HAVE TO ASK HER OUT ON A CULTURE FESTIVAL DATE BEFORE THEN!
Festival Committee Members'
BUT HOW?!
HOW DO I ASK HER OUT?!

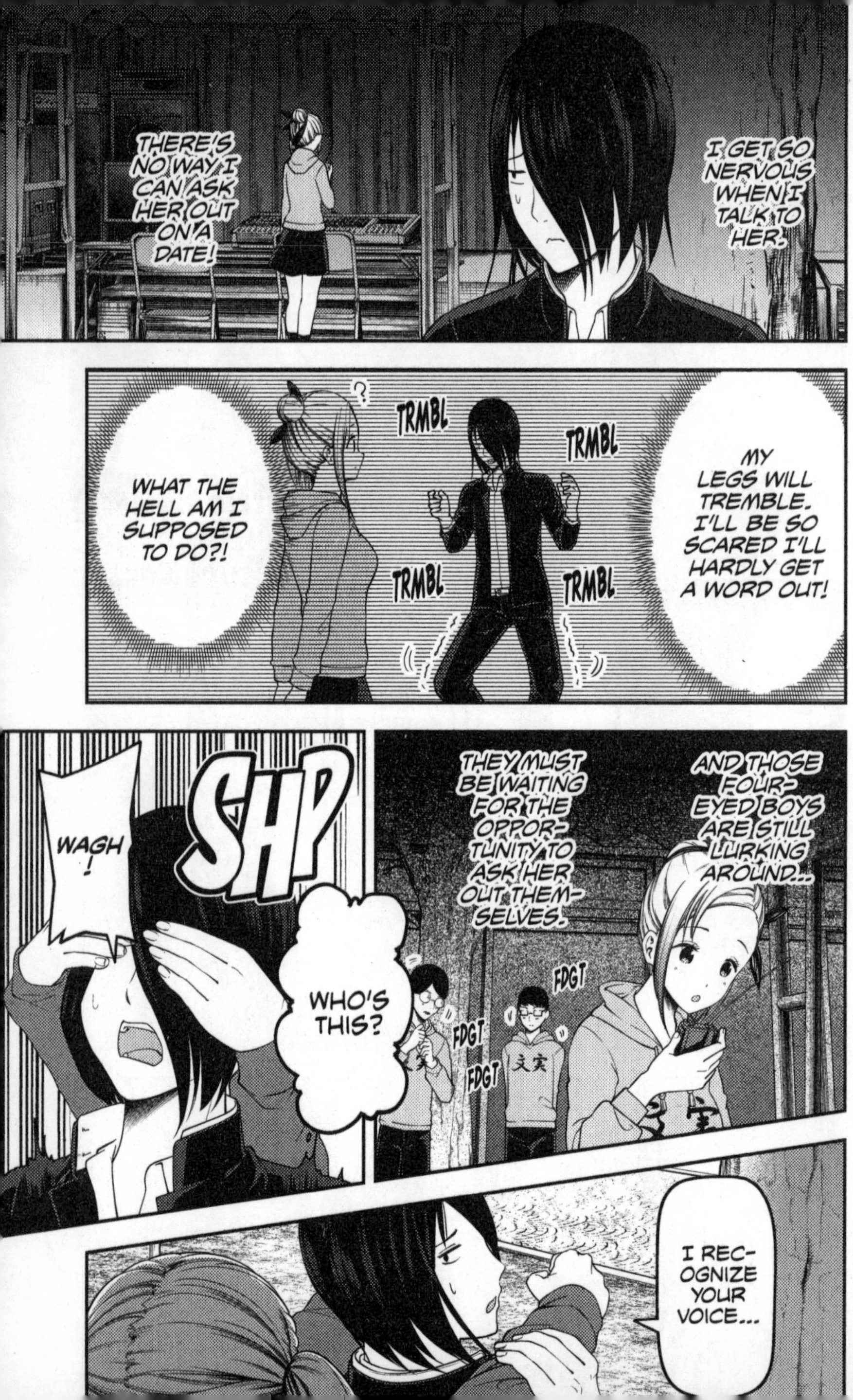
I GET SO NERVOUS WHEN I TALK TO HER.
THERE'S NO WAY I CAN ASK HER OUT ON A DATE!
MY LEGS WILL TREMBLE. I'LL BE SO SCARED I'LL HARDLY GET A WORD OUT!
TRMBL
TRMBL
TRMBL
TRMBL
WHAT THE HELL AM I SUPPOSED TO DO?!
AND THOSE FOUR-EYED BOYS ARE STILL LURKING AROUND...
THEY MUST BE WAITING FOR THE OPPORTUNITY TO ASK HER OUT THEMSELVES.
FDGT
FDGT
FDGT
SHP
WAGH!
WHO'S THIS?
I RECOGNIZE YOUR VOICE...

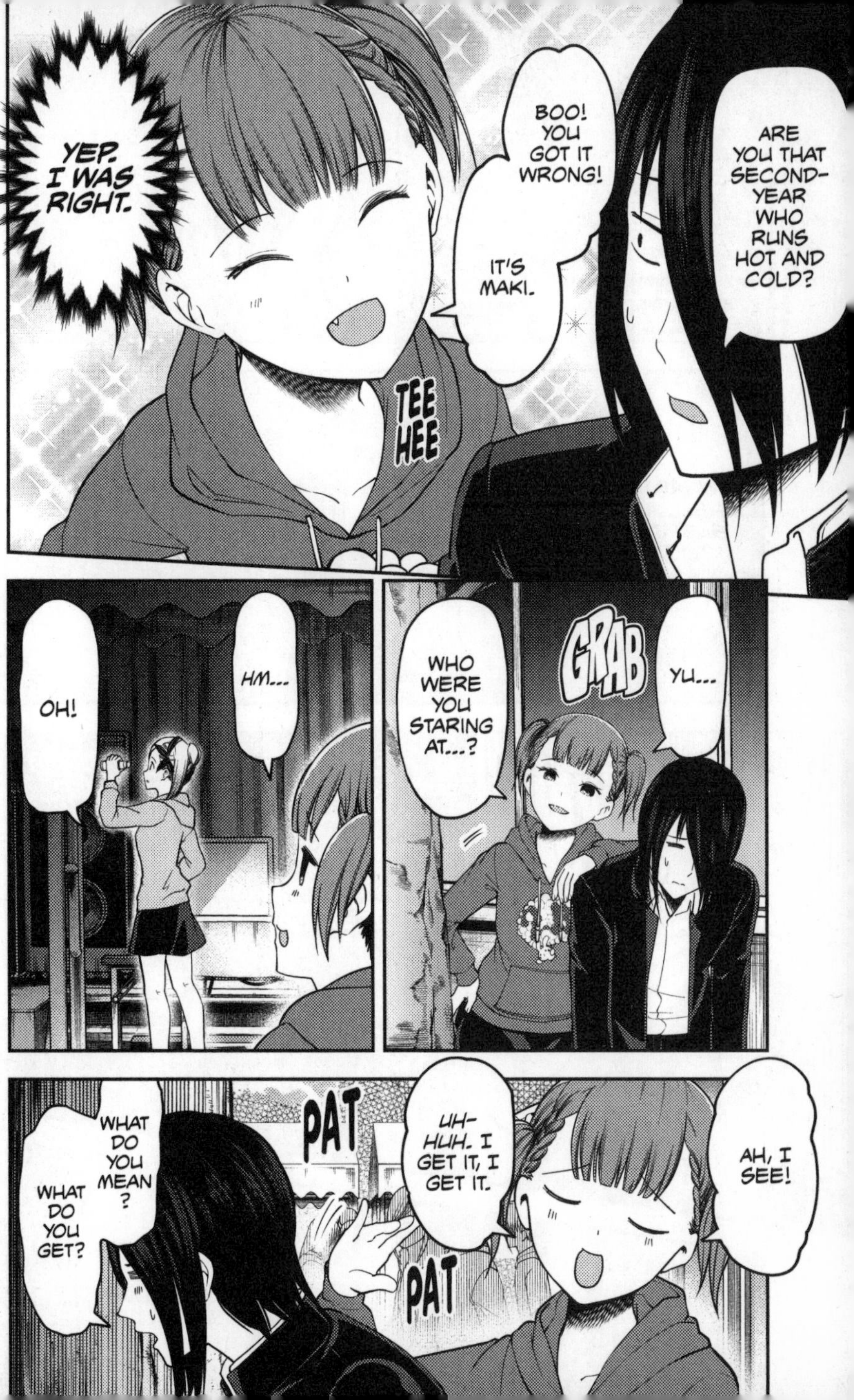
ARE YOU THAT SECOND-YEAR WHO RUNS HOT AND COLD?
BOO! YOU GOT IT WRONG!
IT'S MAKI.
TEE HEE
YEP. I WAS RIGHT.
YU...
GRAB
WHO WERE YOU STARING AT...?
HM...
OH!
AH, I SEE!
UH-HUH. I GET IT, I GET IT.
PAT
PAT
WHAT DO YOU MEAN?
WHAT DO YOU GET?

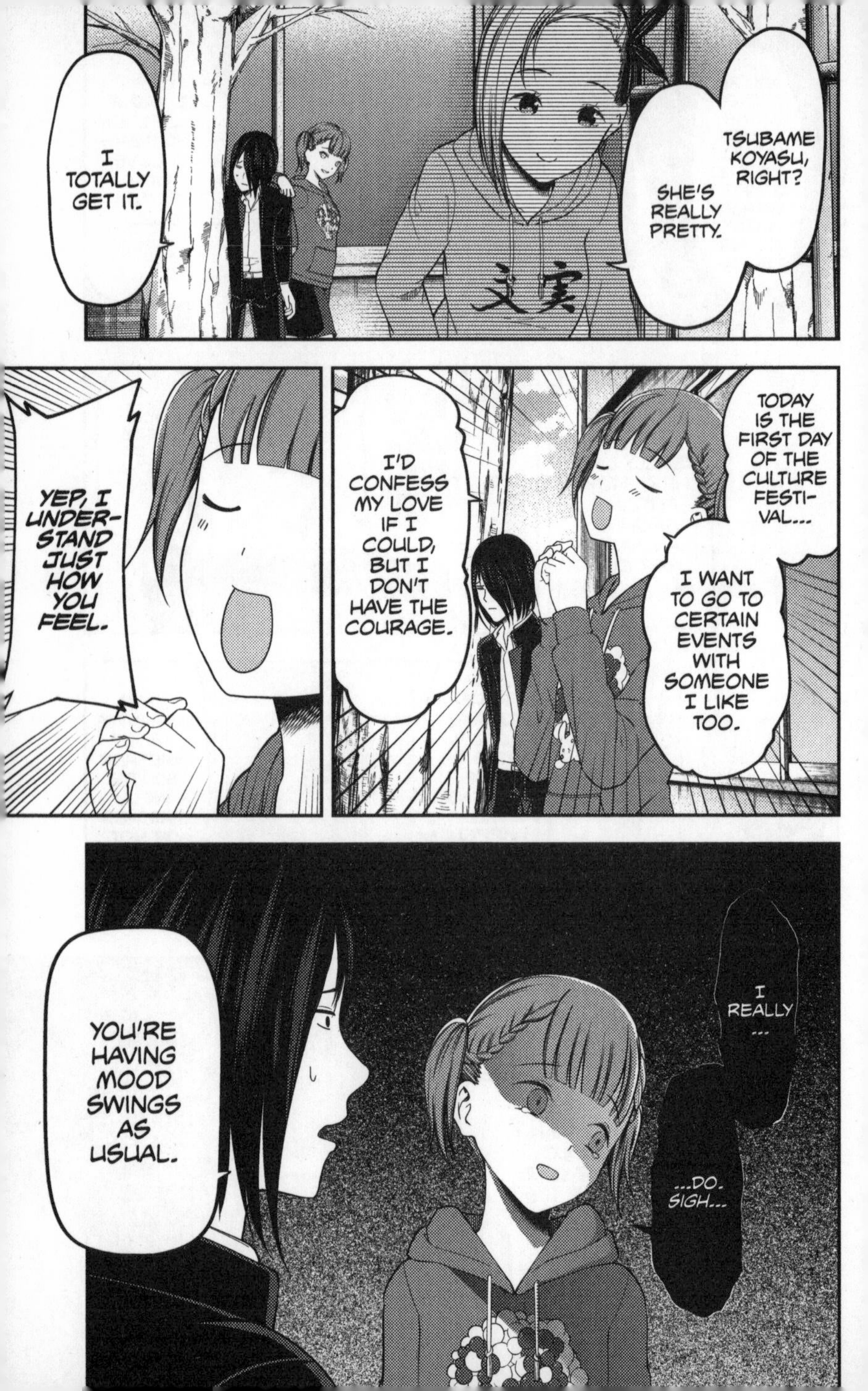
TSUBAME KOYASU, RIGHT?
SHE'S REALLY PRETTY.
文実
I TOTALLY GET IT.
TODAY IS THE FIRST DAY OF THE CULTURE FESTI-VAL...
I WANT TO GO TO CERTAIN EVENTS WITH SOMEONE I LIKE TOO.
I'D CONFESS MY LOVE IF I COULD, BUT I DON'T HAVE THE COURAGE.
YEP, I UNDER-STAND JUST HOW YOU FEEL.
I REALLY...
...DO. SIGH...
YOU'RE HAVING MOOD SWINGS AS USUAL.

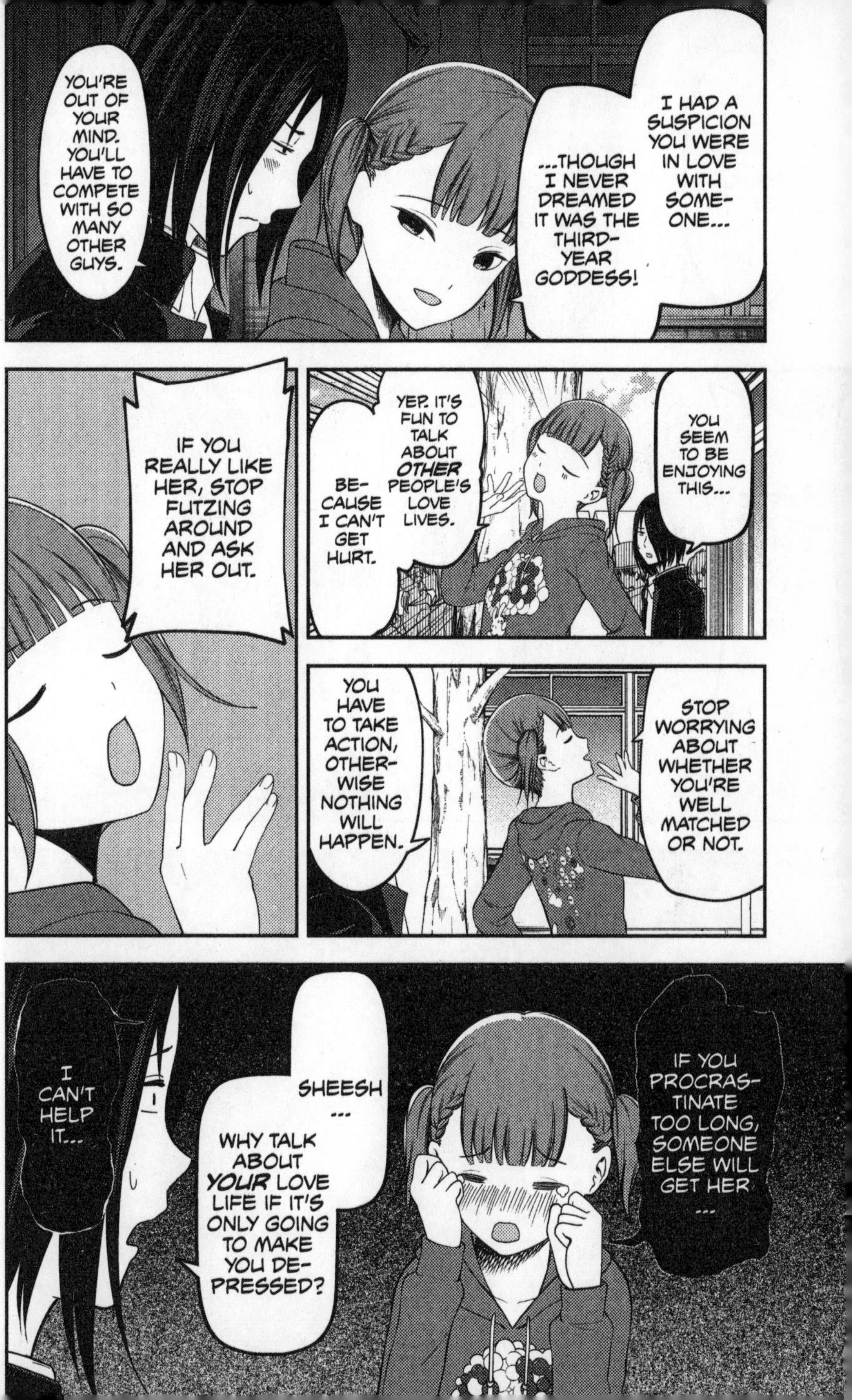
I HAD A SUSPICION YOU WERE IN LOVE WITH SOME-ONE...
...THOUGH I NEVER DREAMED IT WAS THE THIRD-YEAR GODDESS!
YOU'RE OUT OF YOUR MIND. YOU'LL HAVE TO COMPETE WITH SO MANY OTHER GUYS.
YOU SEEM TO BE ENJOYING THIS...
YEP. IT'S FUN TO TALK ABOUT *OTHER* PEOPLE'S LOVE LIVES.
BE-CAUSE I CAN'T GET HURT.
STOP WORRYING ABOUT WHETHER YOU'RE WELL MATCHED OR NOT.
YOU HAVE TO TAKE ACTION, OTHER-WISE NOTHING WILL HAPPEN.
IF YOU REALLY LIKE HER, STOP FUTZING AROUND AND ASK HER OUT.
IF YOU PROCRAS-TINATE TOO LONG, SOMEONE ELSE WILL GET HER...
SHEESH...
WHY TALK ABOUT *YOUR* LOVE LIFE IF IT'S ONLY GOING TO MAKE YOU DE-PRESSED?
I CAN'T HELP IT...

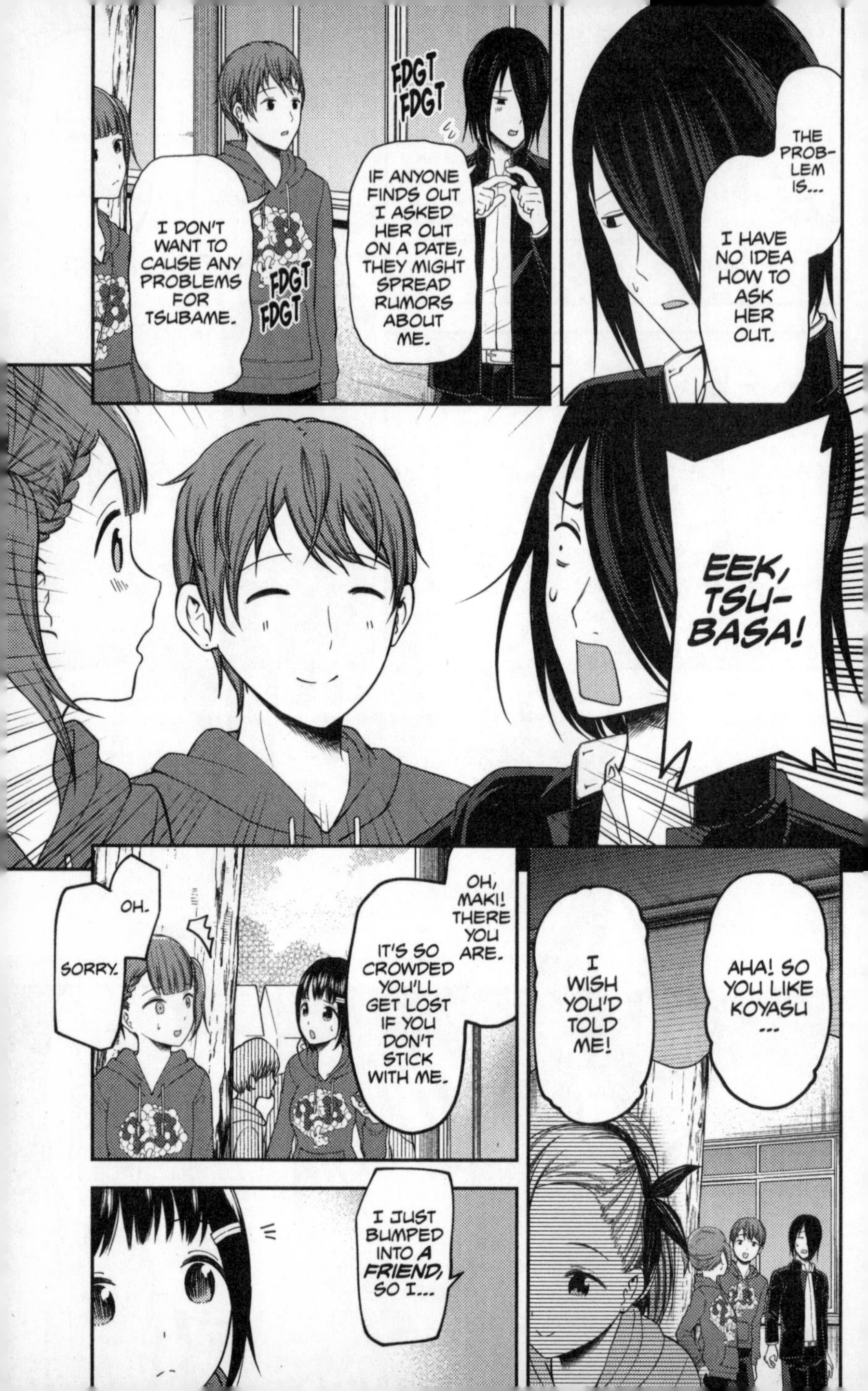
THE PROBLEM IS...
I HAVE NO IDEA HOW TO ASK HER OUT.
FDGT FDGT
IF ANYONE FINDS OUT I ASKED HER OUT ON A DATE, THEY MIGHT SPREAD RUMORS ABOUT ME.
FDGT FDGT
I DON'T WANT TO CAUSE ANY PROBLEMS FOR TSUBAME.
EEK, TSU-BASA!
AHA! SO YOU LIKE KOYASU...
I WISH YOU'D TOLD ME!
OH, MAKI! THERE YOU ARE.
IT'S SO CROWDED YOU'LL GET LOST IF YOU DON'T STICK WITH ME.
OH.
SORRY.
I JUST BUMPED INTO A *FRIEND,* SO I...

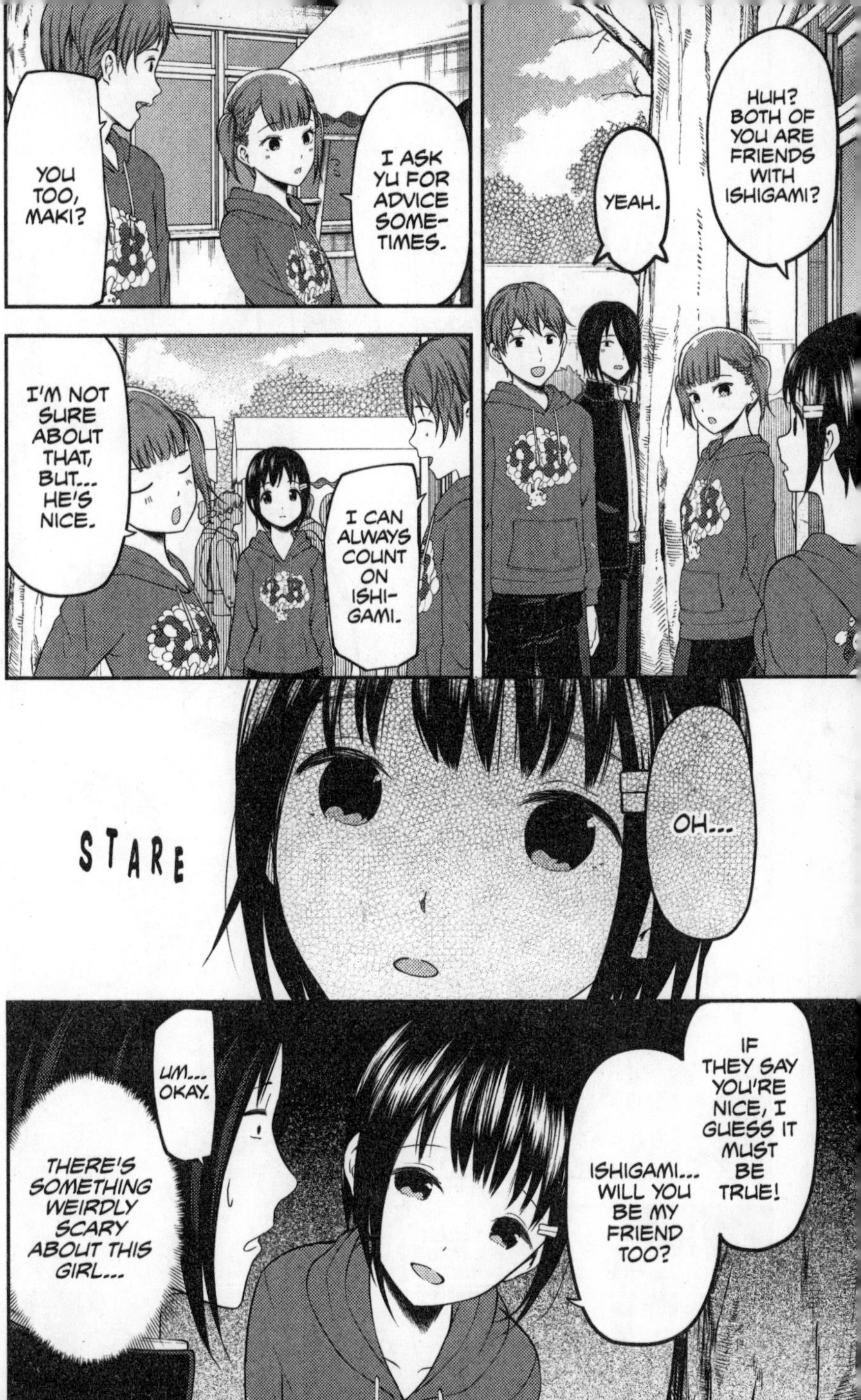
HUH? BOTH OF YOU ARE FRIENDS WITH ISHIGAMI?
YEAH.
I ASK YU FOR ADVICE SOME-TIMES.
YOU TOO, MAKI?
I CAN ALWAYS COUNT ON ISHI-GAMI.
I'M NOT SURE ABOUT THAT, BUT... HE'S NICE.
OH...
STARE
IF THEY SAY YOU'RE NICE, I GUESS IT MUST BE TRUE!
ISHIGAMI... WILL YOU BE MY FRIEND TOO?
UM... OKAY.
THERE'S SOMETHING WEIRDLY SCARY ABOUT THIS GIRL...

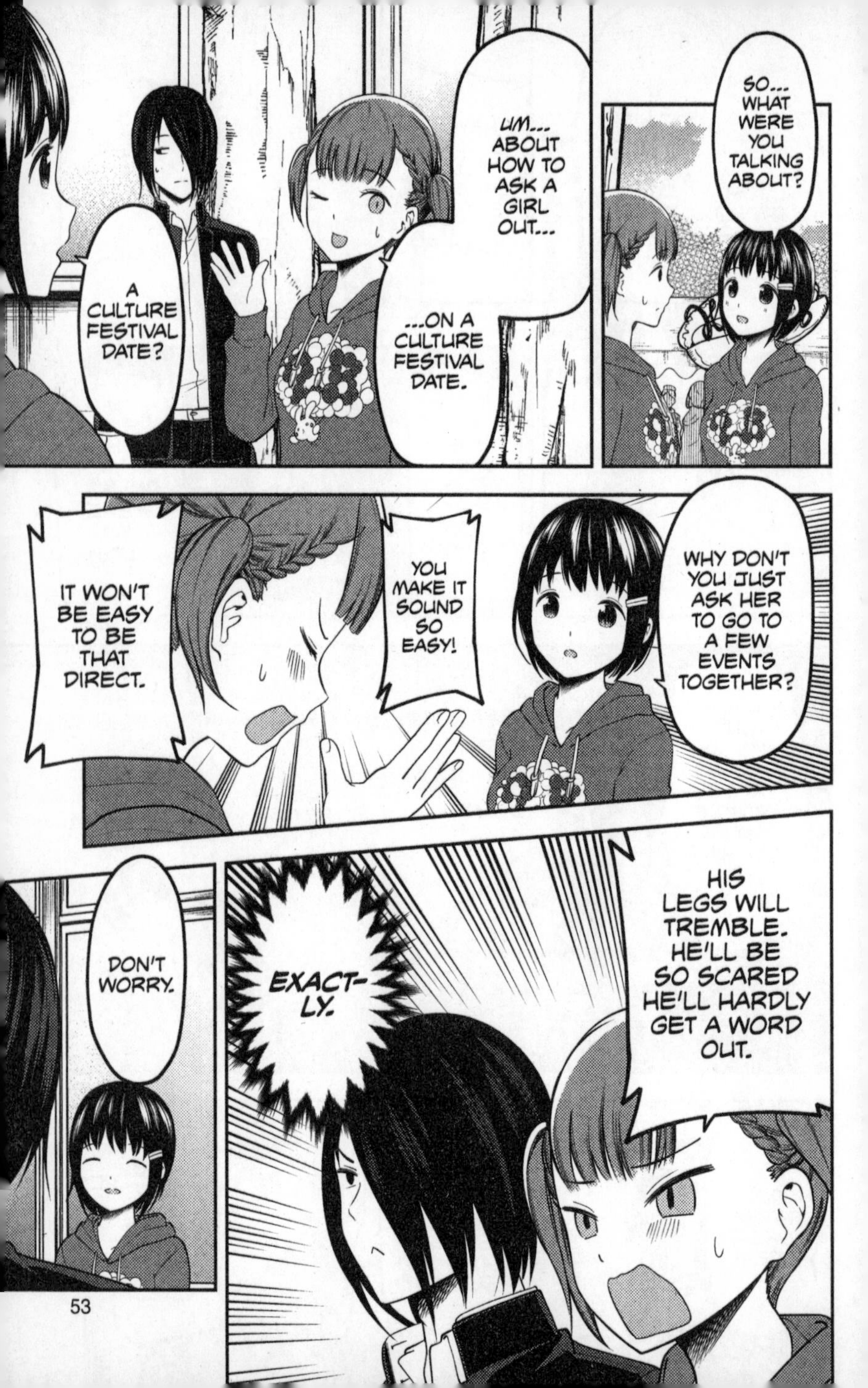
SO... WHAT WERE YOU TALKING ABOUT?
UM... ABOUT HOW TO ASK A GIRL OUT...
...ON A CULTURE FESTIVAL DATE.
A CULTURE FESTIVAL DATE?
WHY DON'T YOU JUST ASK HER TO GO TO A FEW EVENTS TOGETHER?
YOU MAKE IT SOUND SO EASY!
IT WON'T BE EASY TO BE THAT DIRECT.
HIS LEGS WILL TREMBLE. HE'LL BE SO SCARED HE'LL HARDLY GET A WORD OUT.
EXACT-LY.
DON'T WORRY.

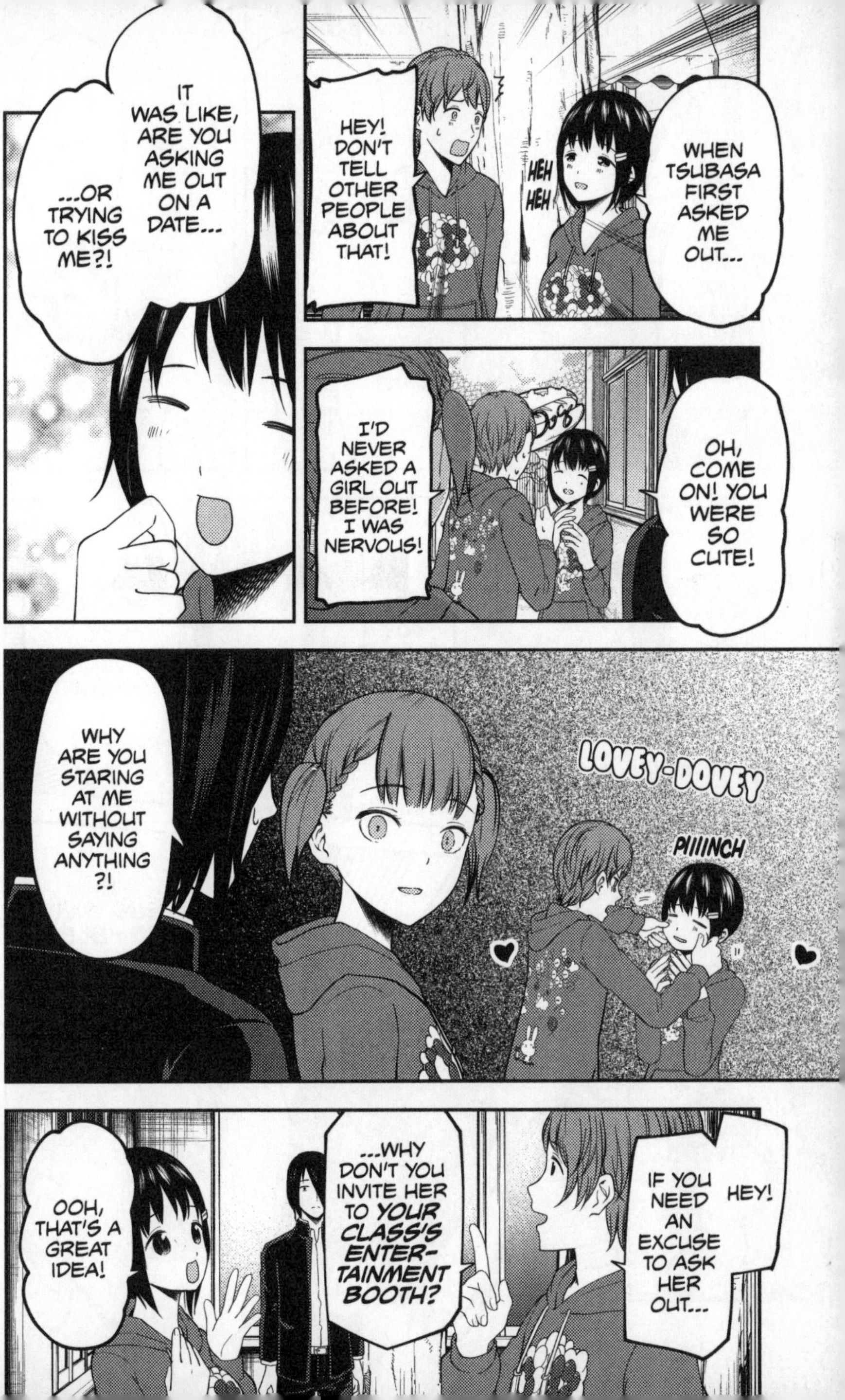
WHEN TSUBASA FIRST ASKED ME OUT...
HEH HEH
HEY! DON'T TELL OTHER PEOPLE ABOUT THAT!
OH, COME ON! YOU WERE SO CUTE!
I'D NEVER ASKED A GIRL OUT BEFORE! I WAS NERVOUS!
IT WAS LIKE, ARE YOU ASKING ME OUT ON A DATE...
...OR TRYING TO KISS ME?!
LOVEY-DOVEY
PIIIINCH
WHY ARE YOU STARING AT ME WITHOUT SAYING ANYTHING?!
HEY!
IF YOU NEED AN EXCUSE TO ASK HER OUT...
...WHY DON'T YOU INVITE HER TO *YOUR CLASS'S ENTERTAINMENT BOOTH?*
OOH, THAT'S A GREAT IDEA!

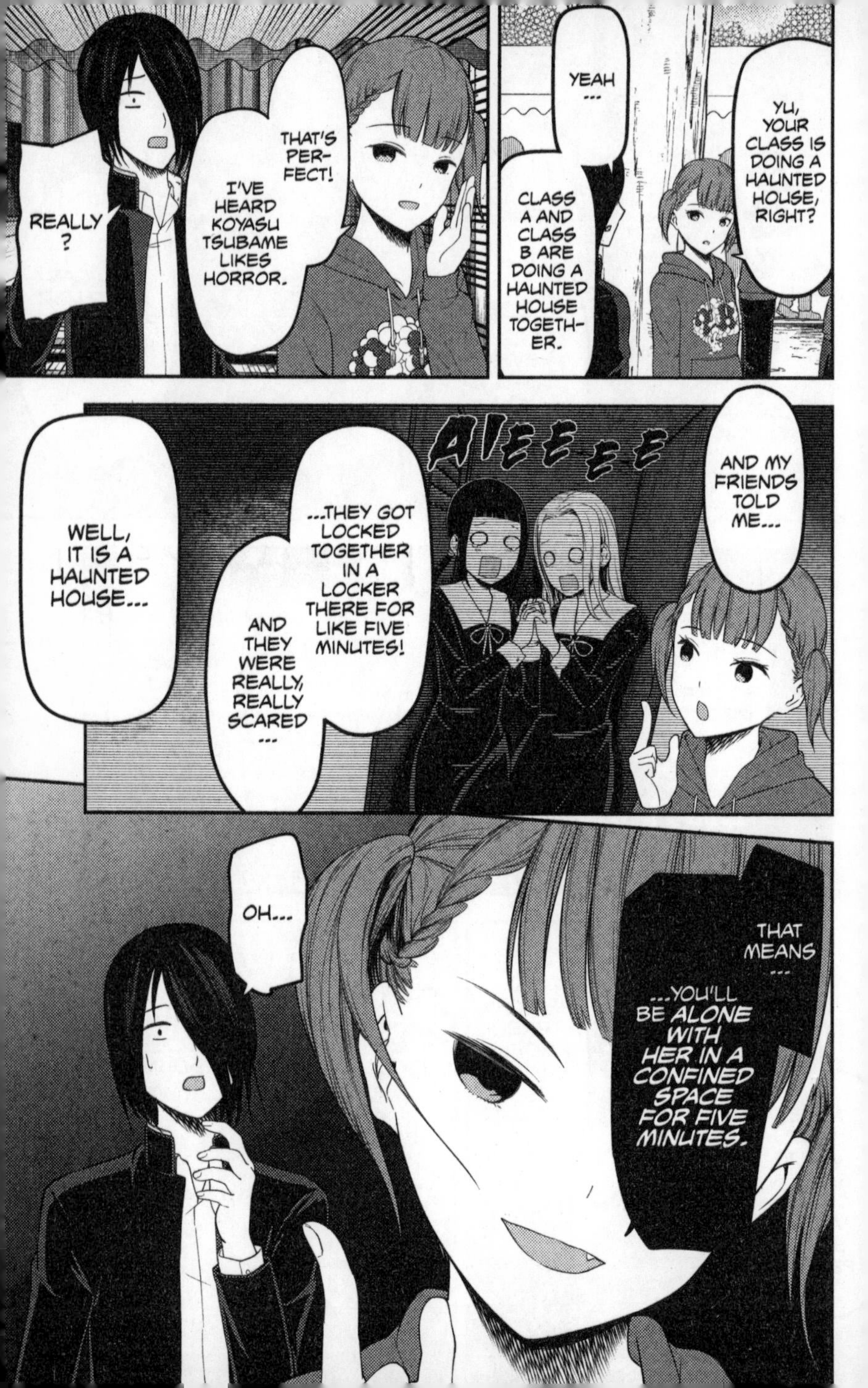
YU, YOUR CLASS IS DOING A HAUNTED HOUSE, RIGHT?
YEAH...
CLASS A AND CLASS B ARE DOING A HAUNTED HOUSE TOGETHER.
THAT'S PERFECT!
I'VE HEARD KOYASU TSUBAME LIKES HORROR.
REALLY?
AND MY FRIENDS TOLD ME...
AIEEE-E-E
...THEY GOT LOCKED TOGETHER IN A LOCKER THERE FOR LIKE FIVE MINUTES!
AND THEY WERE REALLY, REALLY SCARED...
WELL, IT IS A HAUNTED HOUSE...
THAT MEANS...
...YOU'LL BE ALONE WITH HER IN A CONFINED SPACE FOR FIVE MINUTES.
OH...

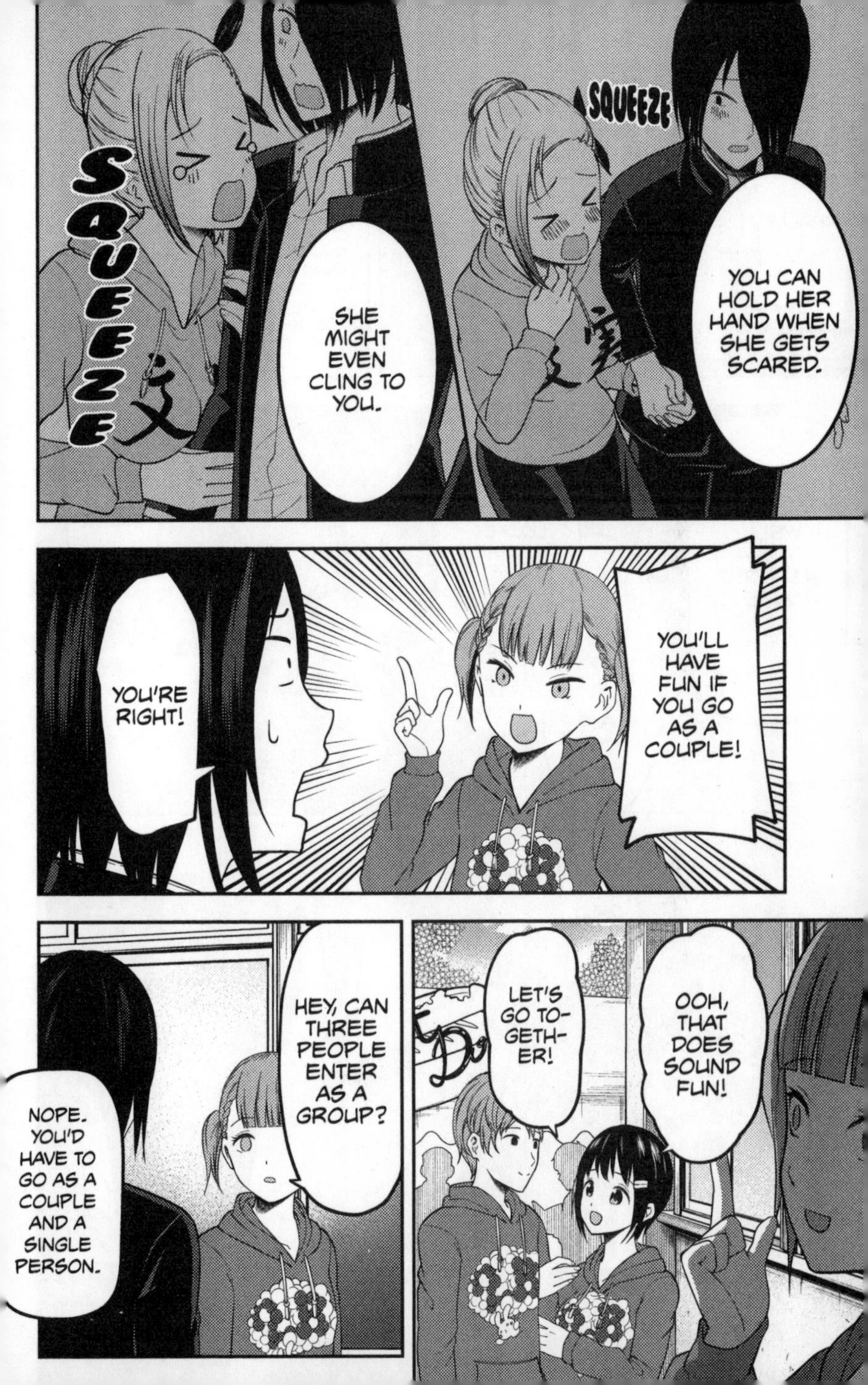
SQUEEZE
YOU CAN HOLD HER HAND WHEN SHE GETS SCARED.
SHE MIGHT EVEN CLING TO YOU.
SQUEEZE
YOU'LL HAVE FUN IF YOU GO AS A COUPLE!
YOU'RE RIGHT!
OOH, THAT DOES SOUND FUN!
LET'S GO TO-GETH-ER!
HEY, CAN THREE PEOPLE ENTER AS A GROUP?
NOPE. YOU'D HAVE TO GO AS A COUPLE AND A SINGLE PERSON.

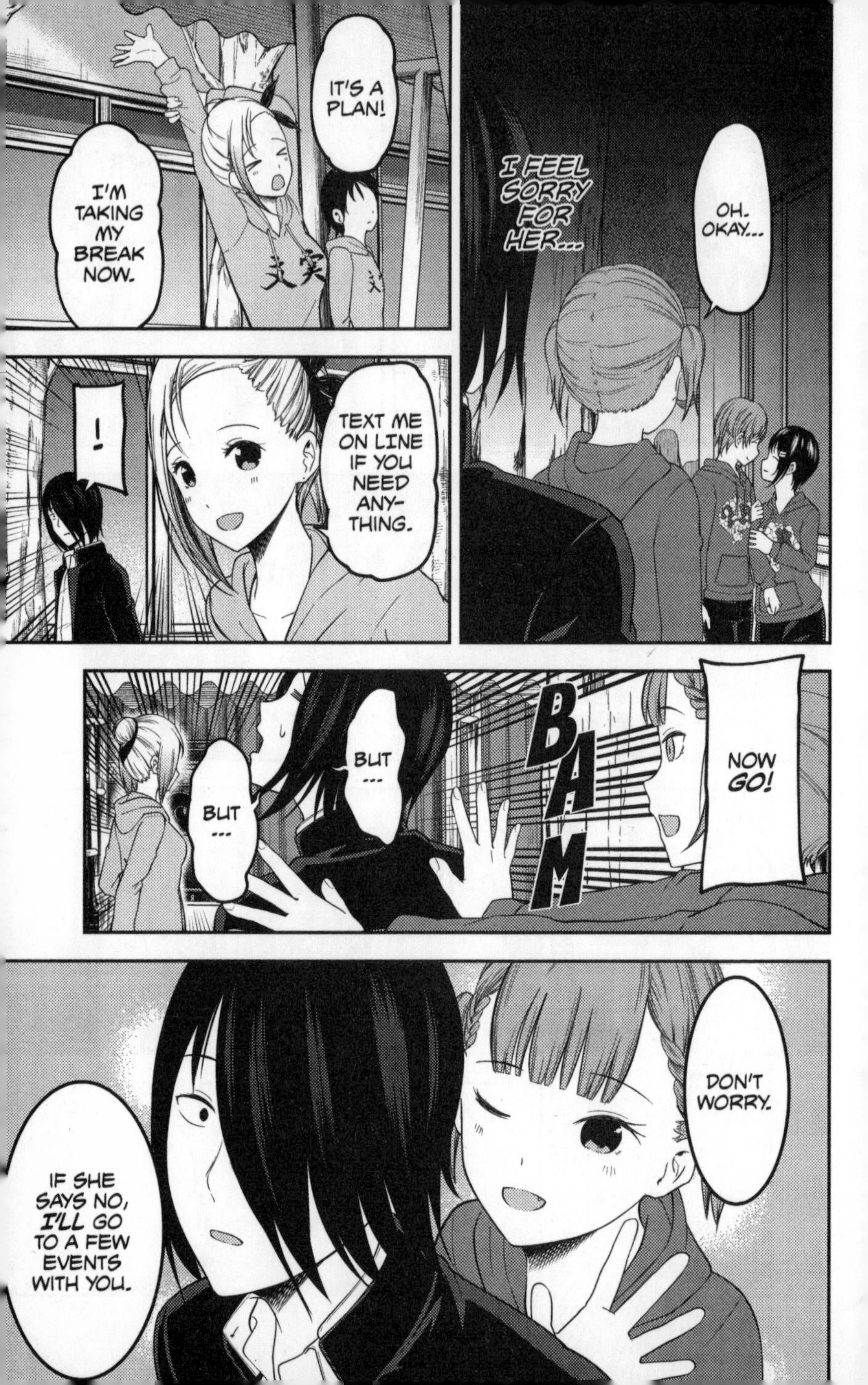
OH. OKAY...
I FEEL SORRY FOR HER...
IT'S A PLAN!
I'M TAKING MY BREAK NOW.
TEXT ME ON LINE IF YOU NEED ANYTHING.
!
NOW GO!
BAM
BUT ...
BUT ...
DON'T WORRY.
IF SHE SAYS NO, I'LL GO TO A FEW EVENTS WITH YOU.

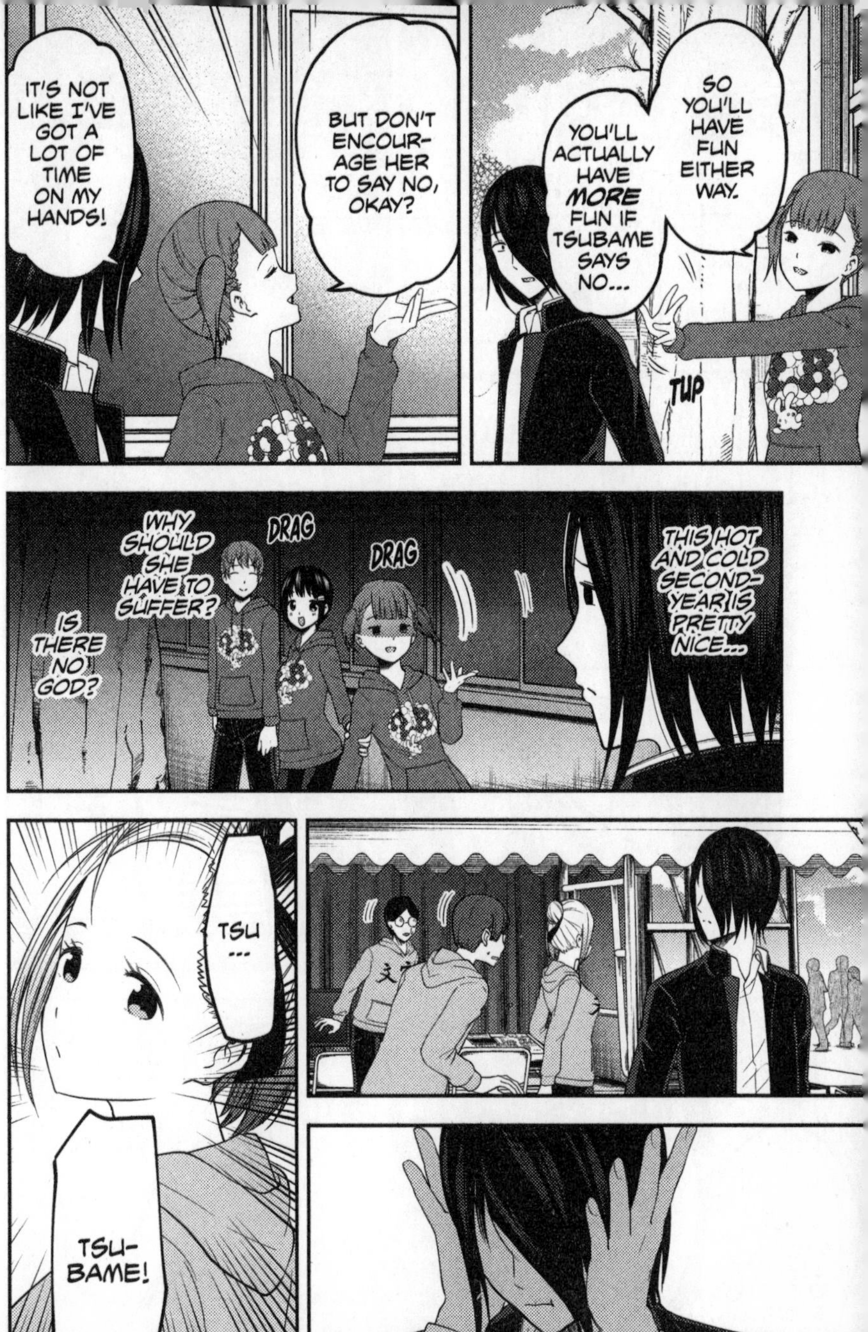
SO YOU'LL HAVE FUN EITHER WAY.
YOU'LL ACTUALLY HAVE **MORE** FUN IF TSUBAME SAYS NO...
TUP
BUT DON'T ENCOURAGE HER TO SAY NO, OKAY?
IT'S NOT LIKE I'VE GOT A LOT OF TIME ON MY HANDS!
THIS HOT AND COLD SECOND-YEAR IS PRETTY NICE...
DRAG
DRAG
WHY SHOULD SHE HAVE TO SUFFER?
IS THERE NO GOD?
TSU...
TSU-BAME!

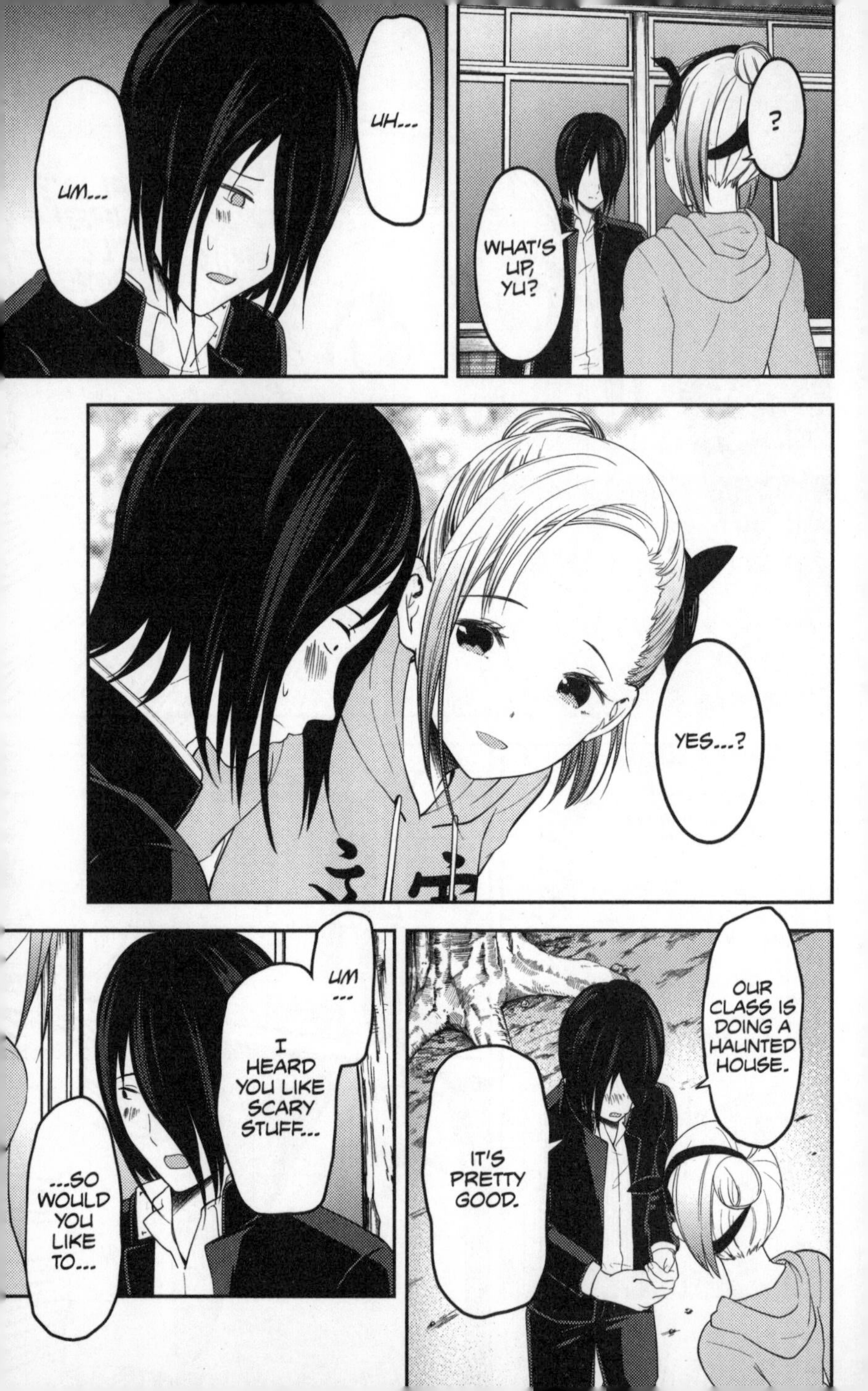
?
WHAT'S UP, YU?
UH...
UM...
YES...?
OUR CLASS IS DOING A HAUNTED HOUSE.
IT'S PRETTY GOOD.
UM...
I HEARD YOU LIKE SCARY STUFF...
...SO WOULD YOU LIKE TO...

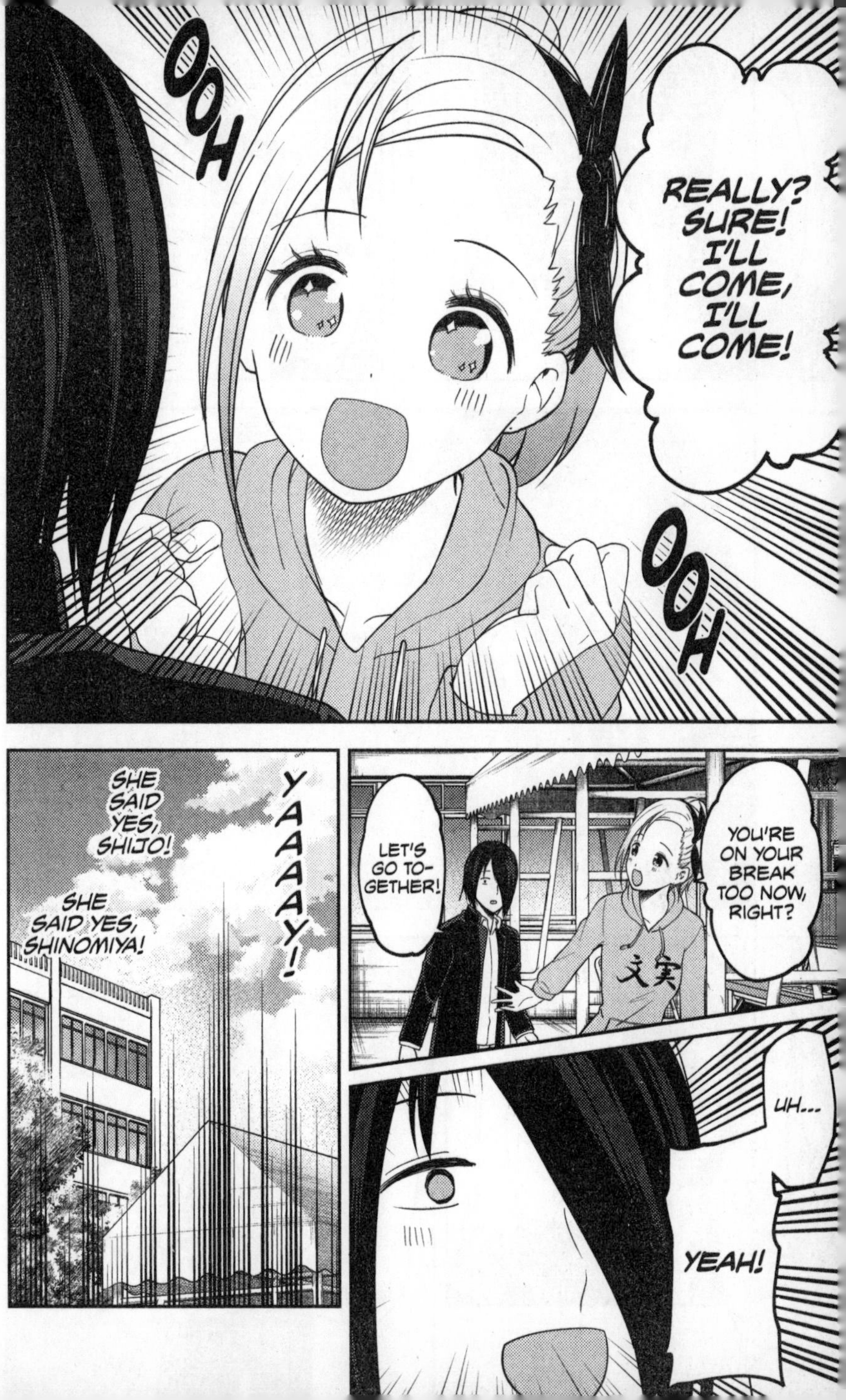
REALLY? SURE! I'LL COME, I'LL COME!
OOH
OOH
YOU'RE ON YOUR BREAK TOO NOW, RIGHT?
LET'S GO TO-GETHER!
UH...
YEAH!
YAAAAAY!
SHE SAID YES, SHIJO!
SHE SAID YES, SHINOMIYA!

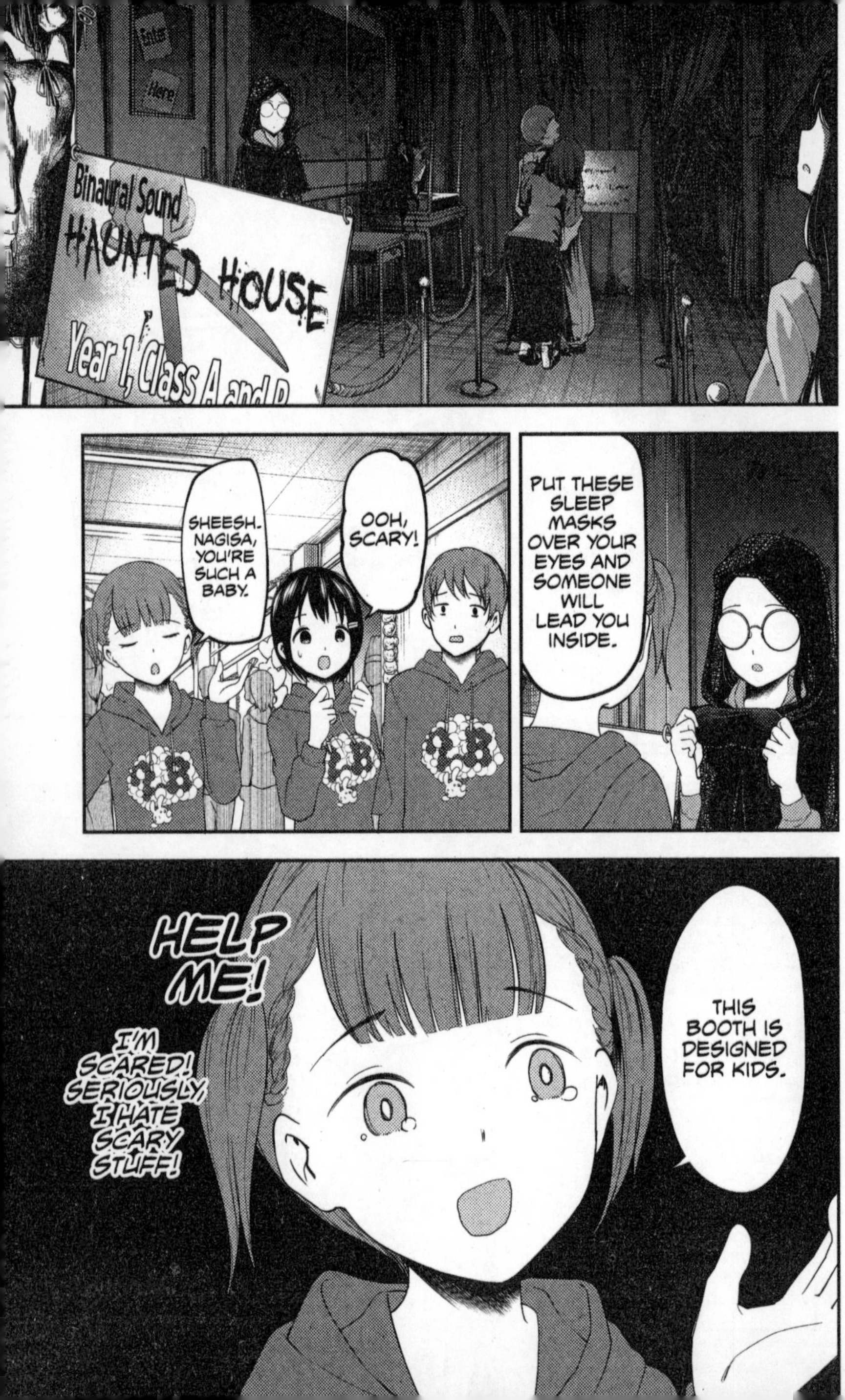
Enter Here!
Binaural Sound
HAUNTED HOUSE
Year 1, Class A and
PUT THESE SLEEP MASKS OVER YOUR EYES AND SOMEONE WILL LEAD YOU INSIDE.
OOH, SCARY!
SHEESH. NAGISA, YOU'RE SUCH A BABY.
THIS BOOTH IS DESIGNED FOR KIDS.
HELP ME!
I'M SCARED! SERIOUSLY, I HATE SCARY STUFF!

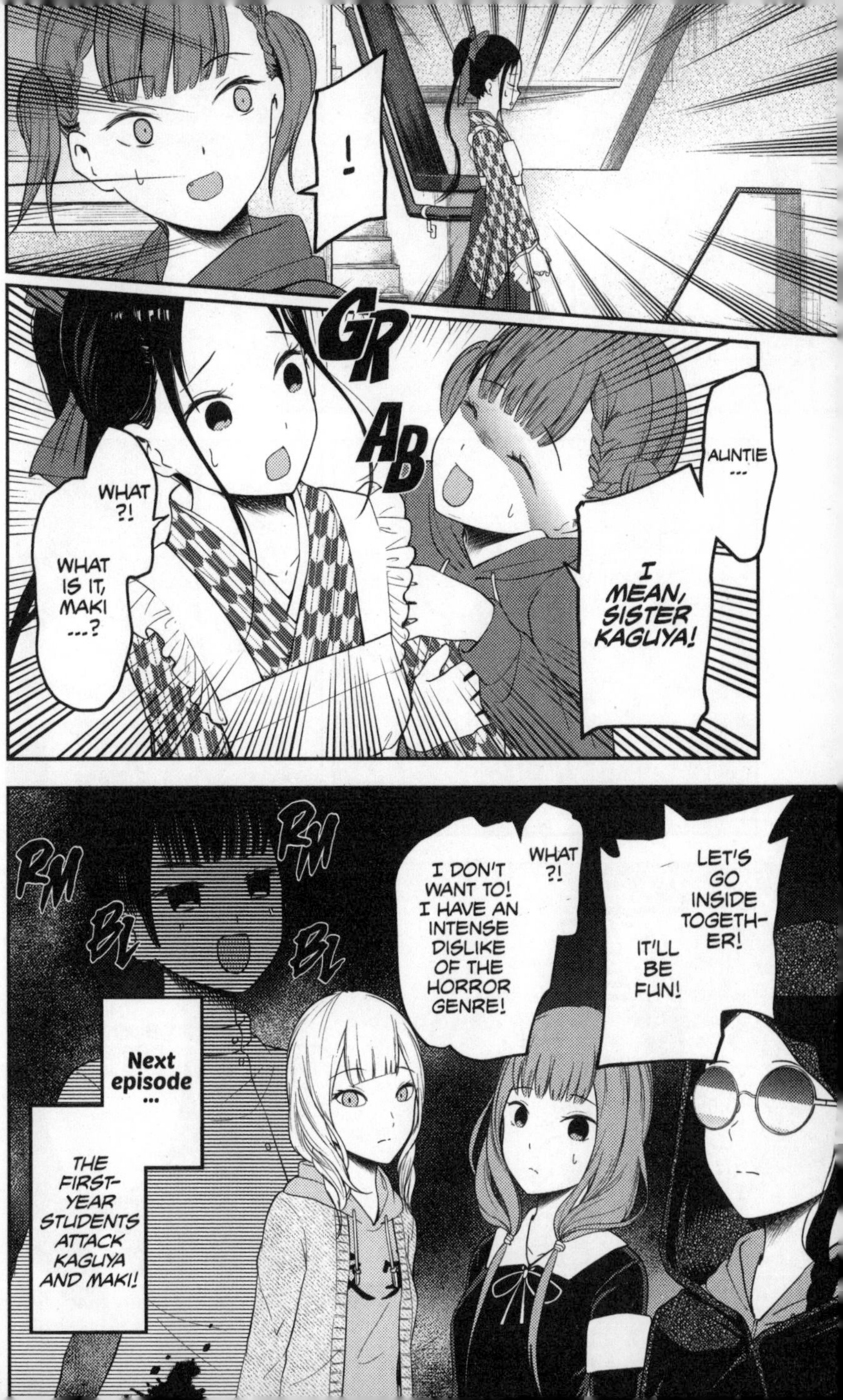
!
GRAB
AUNTIE...
I MEAN, SISTER KAGUYA!
WHAT?!
WHAT IS IT, MAKI...?
LET'S GO INSIDE TOGETHER!
IT'LL BE FUN!
WHAT?!
I DON'T WANT TO! I HAVE AN INTENSE DISLIKE OF THE HORROR GENRE!
RM BL
RM BL
Next episode...
THE FIRST-YEAR STUDENTS ATTACK KAGUYA AND MAKI!

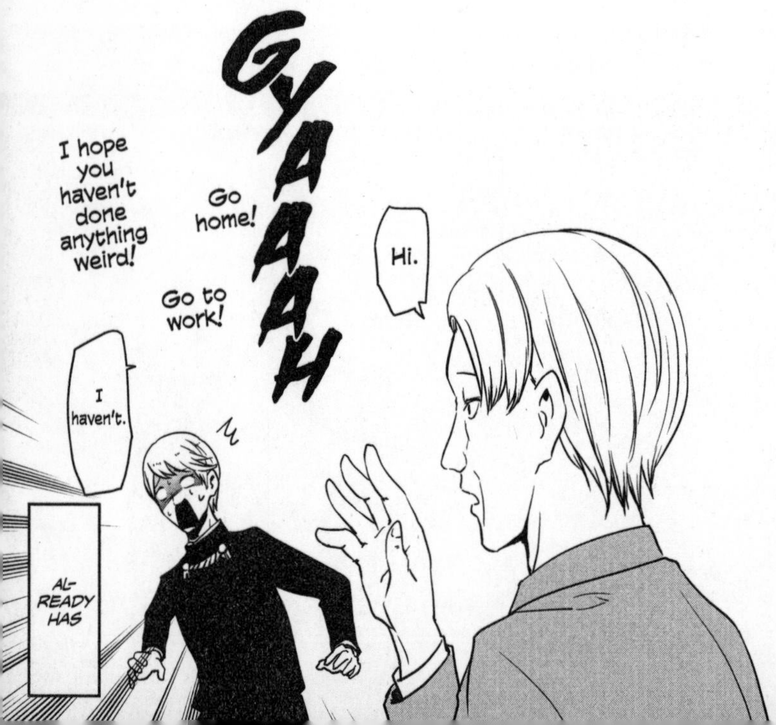
Hi.
GYAAAH
Go home!
I hope you haven't done anything weird!
Go to work!
I haven't.
AL-READY HAS

KAGUYA-SAMA
LOVE IS WAR

Battle 125 Kozue Makihara Wants to Have Fun

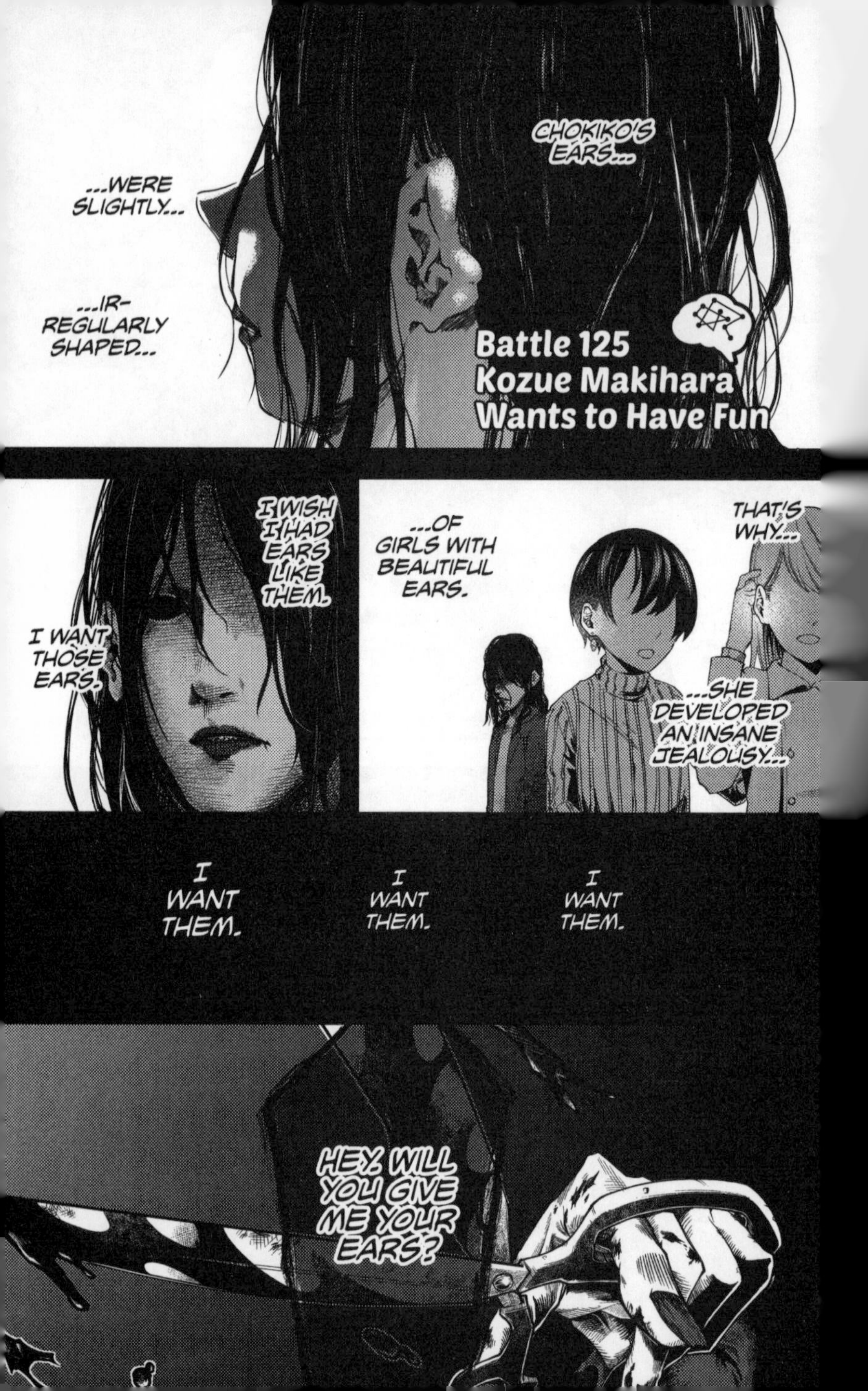
CHOKIKO'S EARS...
...WERE SLIGHTLY...
...IR-REGULARLY SHAPED...
Battle 125 Kozue Makihara Wants to Have Fun
THAT'S WHY...
...SHE DEVELOPED AN INSANE JEALOUSY...
...OF GIRLS WITH BEAUTIFUL EARS.
I WISH I HAD EARS LIKE THEM.
I WANT THOSE EARS.
I WANT THEM.
I WANT THEM.
I WANT THEM.
HEY, WILL YOU GIVE ME YOUR EARS?

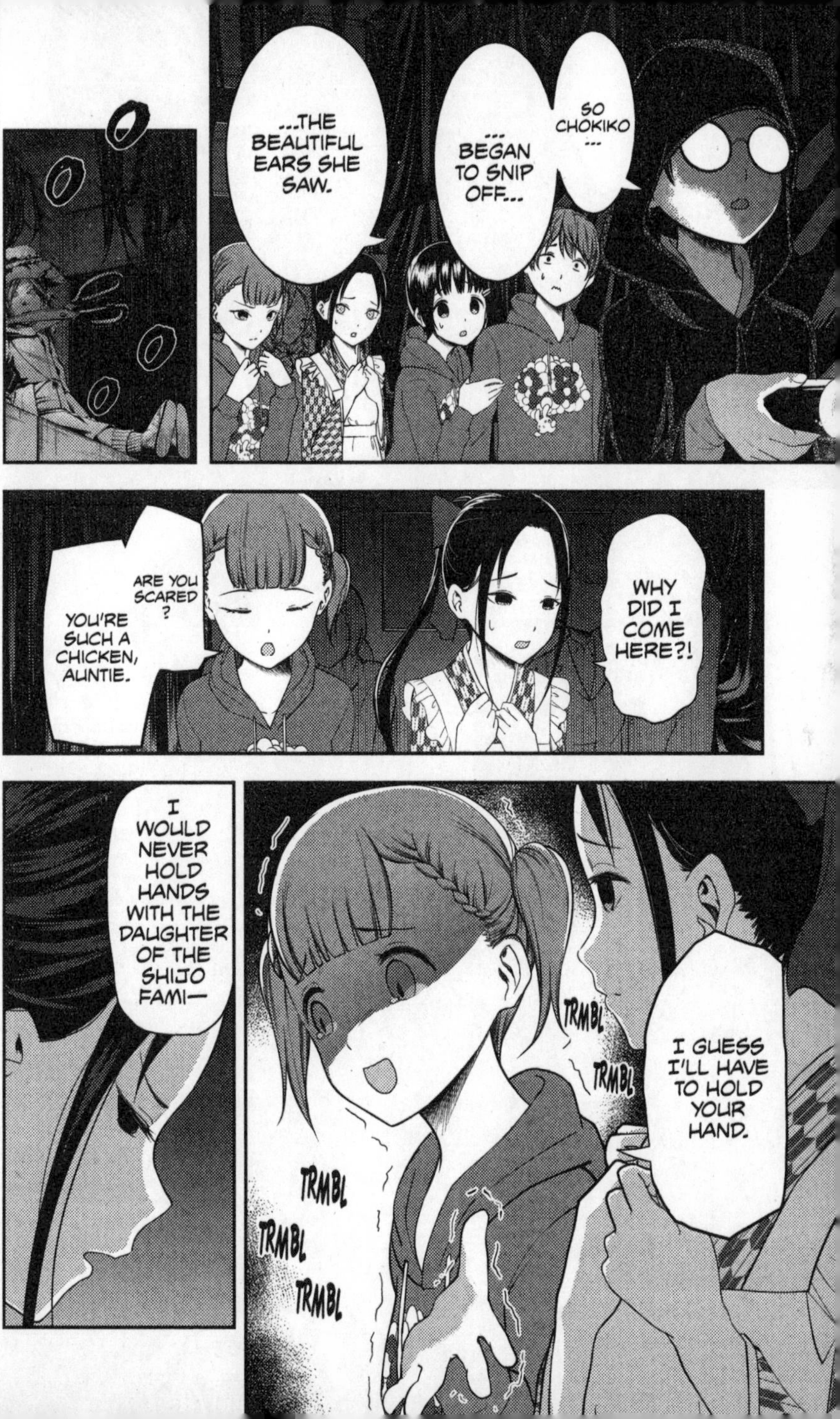
SO CHOKIKO ...
...BEGAN TO SNIP OFF...
...THE BEAUTIFUL EARS SHE SAW.
WHY DID I COME HERE?!
ARE YOU SCARED?
YOU'RE SUCH A CHICKEN, AUNTIE.
I GUESS I'LL HAVE TO HOLD YOUR HAND.
TRMBL
TRMBL
TRMBL
TRMBL
TRMBL
I WOULD NEVER HOLD HANDS WITH THE DAUGHTER OF THE SHIJO FAMI—

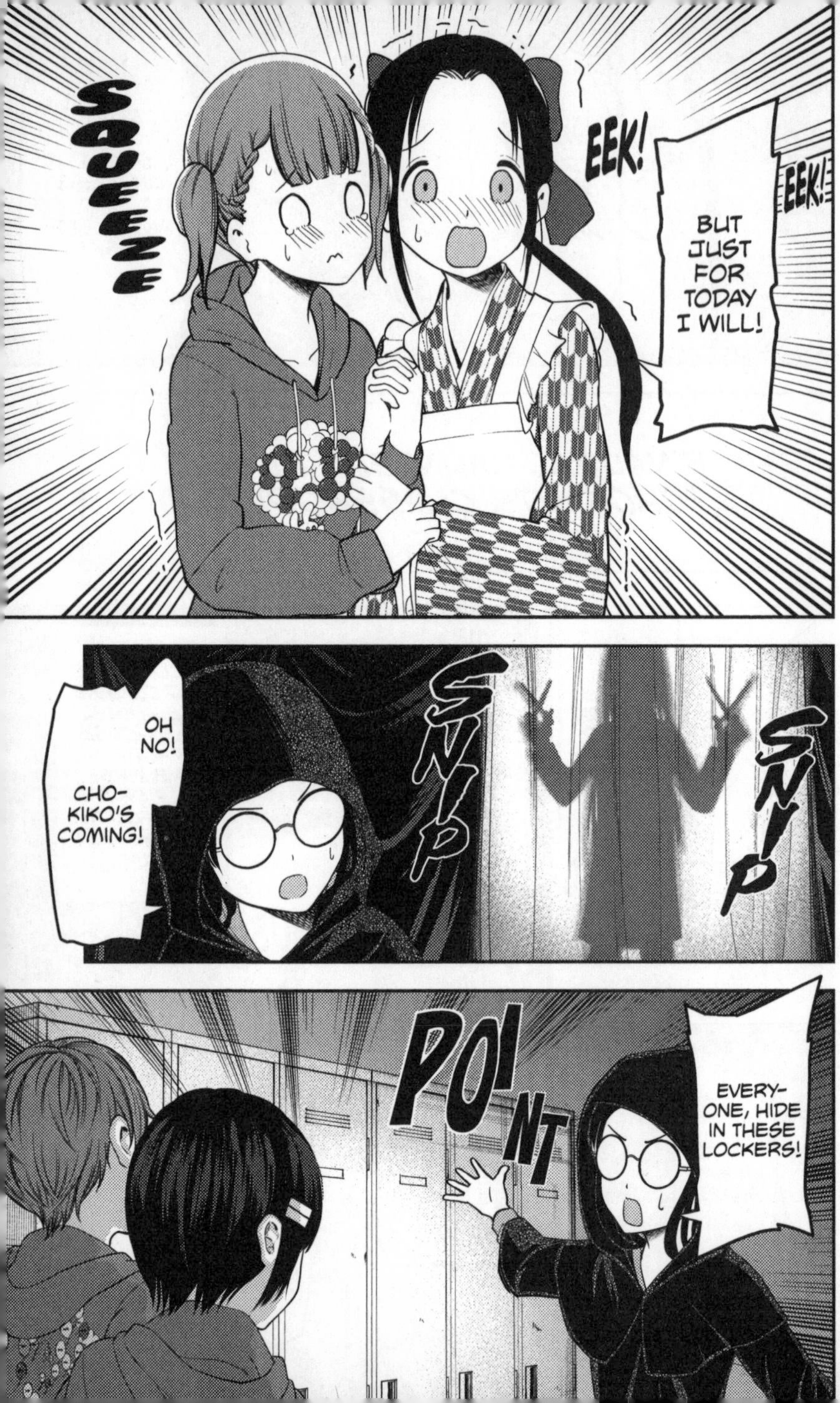
BUT JUST FOR TODAY I WILL!
EEK!
EEK!
SQUEEZE
SNIP
SNIP
OH NO!
CHO-KIKO'S COMING!
EVERY-ONE, HIDE IN THESE LOCKERS!
POINT

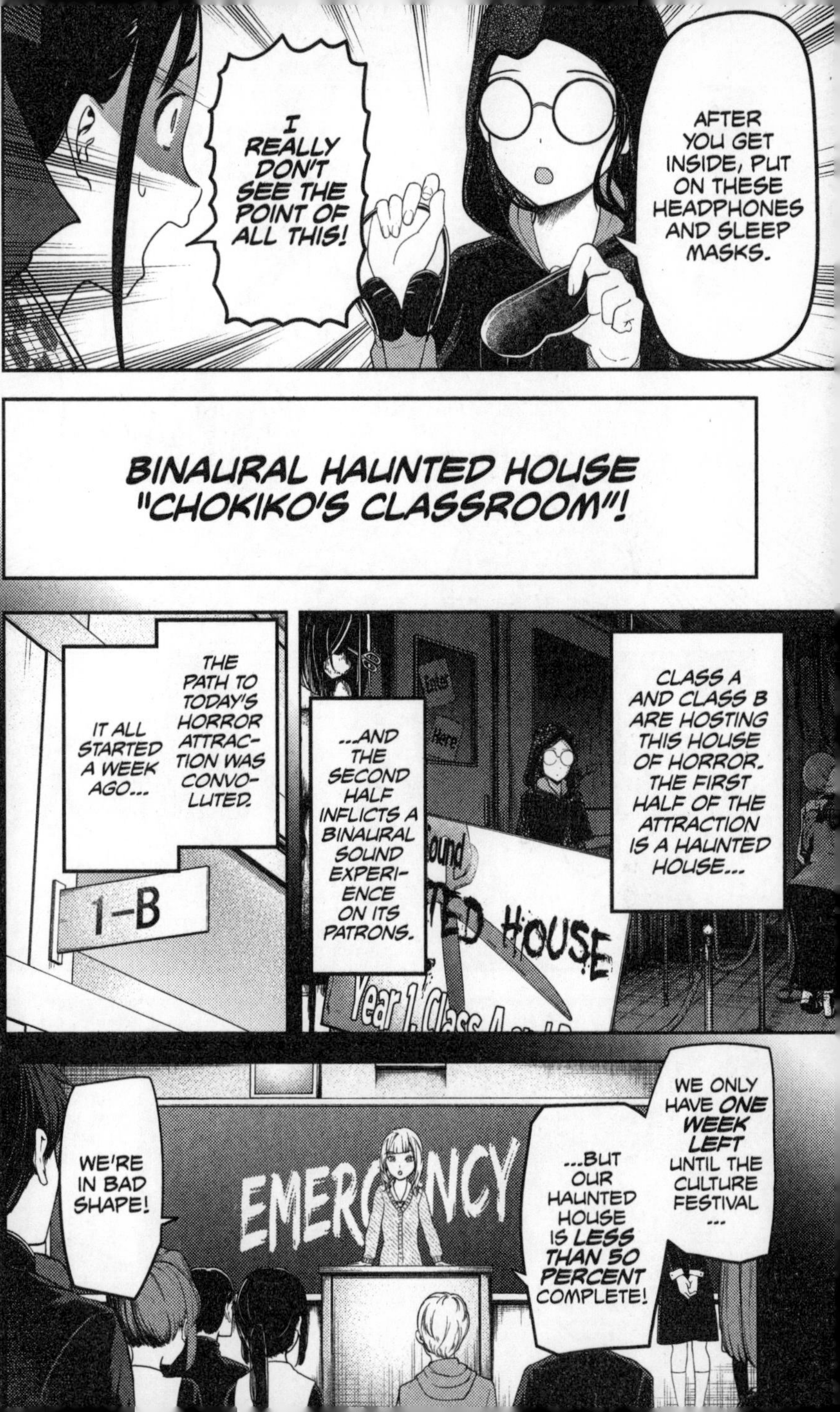
AFTER YOU GET INSIDE, PUT ON THESE HEADPHONES AND SLEEP MASKS.
I REALLY DON'T SEE THE POINT OF ALL THIS!
BINAURAL HAUNTED HOUSE "CHOKIKO'S CLASSROOM"!
CLASS A AND CLASS B ARE HOSTING THIS HOUSE OF HORROR. THE FIRST HALF OF THE ATTRACTION IS A HAUNTED HOUSE...
...AND THE SECOND HALF INFLICTS A BINAURAL SOUND EXPERIENCE ON ITS PATRONS.
Enter Here
THE PATH TO TODAY'S HORROR ATTRACTION WAS CONVOLUTED.
IT ALL STARTED A WEEK AGO...
1-B
WE ONLY HAVE ONE WEEK LEFT UNTIL THE CULTURE FESTIVAL...
...BUT OUR HAUNTED HOUSE IS LESS THAN 50 PERCENT COMPLETE!
WE'RE IN BAD SHAPE!

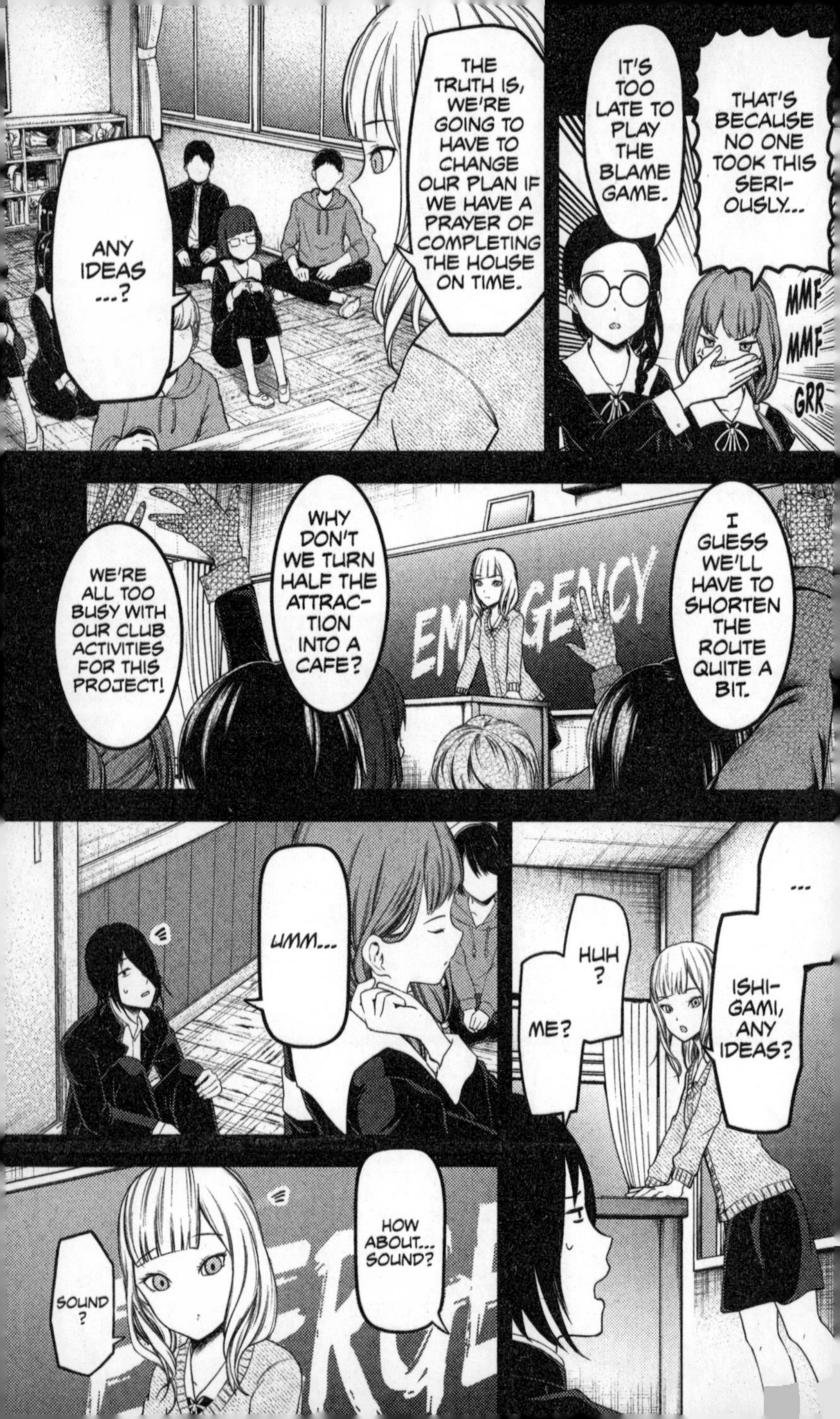

THAT'S BECAUSE NO ONE TOOK THIS SERI-OUSLY...
IT'S TOO LATE TO PLAY THE BLAME GAME.
MMF
MMF
GRR
THE TRUTH IS, WE'RE GOING TO HAVE TO CHANGE OUR PLAN IF WE HAVE A PRAYER OF COMPLETING THE HOUSE ON TIME.
ANY IDEAS ...?
I GUESS WE'LL HAVE TO SHORTEN THE ROUTE QUITE A BIT.
WHY DON'T WE TURN HALF THE ATTRAC-TION INTO A CAFE?
WE'RE ALL TOO BUSY WITH OUR CLUB ACTIVITIES FOR THIS PROJECT!
...
ISHI-GAMI, ANY IDEAS?
HUH?
ME?
UMM...
HOW ABOUT... SOUND?
SOUND?

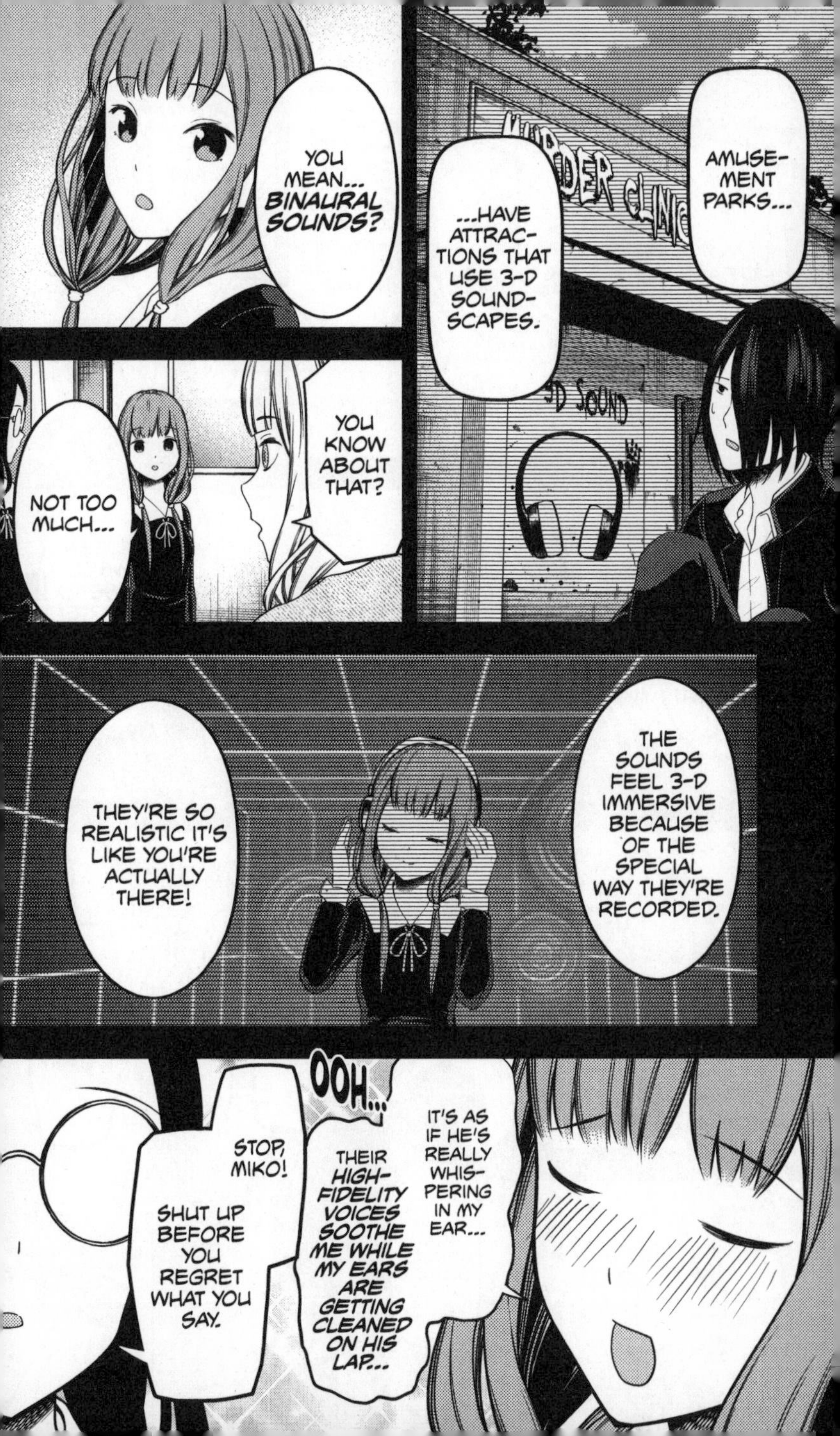

AMUSEMENT PARKS...
...HAVE ATTRACTIONS THAT USE 3-D SOUNDSCAPES.
3D SOUND
YOU MEAN... BINAURAL SOUNDS?
YOU KNOW ABOUT THAT?
NOT TOO MUCH...
THE SOUNDS FEEL 3-D IMMERSIVE BECAUSE OF THE SPECIAL WAY THEY'RE RECORDED.
THEY'RE SO REALISTIC IT'S LIKE YOU'RE ACTUALLY THERE!
OOH...
IT'S AS IF HE'S REALLY WHISPERING IN MY EAR...
THEIR HIGH-FIDELITY VOICES SOOTHE ME WHILE MY EARS ARE GETTING CLEANED ON HIS LAP...
STOP, MIKO!
SHUT UP BEFORE YOU REGRET WHAT YOU SAY.

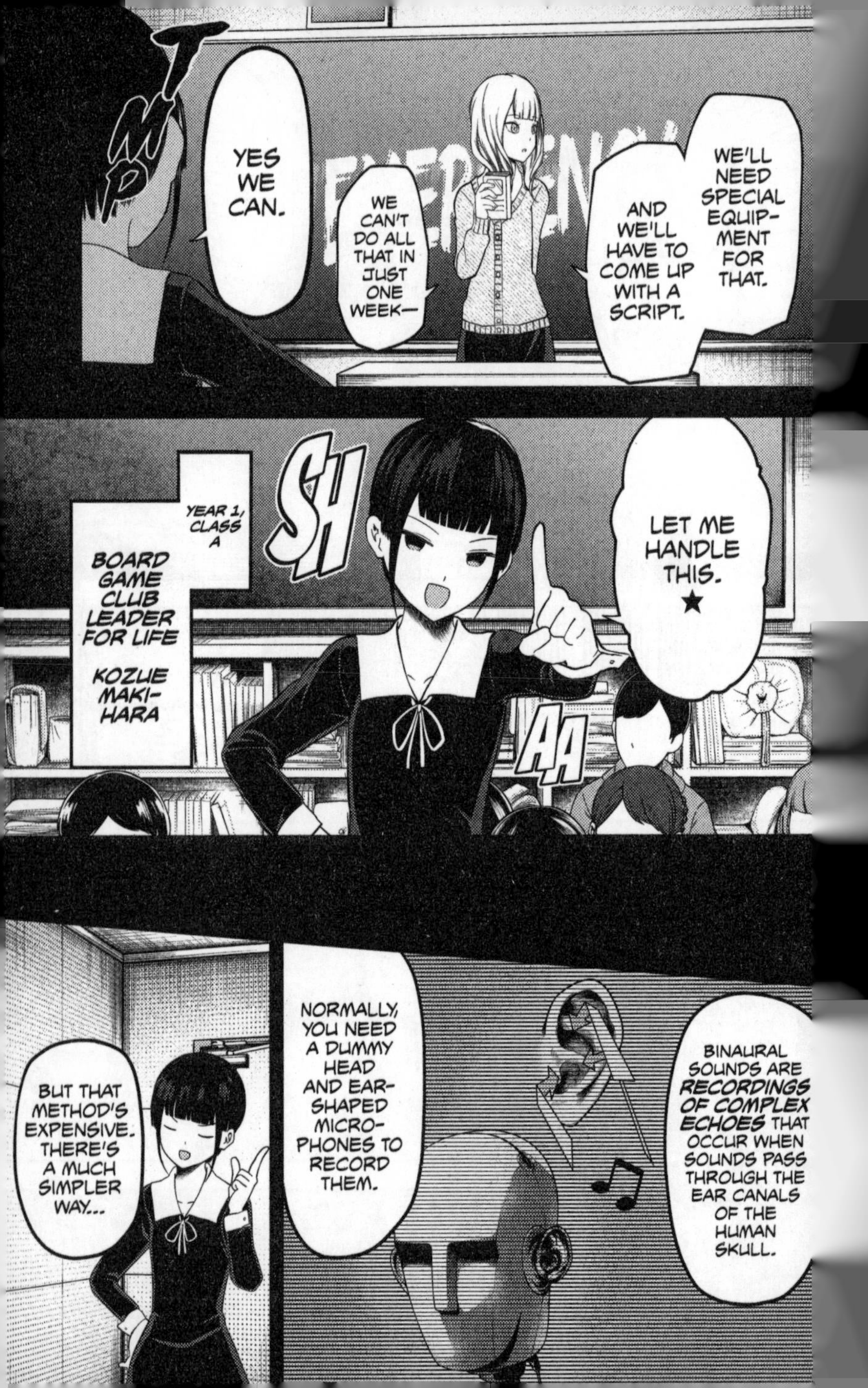
WE'LL NEED SPECIAL EQUIPMENT FOR THAT.
AND WE'LL HAVE TO COME UP WITH A SCRIPT.
WE CAN'T DO ALL THAT IN JUST ONE WEEK—
YES WE CAN.
TMP
LET ME HANDLE THIS. ★
SH
AA
YEAR 1, CLASS A
BOARD GAME CLUB LEADER FOR LIFE
KOZUE MAKIHARA
BINAURAL SOUNDS ARE ***RECORDINGS OF COMPLEX ECHOES*** THAT OCCUR WHEN SOUNDS PASS THROUGH THE EAR CANALS OF THE HUMAN SKULL.
NORMALLY, YOU NEED A DUMMY HEAD AND EAR-SHAPED MICROPHONES TO RECORD THEM.
BUT THAT METHOD'S EXPENSIVE. THERE'S A MUCH SIMPLER WAY...

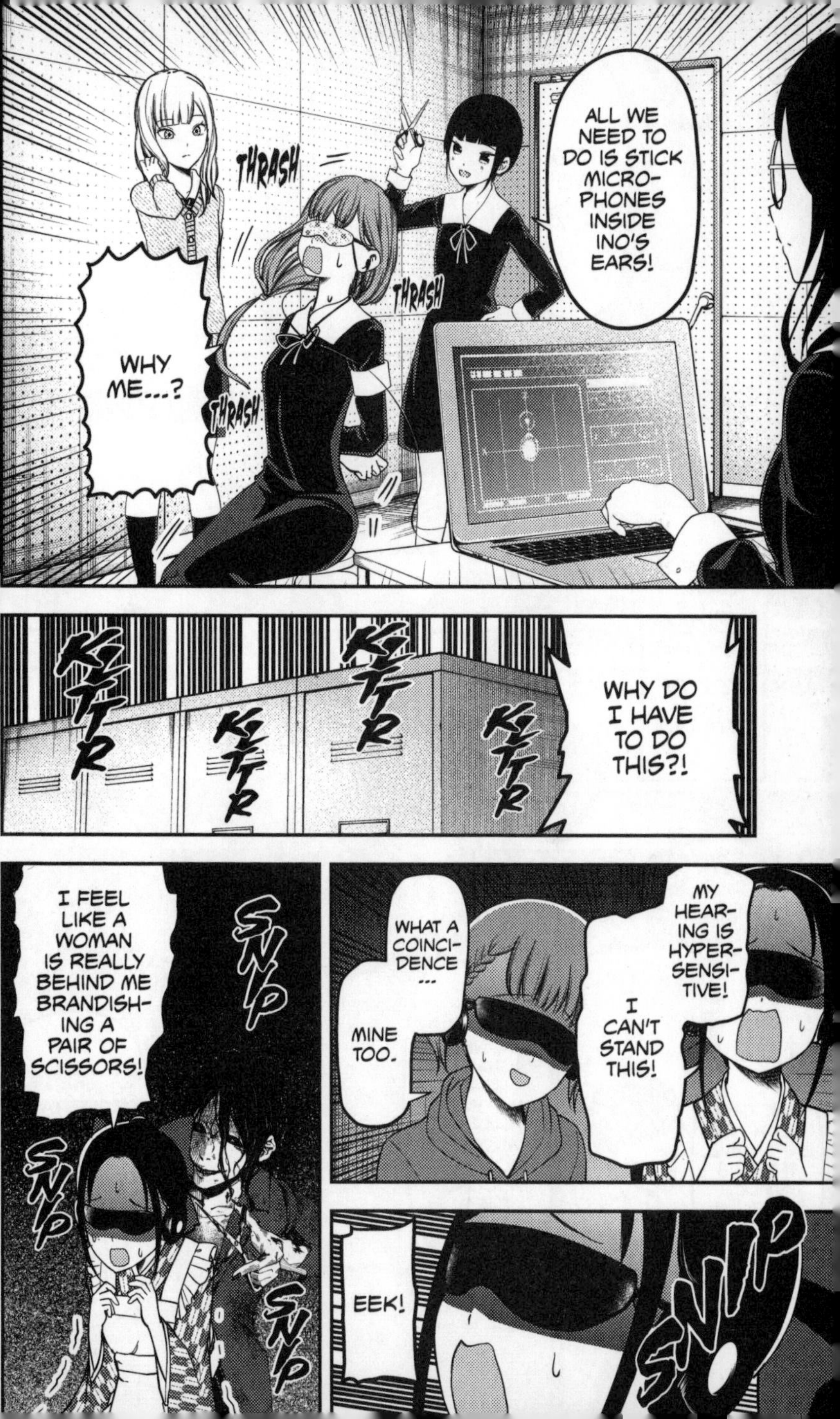
ALL WE NEED TO DO IS STICK MICROPHONES INSIDE INO'S EARS!
THRASH
THRASH
THRASH
WHY ME...?
WHY DO I HAVE TO DO THIS?!
KTTR
KTTR
KTTR
KTTR
MY HEARING IS HYPERSENSITIVE!
I CAN'T STAND THIS!
WHAT A COINCIDENCE...
MINE TOO.
SNIP
EEK!
I FEEL LIKE A WOMAN IS REALLY BEHIND ME BRANDISHING A PAIR OF SCISSORS!
SNIP
SNIP
SNIP

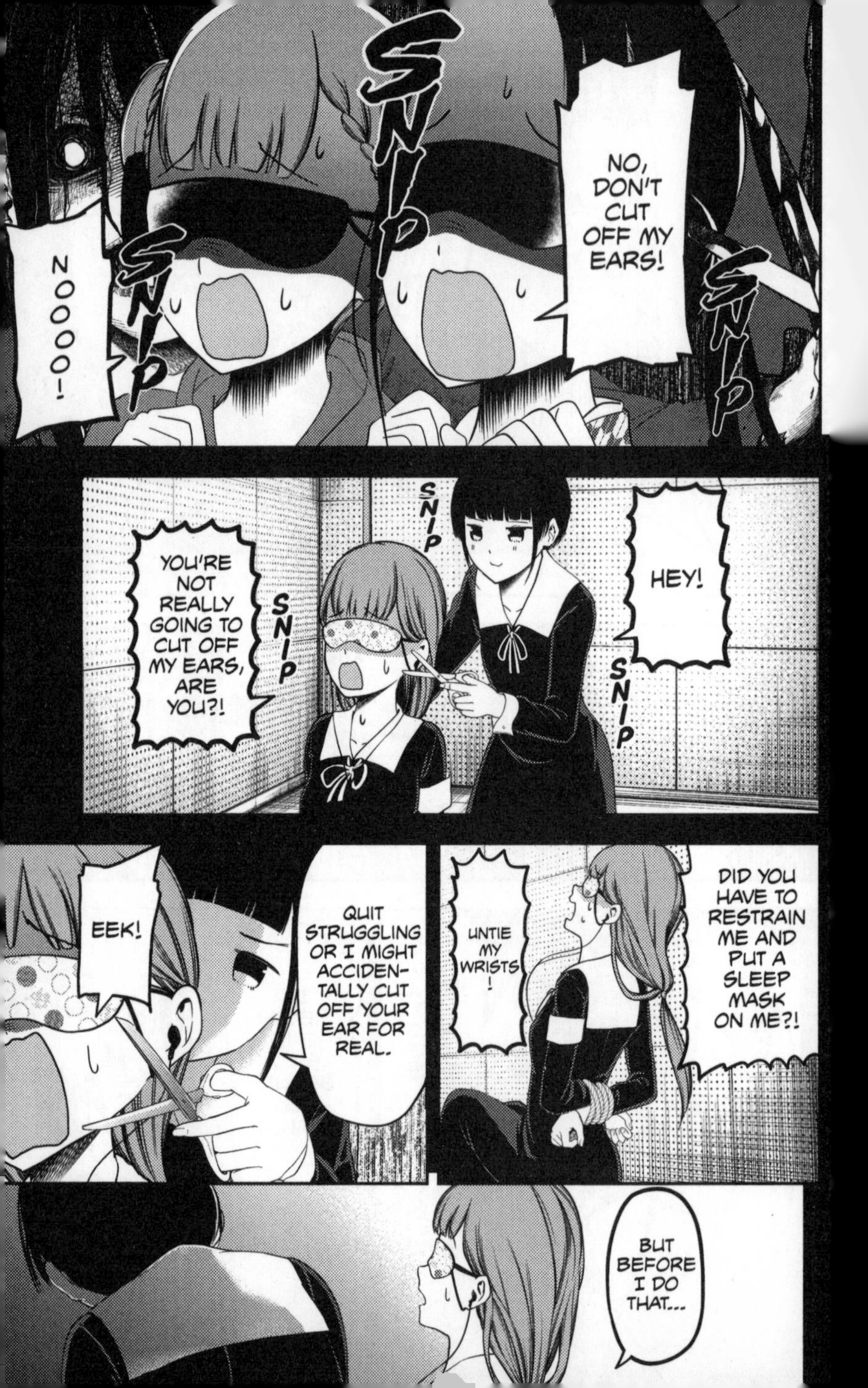
SNIP
NO, DON'T CUT OFF MY EARS!
SNIP
SNIP
NOOOO!
HEY!
SNIP
SNIP
SNIP
YOU'RE NOT REALLY GOING TO CUT OFF MY EARS, ARE YOU?!
SNIP
DID YOU HAVE TO RESTRAIN ME AND PUT A SLEEP MASK ON ME?!
UNTIE MY WRISTS!
QUIT STRUGGLING OR I MIGHT ACCIDENTALLY CUT OFF YOUR EAR FOR REAL.
EEK!
BUT BEFORE I DO THAT...

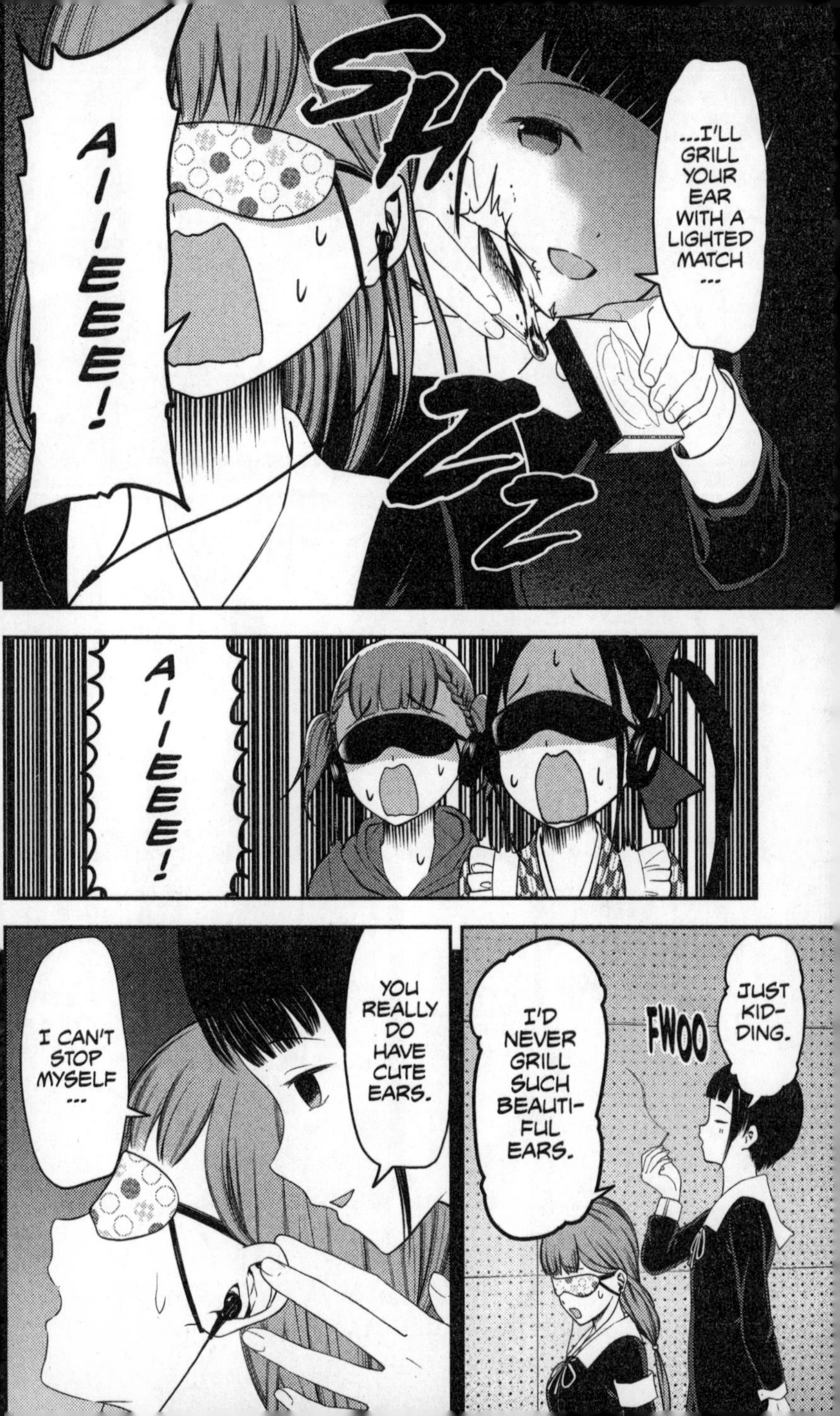

...I'LL GRILL YOUR EAR WITH A LIGHTED MATCH ...
SHZZZ
AIIEEEE!
AIIEEE!
JUST KID-DING.
FWOO
I'D NEVER GRILL SUCH BEAUTI-FUL EARS.
YOU REALLY DO HAVE CUTE EARS.
I CAN'T STOP MYSELF ...

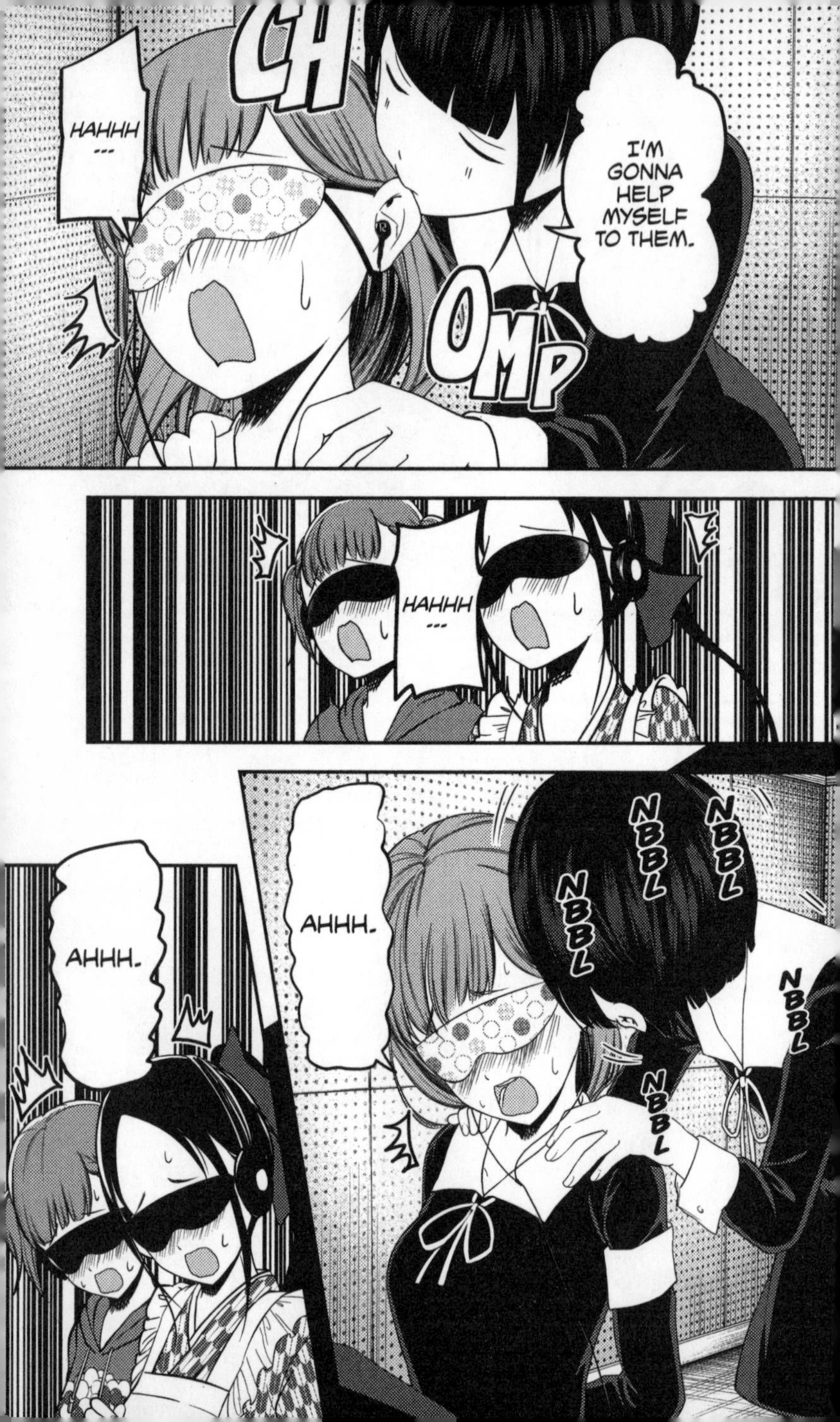
CH
I'M GONNA HELP MYSELF TO THEM.
OMP
HAHHH ---
HAHHH ---
NBBL
NBBL
NBBL
AHHH.
NBBL
NBBL
AHHH.

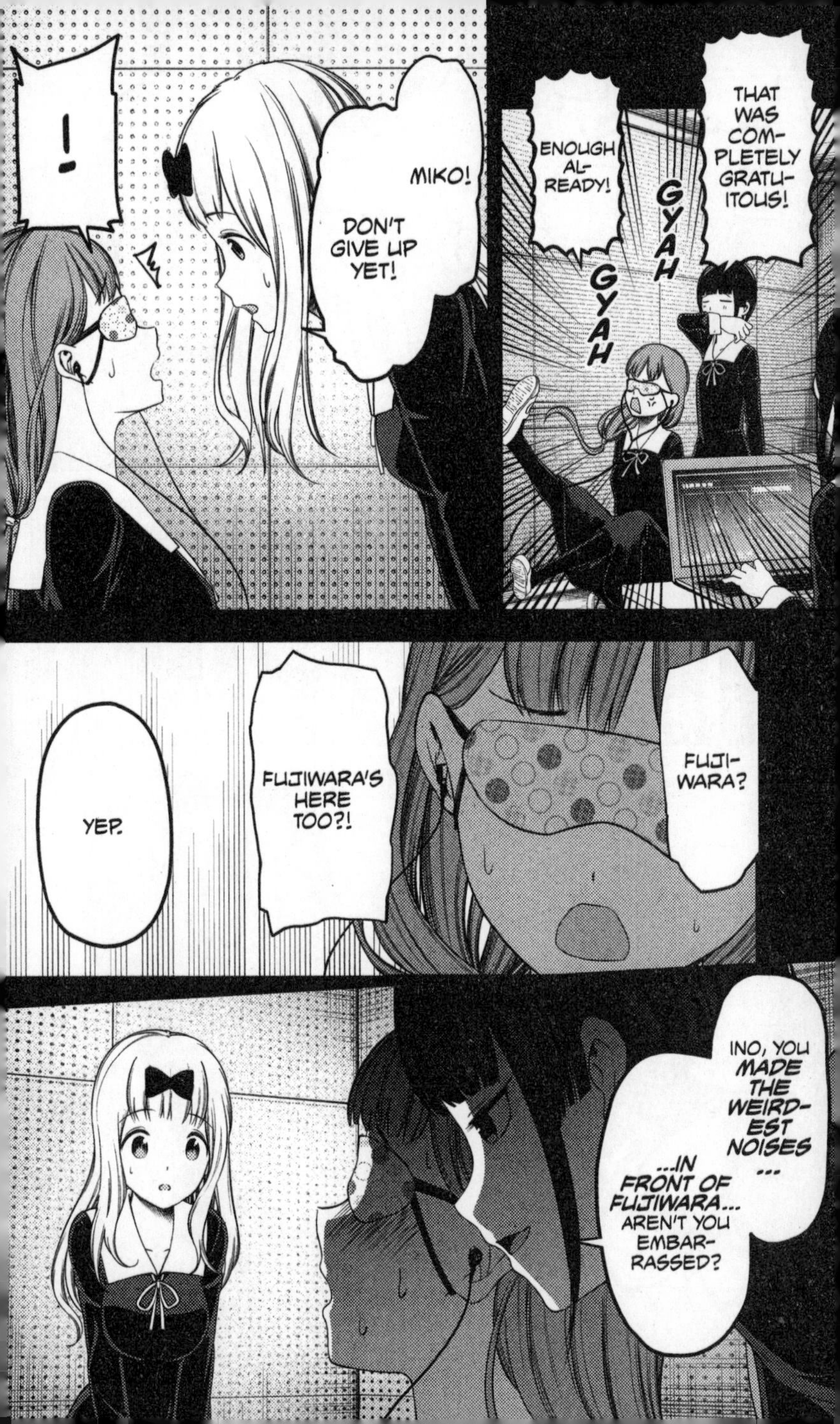
THAT WAS COM-PLETELY GRATU-ITOUS!
GYAH GYAH
ENOUGH AL-READY!
GYAH GYAH
MIKO!
DON'T GIVE UP YET!
!
FUJI-WARA?
FUJIWARA'S HERE TOO?!
YEP.
INO, YOU MADE THE WEIRD-EST NOISES ...
...IN FRONT OF FUJIWARA... AREN'T YOU EMBAR-RASSED?

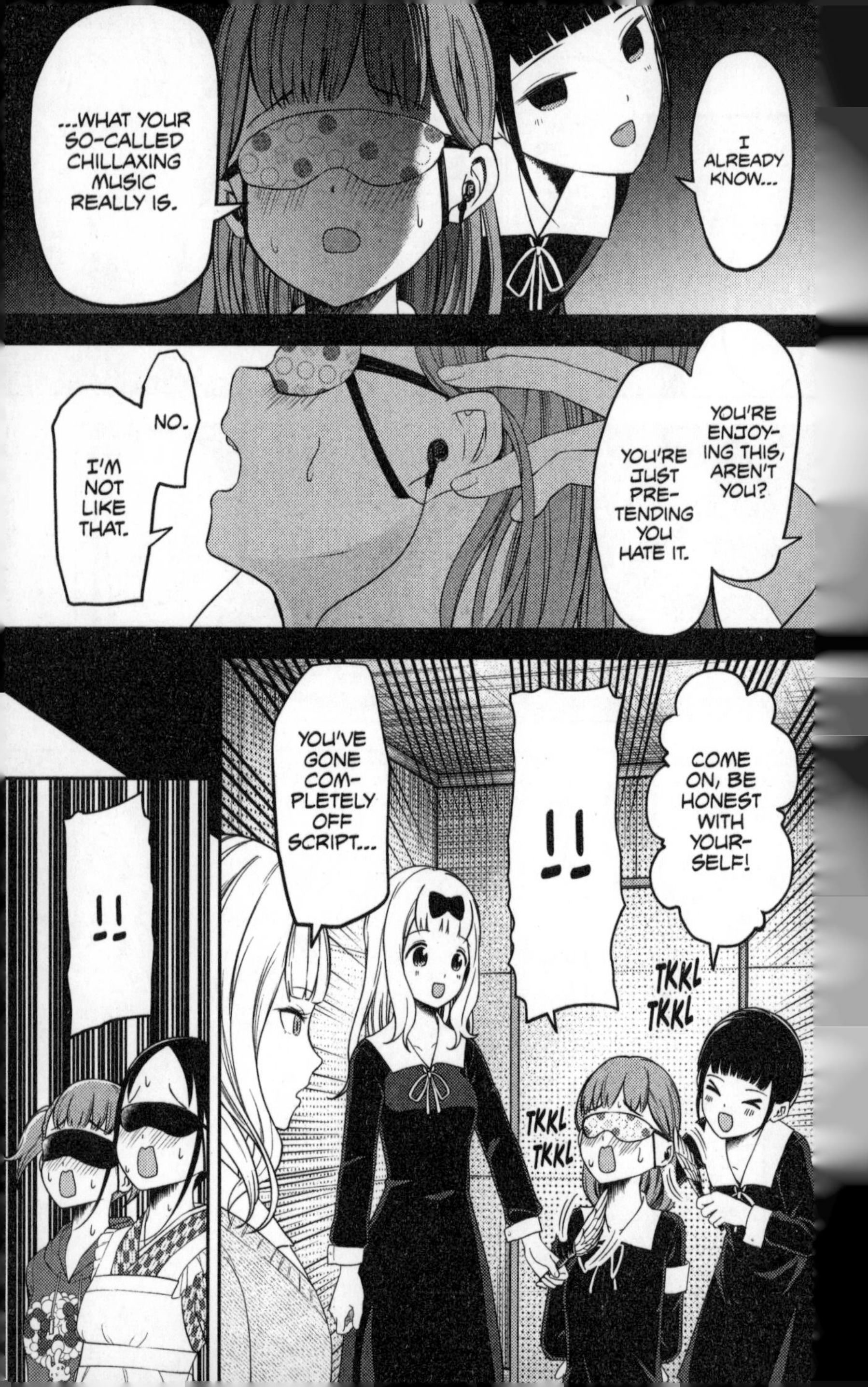
I ALREADY KNOW...
...WHAT YOUR SO-CALLED CHILLAXING MUSIC REALLY IS.
YOU'RE ENJOYING THIS, AREN'T YOU?
YOU'RE JUST PRETENDING YOU HATE IT.
NO.
I'M NOT LIKE THAT.
COME ON, BE HONEST WITH YOURSELF!
TKKL TKKL
!!
YOU'VE GONE COMPLETELY OFF SCRIPT...
TKKL TKKL
!!

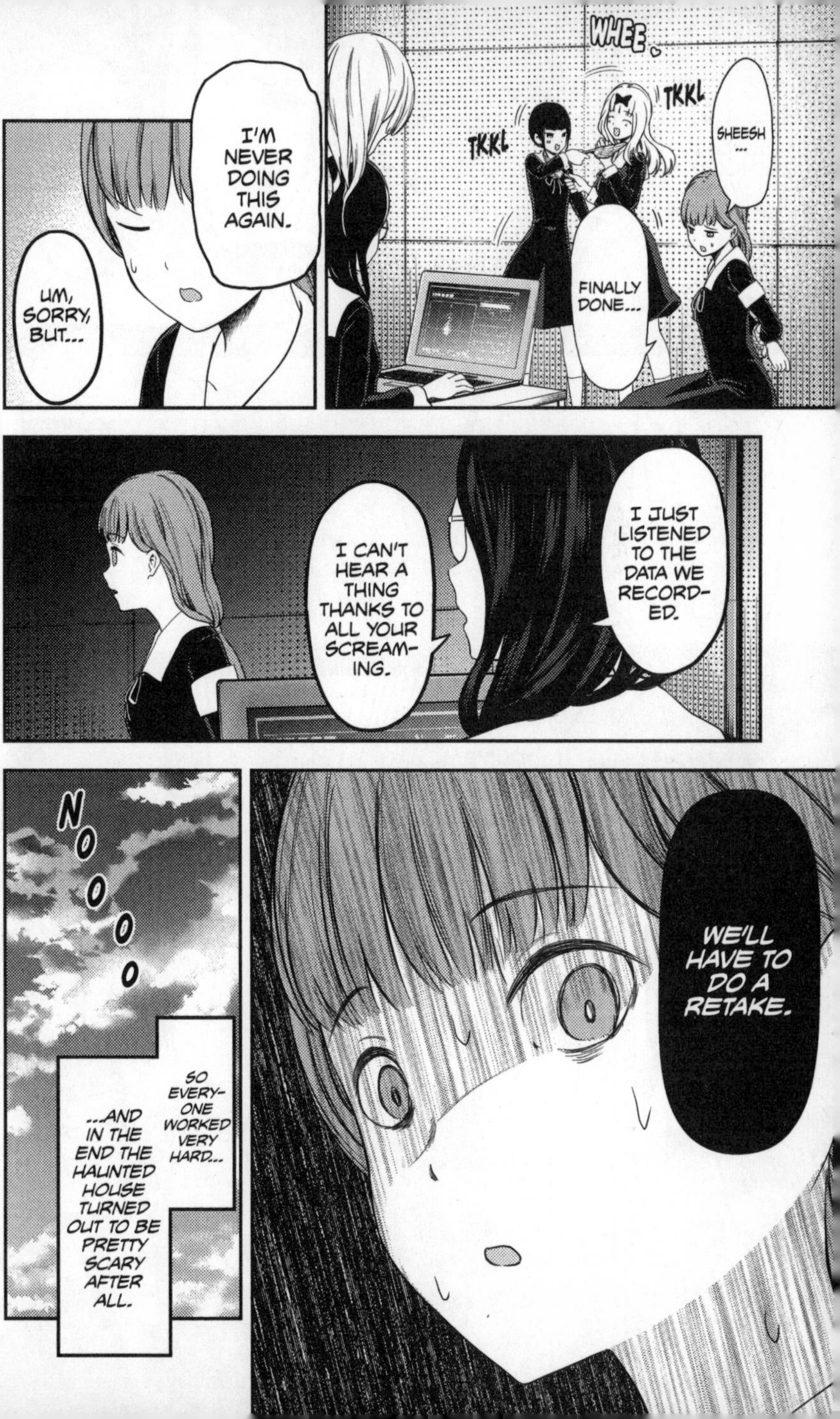
WHEE
TKKL
SHEESH...
TKKL
FINALLY DONE...
I'M NEVER DOING THIS AGAIN.
UM, SORRY, BUT...
I JUST LISTENED TO THE DATA WE RECORDED.
I CAN'T HEAR A THING THANKS TO ALL YOUR SCREAMING.
WE'LL HAVE TO DO A RETAKE.
NOOOOO
SO EVERYONE WORKED VERY HARD...
...AND IN THE END THE HAUNTED HOUSE TURNED OUT TO BE PRETTY SCARY AFTER ALL.

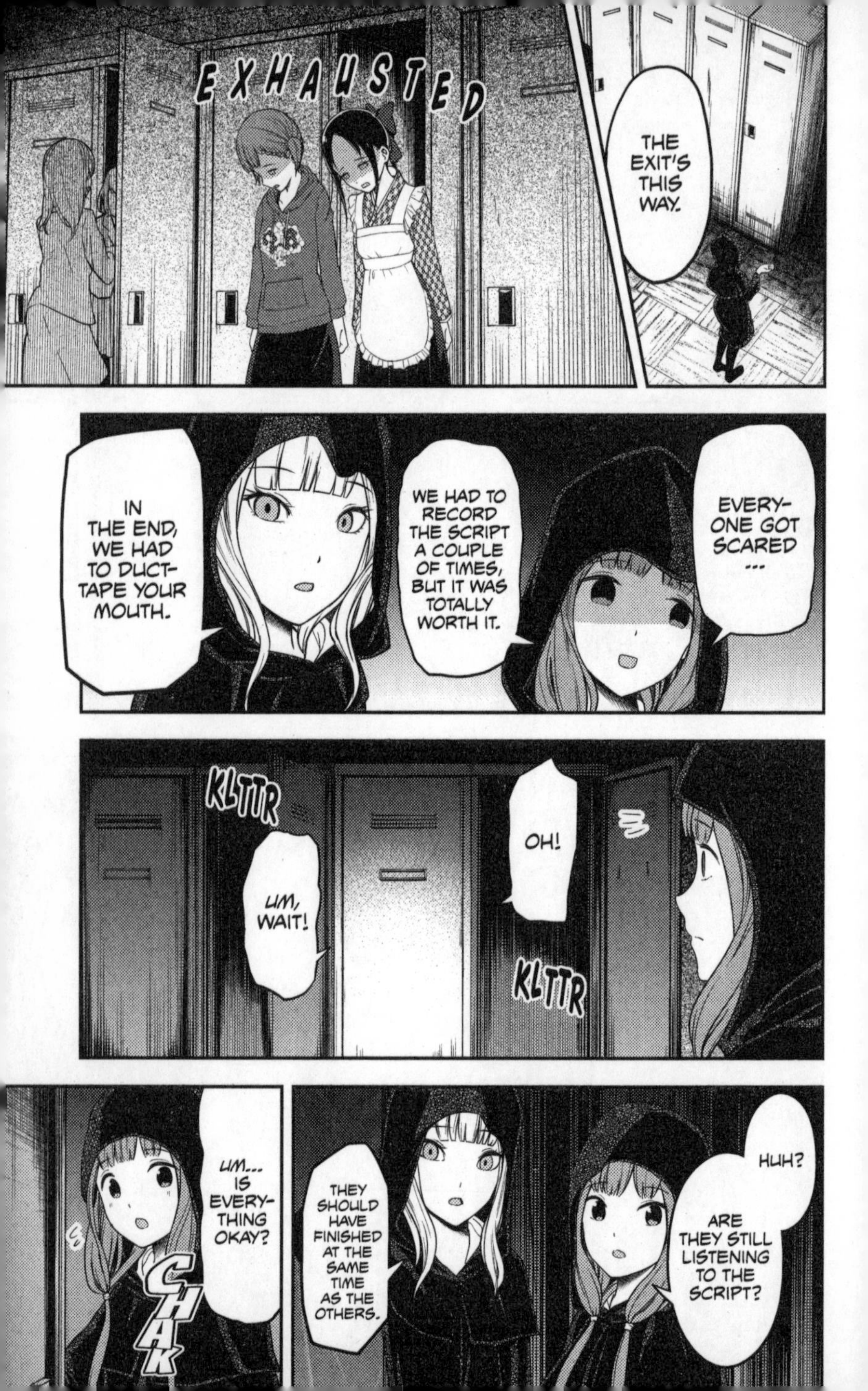
THE EXIT'S THIS WAY.
EXHAUSTED
EVERY-ONE GOT SCARED ...
WE HAD TO RECORD THE SCRIPT A COUPLE OF TIMES, BUT IT WAS TOTALLY WORTH IT.
IN THE END, WE HAD TO DUCT-TAPE YOUR MOUTH.
OH!
KLTTR
UM, WAIT!
KLTTR
HUH?
ARE THEY STILL LISTENING TO THE SCRIPT?
THEY SHOULD HAVE FINISHED AT THE SAME TIME AS THE OTHERS.
UM... IS EVERY-THING OKAY?
CHAK

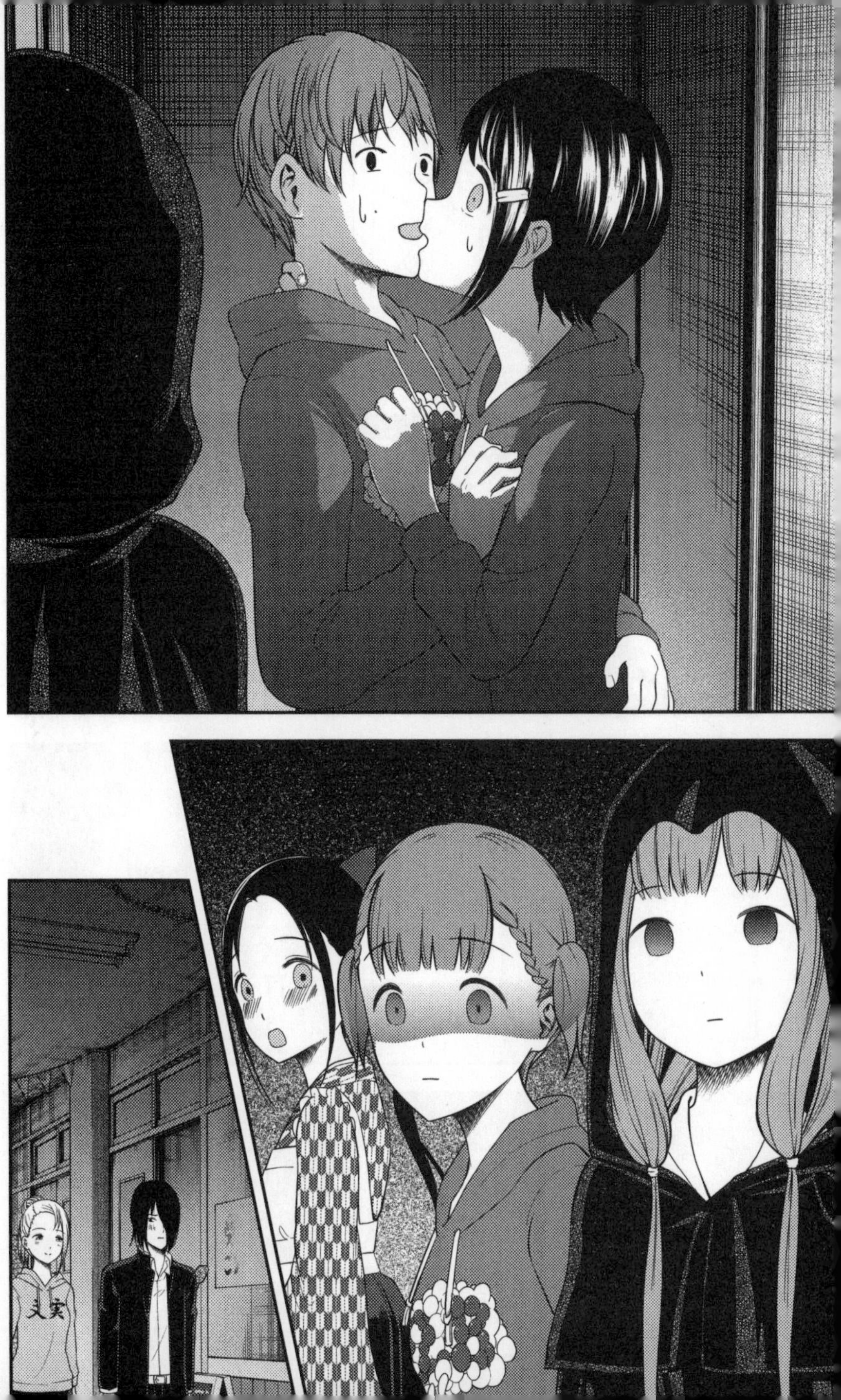

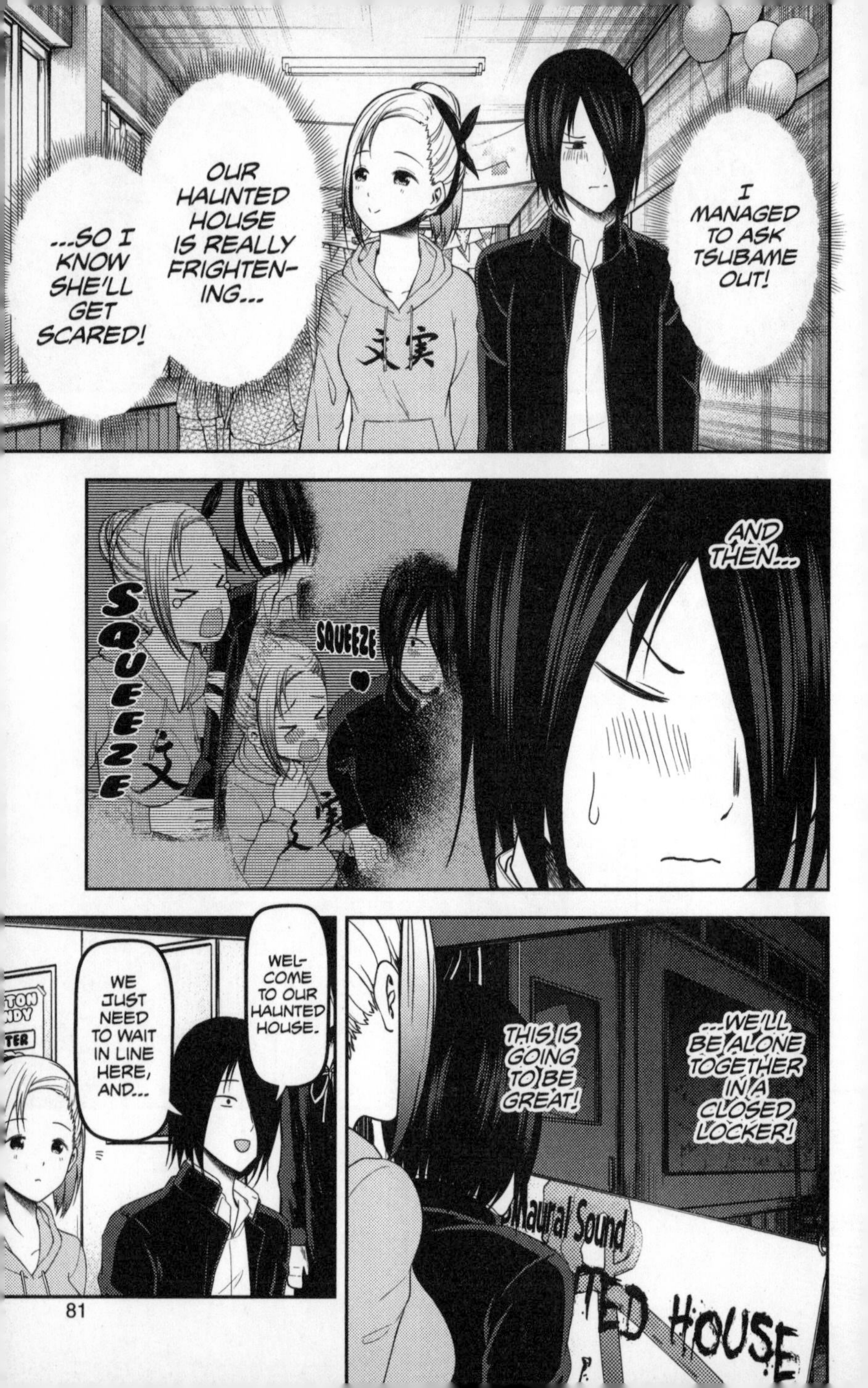
I MANAGED TO ASK TSUBAME OUT!
OUR HAUNTED HOUSE IS REALLY FRIGHTENING...
...SO I KNOW SHE'LL GET SCARED!
AND THEN...
SQUEEZE
SQUEEZE
...WE'LL BE ALONE TOGETHER IN A CLOSED LOCKER!
THIS IS GOING TO BE GREAT!
WELCOME TO OUR HAUNTED HOUSE.
WE JUST NEED TO WAIT IN LINE HERE, AND...

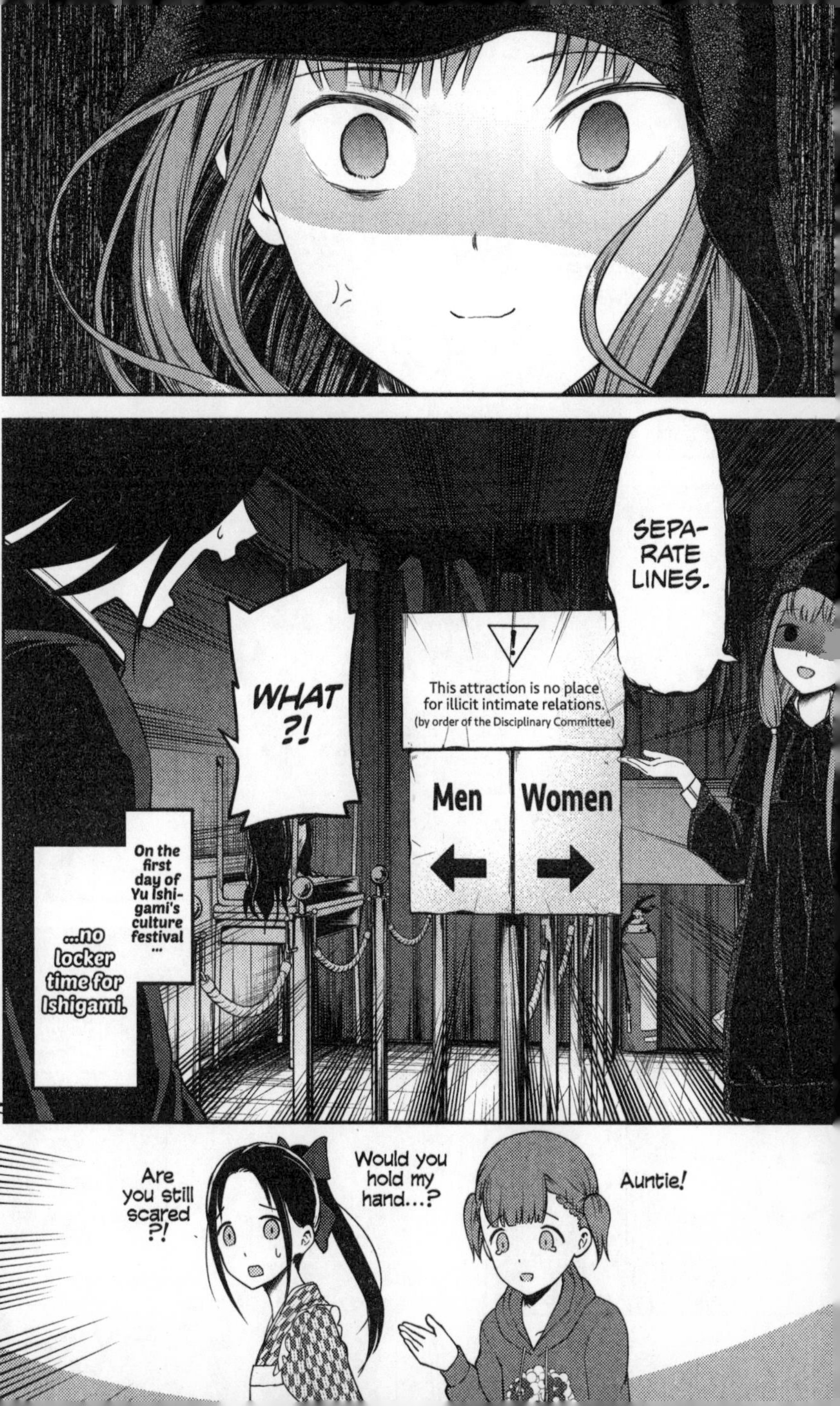
SEPA-RATE LINES.
This attraction is no place for illicit intimate relations.
(by order of the Disciplinary Committee)
Men
Women
WHAT?!
On the first day of Yu Ishigami's culture festival...
...no locker time for Ishigami.
Auntie!
Would you hold my hand...?
Are you still scared?!

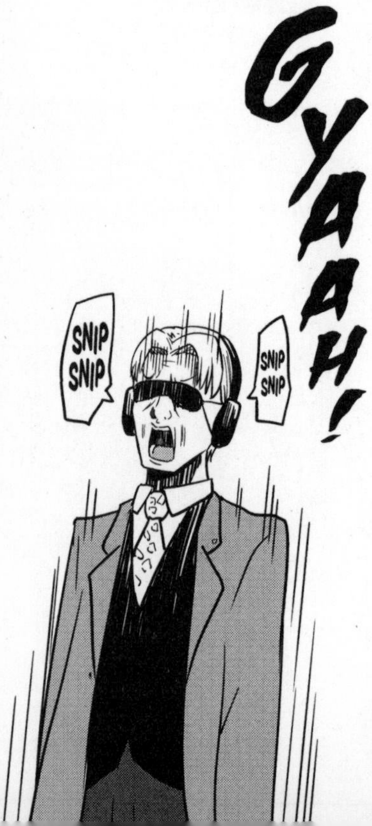
GYAAH!
SNIP SNIP
SNIP SNIP

KAGUYA-SAMA
LOVE IS WAR

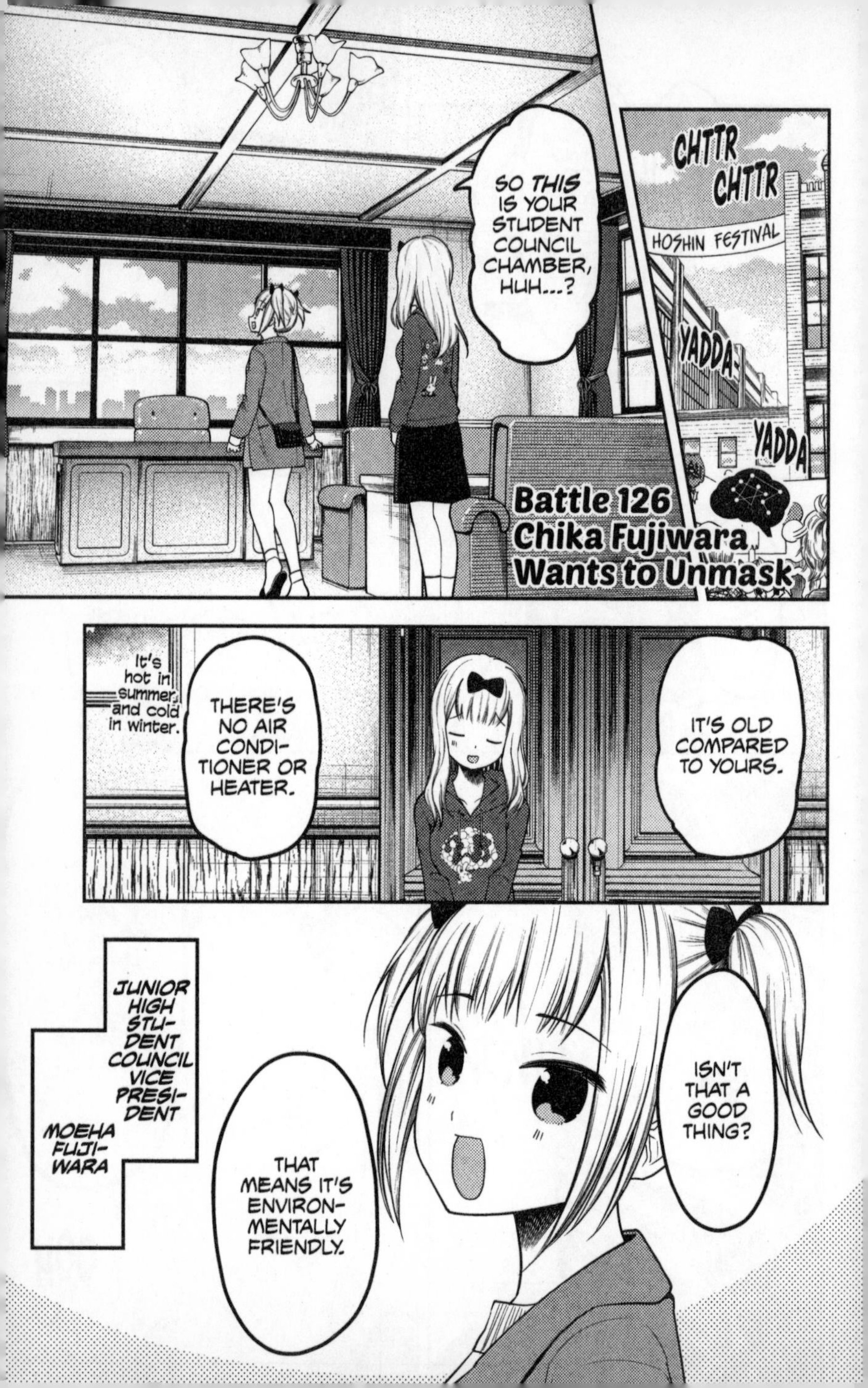
CHTTR CHTTR
HOSHIN FESTIVAL
YADDA-YADDA
Battle 126 Chika Fujiwara Wants to Unmask
SO THIS IS YOUR STUDENT COUNCIL CHAMBER, HUH...?
IT'S OLD COMPARED TO YOURS.
THERE'S NO AIR CONDITIONER OR HEATER.
It's hot in summer and cold in winter.
ISN'T THAT A GOOD THING?
THAT MEANS IT'S ENVIRONMENTALLY FRIENDLY.
JUNIOR HIGH STUDENT COUNCIL VICE PRESIDENT MOEHA FUJIWARA

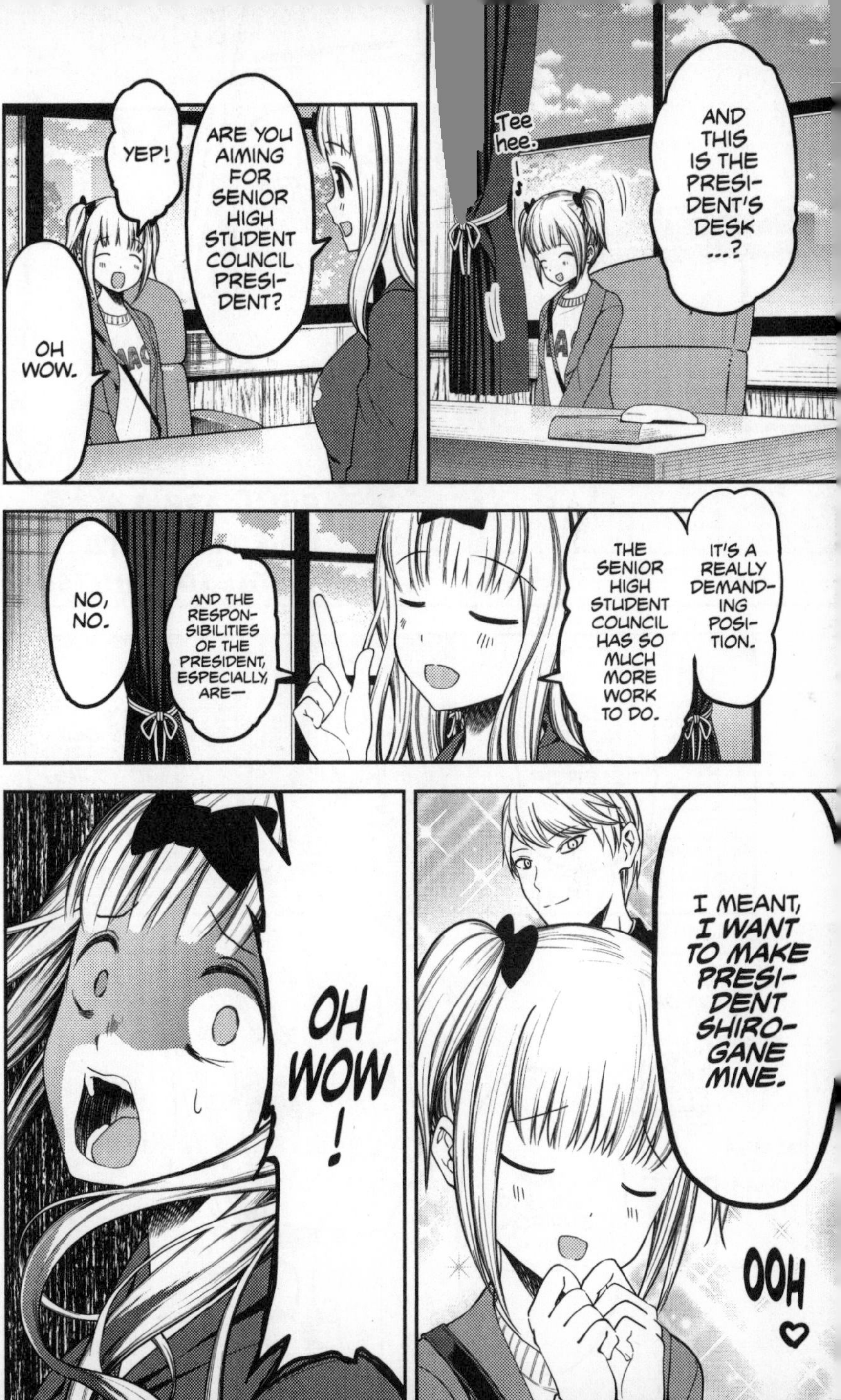
AND THIS IS THE PRESIDENT'S DESK...?
Tee hee.
ARE YOU AIMING FOR SENIOR HIGH STUDENT COUNCIL PRESIDENT?
YEP!
OH WOW.
IT'S A REALLY DEMANDING POSITION.
THE SENIOR HIGH STUDENT COUNCIL HAS SO MUCH MORE WORK TO DO.
AND THE RESPONSIBILITIES OF THE PRESIDENT, ESPECIALLY, ARE—
NO, NO.
I MEANT, *I WANT TO MAKE PRESIDENT SHIROGANE MINE.*
OOH ♥
OH WOW!

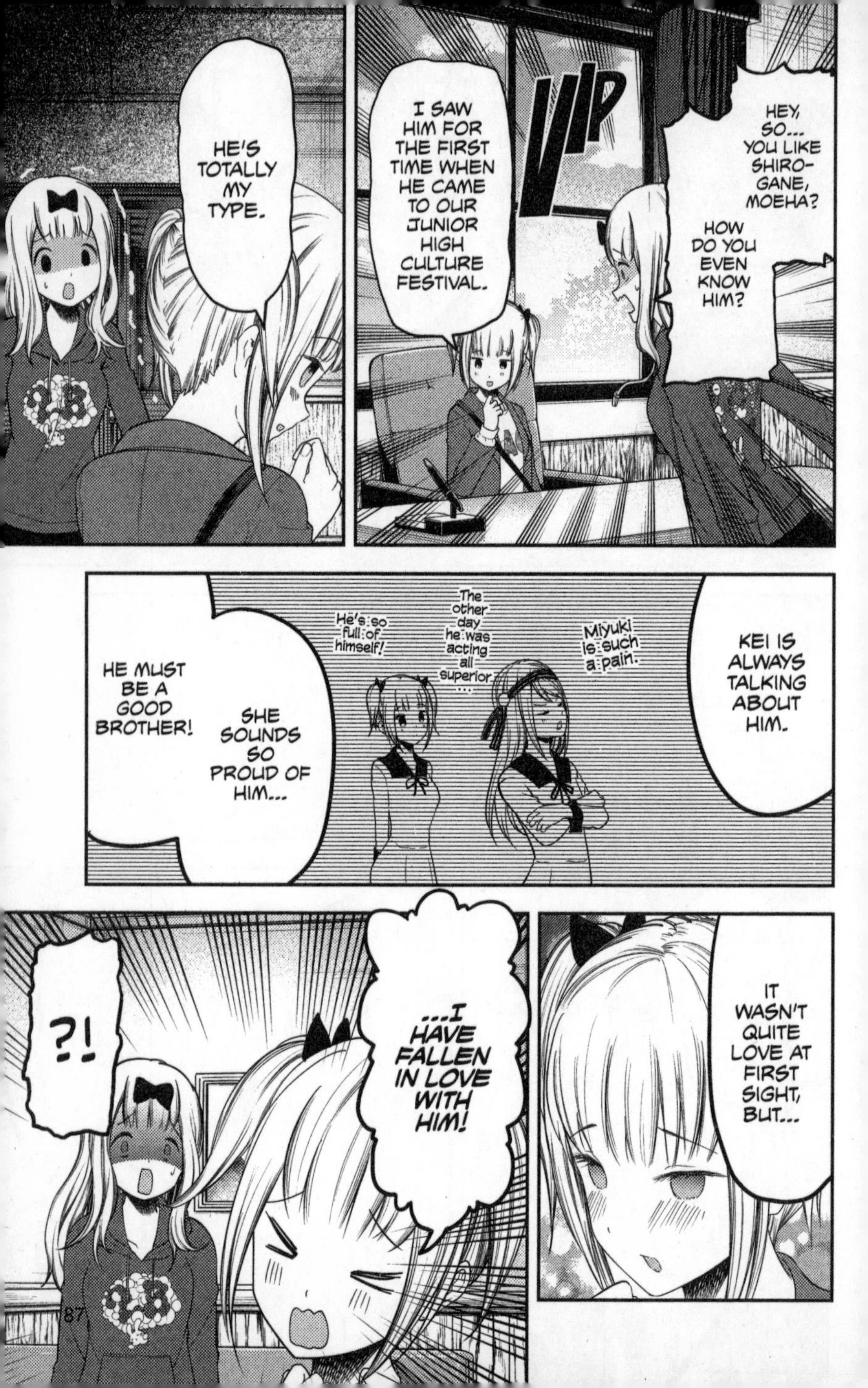
HEY, SO... YOU LIKE SHIRO-GANE, MOEHA?
HOW DO YOU EVEN KNOW HIM?
I SAW HIM FOR THE FIRST TIME WHEN HE CAME TO OUR JUNIOR HIGH CULTURE FESTIVAL.
HE'S TOTALLY MY TYPE.
KEI IS ALWAYS TALKING ABOUT HIM.
Miyuki is such a pain.
The other day he was acting all superior...
He's so full of himself!
SHE SOUNDS SO PROUD OF HIM...
HE MUST BE A GOOD BROTHER!
IT WASN'T QUITE LOVE AT FIRST SIGHT, BUT...
...I HAVE FALLEN IN LOVE WITH HIM!
?!

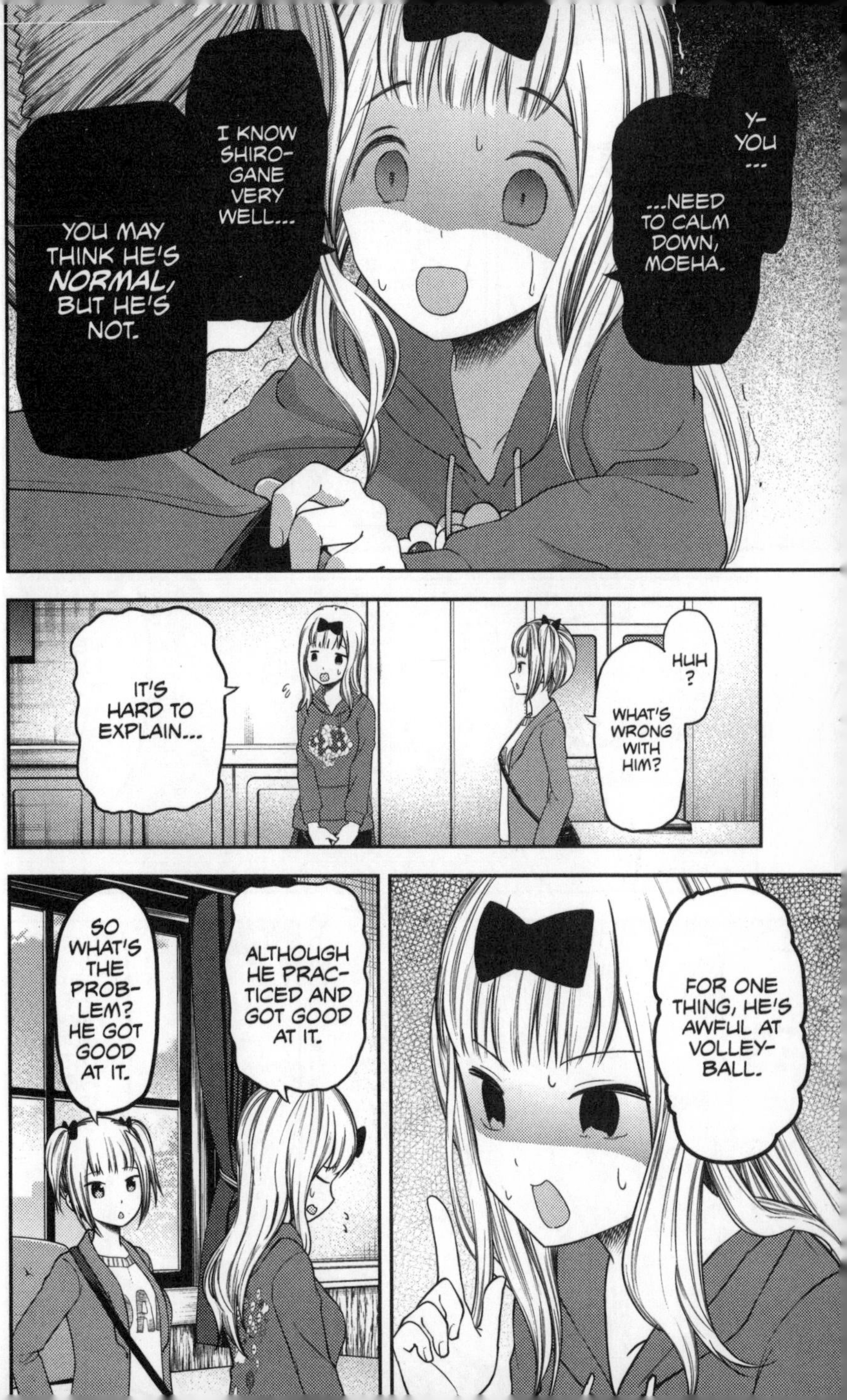
Y-YOU...
...NEED TO CALM DOWN, MOEHA.
I KNOW SHIRO-GANE VERY WELL...
YOU MAY THINK HE'S *NORMAL*, BUT HE'S NOT.
HUH? WHAT'S WRONG WITH HIM?
IT'S HARD TO EXPLAIN...
FOR ONE THING, HE'S AWFUL AT VOLLEY-BALL.
ALTHOUGH HE PRAC-TICED AND GOT GOOD AT IT.
SO WHAT'S THE PROB-LEM? HE GOT GOOD AT IT.

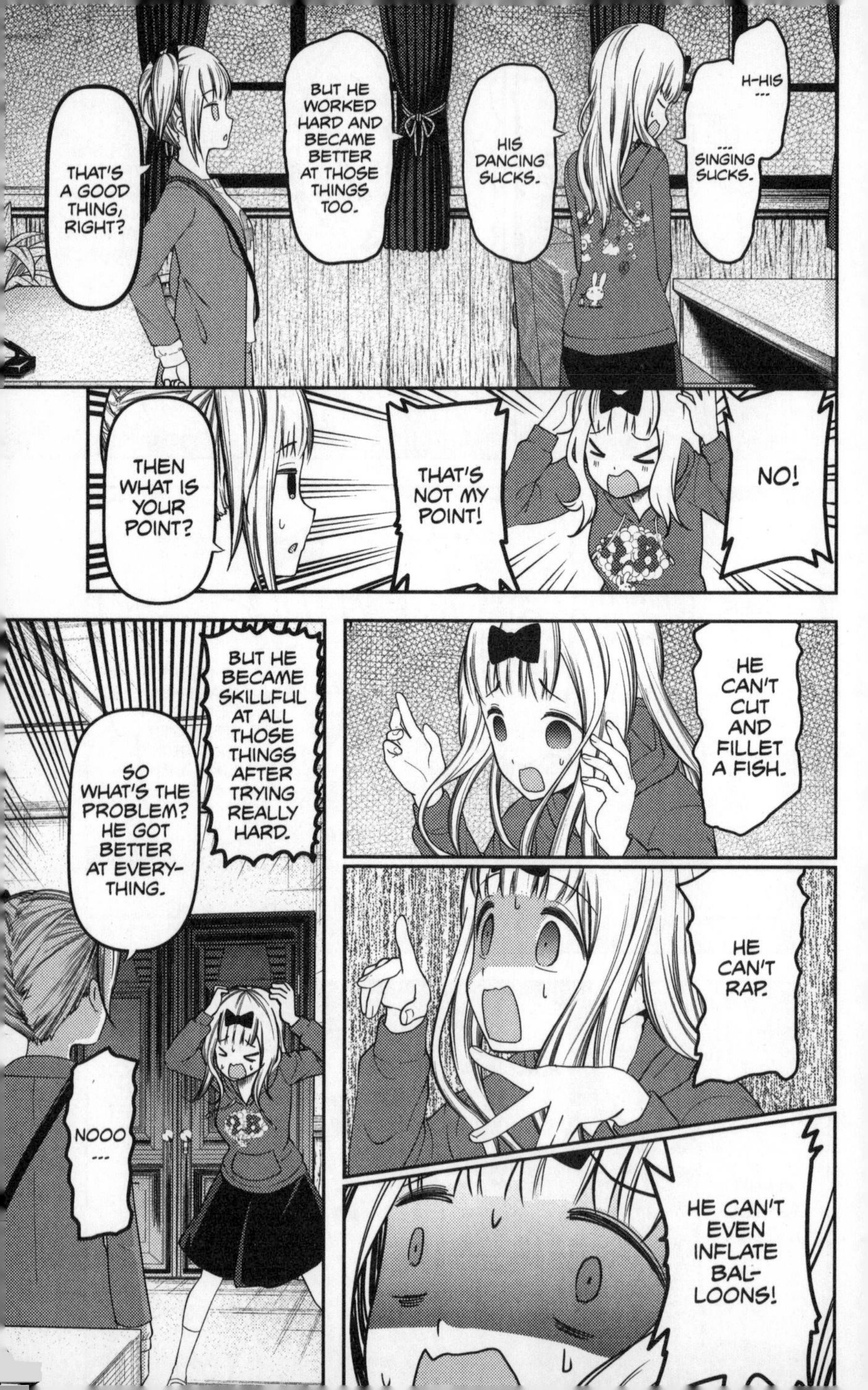
H-HIS --- --- SINGING SUCKS.
HIS DANCING SUCKS.
BUT HE WORKED HARD AND BECAME BETTER AT THOSE THINGS TOO.
THAT'S A GOOD THING, RIGHT?
NO!
THAT'S NOT MY POINT!
THEN WHAT IS YOUR POINT?
HE CAN'T CUT AND FILLET A FISH.
HE CAN'T RAP.
HE CAN'T EVEN INFLATE BAL-LOONS!
BUT HE BECAME SKILLFUL AT ALL THOSE THINGS AFTER TRYING REALLY HARD.
SO WHAT'S THE PROBLEM? HE GOT BETTER AT EVERY-THING.
NOOO ---

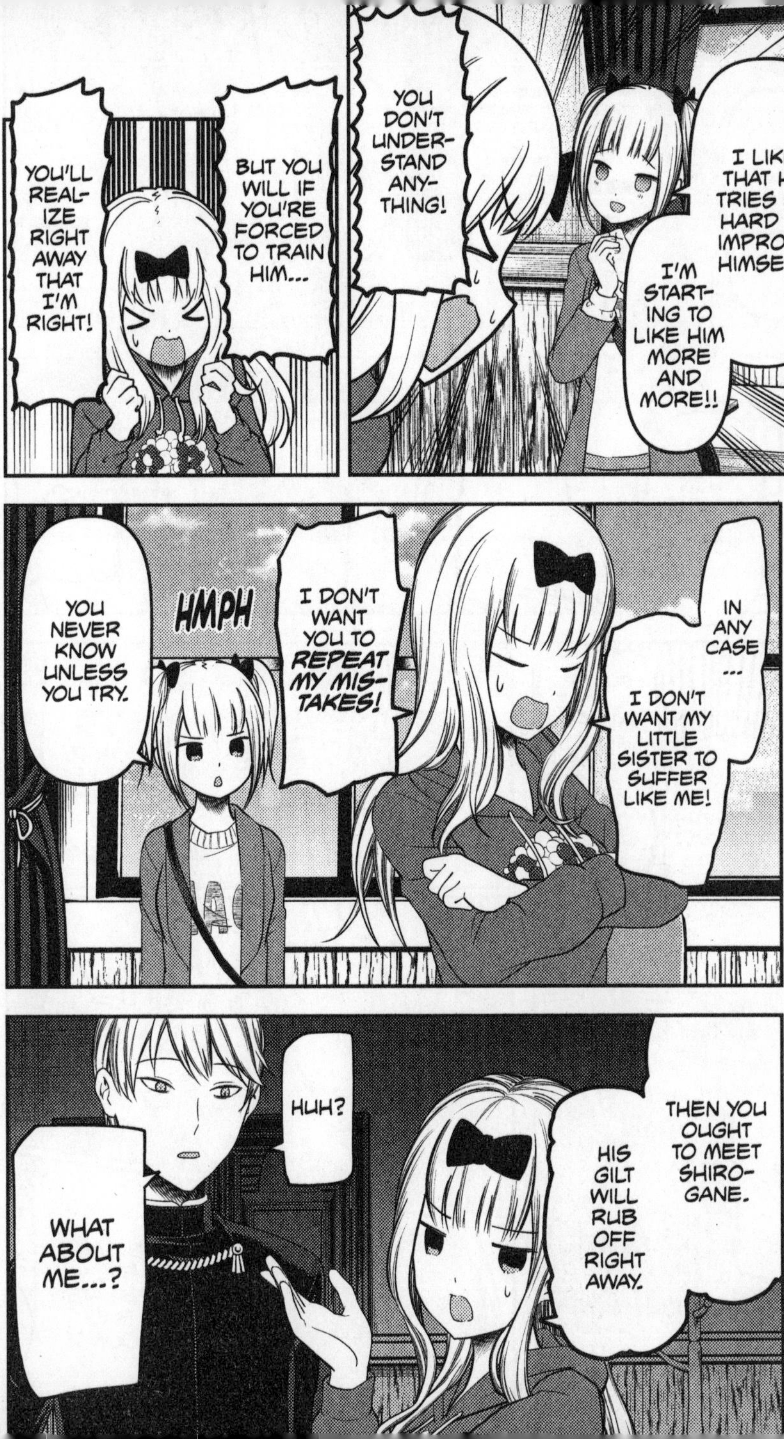
I LIKE THAT HE TRIES SO HARD TO IMPROVE HIMSELF.
I'M STARTING TO LIKE HIM MORE AND MORE!!
YOU DON'T UNDERSTAND ANYTHING!
BUT YOU WILL IF YOU'RE FORCED TO TRAIN HIM...
YOU'LL REALIZE RIGHT AWAY THAT I'M RIGHT!
IN ANY CASE...
I DON'T WANT MY LITTLE SISTER TO SUFFER LIKE ME!
I DON'T WANT YOU TO *REPEAT MY MISTAKES!*
HMPH
YOU NEVER KNOW UNLESS YOU TRY.
THEN YOU OUGHT TO MEET SHIROGANE.
HIS GILT WILL RUB OFF RIGHT AWAY.
HUH?
WHAT ABOUT ME...?

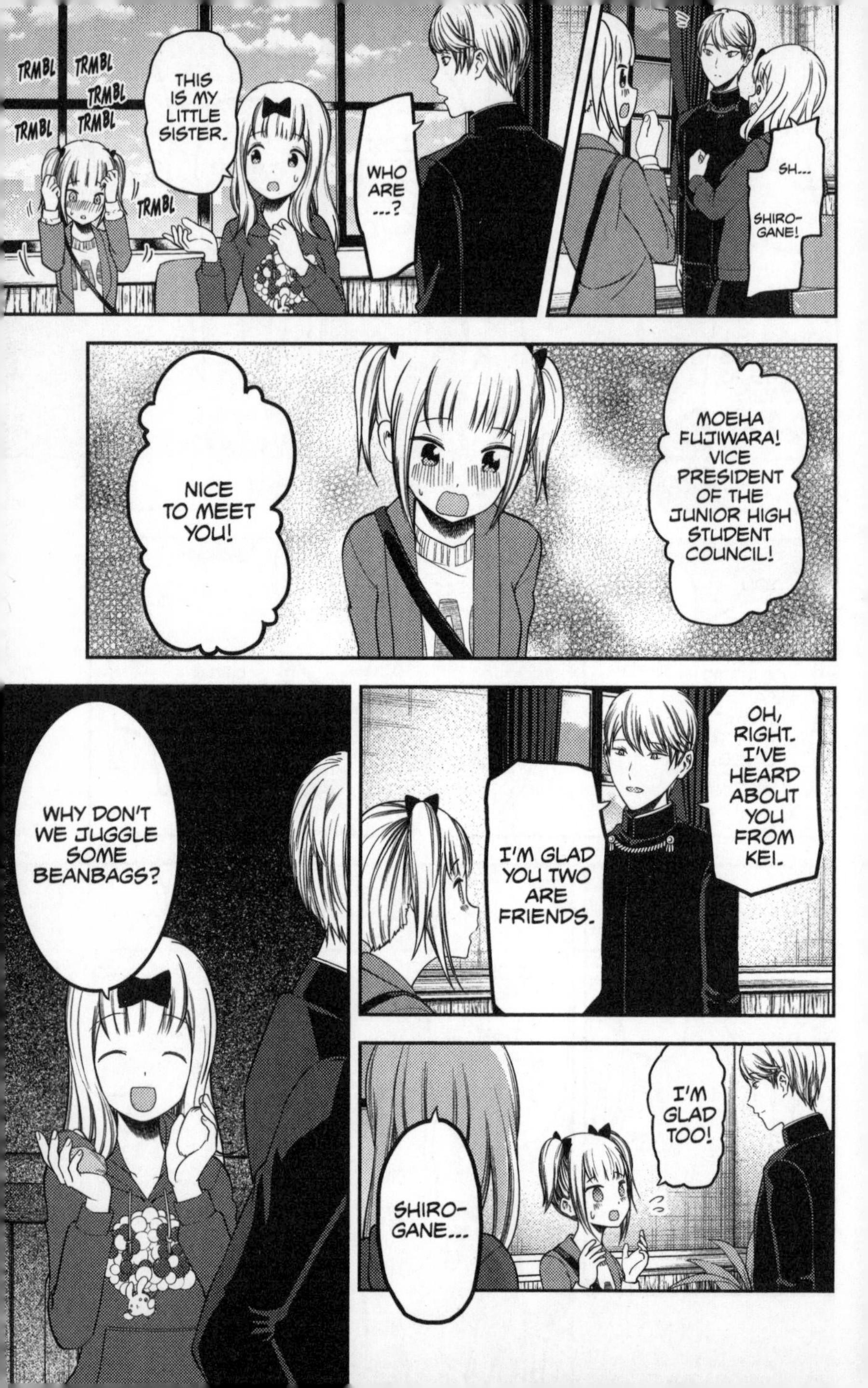
SH...
SHIRO-GANE!
WHO ARE ...?
THIS IS MY LITTLE SISTER.
TRMBL TRMBL TRMBL TRMBL TRMBL TRMBL
MOEHA FUJIWARA! VICE PRESIDENT OF THE JUNIOR HIGH STUDENT COUNCIL!
NICE TO MEET YOU!
OH, RIGHT. I'VE HEARD ABOUT YOU FROM KEI.
I'M GLAD YOU TWO ARE FRIENDS.
I'M GLAD TOO!
SHIRO-GANE...
WHY DON'T WE JUGGLE SOME BEANBAGS?

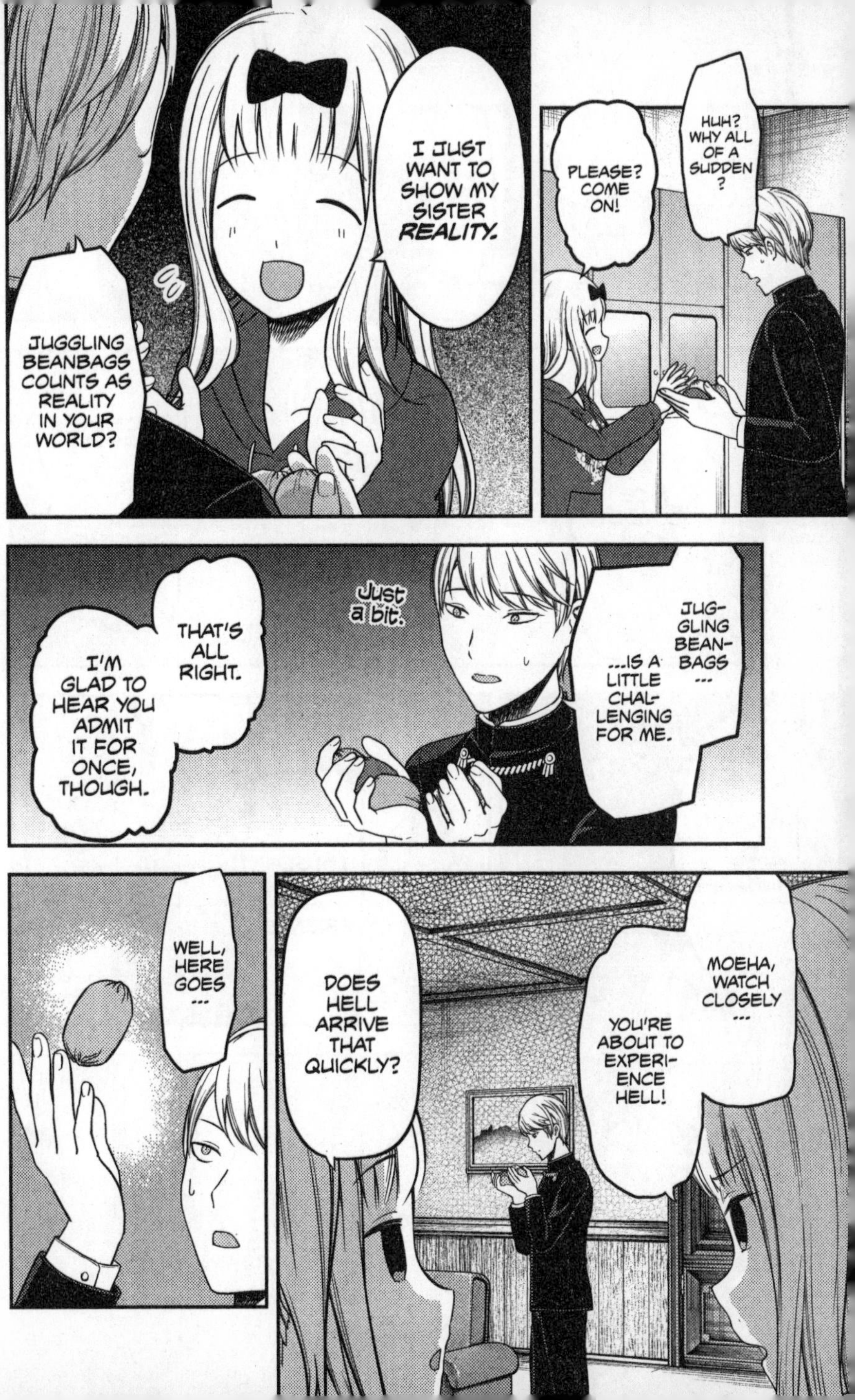

HUH? WHY ALL OF A SUDDEN?
PLEASE? COME ON!
I JUST WANT TO SHOW MY SISTER *REALITY.*
JUGGLING BEANBAGS COUNTS AS REALITY IN YOUR WORLD?
JUGGLING BEANBAGS...
...IS A LITTLE CHALLENGING FOR ME.
Just a bit.
THAT'S ALL RIGHT.
I'M GLAD TO HEAR YOU ADMIT IT FOR ONCE, THOUGH.
MOEHA, WATCH CLOSELY...
YOU'RE ABOUT TO EXPERIENCE HELL!
DOES HELL ARRIVE THAT QUICKLY?
WELL, HERE GOES...

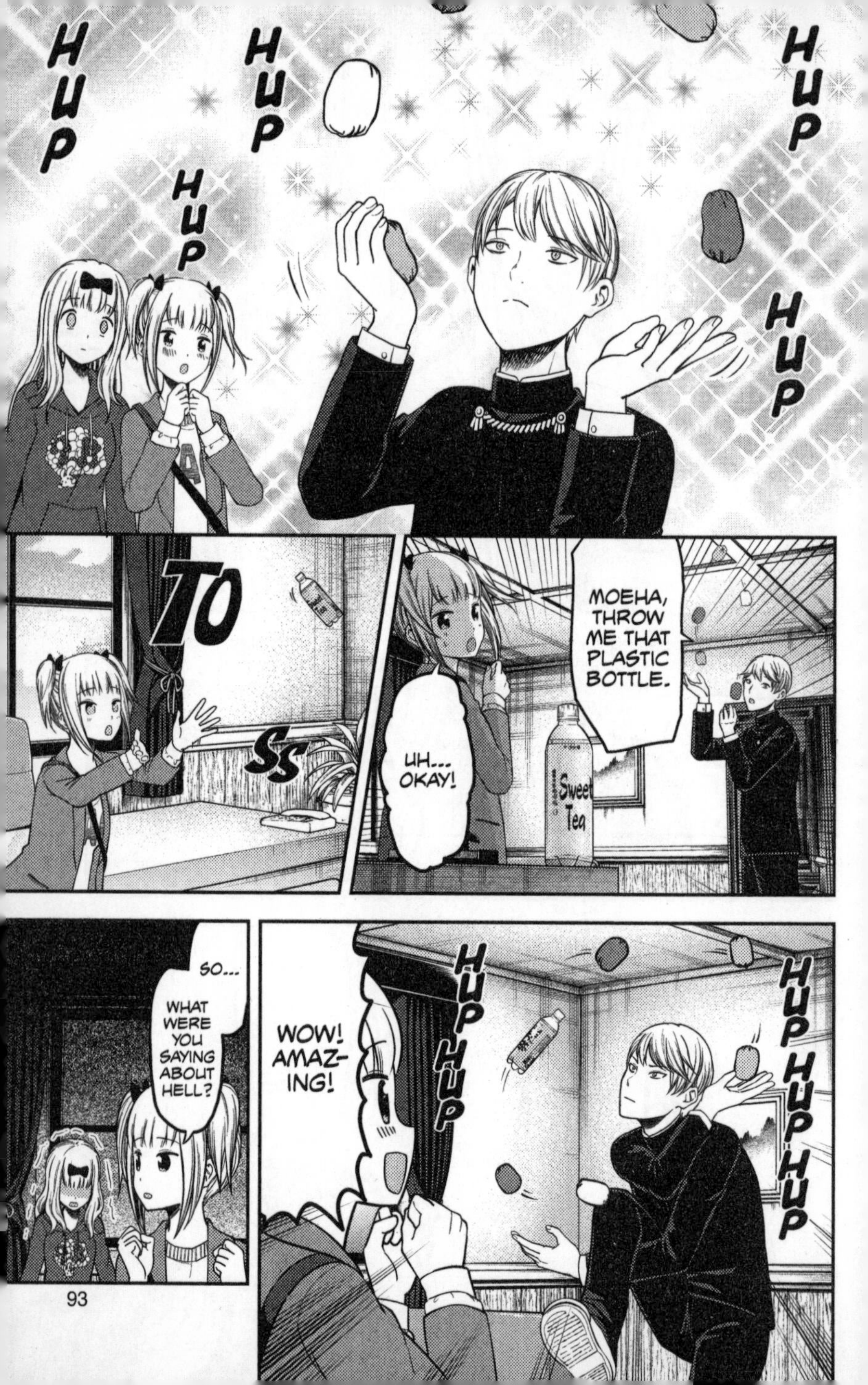
HUP
HUP
HUP
HUP
HUP
HUP
HUP
HUP
MOEHA, THROW ME THAT PLASTIC BOTTLE.
UH... OKAY!
TO
SS
HUP HUP HUP HUP
HUP HUP
WOW! AMAZ-ING!
SO...
WHAT WERE YOU SAYING ABOUT HELL?

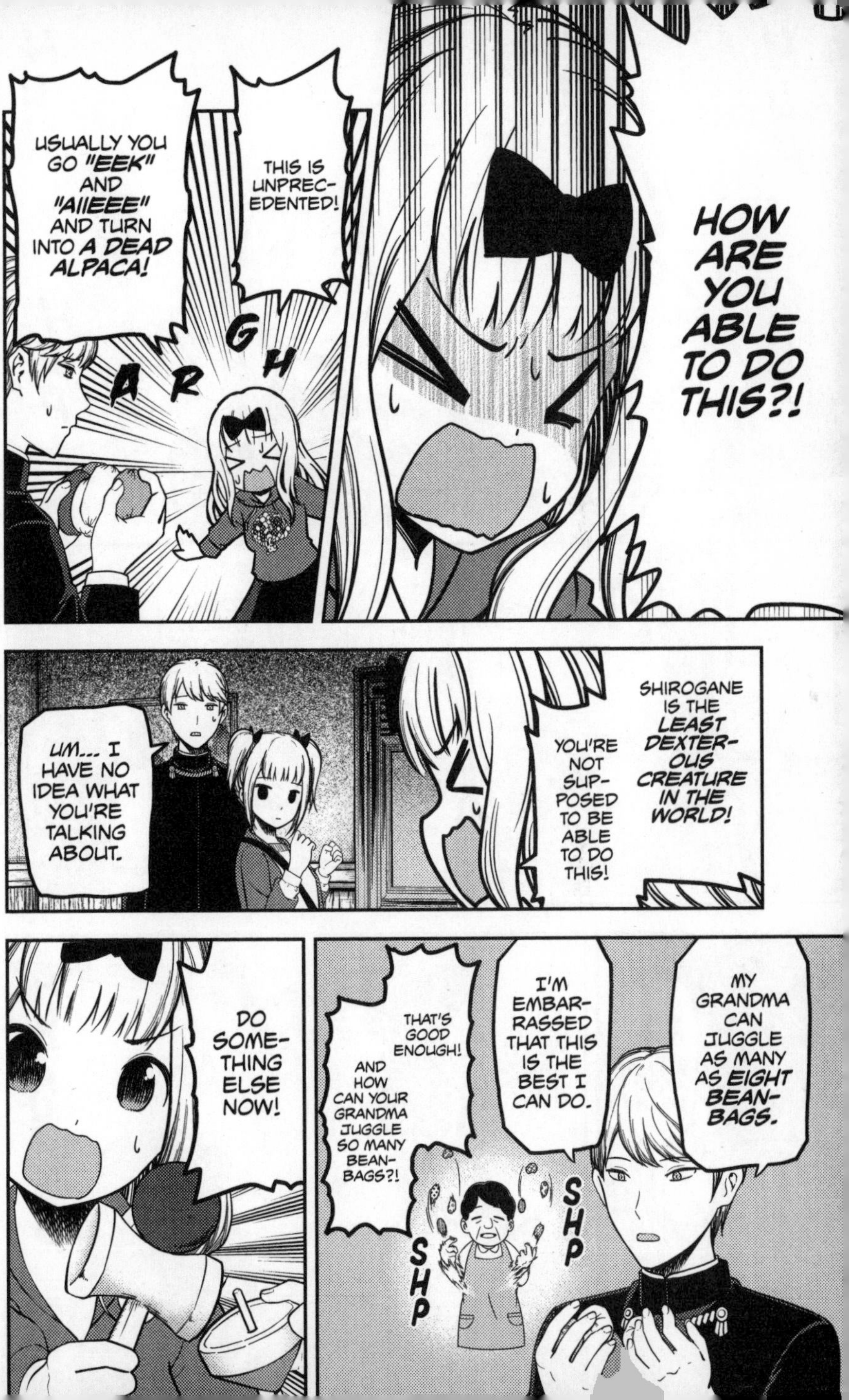
HOW ARE YOU ABLE TO DO THIS?!
THIS IS UNPRECEDENTED!
USUALLY YOU GO "EEK" AND "AIIEEE" AND TURN INTO A DEAD ALPACA!
ARGH
SHIROGANE IS THE LEAST DEXTEROUS CREATURE IN THE WORLD!
YOU'RE NOT SUPPOSED TO BE ABLE TO DO THIS!
UM... I HAVE NO IDEA WHAT YOU'RE TALKING ABOUT.
MY GRANDMA CAN JUGGLE AS MANY AS EIGHT BEANBAGS.
I'M EMBARRASSED THAT THIS IS THE BEST I CAN DO.
THAT'S GOOD ENOUGH!
AND HOW CAN YOUR GRANDMA JUGGLE SO MANY BEANBAGS?!
SHP
SHP
DO SOMETHING ELSE NOW!

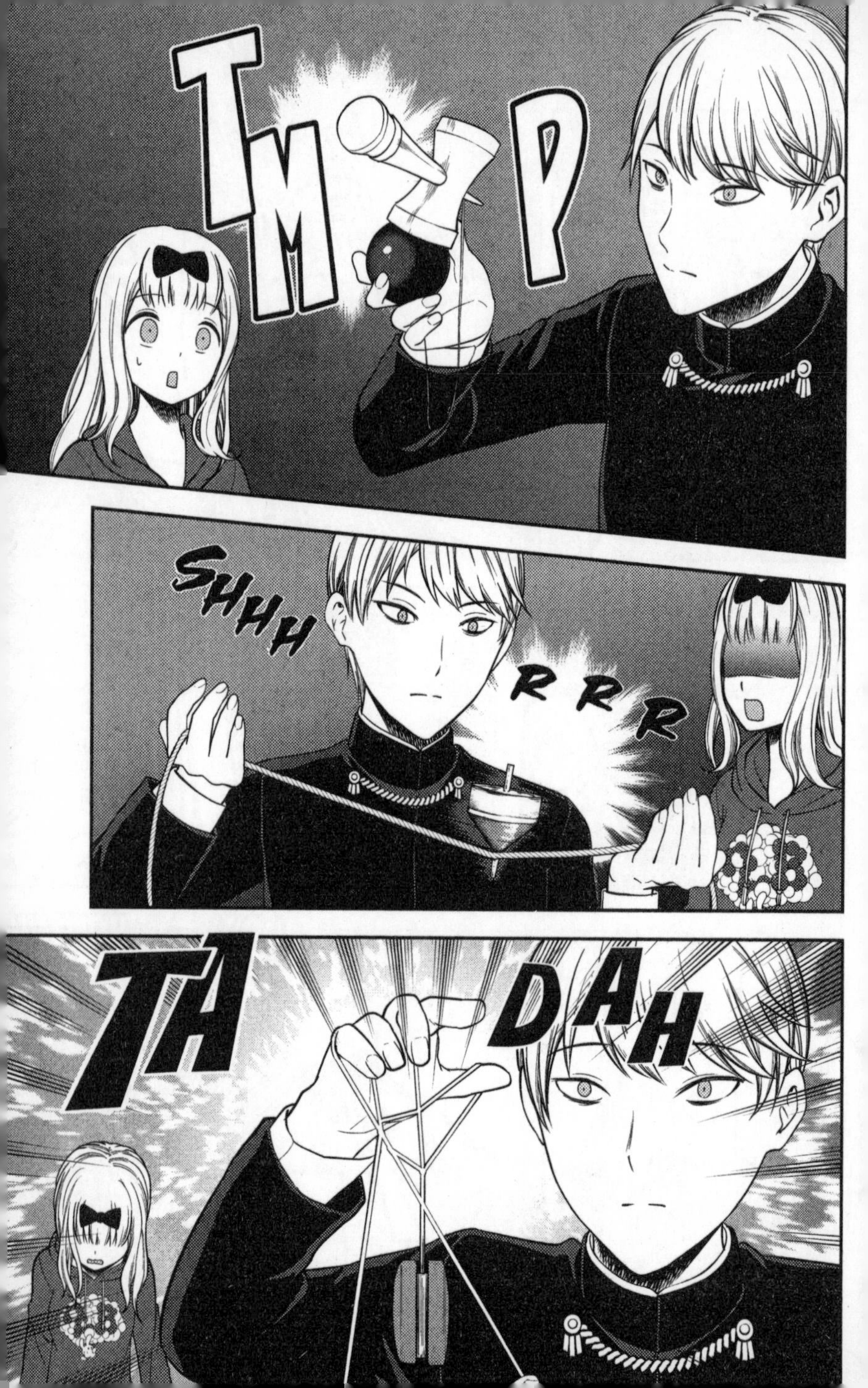
TMP
SHHH
RRR
TA DAH

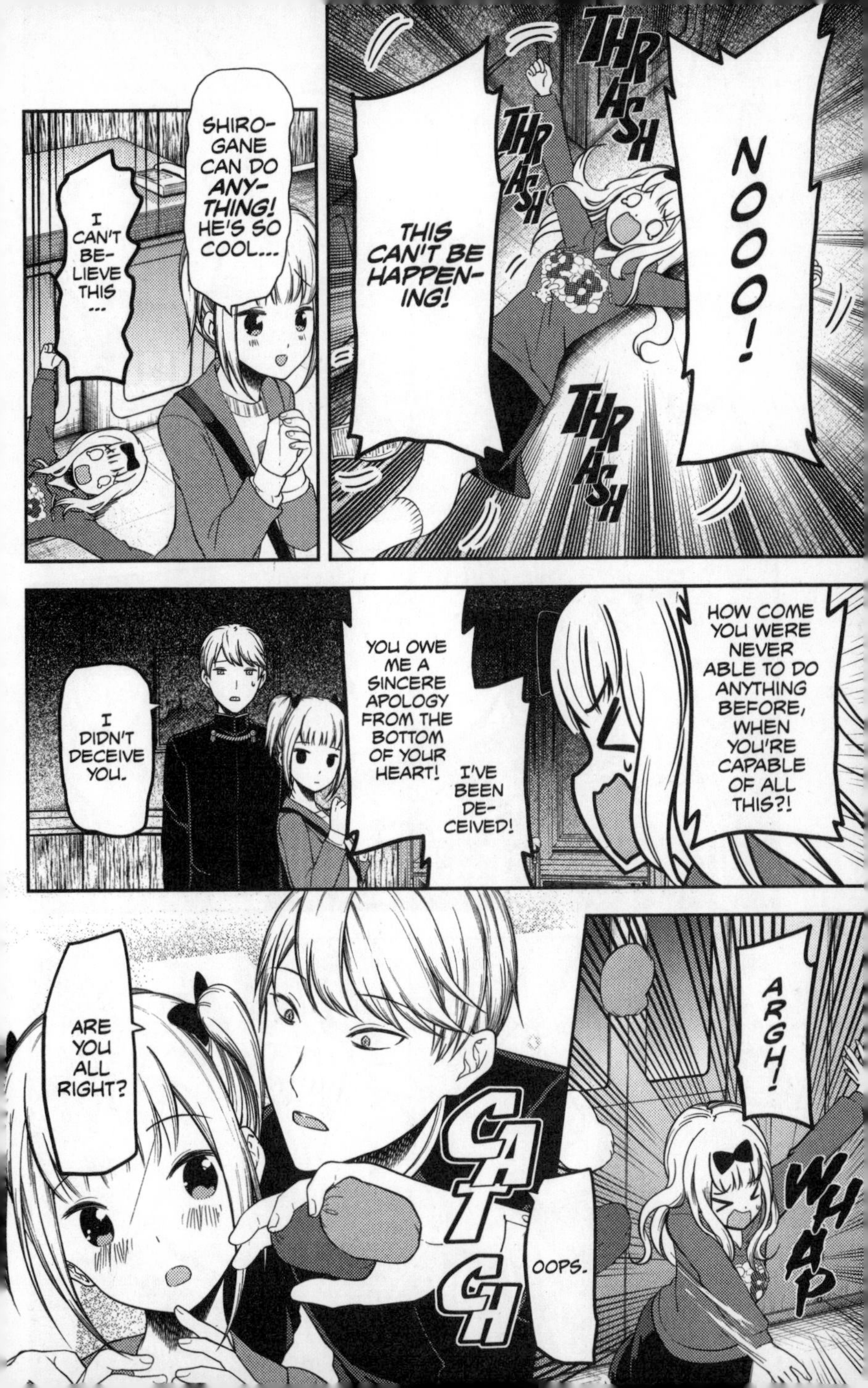

NOOOO!
THRASH
THRASH
THIS CAN'T BE HAPPENING!
THRASH
SHIRO-GANE CAN DO ANY-THING! HE'S SO COOL...
I CAN'T BE-LIEVE THIS...
HOW COME YOU WERE NEVER ABLE TO DO ANYTHING BEFORE, WHEN YOU'RE CAPABLE OF ALL THIS?!
YOU OWE ME A SINCERE APOLOGY FROM THE BOTTOM OF YOUR HEART!
I'VE BEEN DE-CEIVED!
I DIDN'T DECEIVE YOU.
ARGH!
WHAP
CATCH
OOPS.
ARE YOU ALL RIGHT?

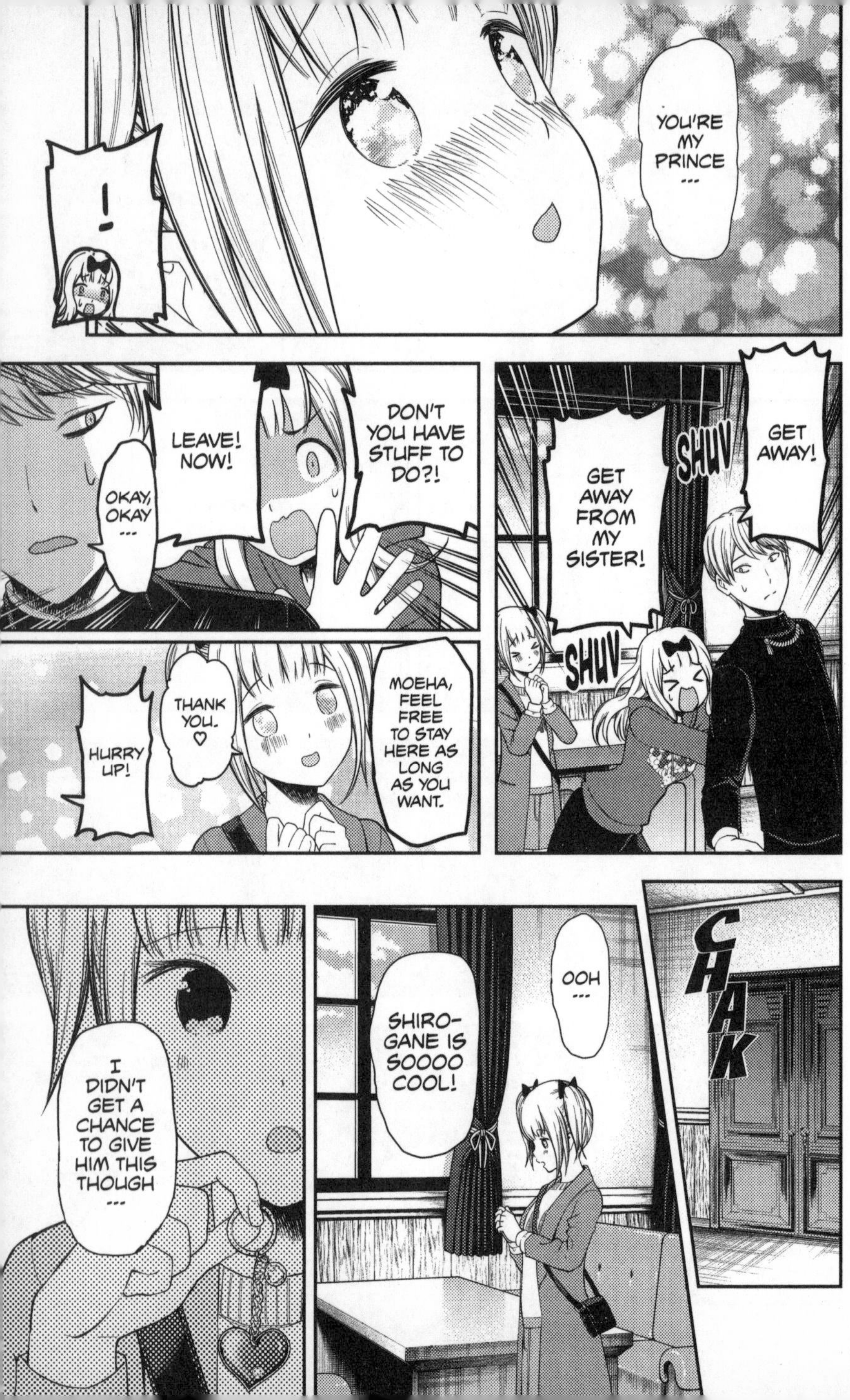
YOU'RE MY PRINCE ...
!
GET AWAY!
SHUV
GET AWAY FROM MY SISTER!
SHUV
DON'T YOU HAVE STUFF TO DO?!
LEAVE! NOW!
OKAY, OKAY ...
MOEHA, FEEL FREE TO STAY HERE AS LONG AS YOU WANT.
THANK YOU. ♡
HURRY UP!
CHAK
OOH ...
SHIRO-GANE IS SOOOO COOL!
I DIDN'T GET A CHANCE TO GIVE HIM THIS THOUGH ...

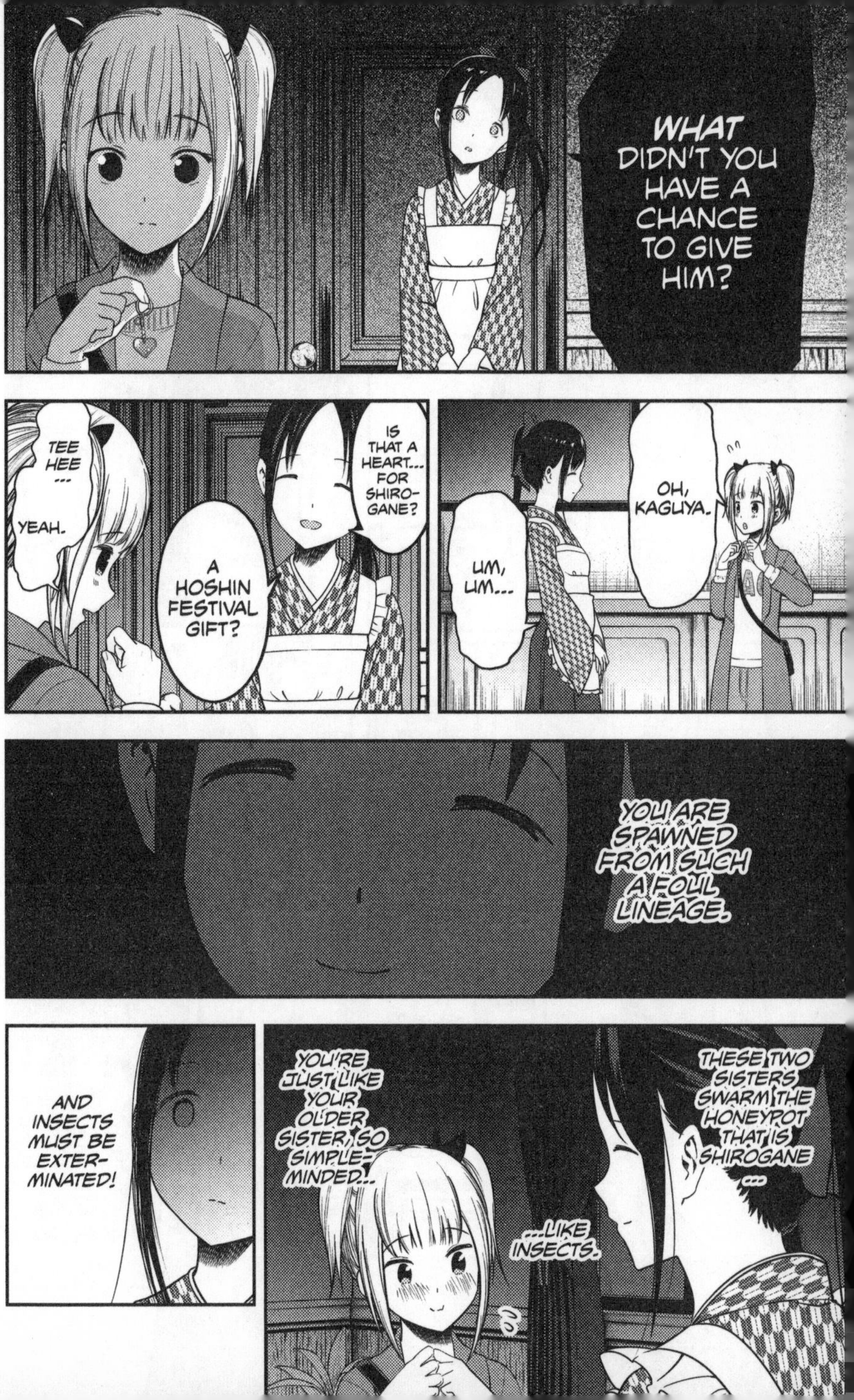
WHAT DIDN'T YOU HAVE A CHANCE TO GIVE HIM?
OH, KAGUYA.
UM, UM...
IS THAT A HEART... FOR SHIROGANE?
A HOSHIN FESTIVAL GIFT?
TEE HEE... YEAH.
YOU ARE SPAWNED FROM SUCH A FOUL LINEAGE.
THESE TWO SISTERS SWARM THE HONEYPOT THAT IS SHIROGANE...
...LIKE INSECTS.
YOU'RE JUST LIKE YOUR OLDER SISTER, SO SIMPLE-MINDED...
AND INSECTS MUST BE EXTERMINATED!

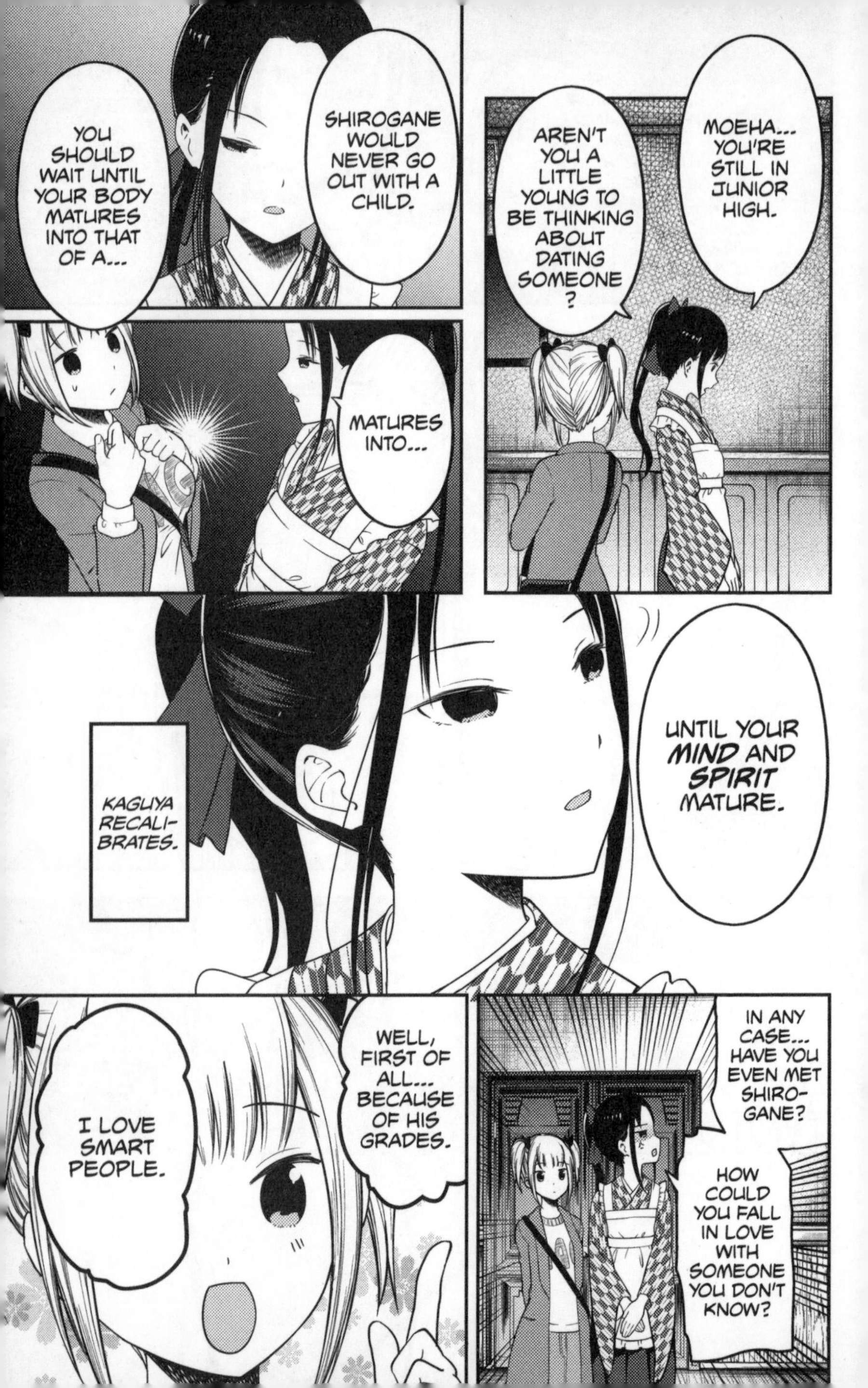

MOEHA... YOU'RE STILL IN JUNIOR HIGH.
AREN'T YOU A LITTLE YOUNG TO BE THINKING ABOUT DATING SOMEONE?
SHIROGANE WOULD NEVER GO OUT WITH A CHILD.
YOU SHOULD WAIT UNTIL YOUR BODY MATURES INTO THAT OF A...
MATURES INTO...
UNTIL YOUR MIND AND SPIRIT MATURE.
KAGUYA RECALI-BRATES.
IN ANY CASE... HAVE YOU EVEN MET SHIRO-GANE?
HOW COULD YOU FALL IN LOVE WITH SOMEONE YOU DON'T KNOW?
WELL, FIRST OF ALL... BECAUSE OF HIS GRADES.
I LOVE SMART PEOPLE.

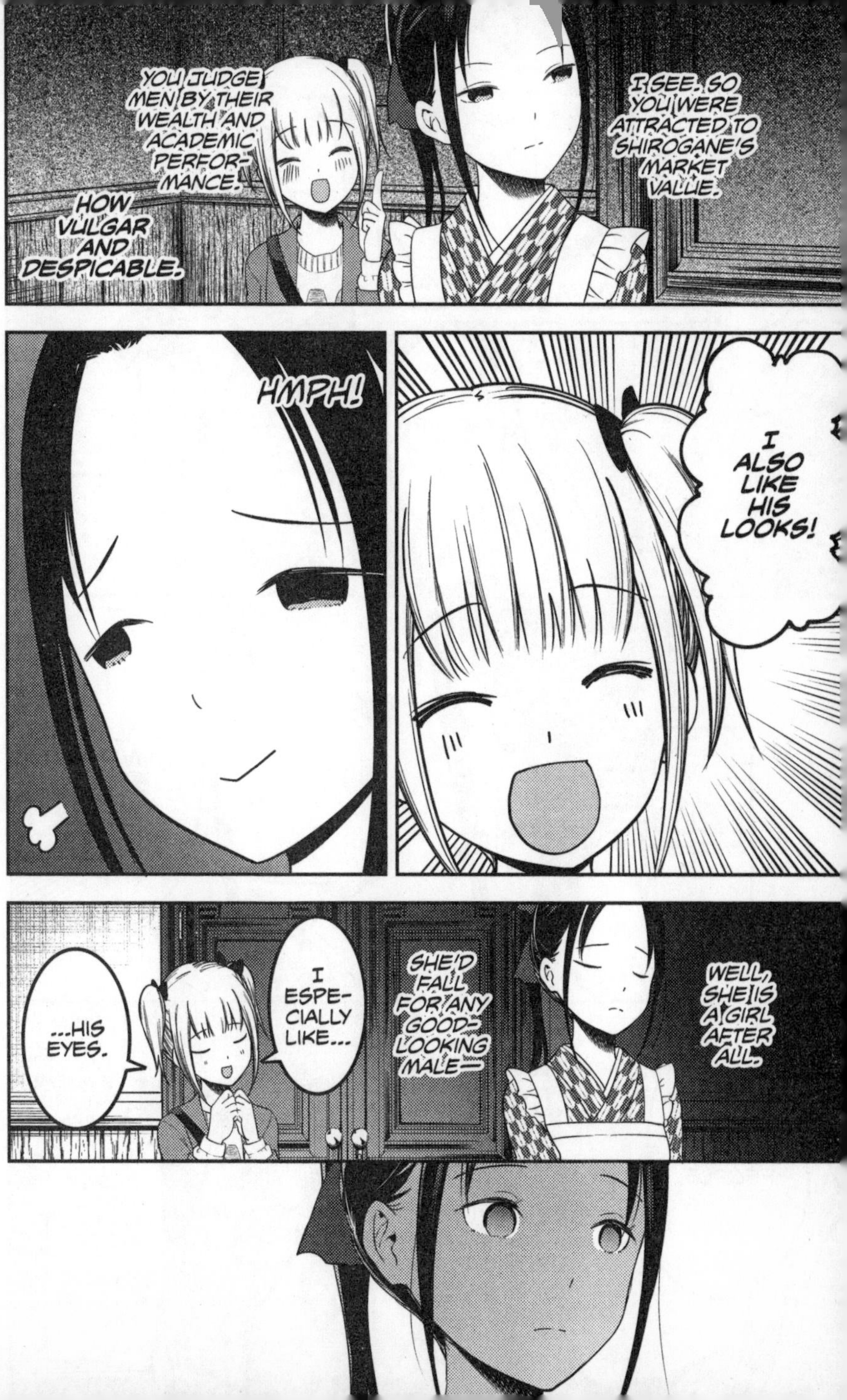
I SEE. SO YOU WERE ATTRACTED TO SHIROGANE'S MARKET VALUE.
YOU JUDGE MEN BY THEIR WEALTH AND ACADEMIC PERFORMANCE.
HOW VULGAR AND DESPICABLE.
I ALSO LIKE HIS LOOKS!
HMPH!
WELL, SHE IS A GIRL AFTER ALL.
SHE'D FALL FOR ANY GOOD-LOOKING MALE—
I ESPECIALLY LIKE...
...HIS EYES.

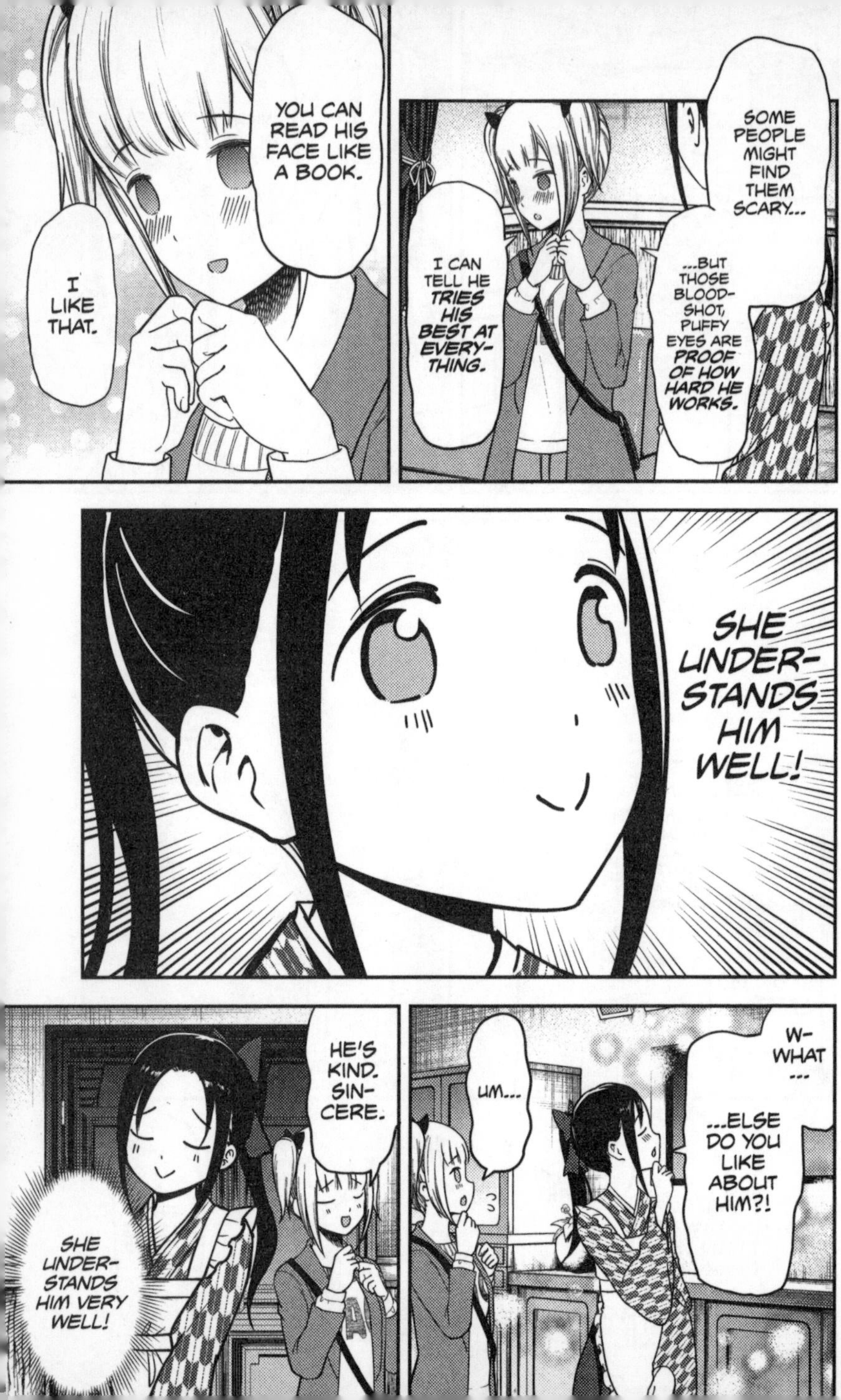
SOME PEOPLE MIGHT FIND THEM SCARY...
...BUT THOSE BLOODSHOT, PUFFY EYES ARE PROOF OF HOW HARD HE WORKS.
I CAN TELL HE TRIES HIS BEST AT EVERYTHING.
YOU CAN READ HIS FACE LIKE A BOOK.
I LIKE THAT.
SHE UNDERSTANDS HIM WELL!
W-WHAT...
...ELSE DO YOU LIKE ABOUT HIM?!
UM...
HE'S KIND. SINCERE.
SHE UNDERSTANDS HIM VERY WELL!

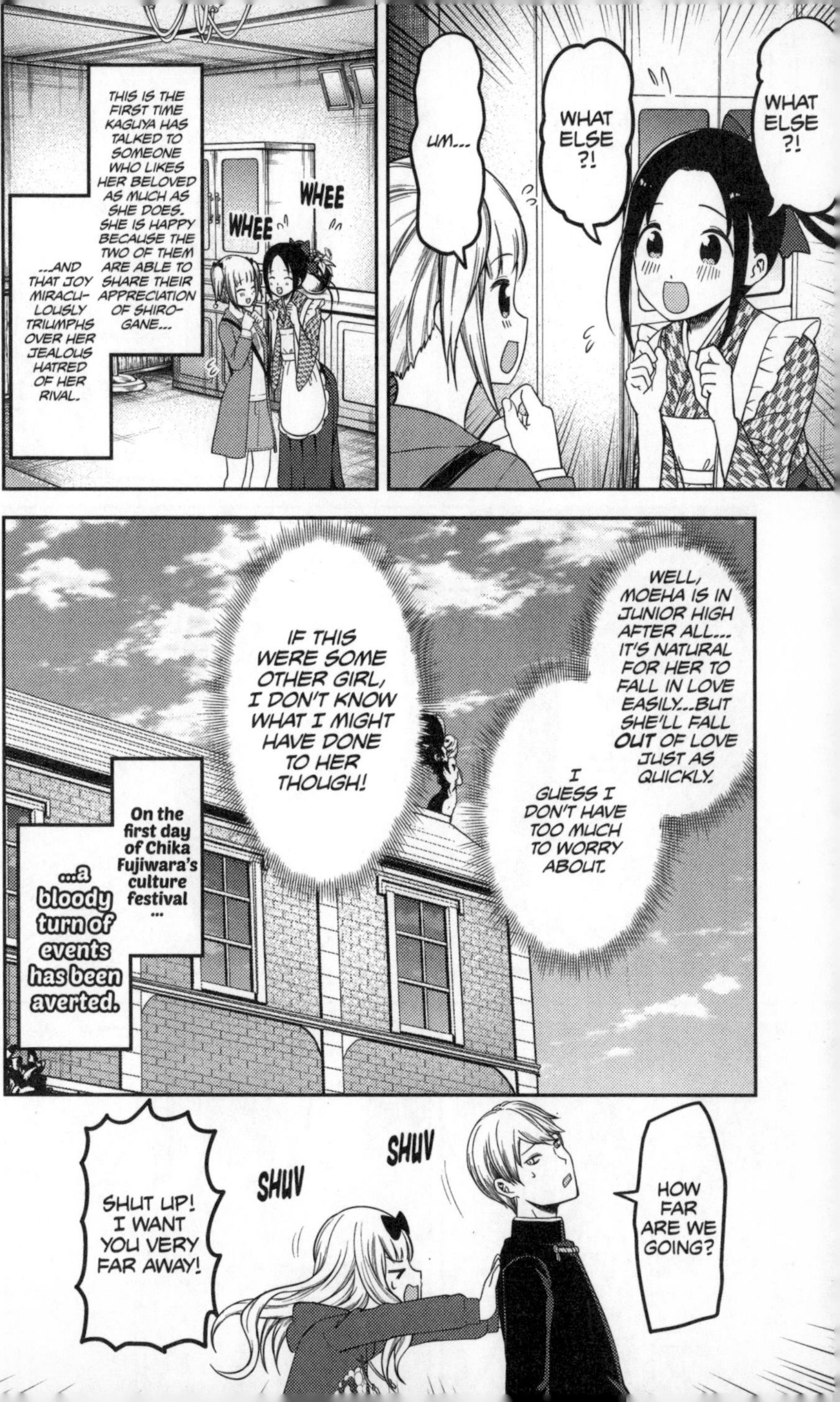
WHAT ELSE ?!
WHAT ELSE ?!
UM...
THIS IS THE FIRST TIME KAGUYA HAS TALKED TO SOMEONE WHO LIKES HER BELOVED AS MUCH AS SHE DOES. SHE IS HAPPY BECAUSE THE TWO OF THEM ARE ABLE TO SHARE THEIR APPRECIATION OF SHIROGANE...
...AND THAT JOY MIRACULOUSLY TRIUMPHS OVER HER JEALOUS HATRED OF HER RIVAL.
WHEE
WHEE
WELL, MOEHA IS IN JUNIOR HIGH AFTER ALL... IT'S NATURAL FOR HER TO FALL IN LOVE EASILY...BUT SHE'LL FALL OUT OF LOVE JUST AS QUICKLY.
I GUESS I DON'T HAVE TOO MUCH TO WORRY ABOUT.
IF THIS WERE SOME OTHER GIRL, I DON'T KNOW WHAT I MIGHT HAVE DONE TO HER THOUGH!
On the first day of Chika Fujiwara's culture festival ...
...a bloody turn of events has been averted.
HOW FAR ARE WE GOING?
SHUV
SHUV
SHUT UP! I WANT YOU VERY FAR AWAY!

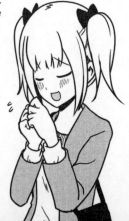

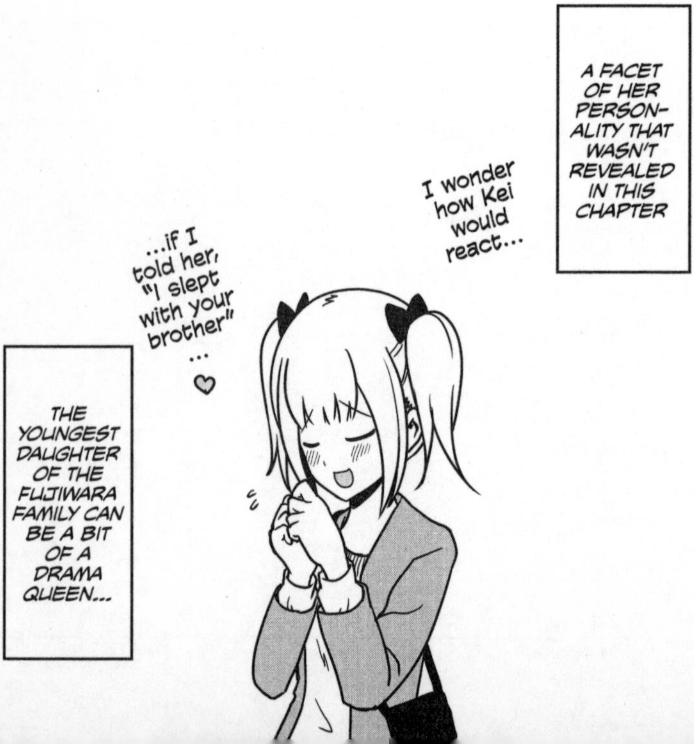

A FACET OF HER PERSON-ALITY THAT WASN'T REVEALED IN THIS CHAPTER

I wonder how Kei would react...

...if I told her, "I slept with your brother"... ♡

THE YOUNGEST DAUGHTER OF THE FUJIWARA FAMILY CAN BE A BIT OF A DRAMA QUEEN...

KAGUYA-SAMA

LOVE IS WAR

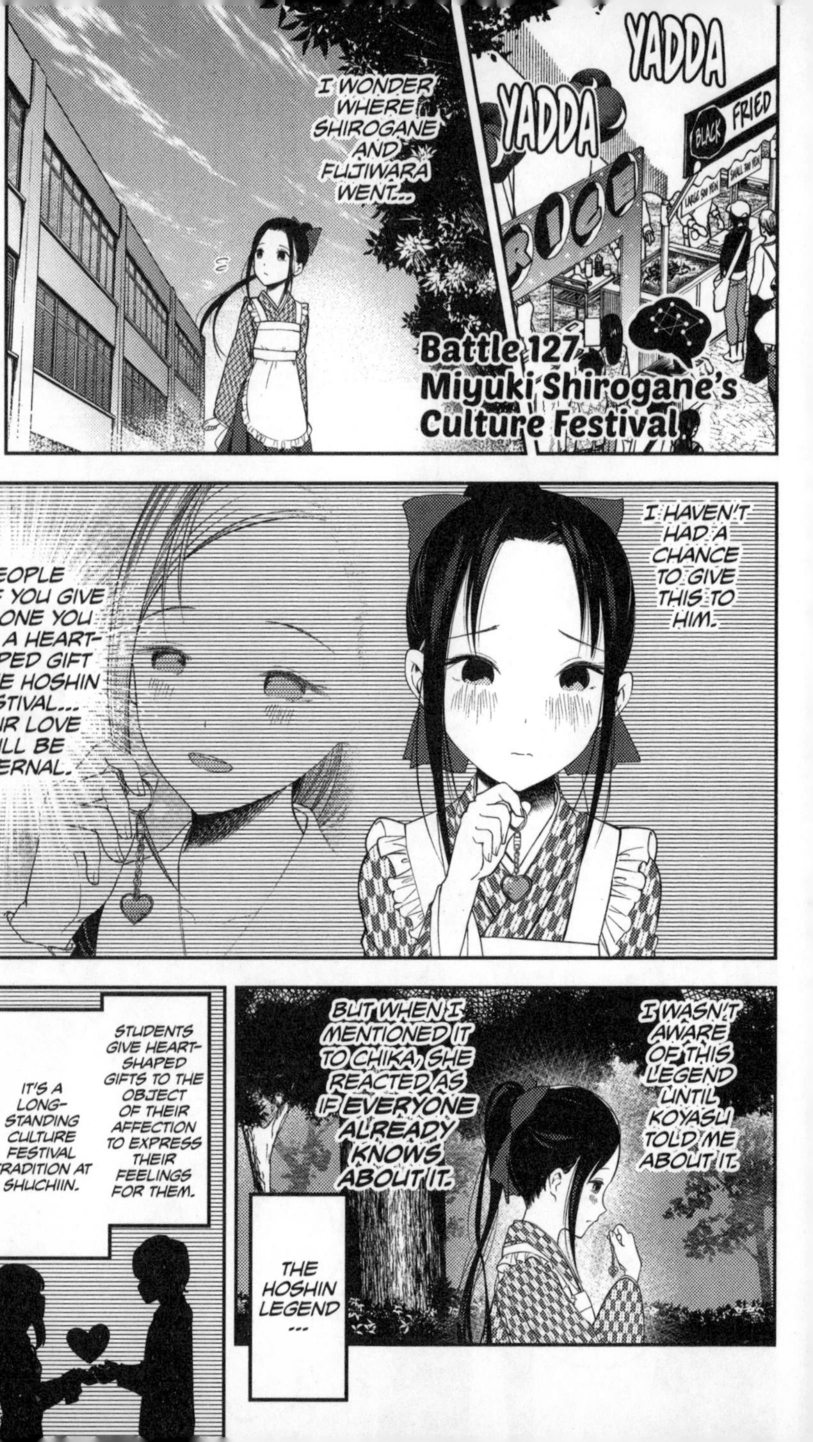

YADDA
YADDA
BLACK FRIED
RICE
Battle 127 Miyuki Shirogane's Culture Festival
I WONDER WHERE SHIROGANE AND FUJIWARA WENT...
I HAVEN'T HAD A CHANCE TO GIVE THIS TO HIM.
PEOPLE SAY IF YOU GIVE THE ONE YOU LOVE A HEART-SHAPED GIFT AT THE HOSHIN FESTIVAL... YOUR LOVE WILL BE ETERNAL.
I WASN'T AWARE OF THIS LEGEND UNTIL KOYASU TOLD ME ABOUT IT.
BUT WHEN I MENTIONED IT TO CHIKA, SHE REACTED AS IF EVERYONE ALREADY KNOWS ABOUT IT.
THE HOSHIN LEGEND...
STUDENTS GIVE HEART-SHAPED GIFTS TO THE OBJECT OF THEIR AFFECTION TO EXPRESS THEIR FEELINGS FOR THEM.
IT'S A LONG-STANDING CULTURE FESTIVAL TRADITION AT SHUCHIIN.

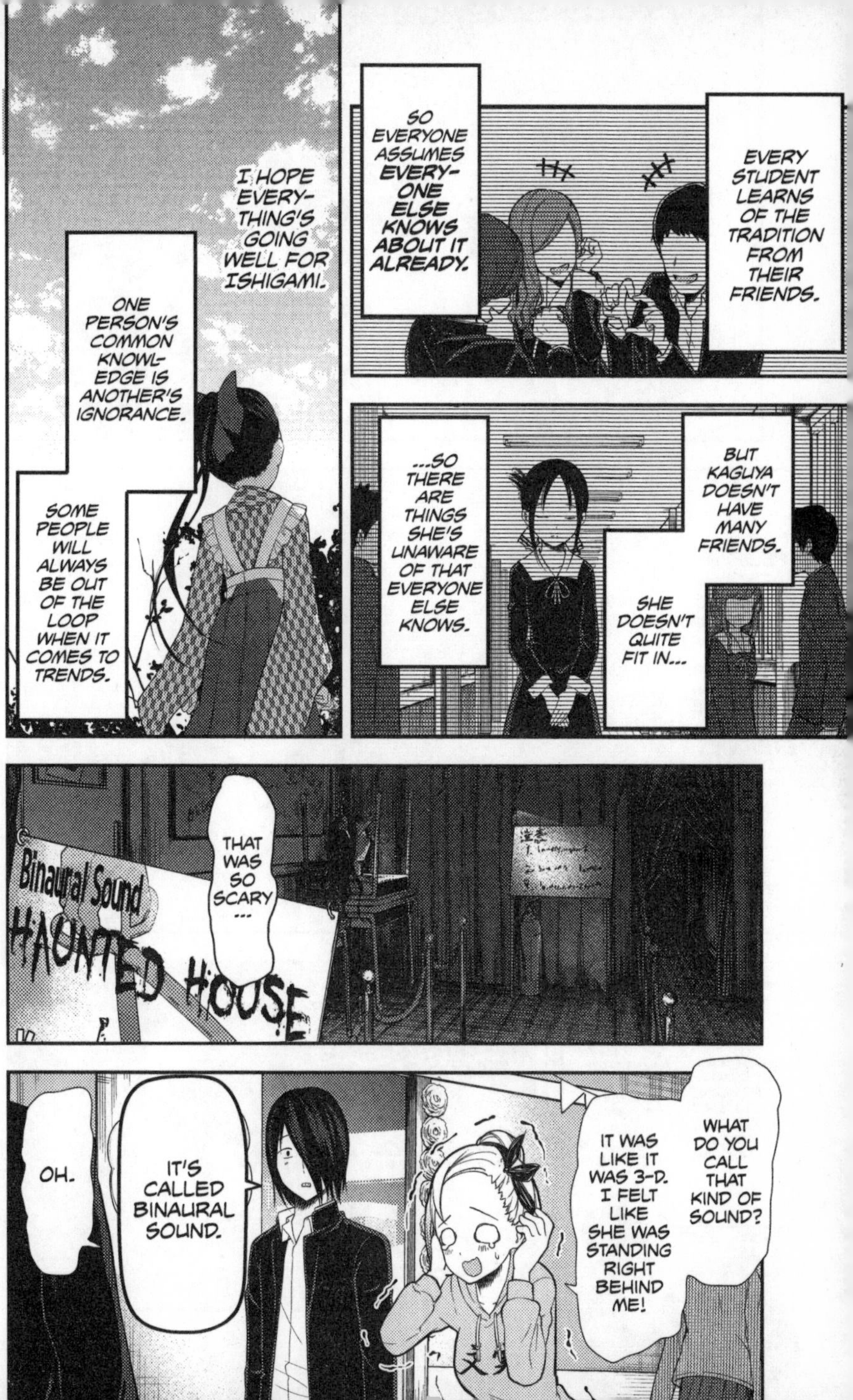
EVERY STUDENT LEARNS OF THE TRADITION FROM THEIR FRIENDS.
SO EVERYONE ASSUMES EVERYONE ELSE KNOWS ABOUT IT ALREADY.
BUT KAGUYA DOESN'T HAVE MANY FRIENDS.
SHE DOESN'T QUITE FIT IN...
...SO THERE ARE THINGS SHE'S UNAWARE OF THAT EVERYONE ELSE KNOWS.
I HOPE EVERYTHING'S GOING WELL FOR ISHIGAMI.
ONE PERSON'S COMMON KNOWLEDGE IS ANOTHER'S IGNORANCE.
SOME PEOPLE WILL ALWAYS BE OUT OF THE LOOP WHEN IT COMES TO TRENDS.
THAT WAS SO SCARY...
Binaural Sound
HAUNTED HOUSE
WHAT DO YOU CALL THAT KIND OF SOUND?
IT WAS LIKE IT WAS 3-D. I FELT LIKE SHE WAS STANDING RIGHT BEHIND ME!
IT'S CALLED BINAURAL SOUND.
OH.

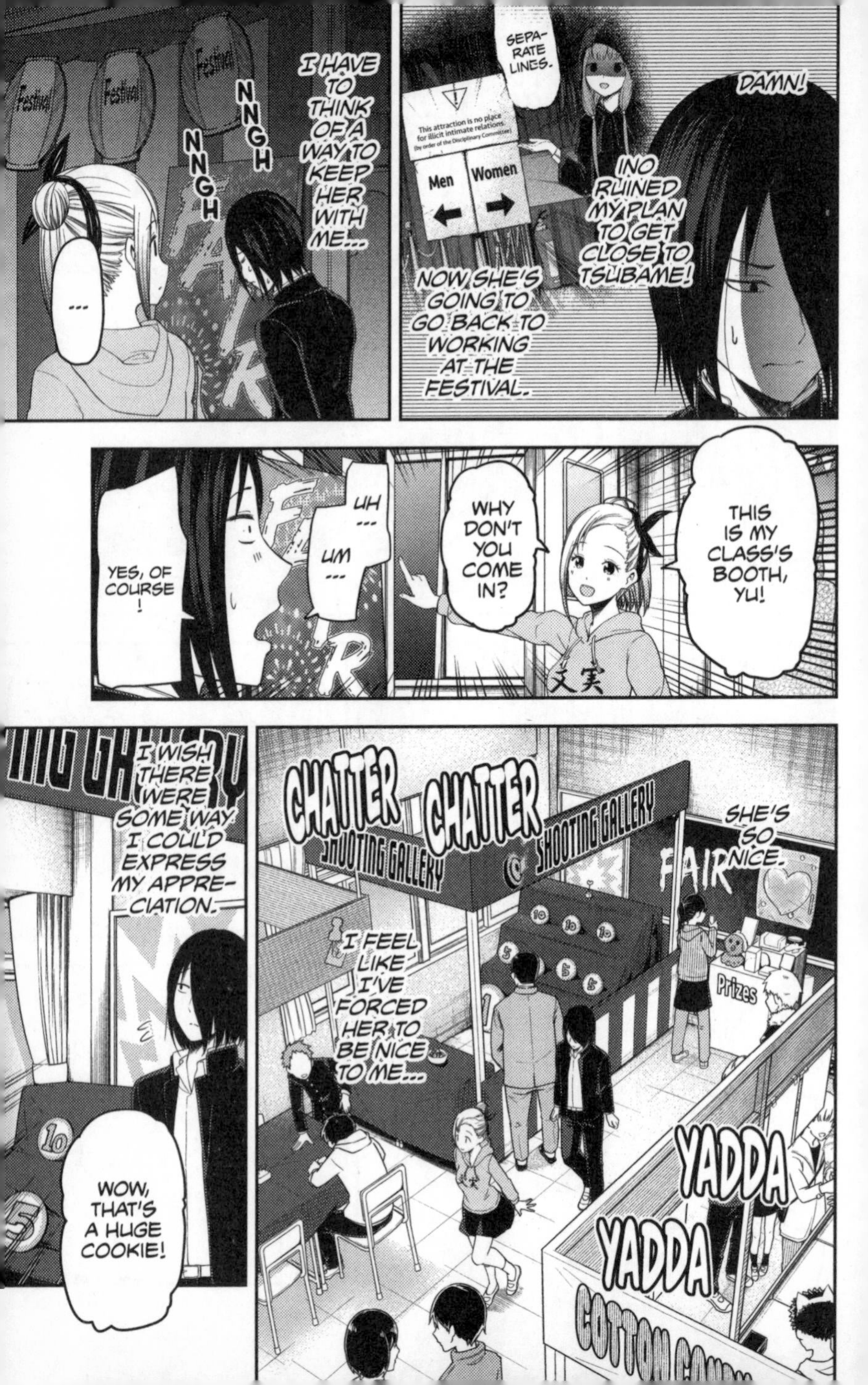
SEPARATE LINES.
This attraction is no place for illicit intimate relations. (by order of the Disciplinary Committee)
Men
Women
DAMN!
INO RUINED MY PLAN TO GET CLOSE TO TSUBAME!
NOW SHE'S GOING TO GO BACK TO WORKING AT THE FESTIVAL.
Festival
Festival
Festival
I HAVE TO THINK OF A WAY TO KEEP HER WITH ME...
NNGH
NNGH
...
THIS IS MY CLASS'S BOOTH, YU!
WHY DON'T YOU COME IN?
UH ---
UM ---
YES, OF COURSE!
CHATTER
CHATTER
SHOOTING GALLERY
SHOOTING GALLERY
SHE'S SO NICE.
FAIR
I FEEL LIKE I'VE FORCED HER TO BE NICE TO ME...
Prizes
YADDA
YADDA
I WISH THERE WERE SOME WAY I COULD EXPRESS MY APPRECIATION.
WOW, THAT'S A HUGE COOKIE!

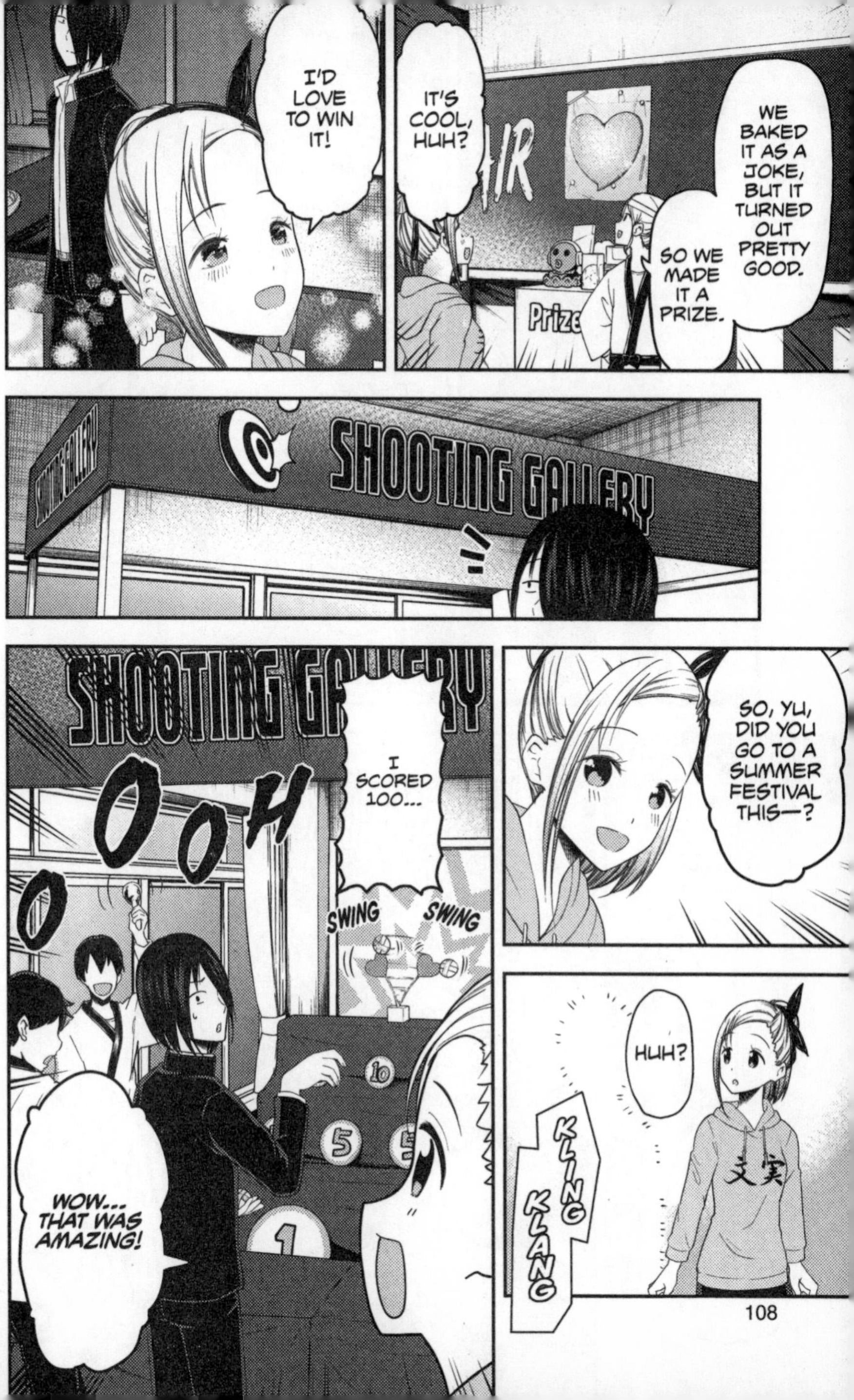
WE BAKED IT AS A JOKE, BUT IT TURNED OUT PRETTY GOOD.
SO WE MADE IT A PRIZE.
Prize
IT'S COOL, HUH?
I'D LOVE TO WIN IT!
SHOOTING GALLERY
SHOOTING GALLERY
SO, YU, DID YOU GO TO A SUMMER FESTIVAL THIS—?
HUH?
KLING KLANG
SHOOTING GALLERY
I SCORED 100...
OOOOH
SWING SWING
WOW... THAT WAS AMAZING!

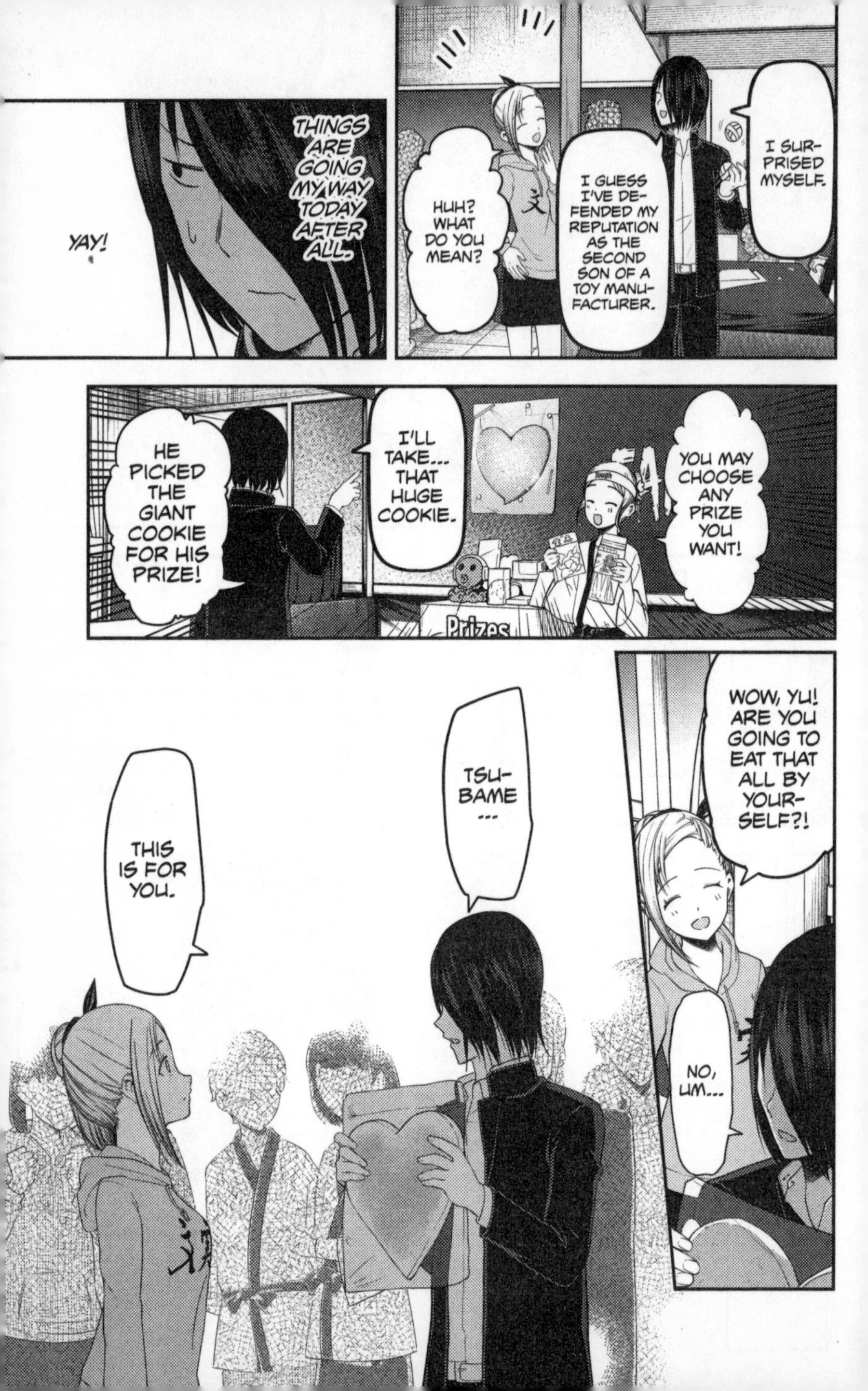
I SURPRISED MYSELF.
I GUESS I'VE DEFENDED MY REPUTATION AS THE SECOND SON OF A TOY MANUFACTURER.
HUH? WHAT DO YOU MEAN?
THINGS ARE GOING MY WAY TODAY AFTER ALL.
YAY!
YOU MAY CHOOSE ANY PRIZE YOU WANT!
Prizes
I'LL TAKE... THAT HUGE COOKIE.
HE PICKED THE GIANT COOKIE FOR HIS PRIZE!
WOW, YU! ARE YOU GOING TO EAT THAT ALL BY YOURSELF?!
NO, UM...
TSUBAME...
THIS IS FOR YOU.

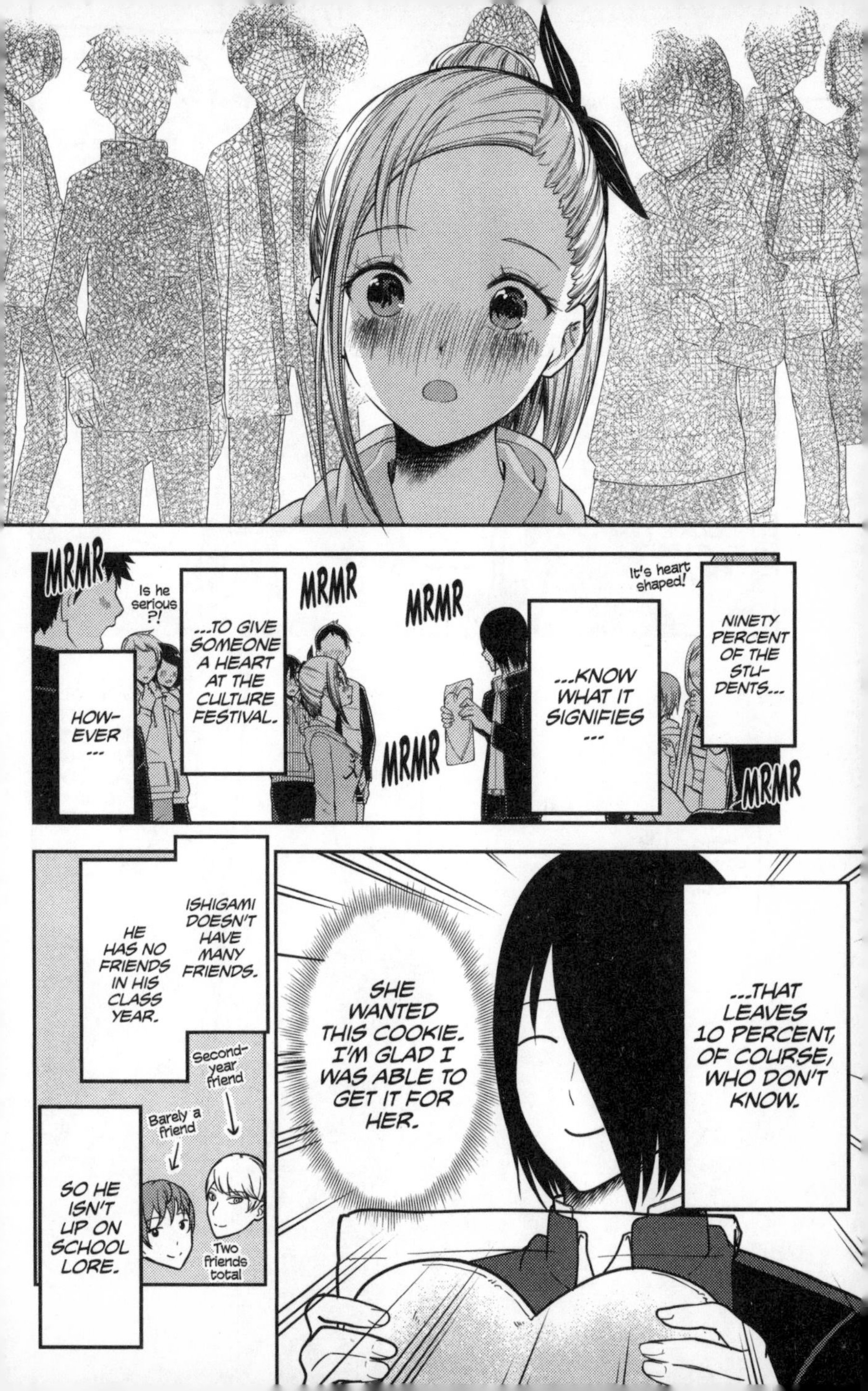
NINETY PERCENT OF THE STU-DENTS...
It's heart shaped!
MRMR
...KNOW WHAT IT SIGNIFIES...
MRMR
MRMR
MRMR
...TO GIVE SOMEONE A HEART AT THE CULTURE FESTIVAL.
Is he serious?!
MRMR
HOW-EVER...
...THAT LEAVES 10 PERCENT, OF COURSE, WHO DON'T KNOW.
SHE WANTED THIS COOKIE. I'M GLAD I WAS ABLE TO GET IT FOR HER.
ISHIGAMI DOESN'T HAVE MANY FRIENDS.
HE HAS NO FRIENDS IN HIS CLASS YEAR.
Second-year friend
Barely a friend
Two friends total
SO HE ISN'T UP ON SCHOOL LORE.

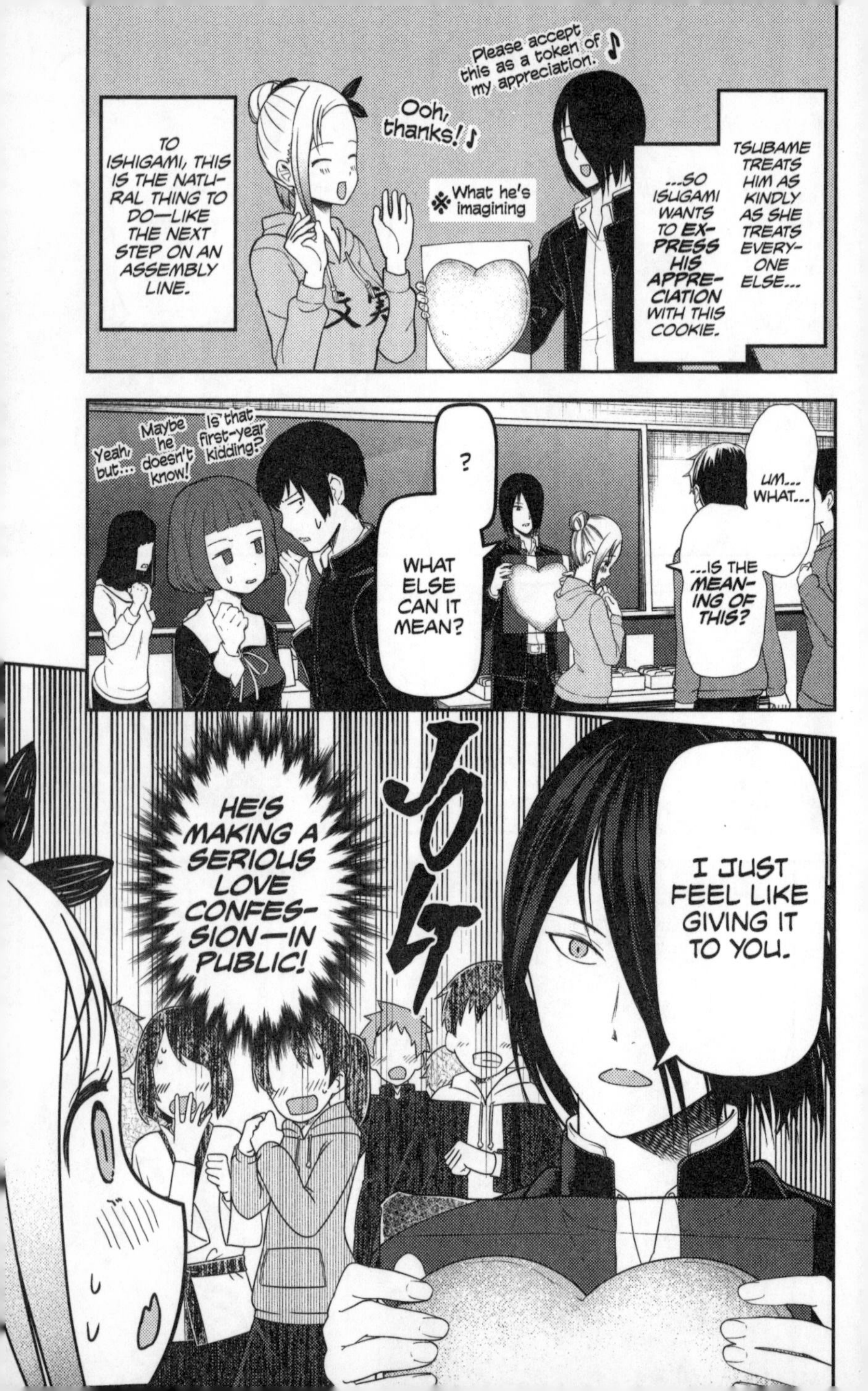
TSUBAME TREATS HIM AS KINDLY AS SHE TREATS EVERYONE ELSE...
...SO ISUGAMI WANTS TO EXPRESS HIS APPRECIATION WITH THIS COOKIE.
Please accept this as a token of my appreciation. ♪
※What he's imagining
Ooh, thanks! ♪
TO ISHIGAMI, THIS IS THE NATURAL THING TO DO—LIKE THE NEXT STEP ON AN ASSEMBLY LINE.
UM... WHAT...
...IS THE MEANING OF THIS?
? WHAT ELSE CAN IT MEAN?
Is that first-year kidding?
Maybe he doesn't know!
Yeah, but...
I JUST FEEL LIKE GIVING IT TO YOU.
JOLT
HE'S MAKING A SERIOUS LOVE CONFESSION—IN PUBLIC!

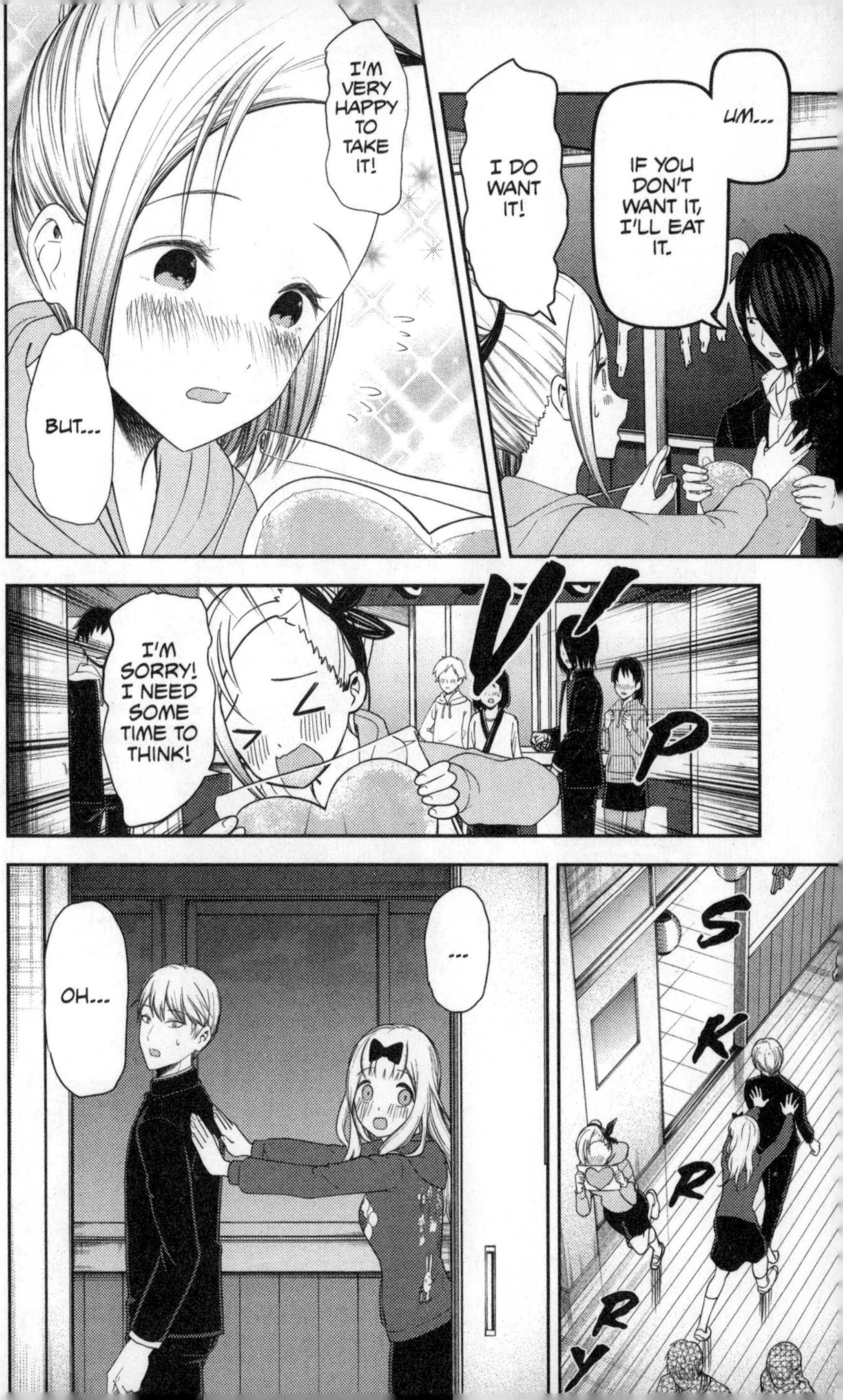
UM...
IF YOU DON'T WANT IT, I'LL EAT IT.
I DO WANT IT!
I'M VERY HAPPY TO TAKE IT!
BUT...
V! P
I'M SORRY! I NEED SOME TIME TO THINK!
SKRRRY
...
OH...

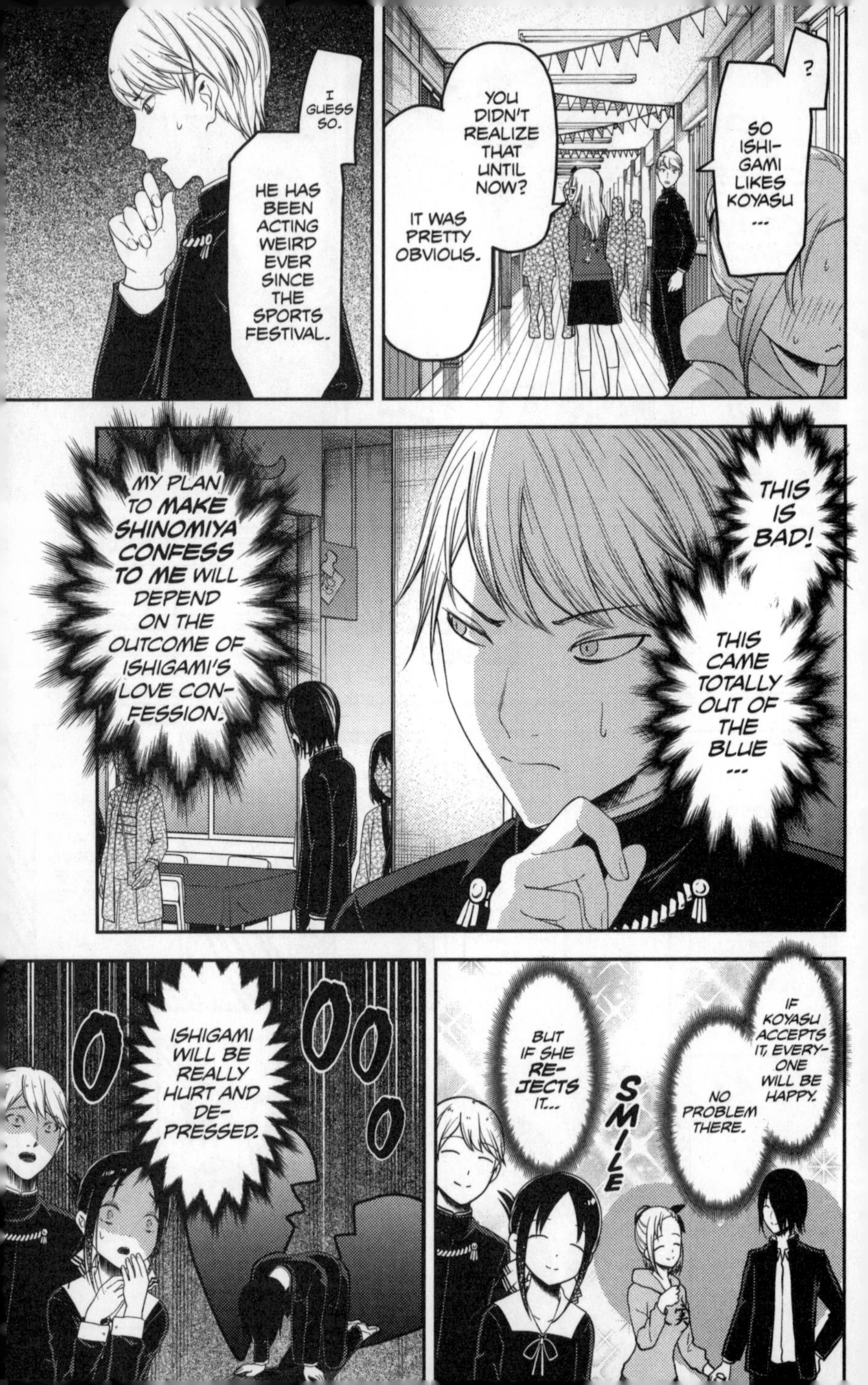
?
SO ISHIGAMI LIKES KOYASU...
YOU DIDN'T REALIZE THAT UNTIL NOW?
IT WAS PRETTY OBVIOUS.
I GUESS SO.
HE HAS BEEN ACTING WEIRD EVER SINCE THE SPORTS FESTIVAL.
THIS IS BAD!
THIS CAME TOTALLY OUT OF THE BLUE...
MY PLAN TO MAKE SHINOMIYA CONFESS TO ME WILL DEPEND ON THE OUTCOME OF ISHIGAMI'S LOVE CONFESSION.
IF KOYASU ACCEPTS IT, EVERYONE WILL BE HAPPY.
NO PROBLEM THERE.
SMILE
BUT IF SHE REJECTS IT...
ISHIGAMI WILL BE REALLY HURT AND DEPRESSED.

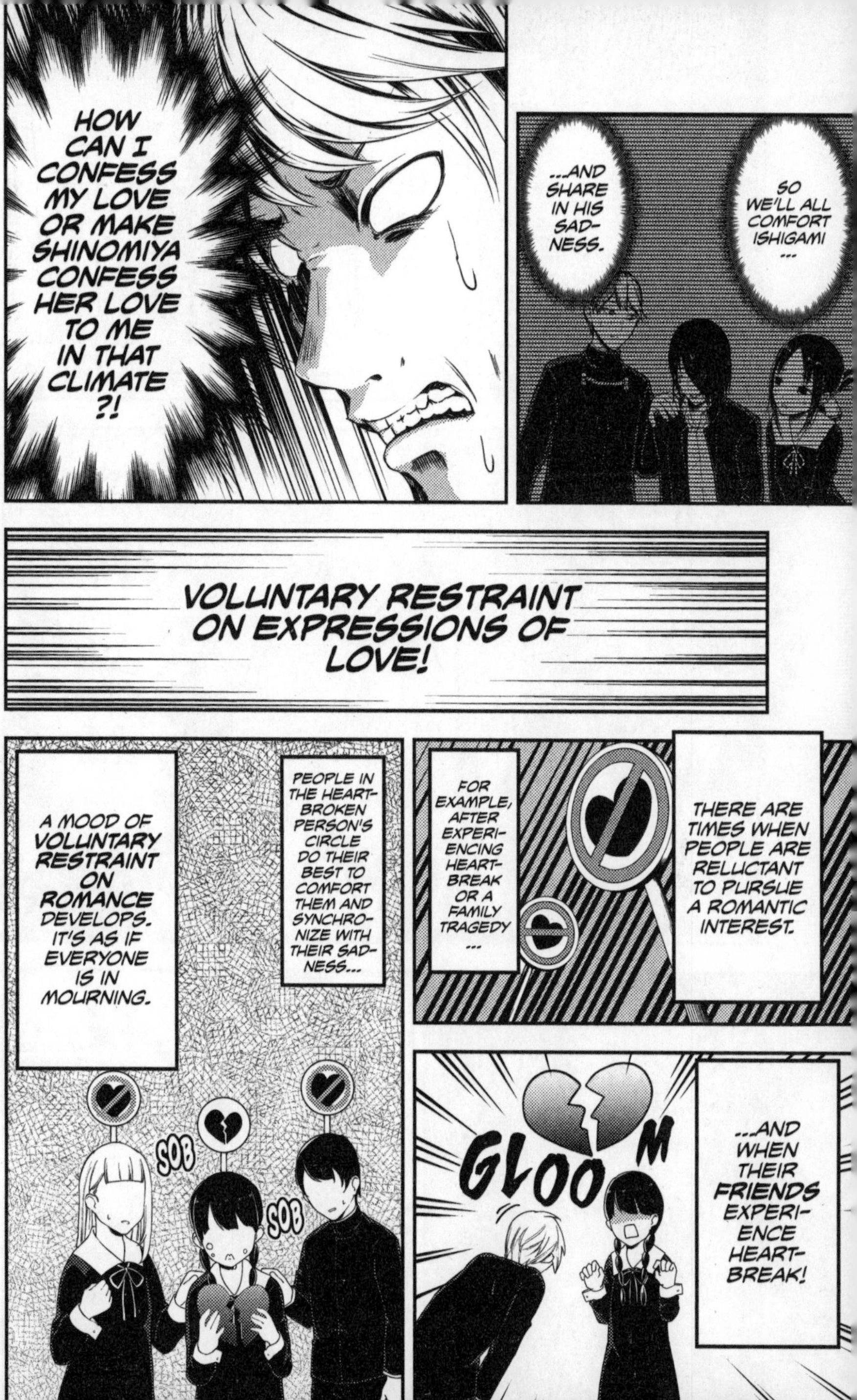
SO WE'LL ALL COMFORT ISHIGAMI...
...AND SHARE IN HIS SADNESS.
HOW CAN I CONFESS MY LOVE OR MAKE SHINOMIYA CONFESS HER LOVE TO ME IN THAT CLIMATE?!
VOLUNTARY RESTRAINT ON EXPRESSIONS OF LOVE!
THERE ARE TIMES WHEN PEOPLE ARE RELUCTANT TO PURSUE A ROMANTIC INTEREST.
FOR EXAMPLE, AFTER EXPERIENCING HEARTBREAK OR A FAMILY TRAGEDY...
...AND WHEN THEIR FRIENDS EXPERIENCE HEARTBREAK!
GLOOOM
PEOPLE IN THE HEARTBROKEN PERSON'S CIRCLE DO THEIR BEST TO COMFORT THEM AND SYNCHRONIZE WITH THEIR SADNESS...
A MOOD OF VOLUNTARY RESTRAINT ON ROMANCE DEVELOPS. IT'S AS IF EVERYONE IS IN MOURNING.
SOB
SOB

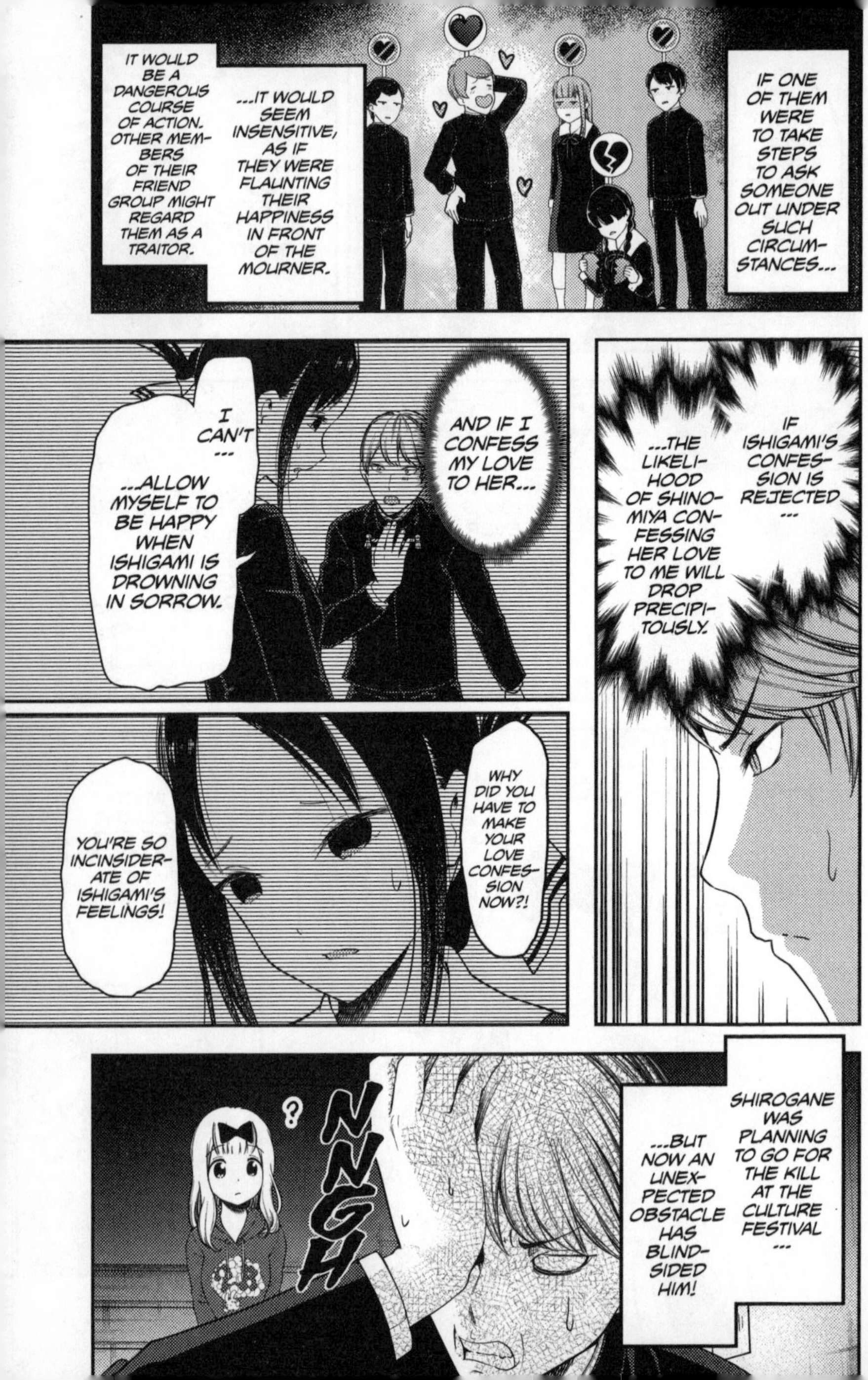
IF ONE OF THEM WERE TO TAKE STEPS TO ASK SOMEONE OUT UNDER SUCH CIRCUMSTANCES...
...IT WOULD SEEM INSENSITIVE, AS IF THEY WERE FLAUNTING THEIR HAPPINESS IN FRONT OF THE MOURNER.
IT WOULD BE A DANGEROUS COURSE OF ACTION. OTHER MEMBERS OF THEIR FRIEND GROUP MIGHT REGARD THEM AS A TRAITOR.
IF ISHIGAMI'S CONFESSION IS REJECTED...
...THE LIKELIHOOD OF SHINOMIYA CONFESSING HER LOVE TO ME WILL DROP PRECIPITOUSLY.
AND IF I CONFESS MY LOVE TO HER...
I CAN'T...
...ALLOW MYSELF TO BE HAPPY WHEN ISHIGAMI IS DROWNING IN SORROW.
WHY DID YOU HAVE TO MAKE YOUR LOVE CONFESSION NOW?!
YOU'RE SO INCINSIDERATE OF ISHIGAMI'S FEELINGS!
SHIROGANE WAS PLANNING TO GO FOR THE KILL AT THE CULTURE FESTIVAL...
...BUT NOW AN UNEXPECTED OBSTACLE HAS BLINDSIDED HIM!
NNGH
?

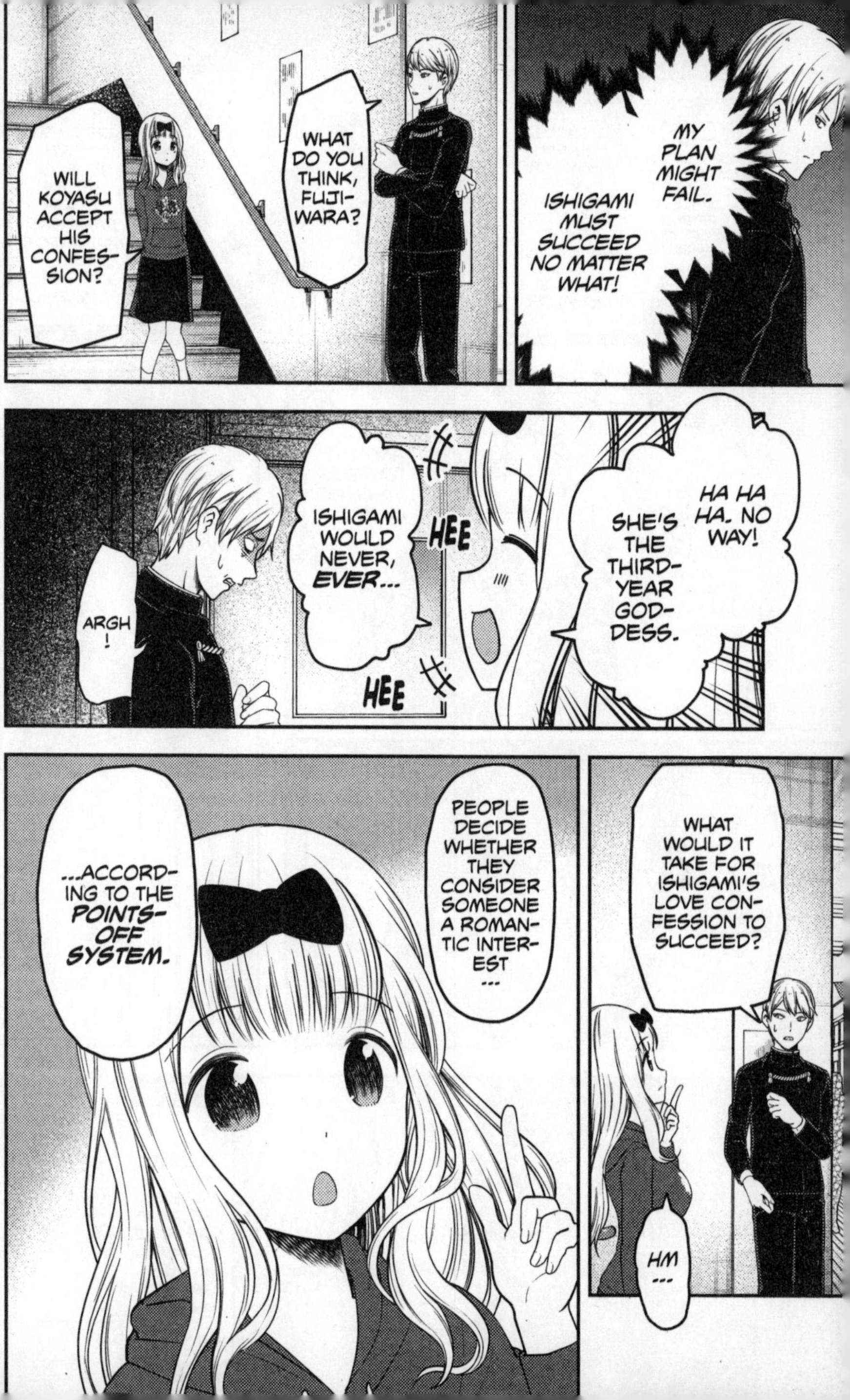
MY PLAN MIGHT FAIL.
ISHIGAMI MUST SUCCEED NO MATTER WHAT!
WHAT DO YOU THINK, FUJIWARA?
WILL KOYASU ACCEPT HIS CONFESSION?
HA HA HA. NO WAY!
SHE'S THE THIRD-YEAR GODDESS.
ISHIGAMI WOULD NEVER, EVER...
HEE
HEE
ARGH!
WHAT WOULD IT TAKE FOR ISHIGAMI'S LOVE CONFESSION TO SUCCEED?
HM...
PEOPLE DECIDE WHETHER THEY CONSIDER SOMEONE A ROMANTIC INTEREST...
...ACCORDING TO THE POINTS-OFF SYSTEM.

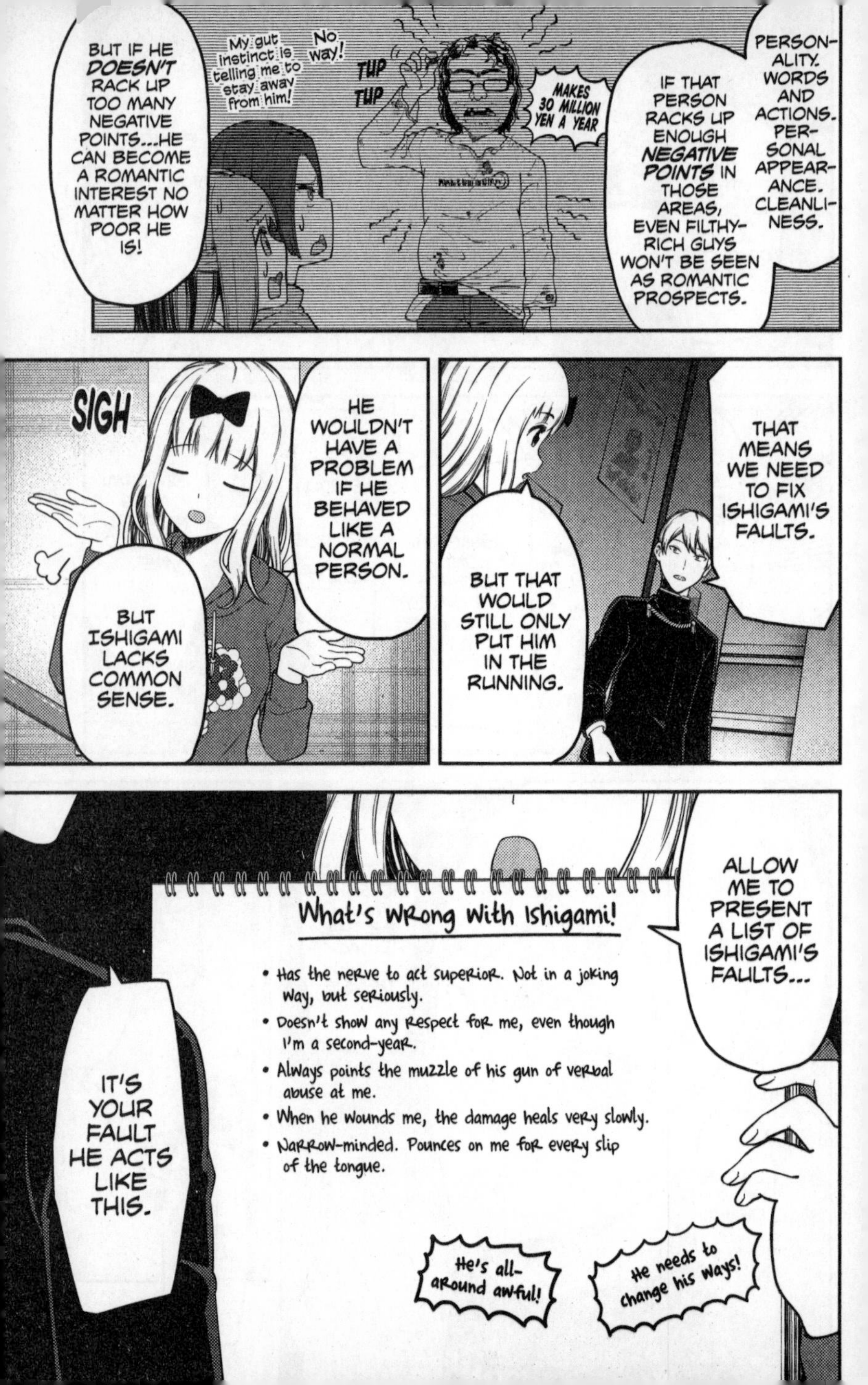
PERSONALITY. WORDS AND ACTIONS. PERSONAL APPEARANCE. CLEANLINESS.
IF THAT PERSON RACKS UP ENOUGH NEGATIVE POINTS IN THOSE AREAS, EVEN FILTHY-RICH GUYS WON'T BE SEEN AS ROMANTIC PROSPECTS.
MAKES 30 MILLION YEN A YEAR
TUP TUP
No way!
My gut instinct is telling me to stay away from him!
BUT IF HE DOESN'T RACK UP TOO MANY NEGATIVE POINTS...HE CAN BECOME A ROMANTIC INTEREST NO MATTER HOW POOR HE IS!
THAT MEANS WE NEED TO FIX ISHIGAMI'S FAULTS.
BUT THAT WOULD STILL ONLY PUT HIM IN THE RUNNING.
HE WOULDN'T HAVE A PROBLEM IF HE BEHAVED LIKE A NORMAL PERSON.
SIGH
BUT ISHIGAMI LACKS COMMON SENSE.
ALLOW ME TO PRESENT A LIST OF ISHIGAMI'S FAULTS...
What's Wrong with Ishigami!
• Has the nerve to act superior. Not in a joking way, but seriously.
• Doesn't show any respect for me, even though I'm a second-year.
• Always points the muzzle of his gun of verbal abuse at me.
• When he wounds me, the damage heals very slowly.
• Narrow-minded. Pounces on me for every slip of the tongue.
He needs to change his ways!
He's all-around awful!
IT'S YOUR FAULT HE ACTS LIKE THIS.

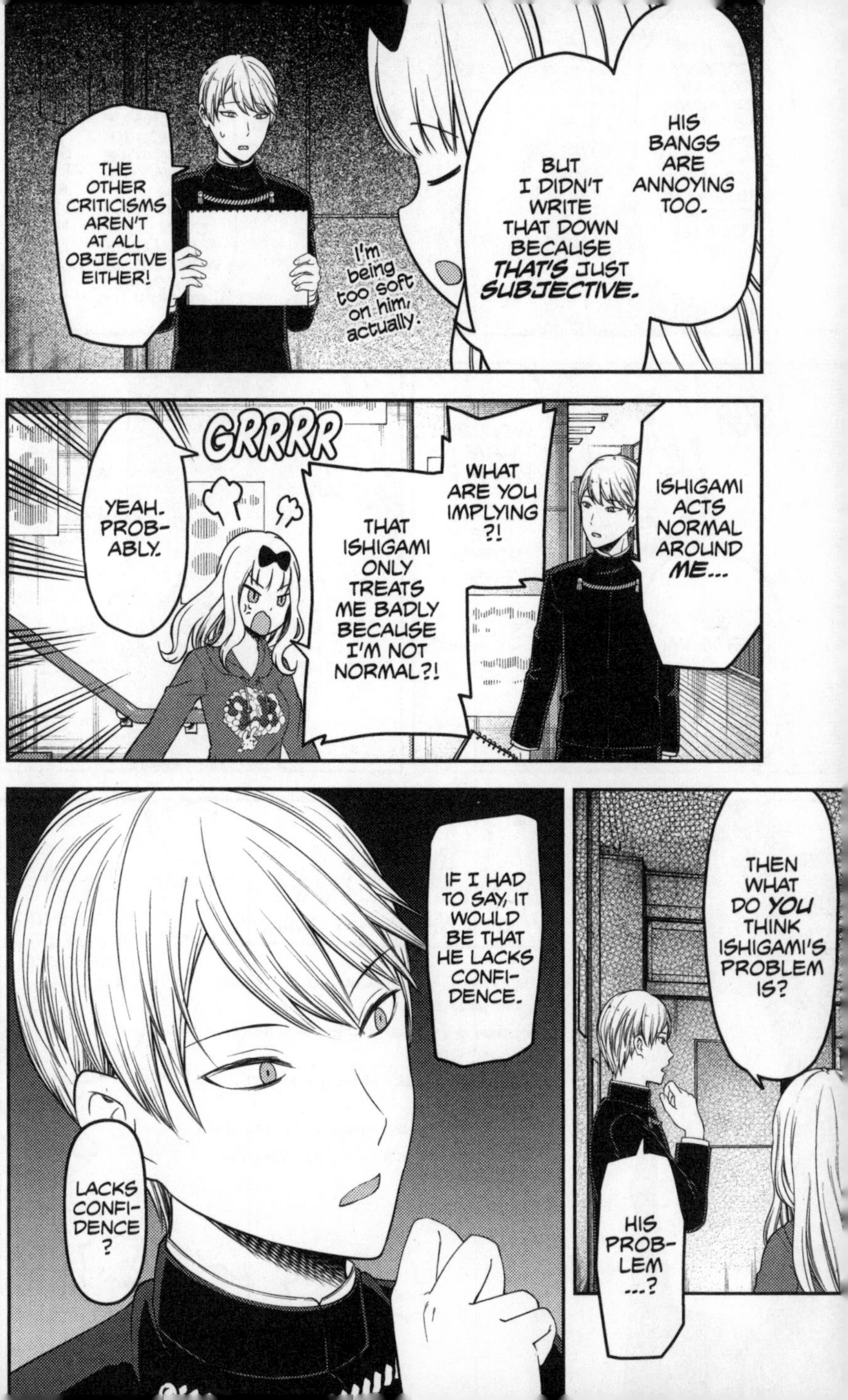
HIS BANGS ARE ANNOYING TOO.
BUT I DIDN'T WRITE THAT DOWN BECAUSE THAT'S JUST SUBJECTIVE.
I'm being too soft on him, actually.
THE OTHER CRITICISMS AREN'T AT ALL OBJECTIVE EITHER!
ISHIGAMI ACTS NORMAL AROUND ME...
WHAT ARE YOU IMPLYING?!
THAT ISHIGAMI ONLY TREATS ME BADLY BECAUSE I'M NOT NORMAL?!
GRRRR
YEAH. PROBABLY.
THEN WHAT DO YOU THINK ISHIGAMI'S PROBLEM IS?
HIS PROBLEM...?
IF I HAD TO SAY, IT WOULD BE THAT HE LACKS CONFIDENCE.
LACKS CONFIDENCE?

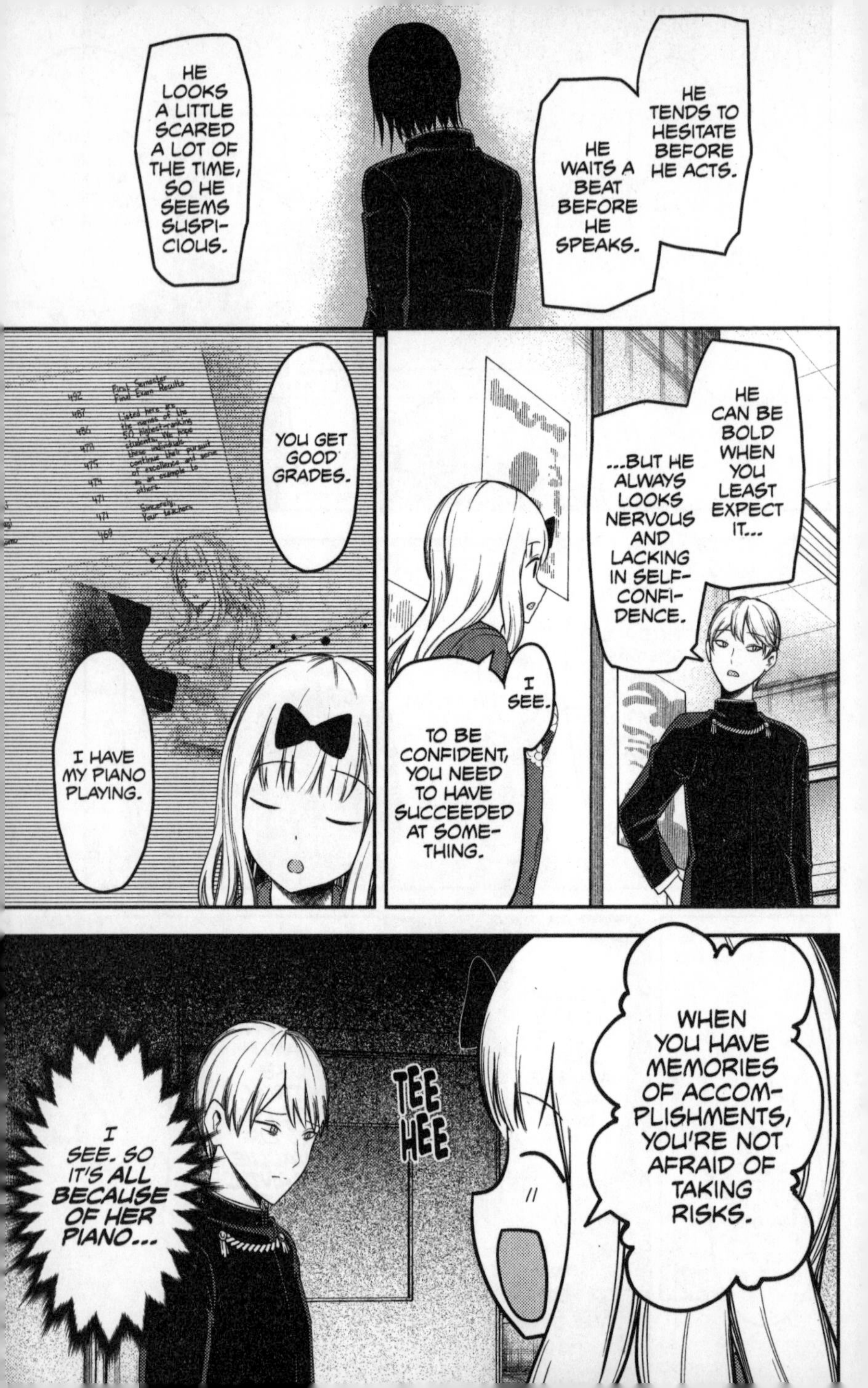
HE TENDS TO HESITATE BEFORE HE ACTS.
HE WAITS A BEAT BEFORE HE SPEAKS.
HE LOOKS A LITTLE SCARED A LOT OF THE TIME, SO HE SEEMS SUSPICIOUS.
HE CAN BE BOLD WHEN YOU LEAST EXPECT IT...
...BUT HE ALWAYS LOOKS NERVOUS AND LACKING IN SELF-CONFIDENCE.
I SEE.
TO BE CONFIDENT, YOU NEED TO HAVE SUCCEEDED AT SOMETHING.
YOU GET GOOD GRADES.
I HAVE MY PIANO PLAYING.
WHEN YOU HAVE MEMORIES OF ACCOMPLISHMENTS, YOU'RE NOT AFRAID OF TAKING RISKS.
TEE HEE
I SEE. SO IT'S ALL BECAUSE OF HER PIANO...

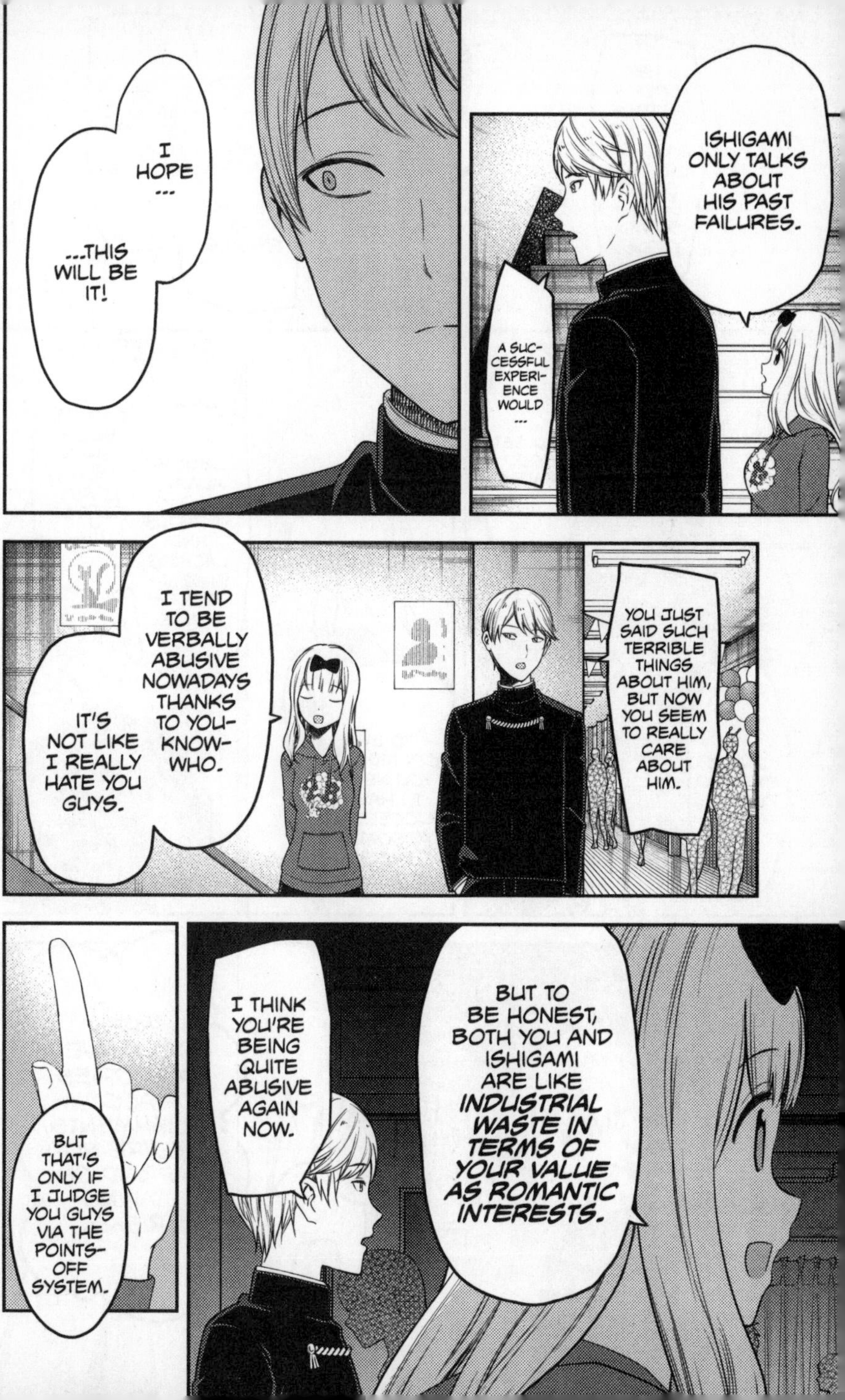

ISHIGAMI ONLY TALKS ABOUT HIS PAST FAILURES.
A SUCCESSFUL EXPERIENCE WOULD...
I HOPE...
...THIS WILL BE IT!
YOU JUST SAID SUCH TERRIBLE THINGS ABOUT HIM, BUT NOW YOU SEEM TO REALLY CARE ABOUT HIM.
I TEND TO BE VERBALLY ABUSIVE NOWADAYS THANKS TO YOU-KNOW-WHO.
IT'S NOT LIKE I REALLY HATE YOU GUYS.
BUT TO BE HONEST, BOTH YOU AND ISHIGAMI ARE LIKE **INDUSTRIAL WASTE IN TERMS OF YOUR VALUE AS ROMANTIC INTERESTS.**
I THINK YOU'RE BEING QUITE ABUSIVE AGAIN NOW.
BUT THAT'S ONLY IF I JUDGE YOU GUYS VIA THE POINTS-OFF SYSTEM.

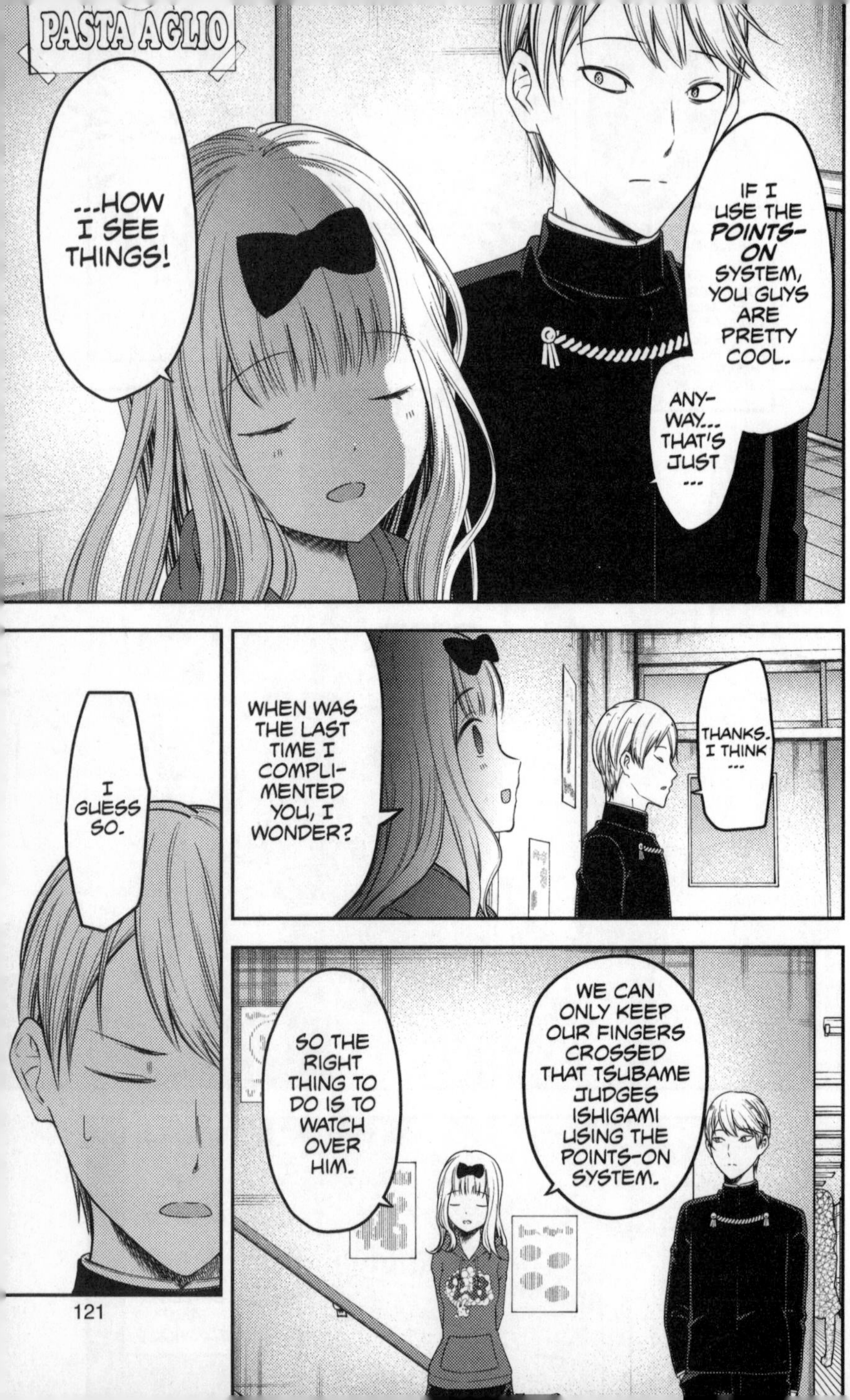
PASTA AGLIO
IF I USE THE POINTS-ON SYSTEM, YOU GUYS ARE PRETTY COOL.
ANY-WAY... THAT'S JUST ...
...HOW I SEE THINGS!
THANKS. I THINK ...
WHEN WAS THE LAST TIME I COMPLIMENTED YOU, I WONDER?
WE CAN ONLY KEEP OUR FINGERS CROSSED THAT TSUBAME JUDGES ISHIGAMI USING THE POINTS-ON SYSTEM.
SO THE RIGHT THING TO DO IS TO WATCH OVER HIM.
I GUESS SO.

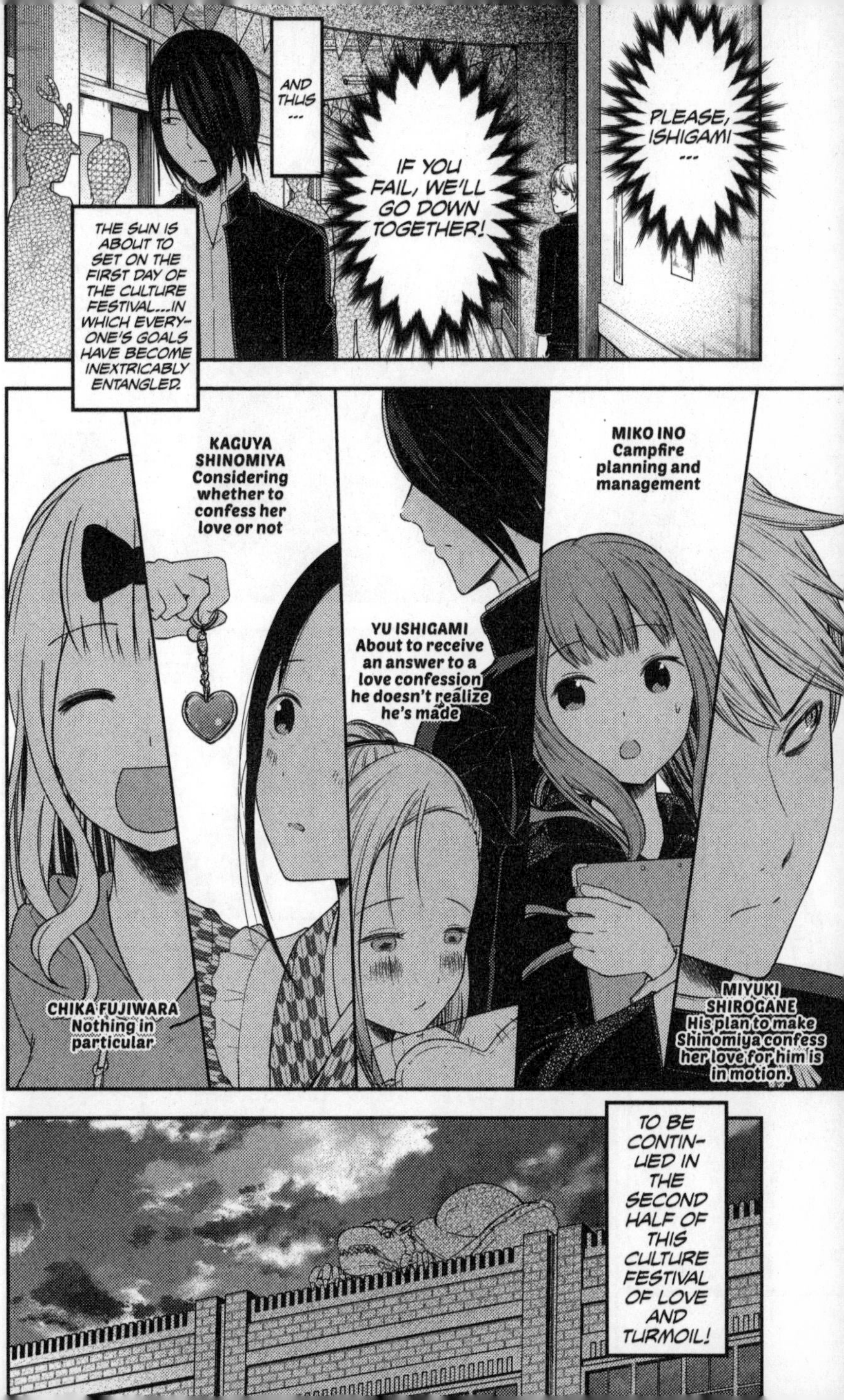
PLEASE, ISHIGAMI...
IF YOU FAIL, WE'LL GO DOWN TOGETHER!
AND THUS...
THE SUN IS ABOUT TO SET ON THE FIRST DAY OF THE CULTURE FESTIVAL...IN WHICH EVERYONE'S GOALS HAVE BECOME INEXTRICABLY ENTANGLED.
MIYUKI SHIROGANE His plan to make Shinomiya confess her love for him is in motion.
MIKO INO Campfire planning and management
YU ISHIGAMI About to receive an answer to a love confession he doesn't realize he's made
KAGUYA SHINOMIYA Considering whether to confess her love or not
CHIKA FUJIWARA Nothing in particular
TO BE CONTINUED IN THE SECOND HALF OF THIS CULTURE FESTIVAL OF LOVE AND TURMOIL!

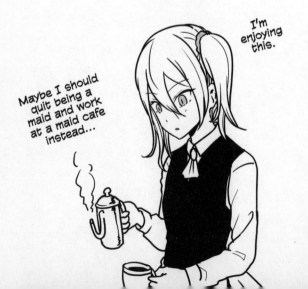

AI HAYASAKA
Will work at the
cosplay cafe
tomorrow too

I'm enjoying this.

Maybe I should quit being a maid and work at a maid cafe instead...

KAGUYA-SAMA

LOVE IS WAR

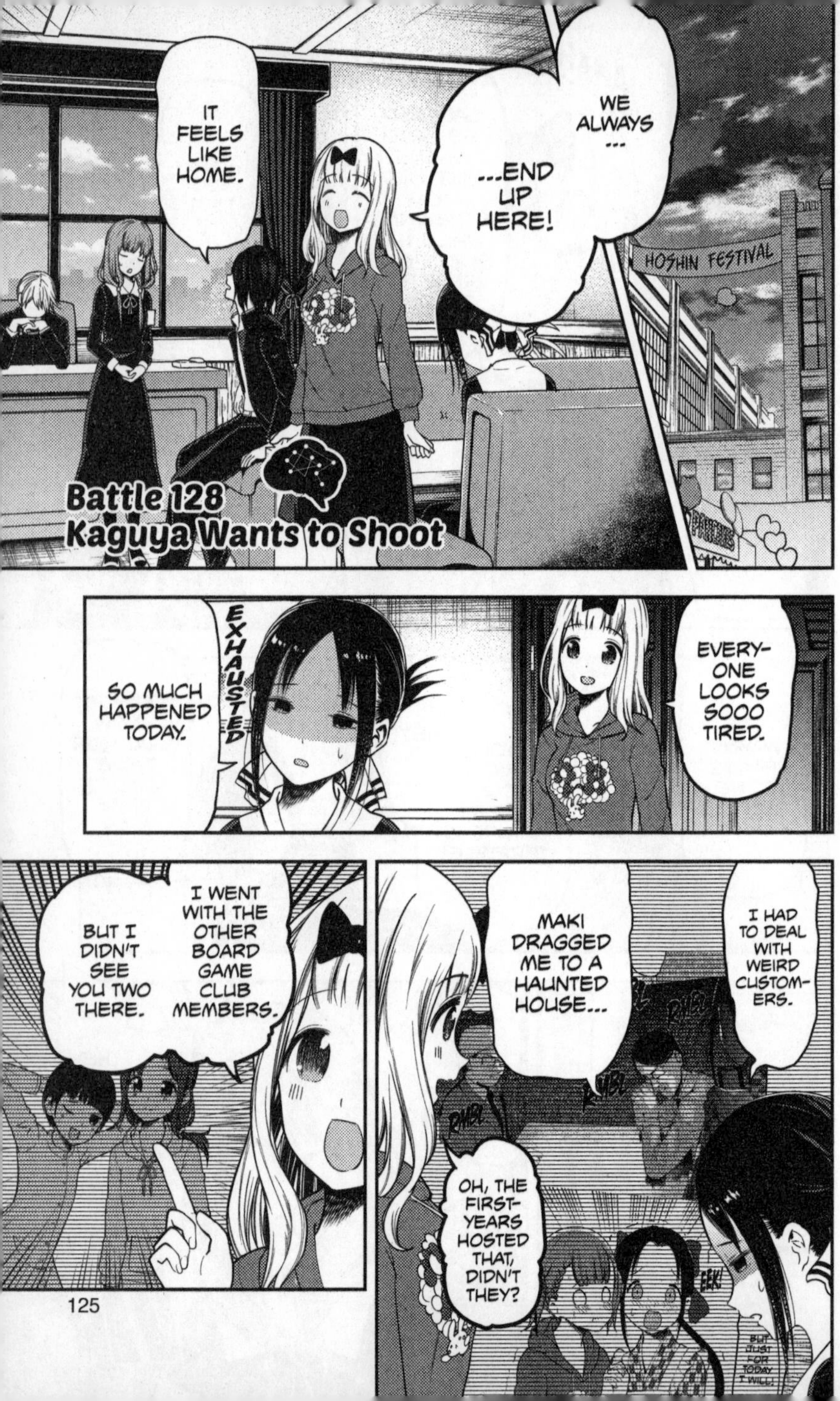
WE ALWAYS ...
...END UP HERE!
IT FEELS LIKE HOME.
HOSHIN FESTIVAL
Battle 128
Kaguya Wants to Shoot
EVERY-ONE LOOKS SOOO TIRED.
EXHAUSTED
SO MUCH HAPPENED TODAY.
I HAD TO DEAL WITH WEIRD CUSTOM-ERS.
MAKI DRAGGED ME TO A HAUNTED HOUSE...
RMBL
RMBL
OH, THE FIRST-YEARS HOSTED THAT, DIDN'T THEY?
EEK!
BUT JUST FOR TODAY I WILL!
I WENT WITH THE OTHER BOARD GAME CLUB MEMBERS.
BUT I DIDN'T SEE YOU TWO THERE.

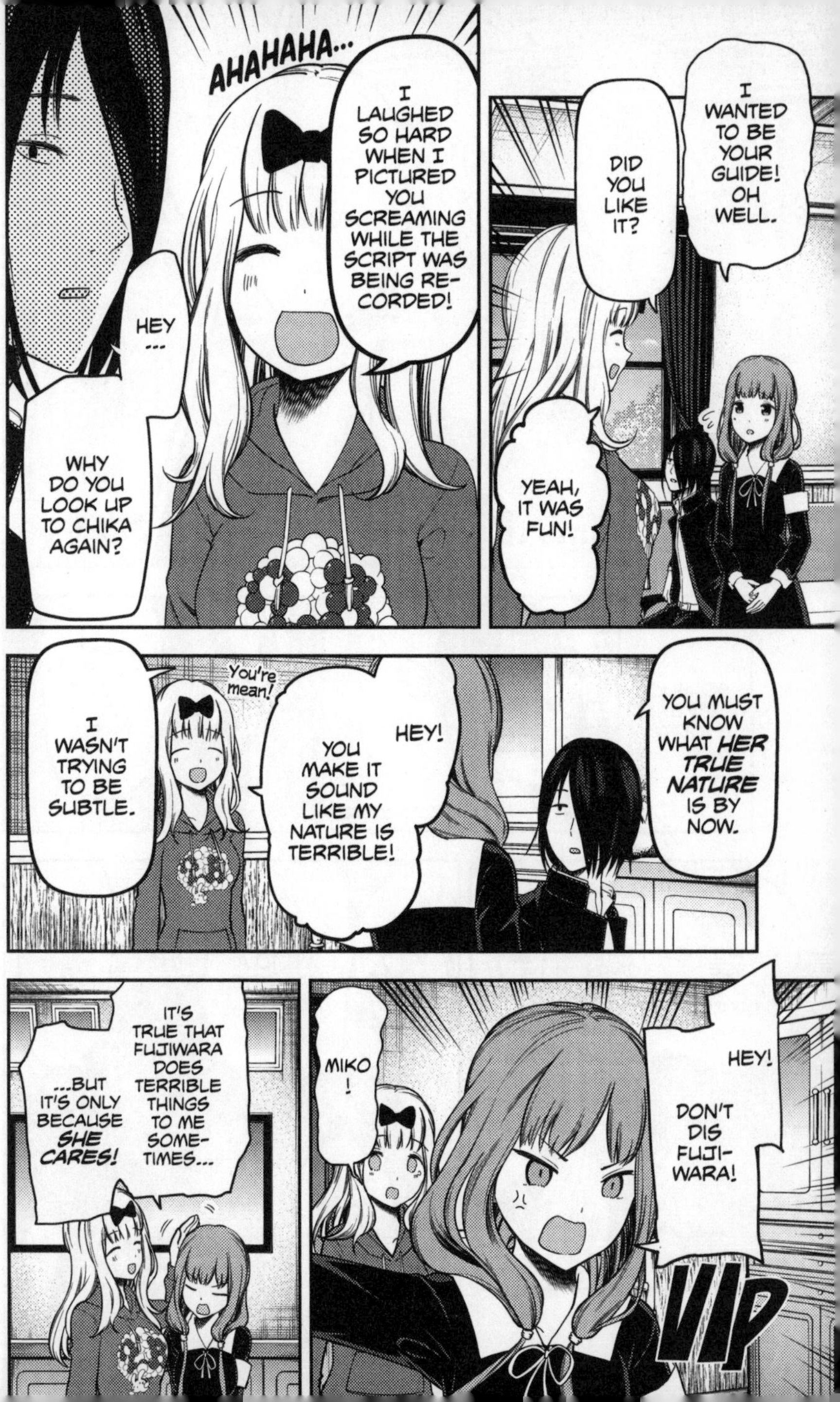
I WANTED TO BE YOUR GUIDE! OH WELL.
DID YOU LIKE IT?
YEAH, IT WAS FUN!
AHAHAHA...
I LAUGHED SO HARD WHEN I PICTURED YOU SCREAMING WHILE THE SCRIPT WAS BEING RE-CORDED!
HEY ...
WHY DO YOU LOOK UP TO CHIKA AGAIN?
YOU MUST KNOW WHAT HER TRUE NATURE IS BY NOW.
HEY! YOU MAKE IT SOUND LIKE MY NATURE IS TERRIBLE!
You're mean!
I WASN'T TRYING TO BE SUBTLE.
HEY! DON'T DIS FUJI-WARA!
VIP
MIKO!
IT'S TRUE THAT FUJIWARA DOES TERRIBLE THINGS TO ME SOME-TIMES...
...BUT IT'S ONLY BECAUSE SHE CARES!

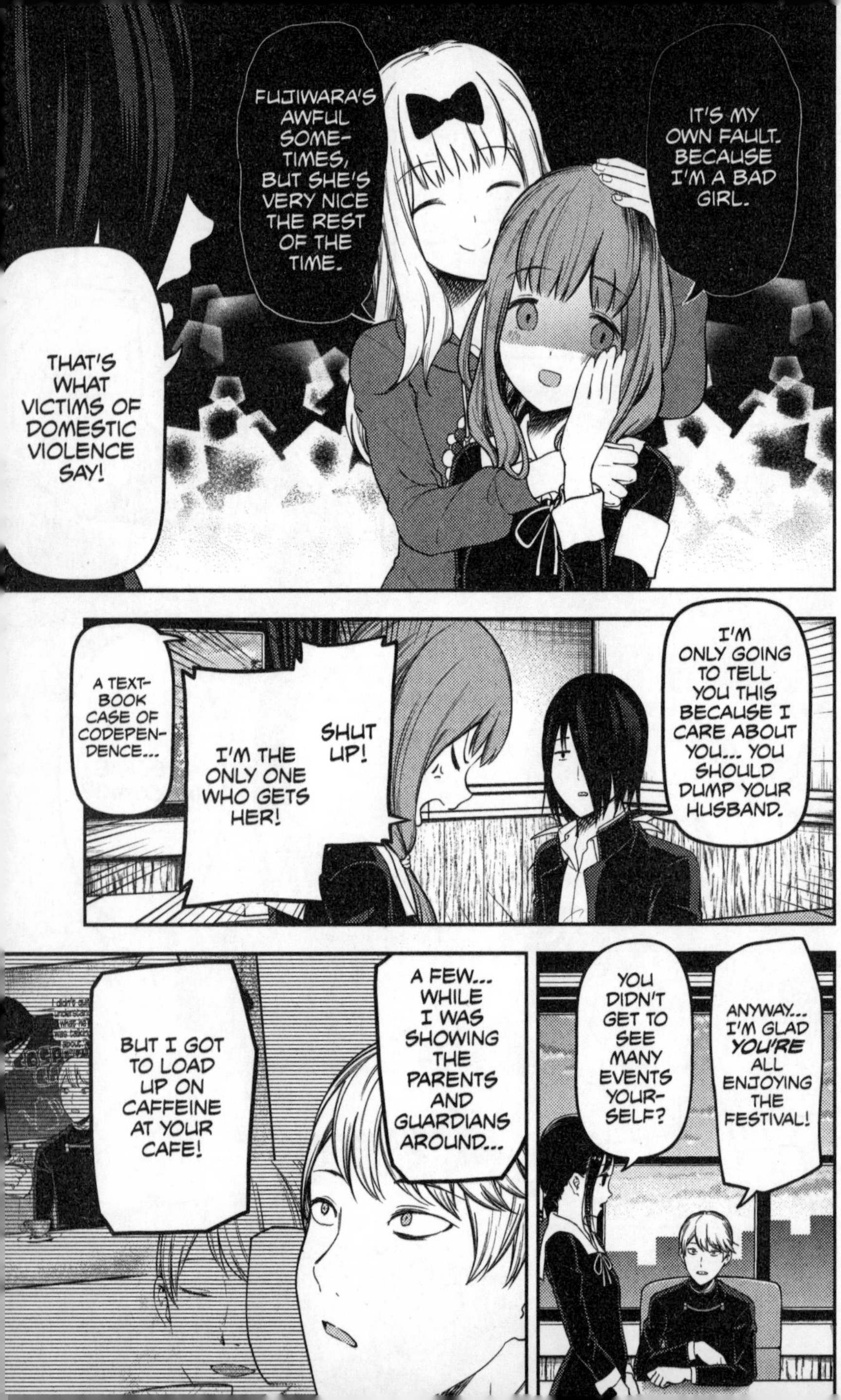
IT'S MY OWN FAULT. BECAUSE I'M A BAD GIRL.
FUJIWARA'S AWFUL SOMETIMES, BUT SHE'S VERY NICE THE REST OF THE TIME.
THAT'S WHAT VICTIMS OF DOMESTIC VIOLENCE SAY!
I'M ONLY GOING TO TELL YOU THIS BECAUSE I CARE ABOUT YOU... YOU SHOULD DUMP YOUR HUSBAND.
SHUT UP!
I'M THE ONLY ONE WHO GETS HER!
A TEXTBOOK CASE OF CODEPENDENCE...
ANYWAY... I'M GLAD ***YOU'RE*** ALL ENJOYING THE FESTIVAL!
YOU DIDN'T GET TO SEE MANY EVENTS YOURSELF?
A FEW... WHILE I WAS SHOWING THE PARENTS AND GUARDIANS AROUND...
BUT I GOT TO LOAD UP ON CAFFEINE AT YOUR CAFE!

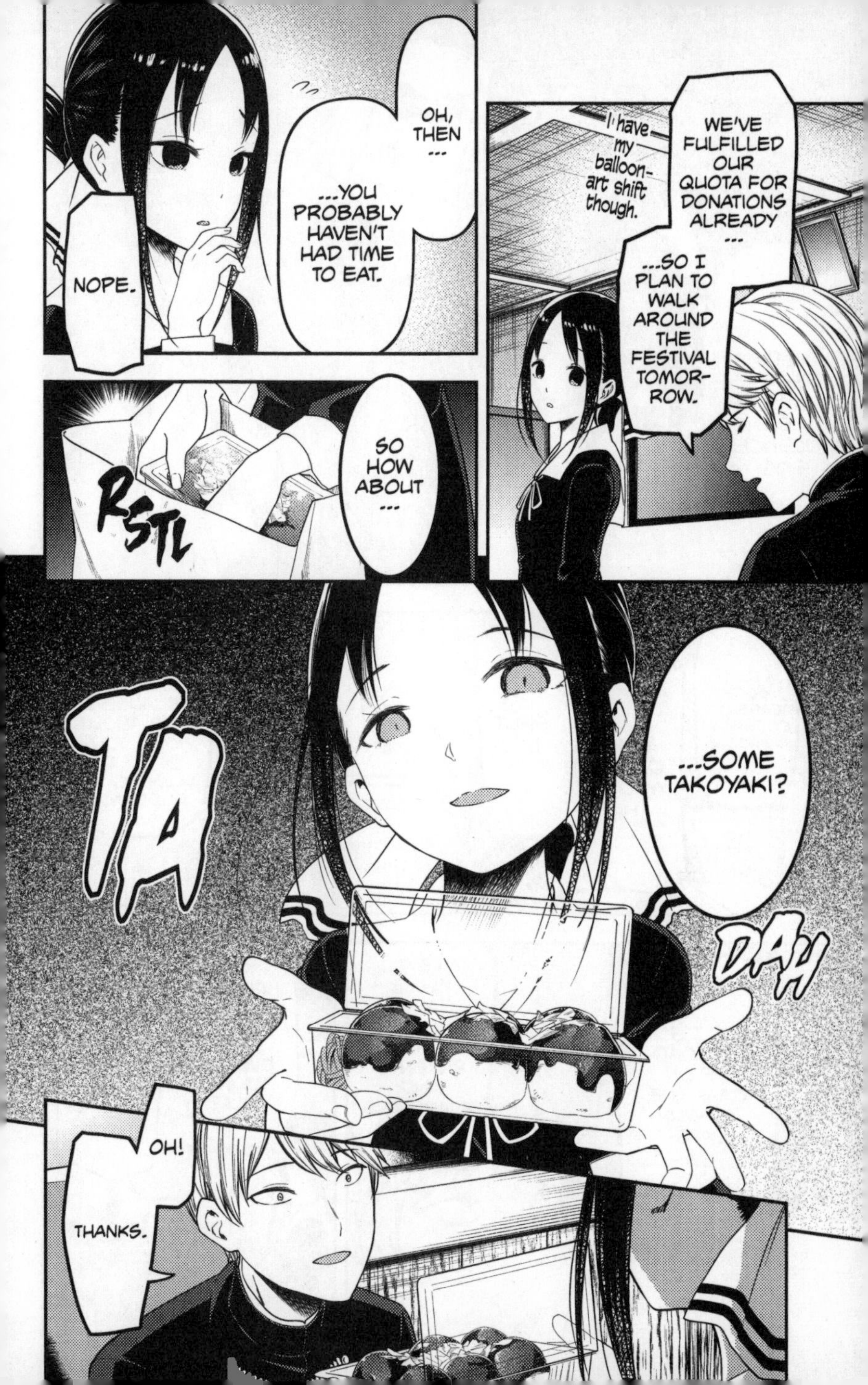
WE'VE FULFILLED OUR QUOTA FOR DONATIONS ALREADY ...
I have my balloon-art shift though.
...SO I PLAN TO WALK AROUND THE FESTIVAL TOMORROW.
OH, THEN ...
...YOU PROBABLY HAVEN'T HAD TIME TO EAT.
NOPE.
SO HOW ABOUT ...
RSTL
...SOME TAKOYAKI?
TA DAH
OH!
THANKS.

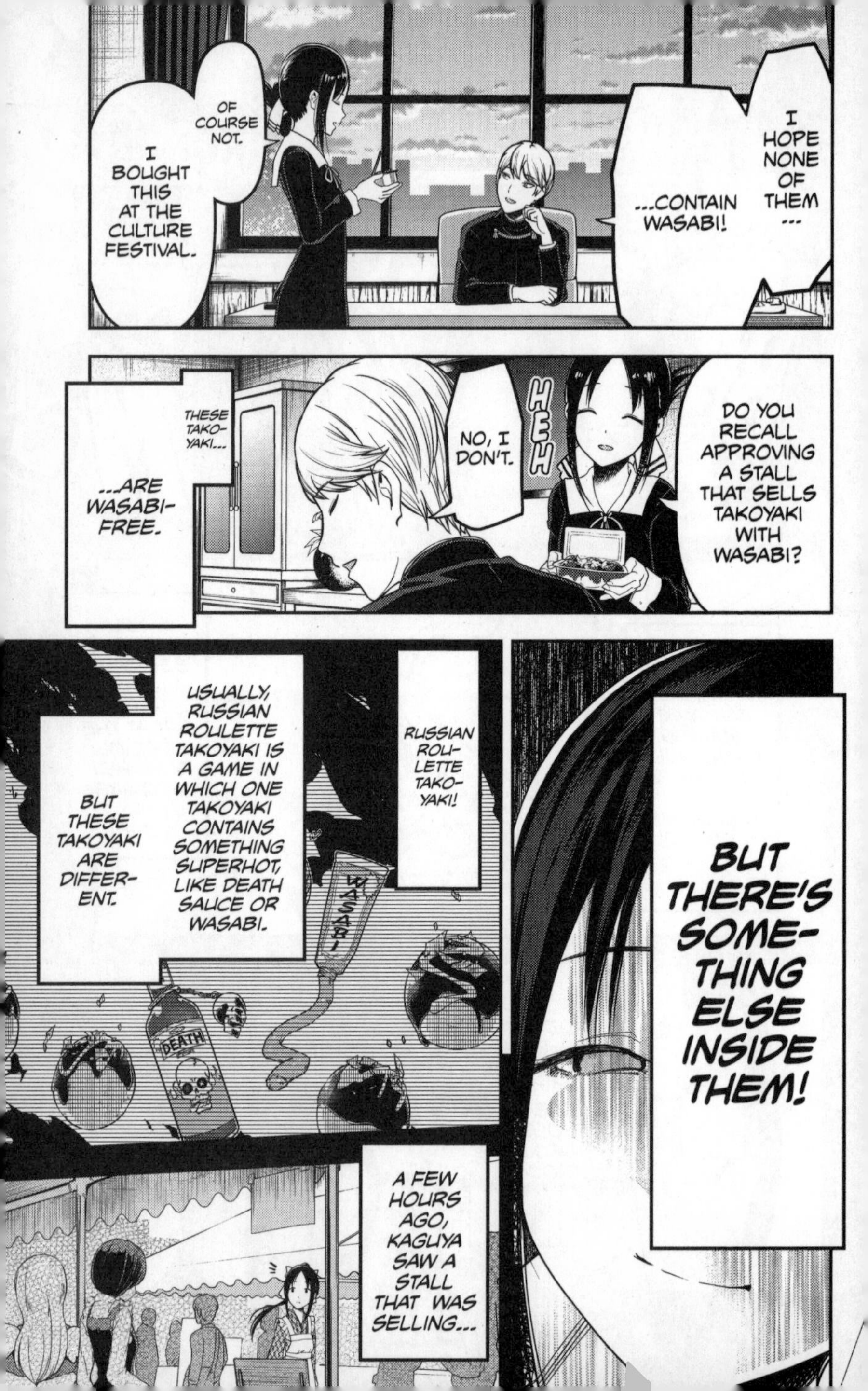
I HOPE NONE OF THEM ...
...CONTAIN WASABI!
OF COURSE NOT.
I BOUGHT THIS AT THE CULTURE FESTIVAL.
DO YOU RECALL APPROVING A STALL THAT SELLS TAKOYAKI WITH WASABI?
HEH
NO, I DON'T.
THESE TAKOYAKI...
...ARE WASABI-FREE.
BUT THERE'S SOME-THING ELSE INSIDE THEM!
RUSSIAN ROU-LETTE TAKO-YAKI!
USUALLY, RUSSIAN ROULETTE TAKOYAKI IS A GAME IN WHICH ONE TAKOYAKI CONTAINS SOMETHING SUPERHOT, LIKE DEATH SAUCE OR WASABI.
BUT THESE TAKOYAKI ARE DIFFER-ENT.
WASABI
DEATH
A FEW HOURS AGO, KAGUYA SAW A STALL THAT WAS SELLING...

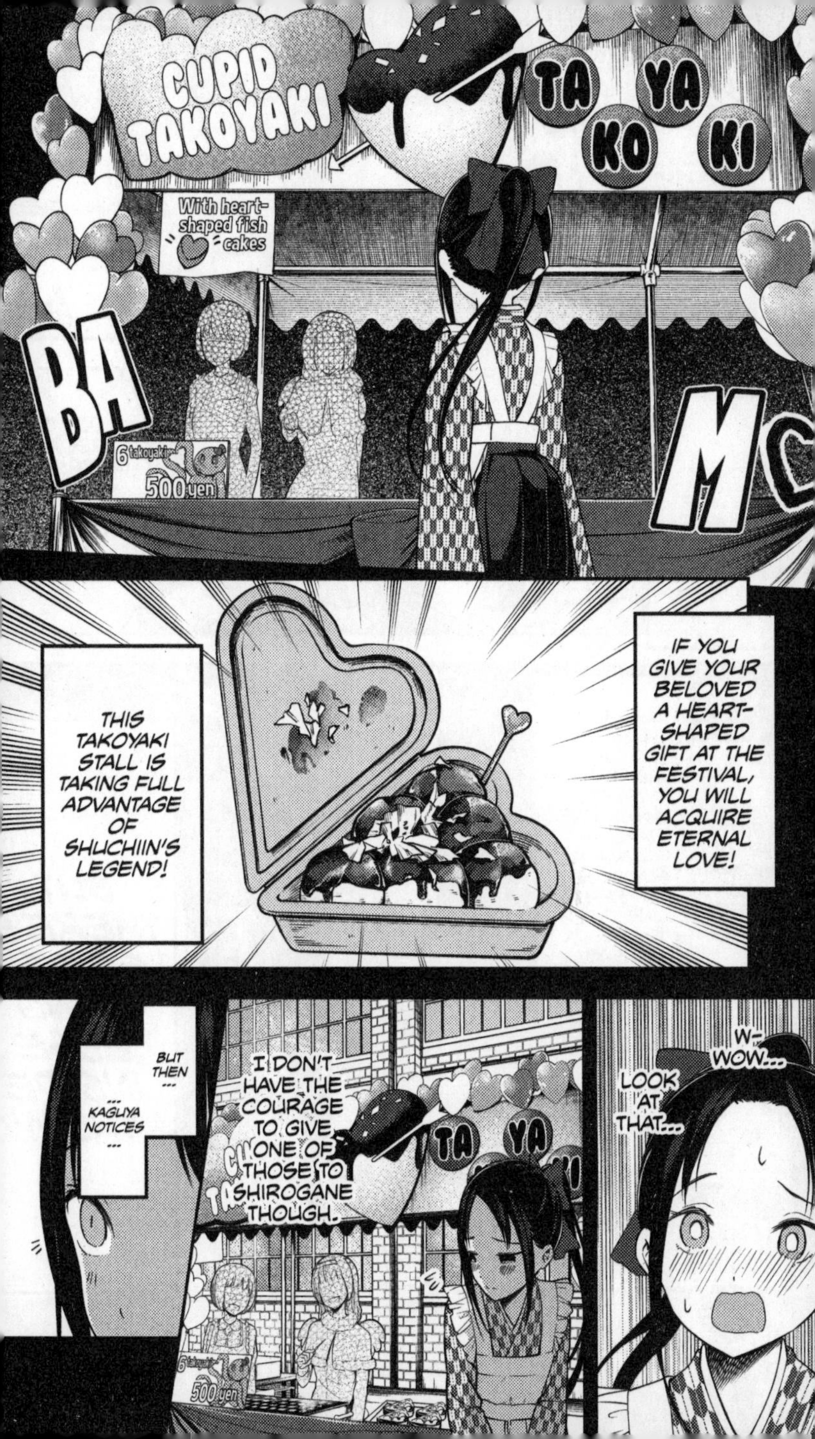

CUPID TAKOYAKI
TA KO YA KI
With heart-shaped fish cakes
6 takoyaki
500 yen
BA
M
IF YOU GIVE YOUR BELOVED A HEART-SHAPED GIFT AT THE FESTIVAL, YOU WILL ACQUIRE ETERNAL LOVE!
THIS TAKOYAKI STALL IS TAKING FULL ADVANTAGE OF SHUCHIIN'S LEGEND!
W-WOW...
LOOK AT THAT...
I DON'T HAVE THE COURAGE TO GIVE ONE OF THOSE TO SHIROGANE THOUGH.
BUT THEN...
...KAGUYA NOTICES...

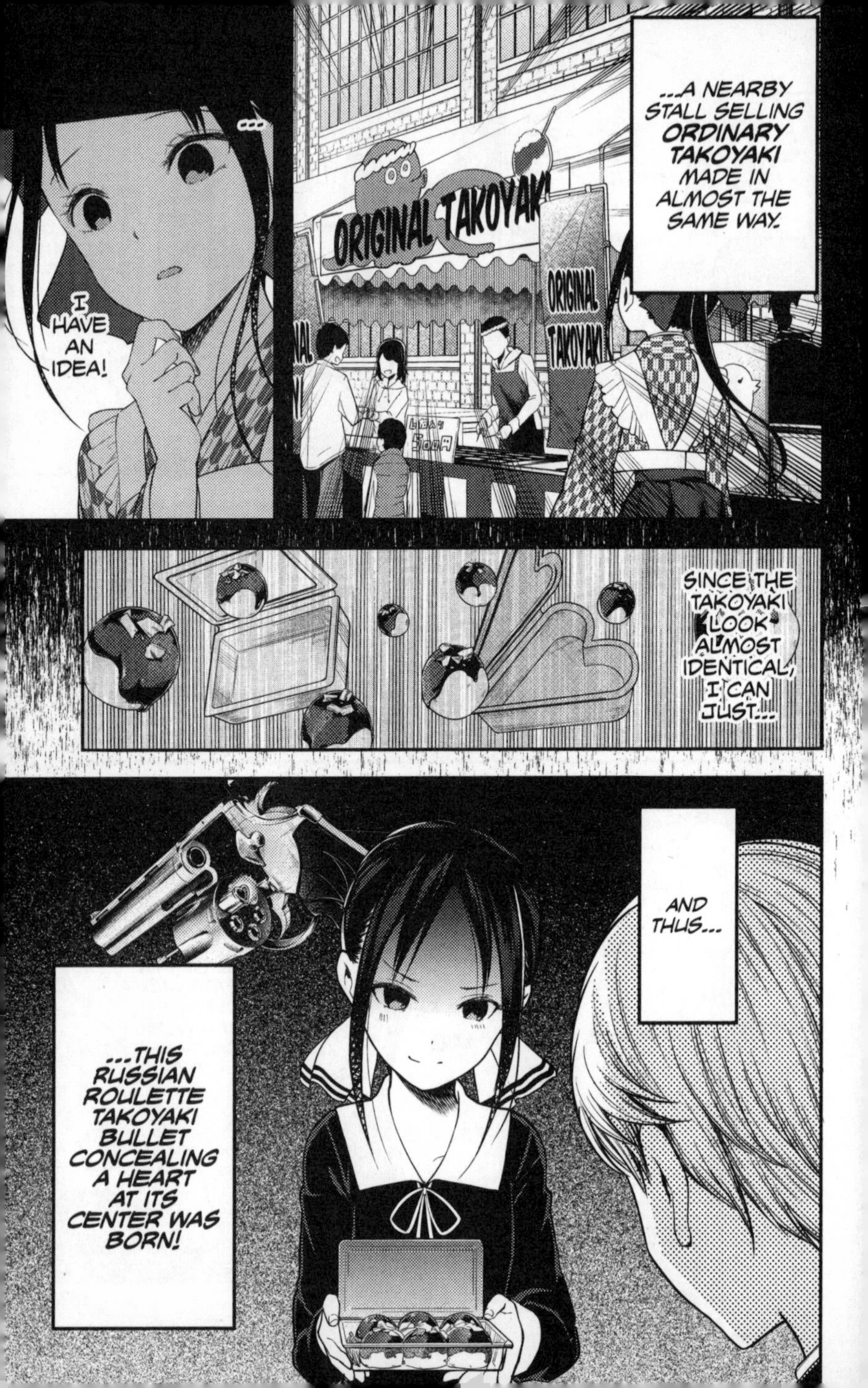

...A NEARBY STALL SELLING ORDINARY TAKOYAKI MADE IN ALMOST THE SAME WAY.
ORIGINAL TAKOYAKI
ORIGINAL TAKOYAKI
...
I HAVE AN IDEA!
SINCE THE TAKOYAKI LOOK ALMOST IDENTICAL, I CAN JUST...
AND THUS...
...THIS RUSSIAN ROULETTE TAKOYAKI BULLET CONCEALING A HEART AT ITS CENTER WAS BORN!

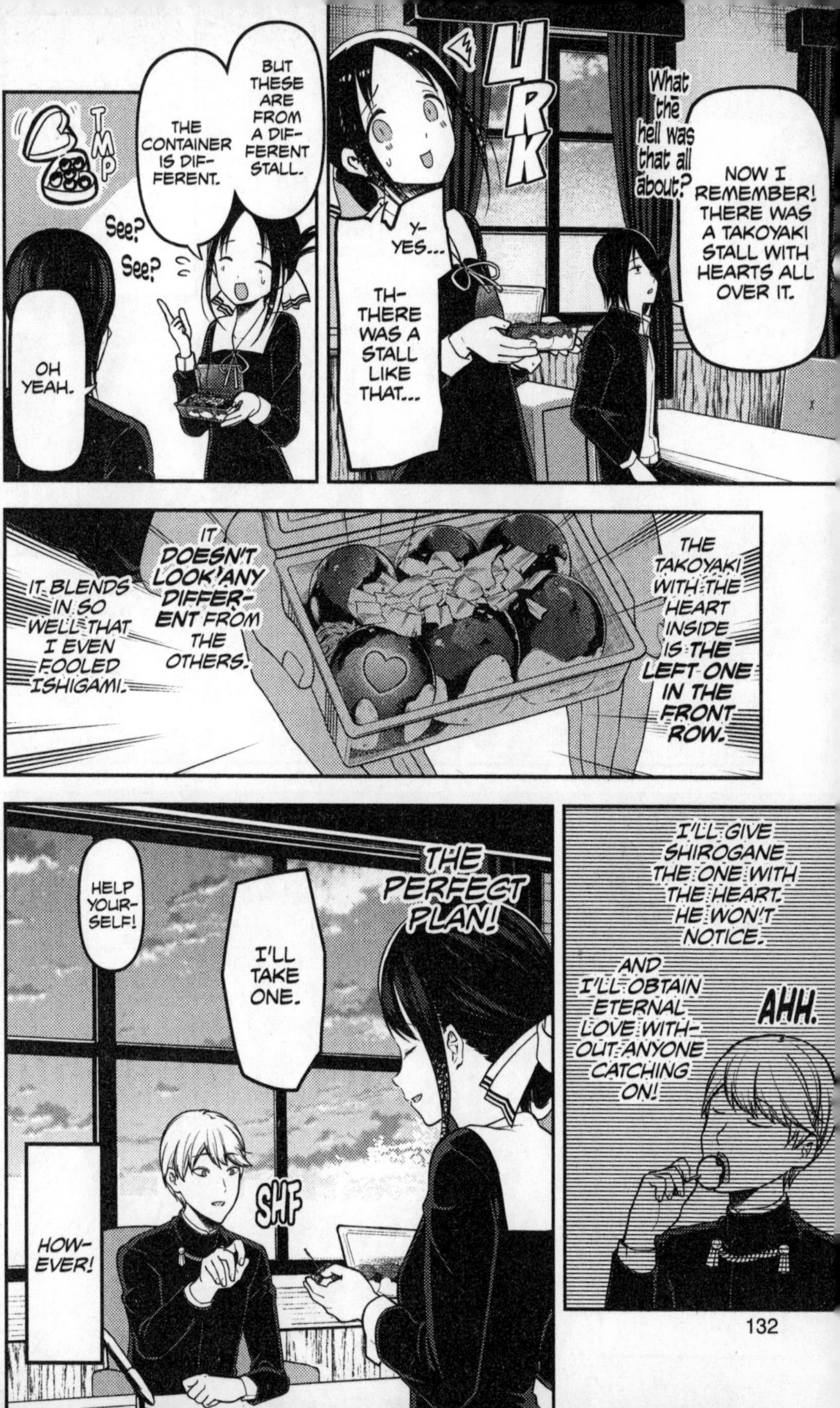
What the hell was that all about?
NOW I REMEMBER! THERE WAS A TAKOYAKI STALL WITH HEARTS ALL OVER IT.
URK
Y-YES...
TH-THERE WAS A STALL LIKE THAT...
BUT THESE ARE FROM A DIFFERENT STALL.
THE CONTAINER IS DIFFERENT.
TMP
See? See?
OH YEAH.
THE TAKOYAKI WITH THE HEART INSIDE IS THE LEFT ONE IN THE FRONT ROW.
IT DOESN'T LOOK ANY DIFFERENT FROM THE OTHERS.
IT BLENDS IN SO WELL THAT I EVEN FOOLED ISHIGAMI.
I'LL GIVE SHIROGANE THE ONE WITH THE HEART. HE WON'T NOTICE.
AND I'LL OBTAIN ETERNAL LOVE WITHOUT ANYONE CATCHING ON!
AHH.
THE PERFECT PLAN!
HELP YOURSELF!
I'LL TAKE ONE.
SHF
HOWEVER!

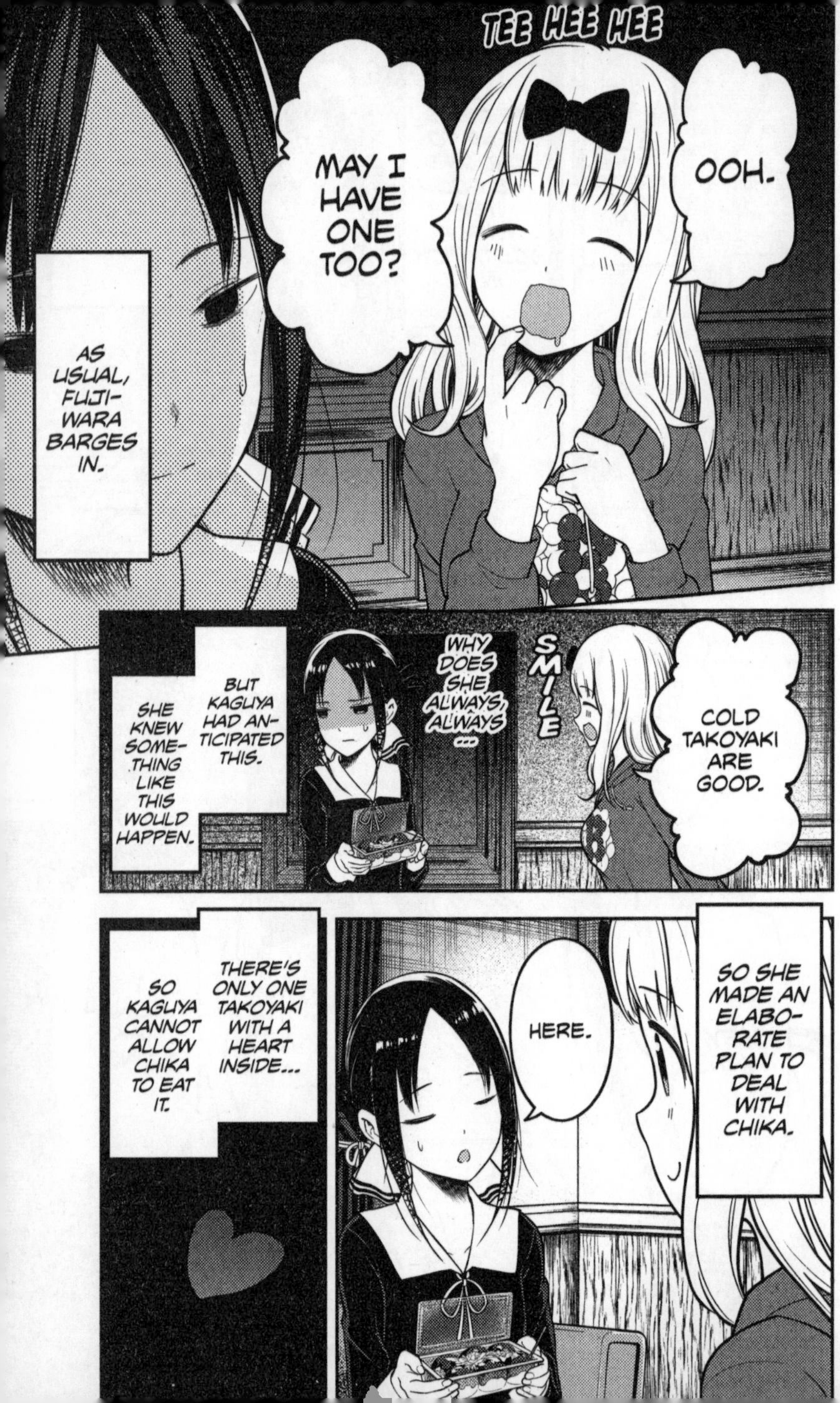
TEE HEE HEE
OOH.
MAY I HAVE ONE TOO?
AS USUAL, FUJIWARA BARGES IN.
COLD TAKOYAKI ARE GOOD.
SMILE
WHY DOES SHE ALWAYS, ALWAYS...
BUT KAGUYA HAD ANTICIPATED THIS.
SHE KNEW SOMETHING LIKE THIS WOULD HAPPEN.
SO SHE MADE AN ELABORATE PLAN TO DEAL WITH CHIKA.
HERE.
THERE'S ONLY ONE TAKOYAKI WITH A HEART INSIDE...
SO KAGUYA CANNOT ALLOW CHIKA TO EAT IT.

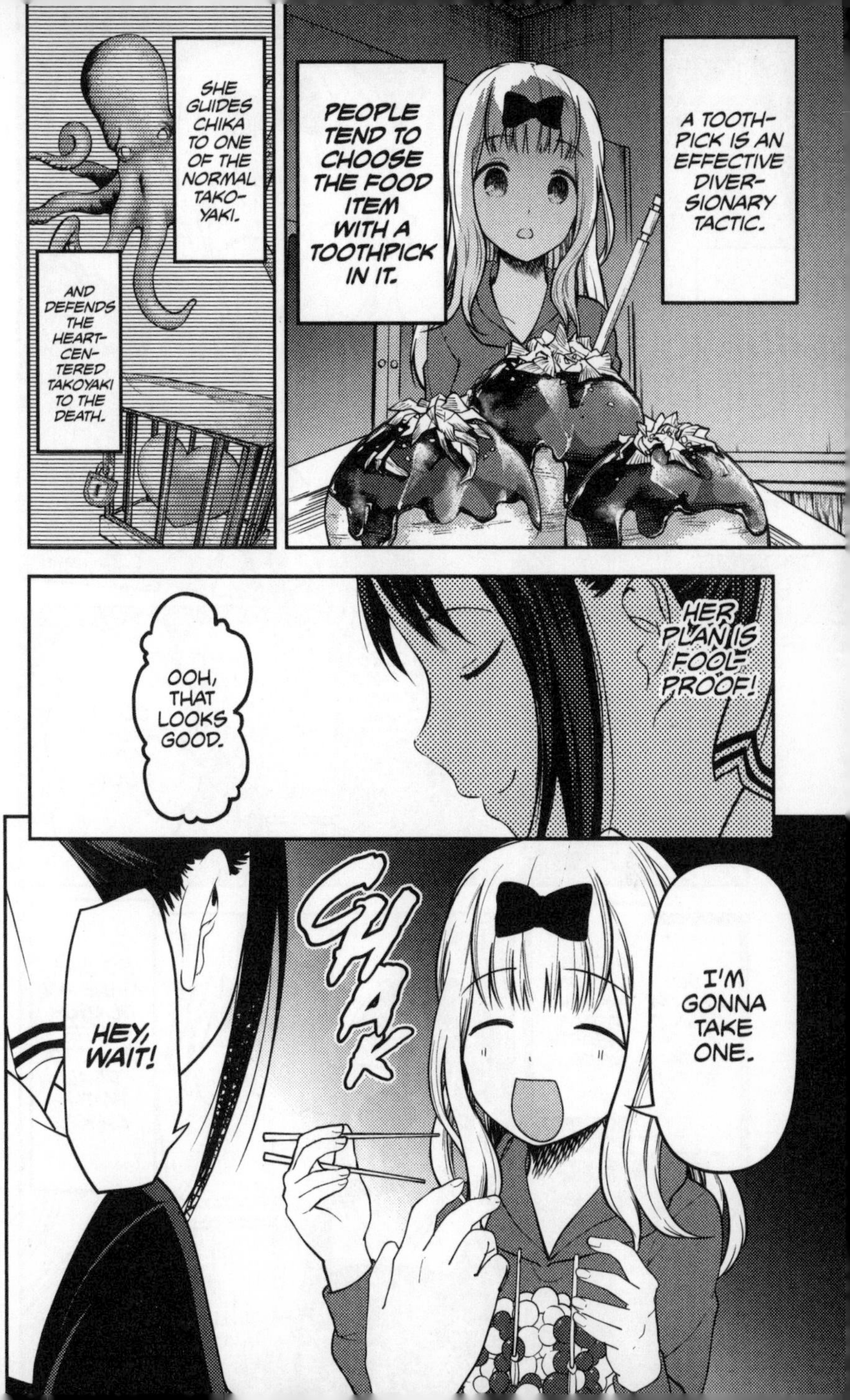
A TOOTH-PICK IS AN EFFECTIVE DIVER-SIONARY TACTIC.
PEOPLE TEND TO CHOOSE THE FOOD ITEM WITH A TOOTHPICK IN IT.
SHE GUIDES CHIKA TO ONE OF THE NORMAL TAKO-YAKI.
AND DEFENDS THE HEART-CEN-TERED TAKOYAKI TO THE DEATH.
HER PLAN IS FOOL-PROOF!
OOH, THAT LOOKS GOOD.
I'M GONNA TAKE ONE.
CHAK
HEY, WAIT!

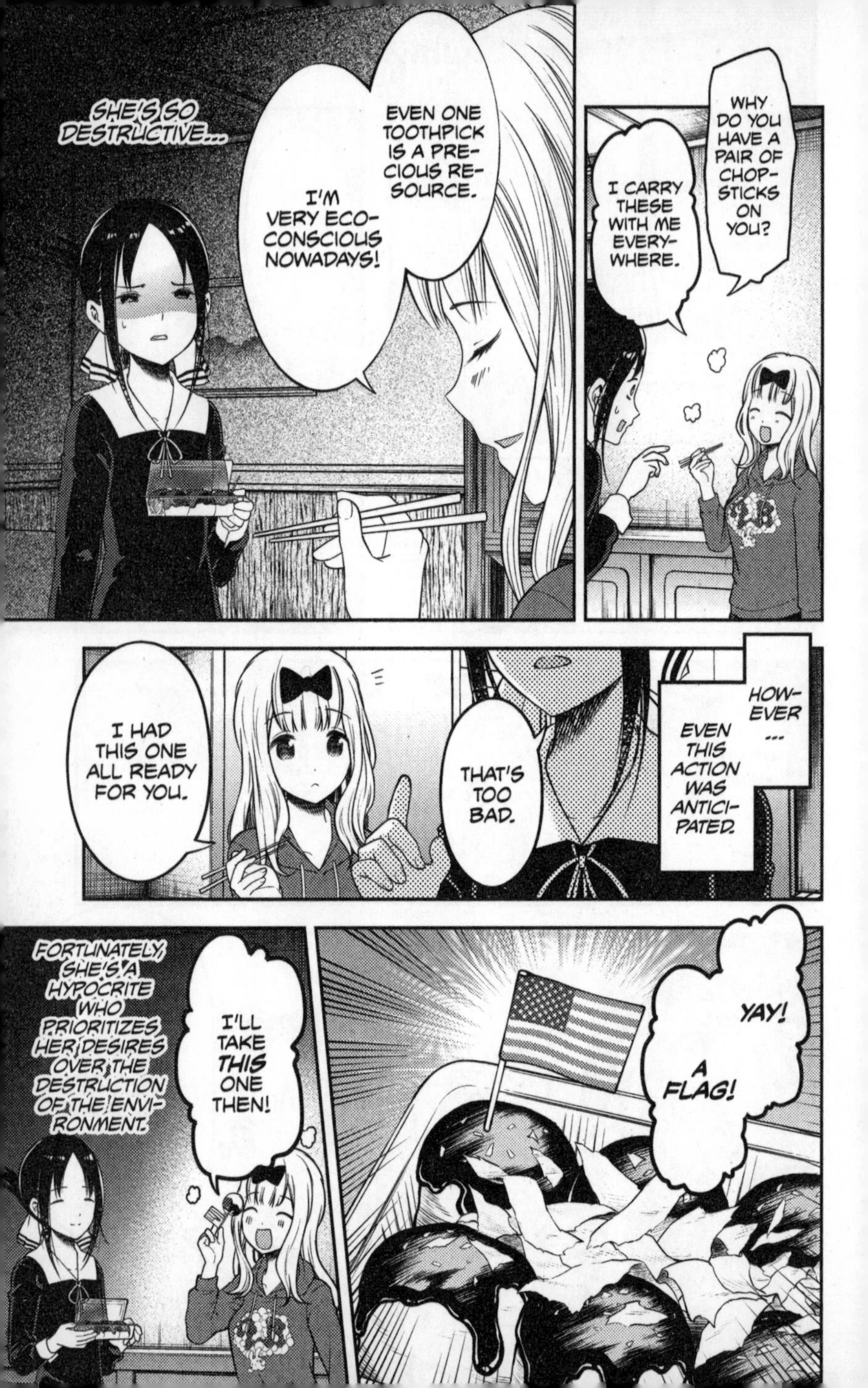
WHY DO YOU HAVE A PAIR OF CHOPSTICKS ON YOU?
I CARRY THESE WITH ME EVERYWHERE.
EVEN ONE TOOTHPICK IS A PRECIOUS RESOURCE.
I'M VERY ECO-CONSCIOUS NOWADAYS!
SHE'S SO DESTRUCTIVE...
HOWEVER...
EVEN THIS ACTION WAS ANTICIPATED.
THAT'S TOO BAD.
I HAD THIS ONE ALL READY FOR YOU.
YAY!
A FLAG!
I'LL TAKE **THIS** ONE THEN!
FORTUNATELY, SHE'S A HYPOCRITE WHO PRIORITIZES HER DESIRES OVER THE DESTRUCTION OF THE ENVIRONMENT.

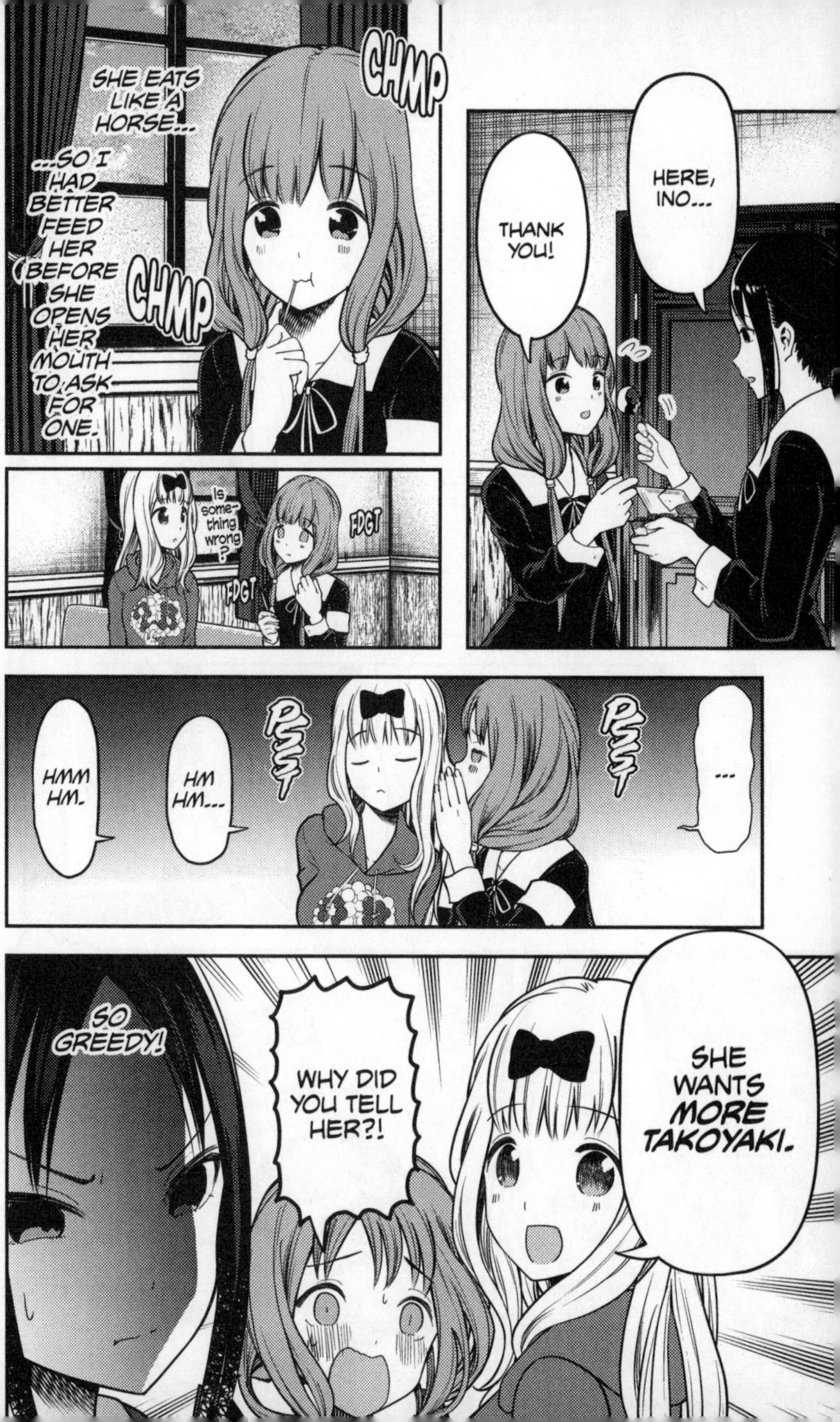
HERE, INO...
THANK YOU!
CHMP
SHE EATS LIKE A HORSE...
...SO I HAD BETTER FEED HER BEFORE SHE OPENS HER MOUTH TO ASK FOR ONE.
CHMP
FDGT
Is something wrong?
FDGT
...
PSST
PSST
HM HM...
HMM HM.
SHE WANTS MORE TAKOYAKI.
WHY DID YOU TELL HER?!
SO GREEDY!

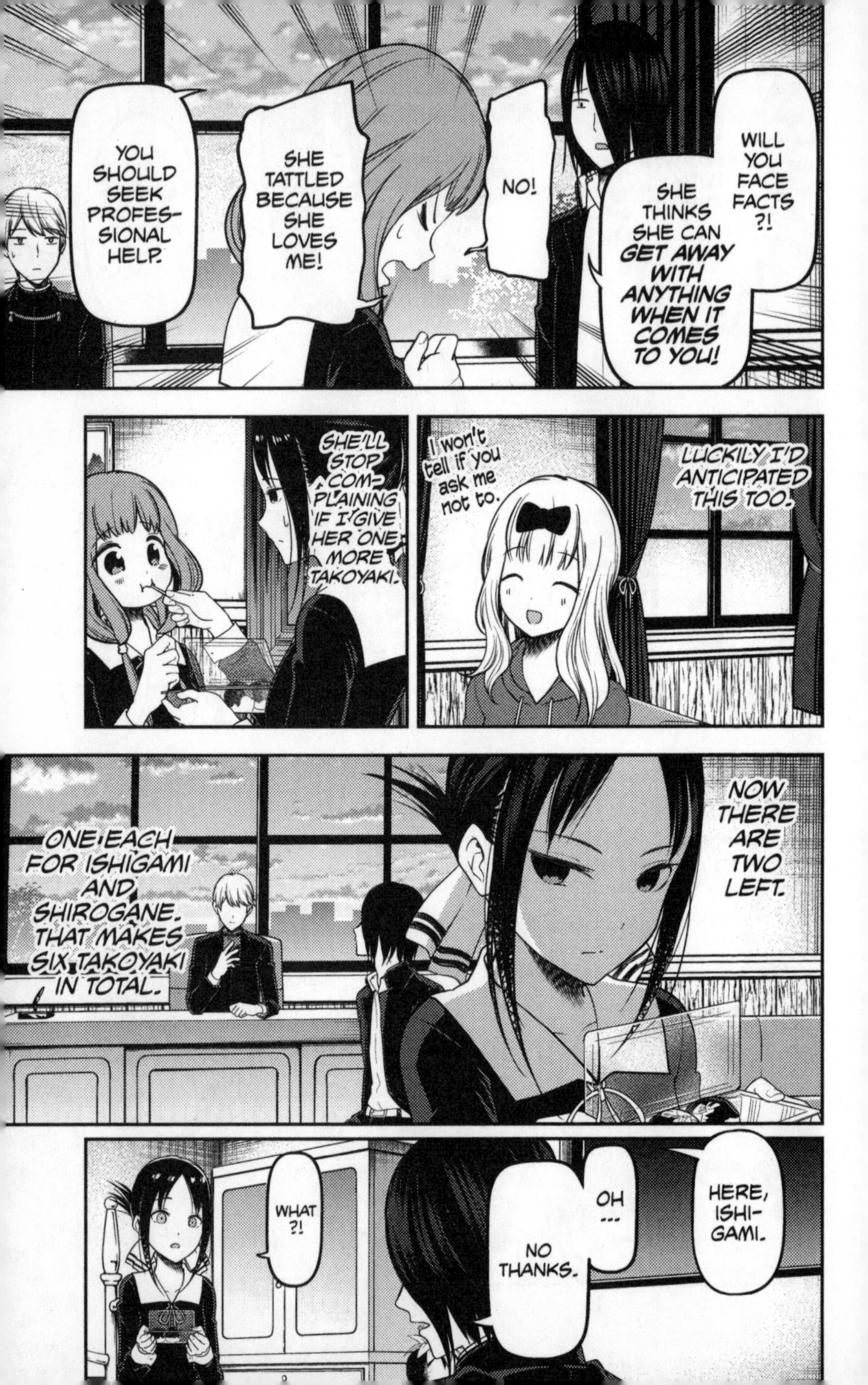
WILL YOU FACE FACTS?!
SHE THINKS SHE CAN GET AWAY WITH ANYTHING WHEN IT COMES TO YOU!
NO!
SHE TATTLED BECAUSE SHE LOVES ME!
YOU SHOULD SEEK PROFESSIONAL HELP.
LUCKILY I'D ANTICIPATED THIS TOO.
I won't tell if you ask me not to.
SHE'LL STOP COMPLAINING IF I GIVE HER ONE MORE TAKOYAKI.
NOW THERE ARE TWO LEFT.
ONE EACH FOR ISHIGAMI AND SHIROGANE. THAT MAKES SIX TAKOYAKI IN TOTAL.
HERE, ISHIGAMI.
OH...
NO THANKS.
WHAT?!

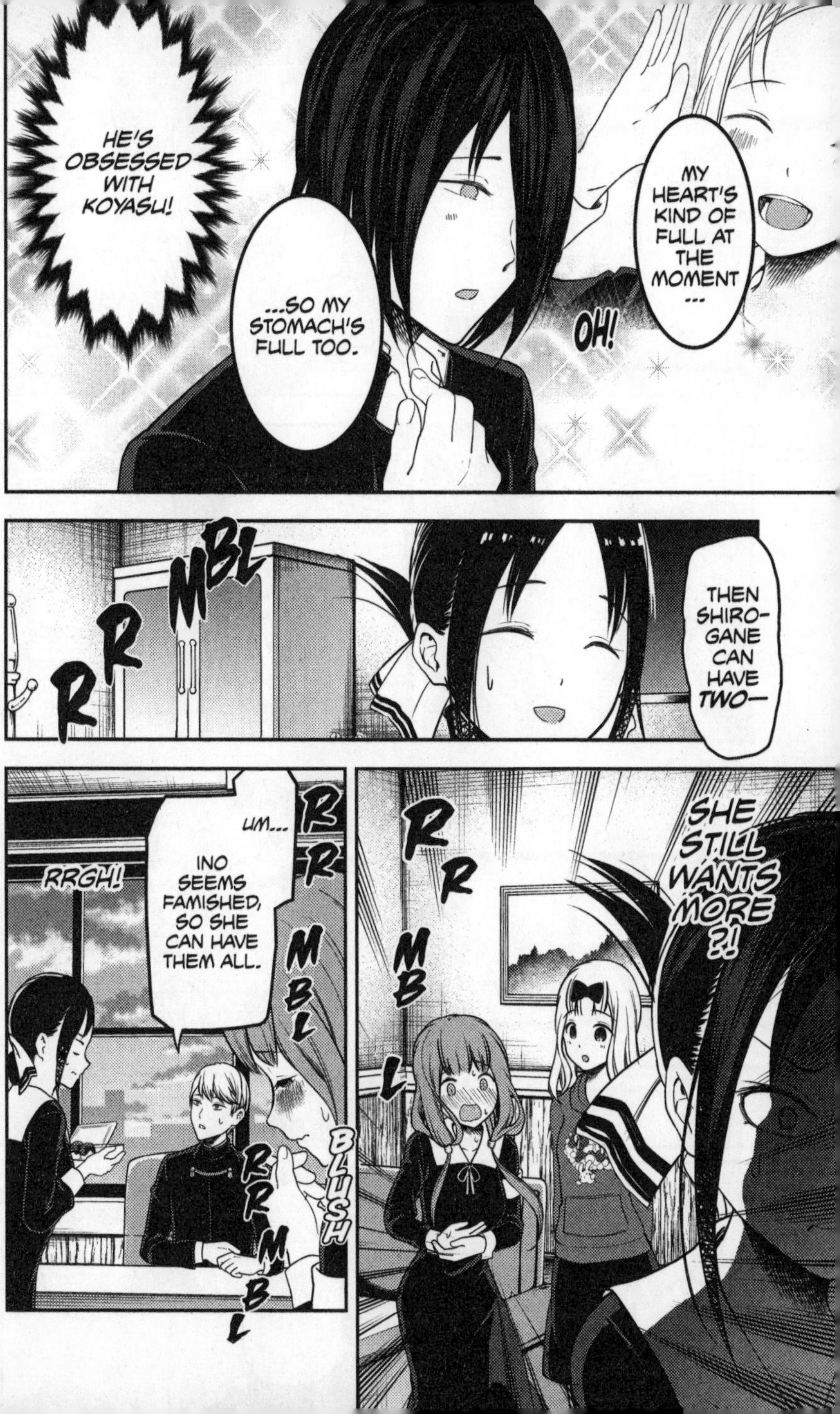
MY HEART'S KIND OF FULL AT THE MOMENT...
OH!
...SO MY STOMACH'S FULL TOO.
HE'S OBSESSED WITH KOYASU!
THEN SHIRO-GANE CAN HAVE TWO—
RRMBL
SHE STILL WANTS MORE?!
RRMBL
RRMBL
UM...
INO SEEMS FAMISHED, SO SHE CAN HAVE THEM ALL.
RRGH!
BLUSH
RRMBL

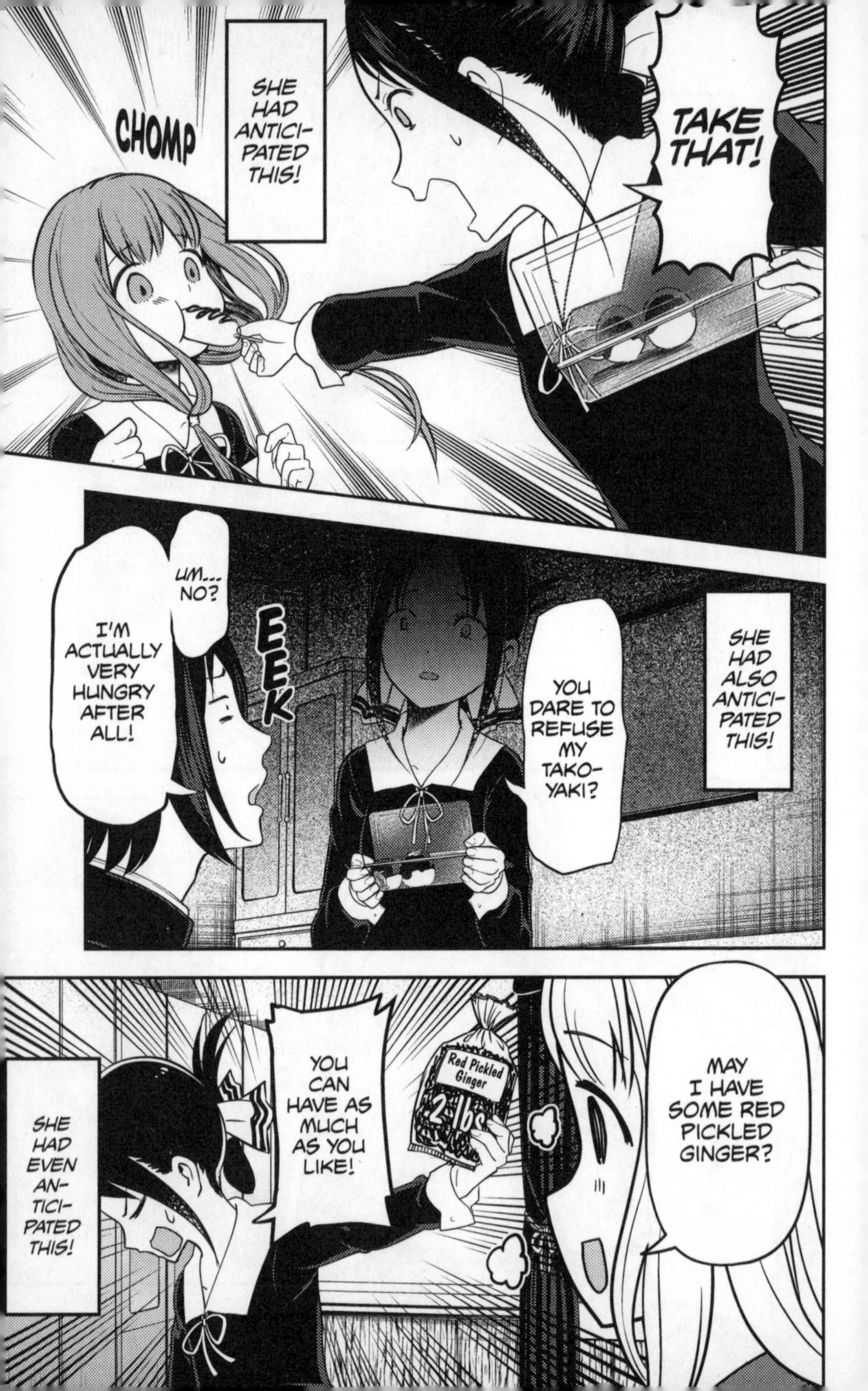
TAKE THAT!
SHE HAD ANTICIPATED THIS!
CHOMP
SHE HAD ALSO ANTICIPATED THIS!
UM... NO?
YOU DARE TO REFUSE MY TAKO-YAKI?
EEK
I'M ACTUALLY VERY HUNGRY AFTER ALL!
MAY I HAVE SOME RED PICKLED GINGER?
Red Pickled Ginger
2 lbs
YOU CAN HAVE AS MUCH AS YOU LIKE!
SHE HAD EVEN ANTICIPATED THIS!

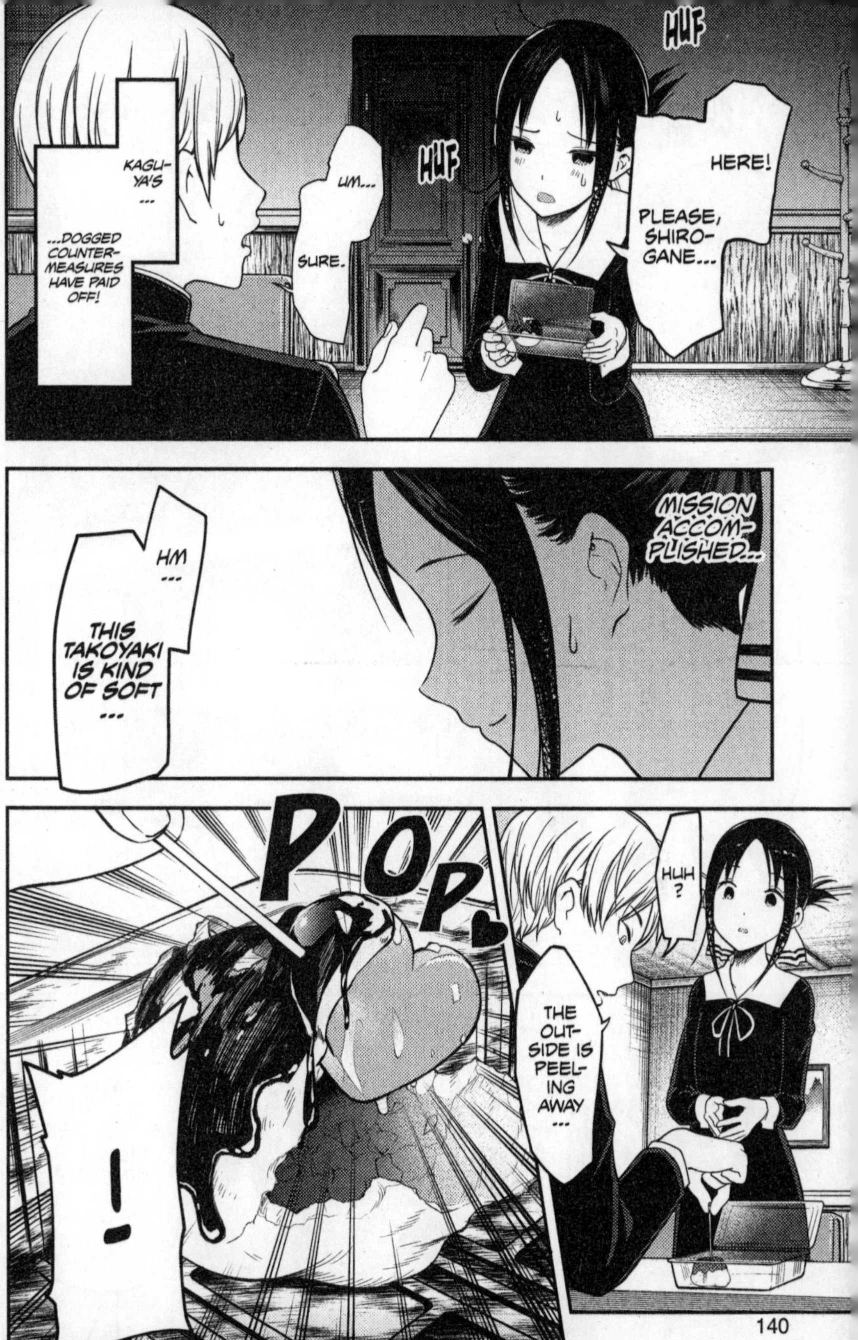
HUF
HERE!
PLEASE, SHIRO-GANE...
HUF
UM... SURE.
KAGUYA'S ...
...DOGGED COUNTER-MEASURES HAVE PAID OFF!
MISSION ACCOMPLISHED...
HM ...
THIS TAKOYAKI IS KIND OF SOFT ...
HUH?
THE OUTSIDE IS PEELING AWAY ...
POP
!

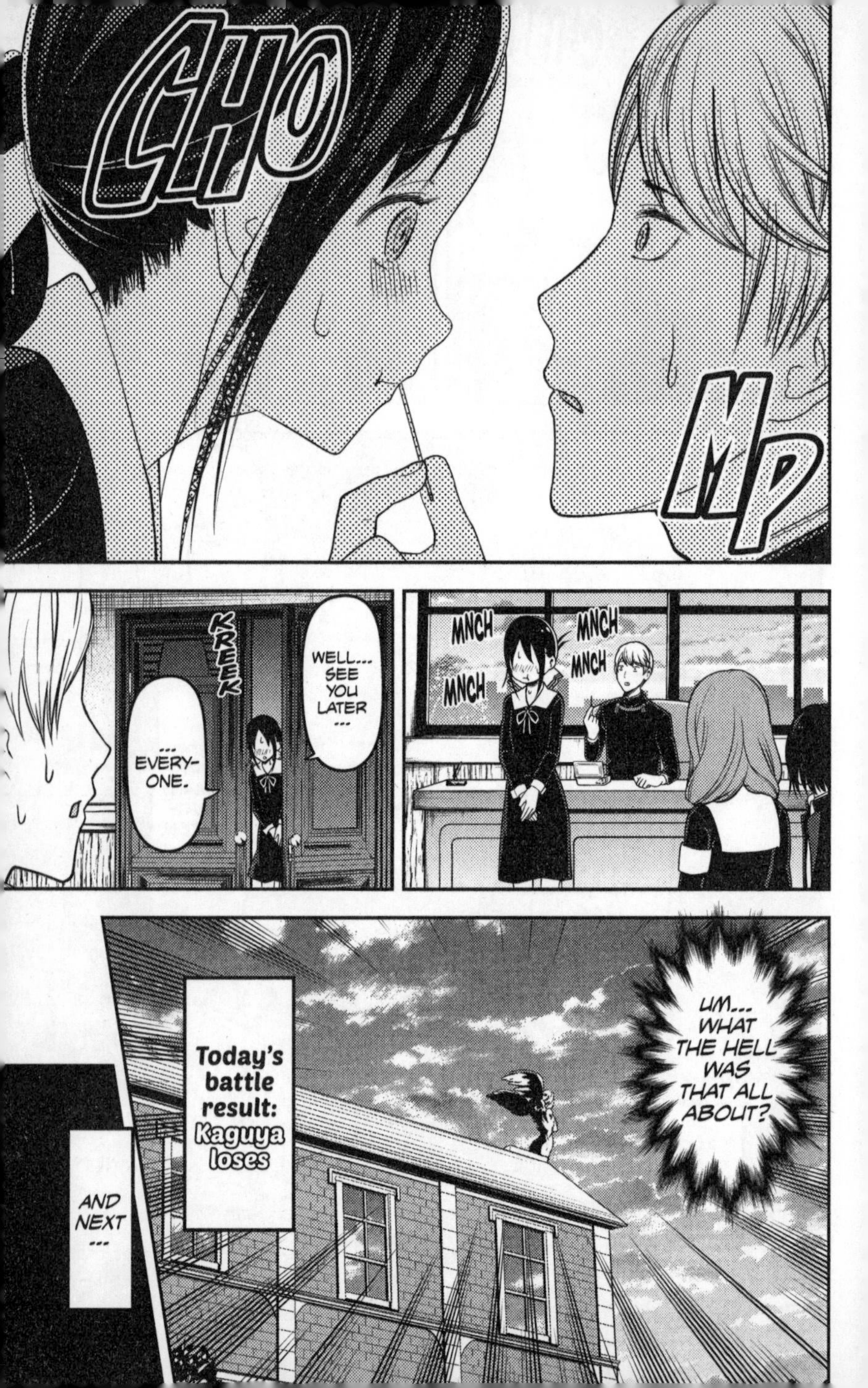
CHO
MP
MNCH
MNCH
MNCH
MNCH
KREEK
WELL... SEE YOU LATER ...
... EVERY-ONE.
UM... WHAT THE HELL WAS THAT ALL ABOUT?
Today's battle result: Kaguya loses
AND NEXT ...

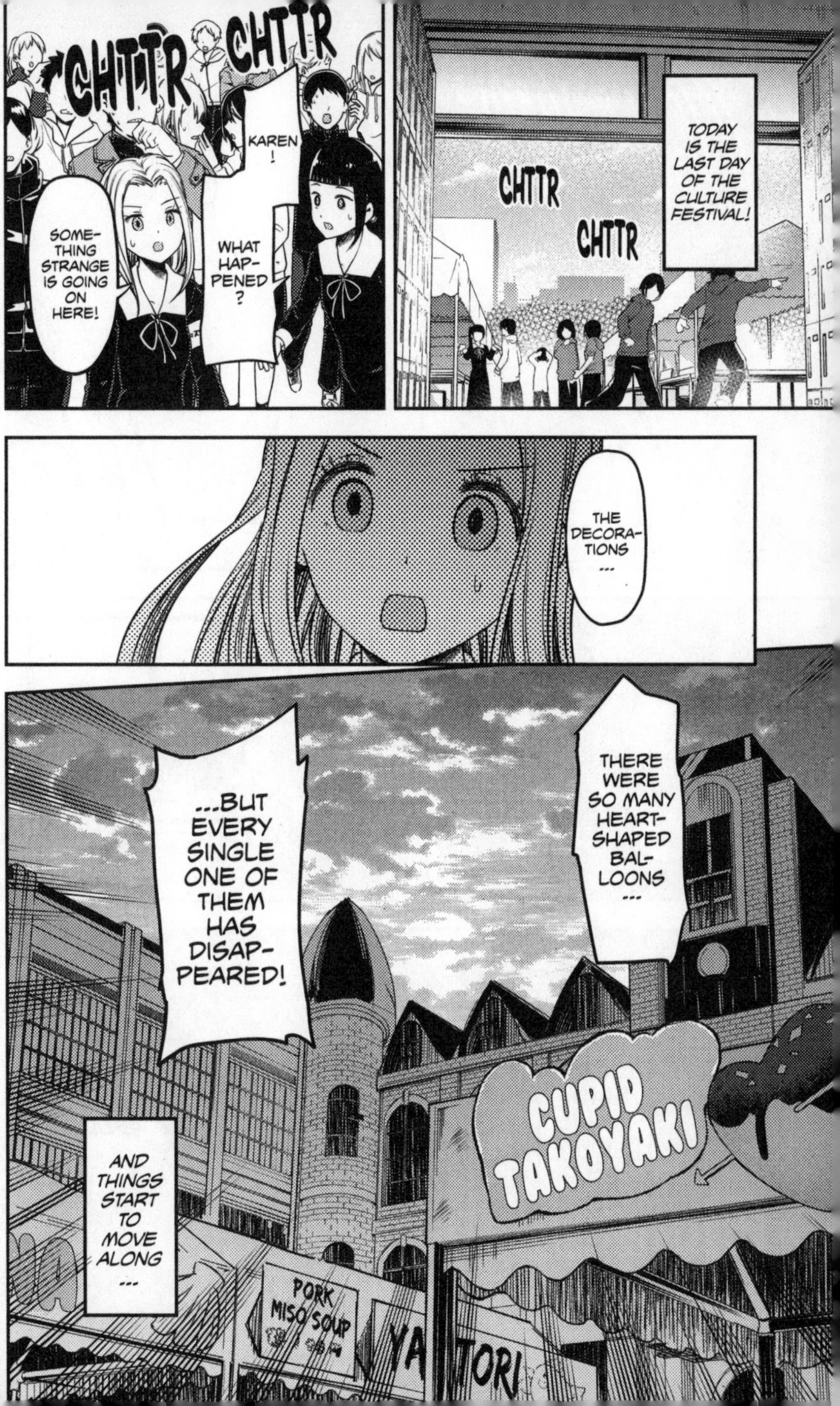
TODAY IS THE LAST DAY OF THE CULTURE FESTIVAL!
CHTTR
CHTTR
CHTTR
CHTTR
KAREN!
WHAT HAP-PENED?
SOME-THING STRANGE IS GOING ON HERE!
THE DECORA-TIONS...
THERE WERE SO MANY HEART-SHAPED BAL-LOONS...
...BUT EVERY SINGLE ONE OF THEM HAS DISAP-PEARED!
CUPID TAKOYAKI
AND THINGS START TO MOVE ALONG...
PORK MISO SOUP
YA TORI

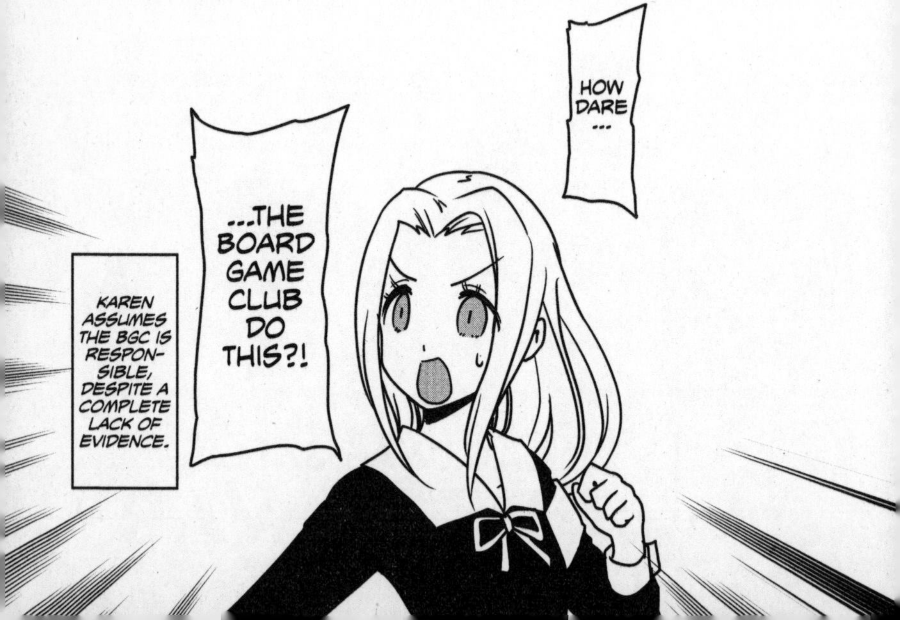
HOW DARE...
...THE BOARD GAME CLUB DO THIS?!
KAREN ASSUMES THE BGC IS RESPONSIBLE, DESPITE A COMPLETE LACK OF EVIDENCE.

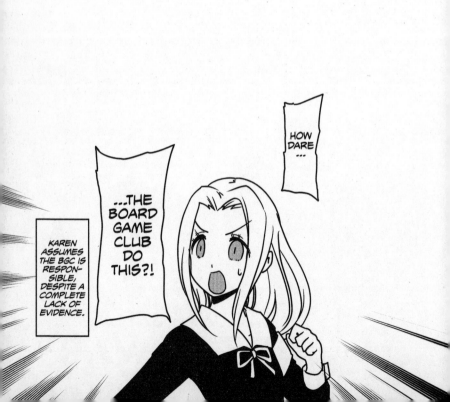

KAGUYA-SAMA

LOVE IS WAR

SECOND DAY OF THE CULTURE FESTIVAL (THE LAST DAY)

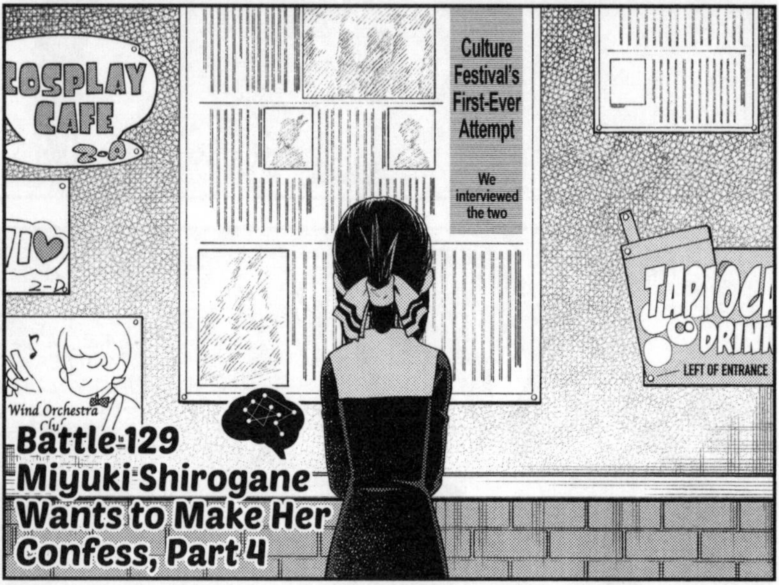
Culture Festival's First-Ever Attempt
We interviewed the two
CAFE
2-A
2-D
TAPIOCA
DRINK
LEFT OF ENTRANCE
Wind Orchestra
Battle 129
Miyuki Shirogane Wants to Make Her Confess, Part 4

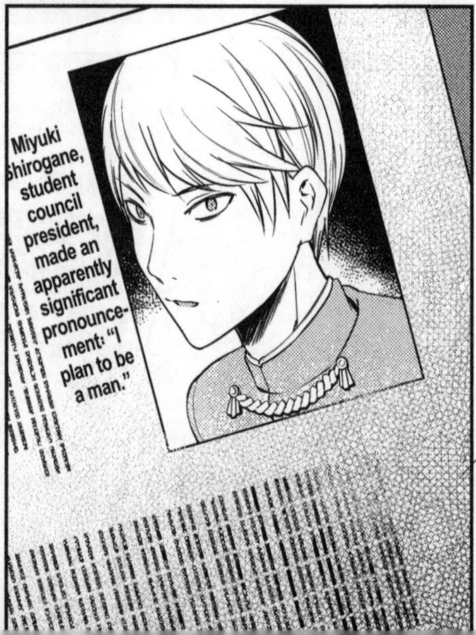
Miyuki Shirogane, student council president, made an apparently significant pronouncement: "I plan to be a man."

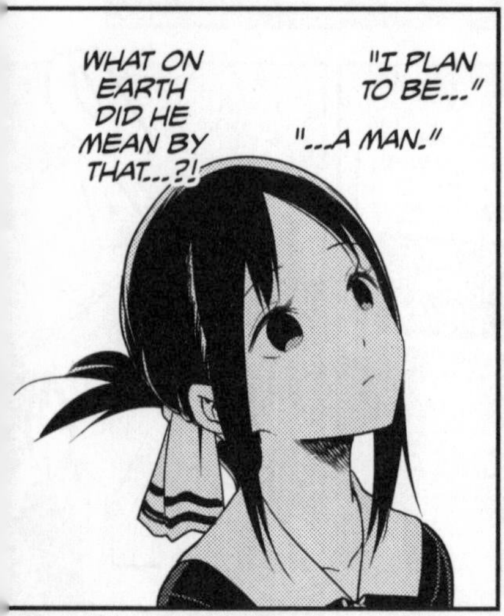
"I PLAN TO BE..."
"...A MAN."
WHAT ON EARTH DID HE MEAN BY THAT...?!

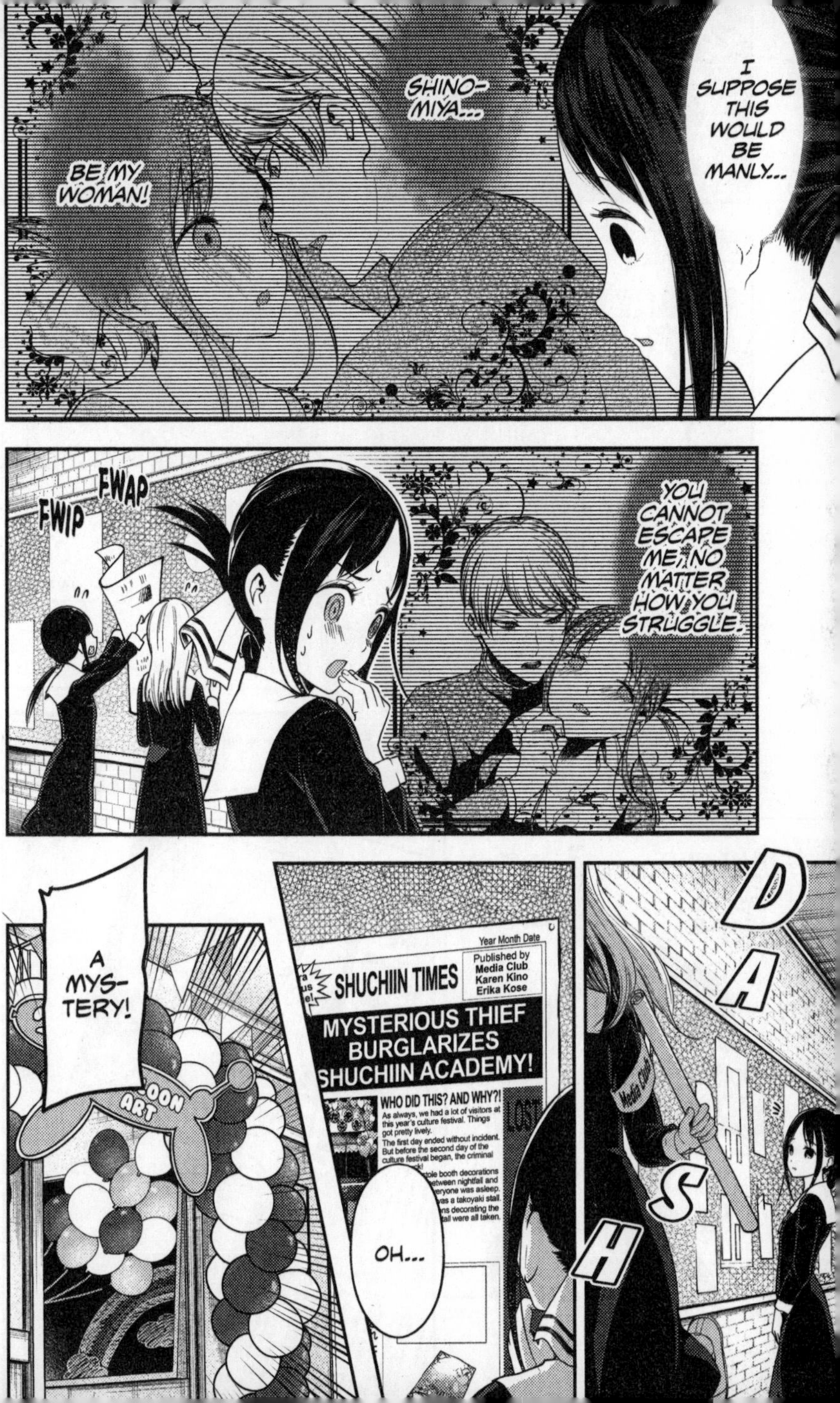
I SUPPOSE THIS WOULD BE MANLY...
SHINO-MIYA...
BE MY WOMAN!
YOU CANNOT ESCAPE ME, NO MATTER HOW YOU STRUGGLE.
FWAP
FWIP
DASH
Media Club
Year Month Date
SHUCHIIN TIMES
Published by Media Club Karen Kino Erika Kose
MYSTERIOUS THIEF BURGLARIZES SHUCHIIN ACADEMY!
WHO DID THIS? AND WHY?!
As always, we had a lot of visitors at this year's culture festival. Things got pretty lively.
The first day ended without incident. But before the second day of the culture festival began, the criminal
LOST
OH...
A MYS-TERY!
OON ART

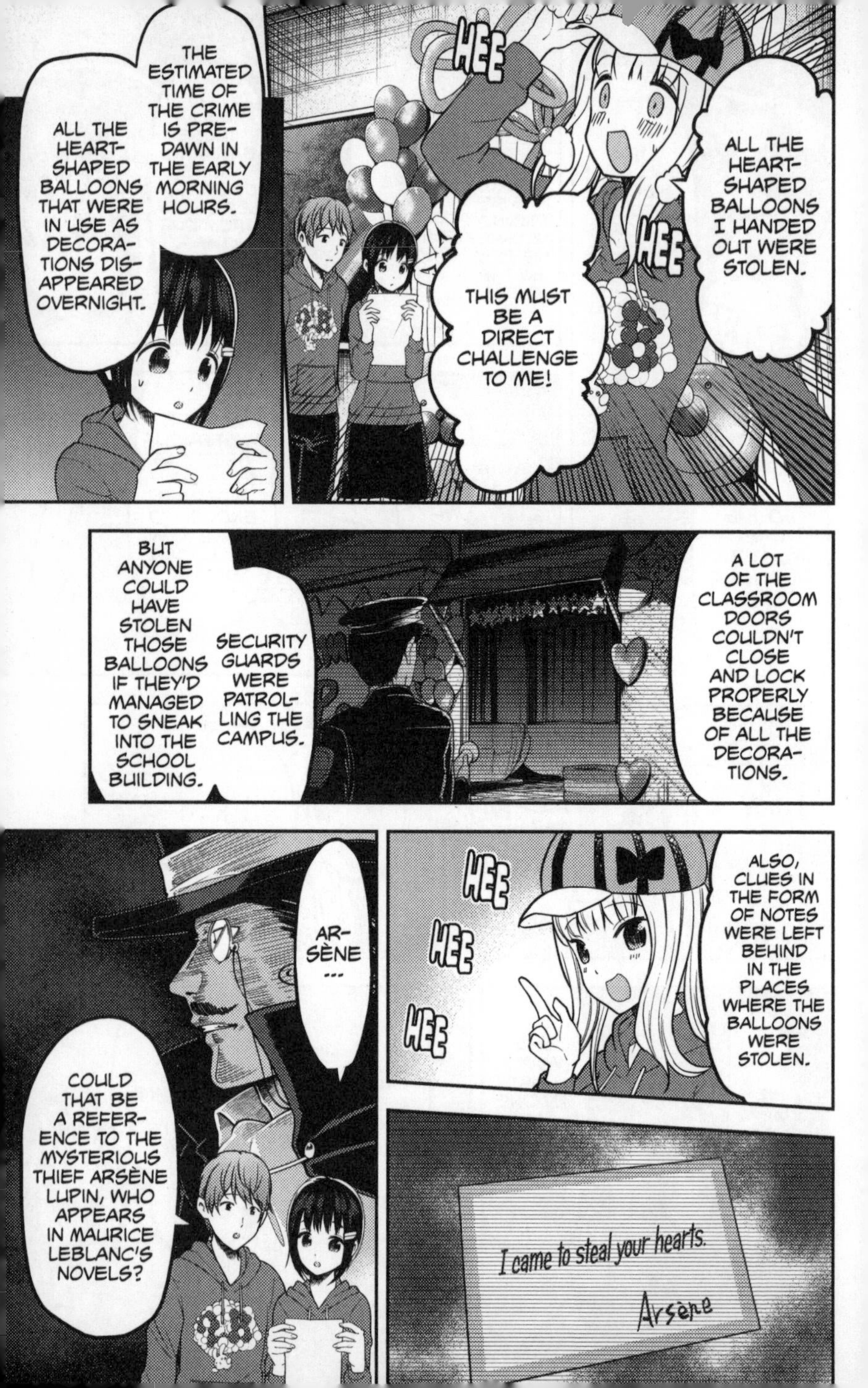
HEE
ALL THE HEART-SHAPED BALLOONS I HANDED OUT WERE STOLEN.
HEE
THIS MUST BE A DIRECT CHALLENGE TO ME!
THE ESTIMATED TIME OF THE CRIME IS PRE-DAWN IN THE EARLY MORNING HOURS.
ALL THE HEART-SHAPED BALLOONS THAT WERE IN USE AS DECORATIONS DISAPPEARED OVERNIGHT.
A LOT OF THE CLASSROOM DOORS COULDN'T CLOSE AND LOCK PROPERLY BECAUSE OF ALL THE DECORATIONS.
SECURITY GUARDS WERE PATROLLING THE CAMPUS.
BUT ANYONE COULD HAVE STOLEN THOSE BALLOONS IF THEY'D MANAGED TO SNEAK INTO THE SCHOOL BUILDING.
HEE
HEE
HEE
ALSO, CLUES IN THE FORM OF NOTES WERE LEFT BEHIND IN THE PLACES WHERE THE BALLOONS WERE STOLEN.
I came to steal your hearts.
Arsène
ARSÈNE...
COULD THAT BE A REFERENCE TO THE MYSTERIOUS THIEF ARSÈNE LUPIN, WHO APPEARS IN MAURICE LEBLANC'S NOVELS?

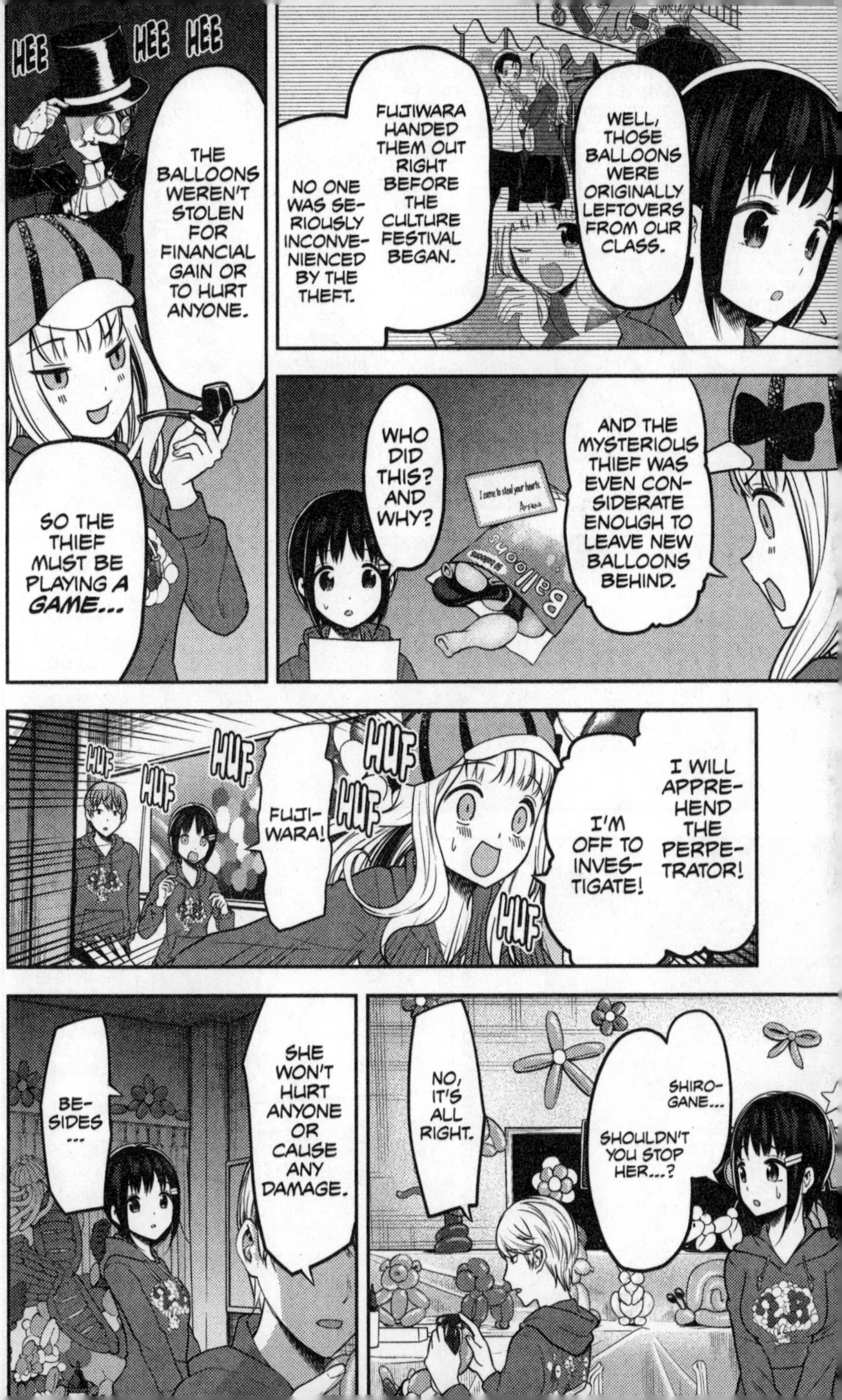
WELL, THOSE BALLOONS WERE ORIGINALLY LEFTOVERS FROM OUR CLASS.
FUJIWARA HANDED THEM OUT RIGHT BEFORE THE CULTURE FESTIVAL BEGAN.
NO ONE WAS SERIOUSLY INCONVENIENCED BY THE THEFT.
AND THE MYSTERIOUS THIEF WAS EVEN CONSIDERATE ENOUGH TO LEAVE NEW BALLOONS BEHIND.
I came to steal your hearts.
Balloons
WHO DID THIS? AND WHY?
HEE HEE HEE
THE BALLOONS WEREN'T STOLEN FOR FINANCIAL GAIN OR TO HURT ANYONE.
SO THE THIEF MUST BE PLAYING A *GAME*...
I WILL APPREHEND THE PERPETRATOR!
I'M OFF TO INVESTIGATE!
HUF HUF HUF HUF
FUJIWARA!
HUF HUF
SHIROGANE...
SHOULDN'T YOU STOP HER...?
NO, IT'S ALL RIGHT.
SHE WON'T HURT ANYONE OR CAUSE ANY DAMAGE.
BESIDES...

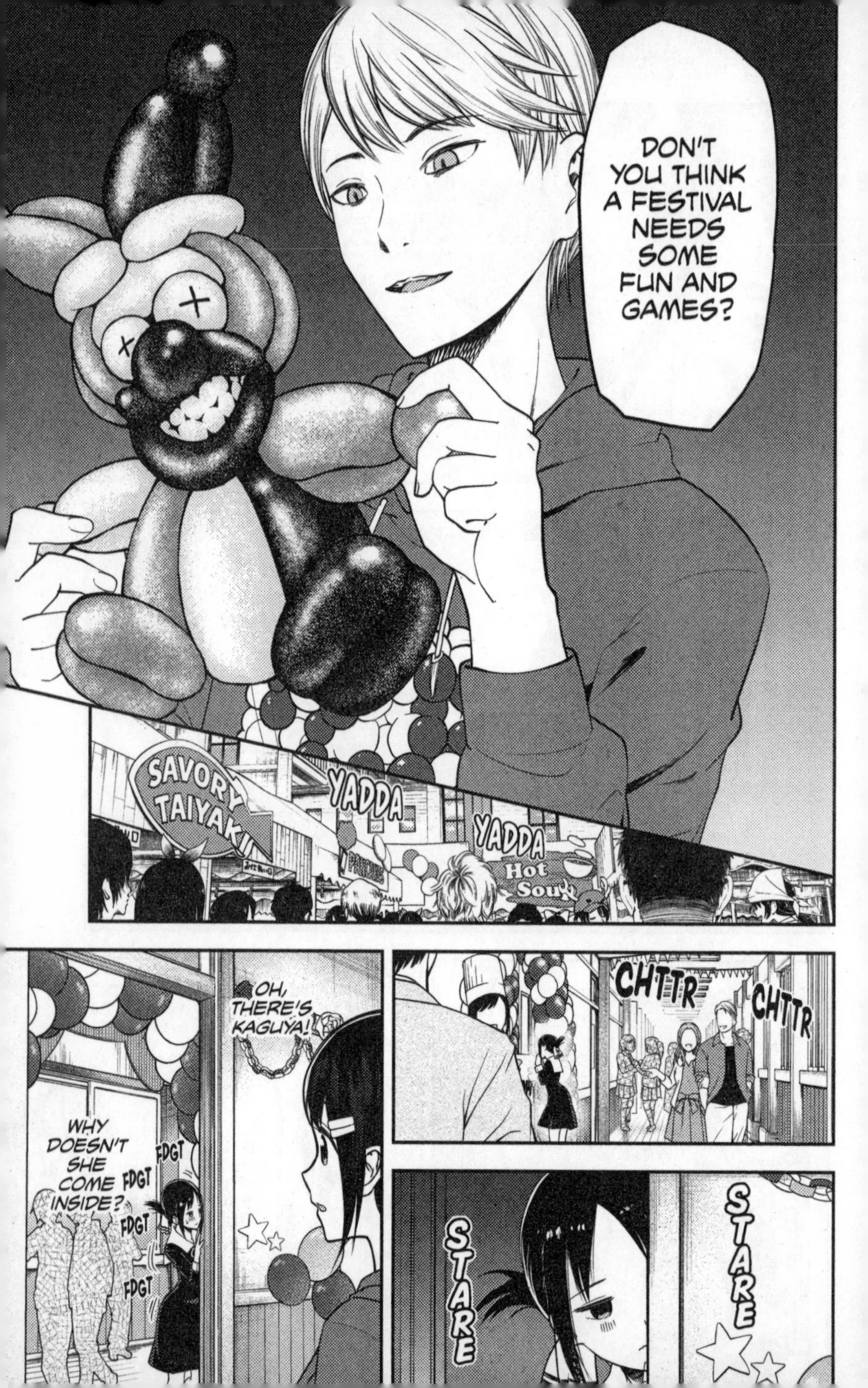

DON'T YOU THINK A FESTIVAL NEEDS SOME FUN AND GAMES?
YADDA
YADDA
Hot
SAVORY TAIYAKI
CHTTR
CHTTR
STARE
STARE
OH, THERE'S KAGUYA!
WHY DOESN'T SHE COME INSIDE?
FDGT
FDGT
FDGT
FDGT

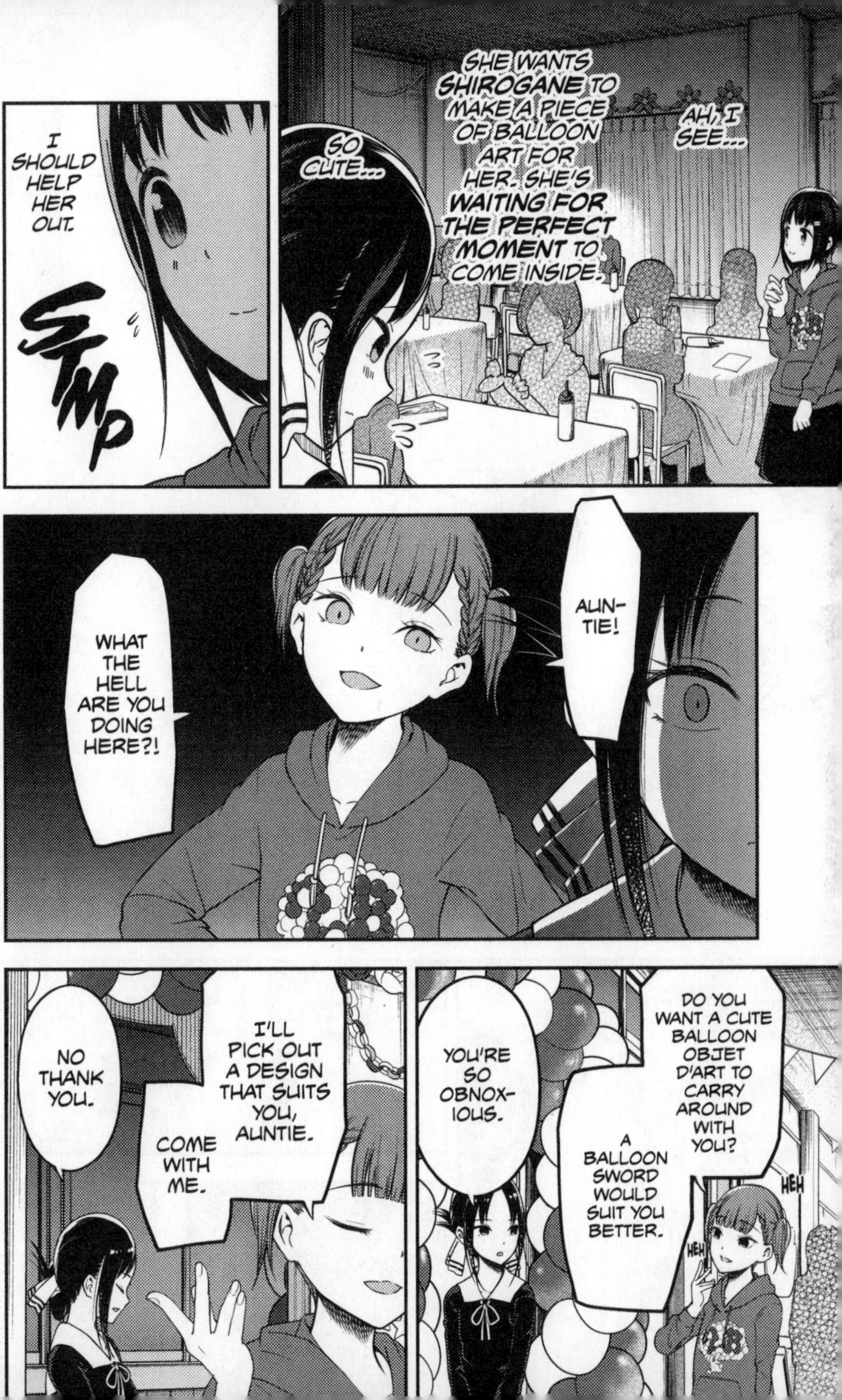
AH, I SEE...
SHE WANTS SHIROGANE TO MAKE A PIECE OF BALLOON ART FOR HER. SHE'S WAITING FOR THE PERFECT MOMENT TO COME INSIDE.
SO CUTE...
I SHOULD HELP HER OUT.
STMP
AUNTIE!
WHAT THE HELL ARE YOU DOING HERE?!
DO YOU WANT A CUTE BALLOON OBJET D'ART TO CARRY AROUND WITH YOU?
HEH
YOU'RE SO OBNOXIOUS.
A BALLOON SWORD WOULD SUIT YOU BETTER.
HEH
I'LL PICK OUT A DESIGN THAT SUITS YOU, AUNTIE.
COME WITH ME.
NO THANK YOU.

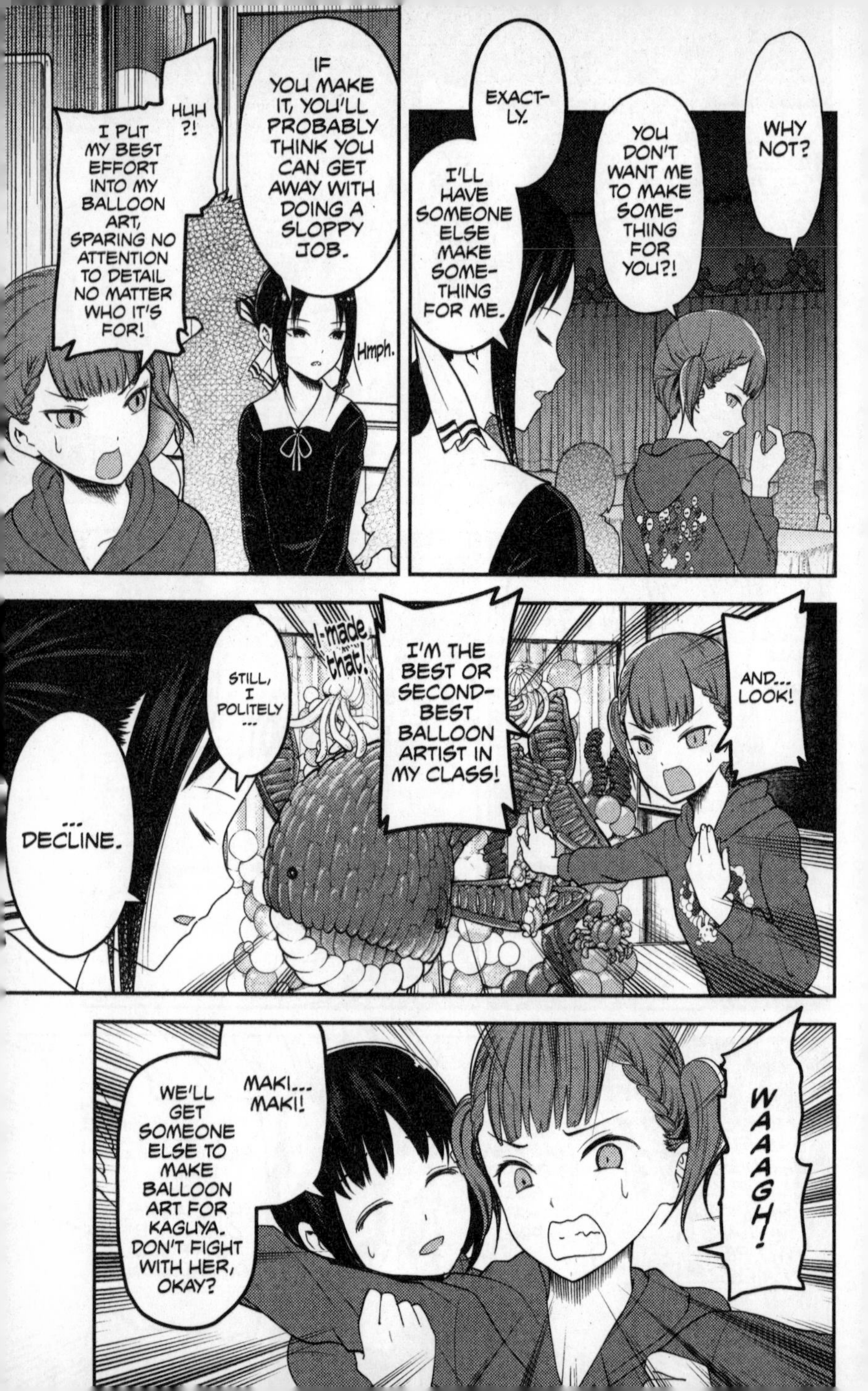
WHY NOT?
YOU DON'T WANT ME TO MAKE SOMETHING FOR YOU?!
EXACTLY.
I'LL HAVE SOMEONE ELSE MAKE SOMETHING FOR ME.
IF YOU MAKE IT, YOU'LL PROBABLY THINK YOU CAN GET AWAY WITH DOING A SLOPPY JOB.
Hmph.
HUH?!
I PUT MY BEST EFFORT INTO MY BALLOON ART, SPARING NO ATTENTION TO DETAIL NO MATTER WHO IT'S FOR!
AND... LOOK!
I'M THE BEST OR SECOND-BEST BALLOON ARTIST IN MY CLASS!
I-made that!
STILL, I POLITELY...
...DECLINE.
WAAAGH!
MAKI... MAKI!
WE'LL GET SOMEONE ELSE TO MAKE BALLOON ART FOR KAGUYA. DON'T FIGHT WITH HER, OKAY?

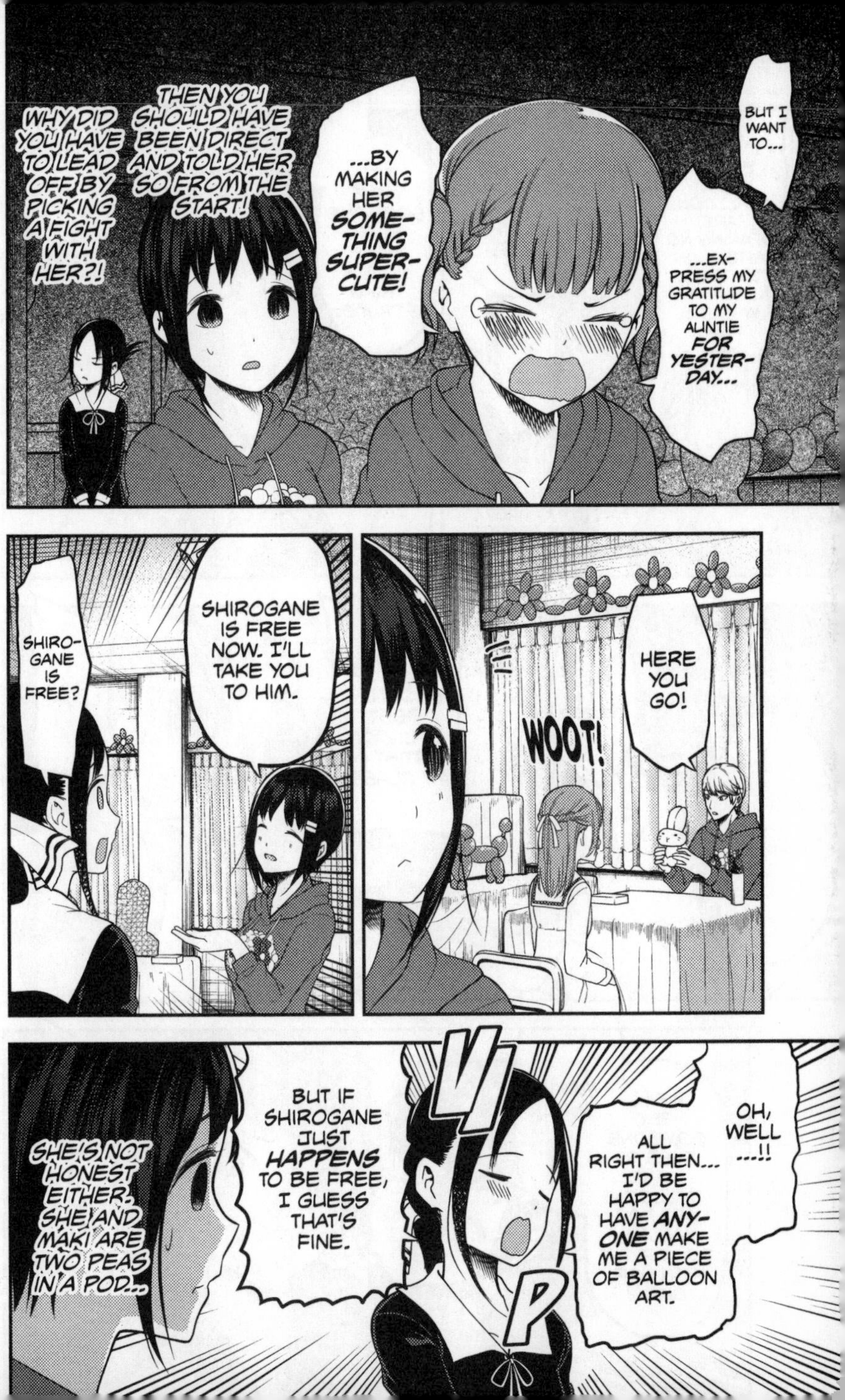
BUT I WANT TO...
...EXPRESS MY GRATITUDE TO MY AUNTIE FOR YESTERDAY...
...BY MAKING HER SOMETHING SUPERCUTE!
THEN YOU SHOULD HAVE BEEN DIRECT AND TOLD HER SO FROM THE START!
WHY DID YOU HAVE TO LEAD OFF BY PICKING A FIGHT WITH HER?!
HERE YOU GO!
WOOT!
SHIROGANE IS FREE NOW. I'LL TAKE YOU TO HIM.
SHIROGANE IS FREE?
OH, WELL...!!
ALL RIGHT THEN... I'D BE HAPPY TO HAVE ANYONE MAKE ME A PIECE OF BALLOON ART.
VP
BUT IF SHIROGANE JUST HAPPENS TO BE FREE, I GUESS THAT'S FINE.
SHE'S NOT HONEST EITHER. SHE AND MAKI ARE TWO PEAS IN A POD...

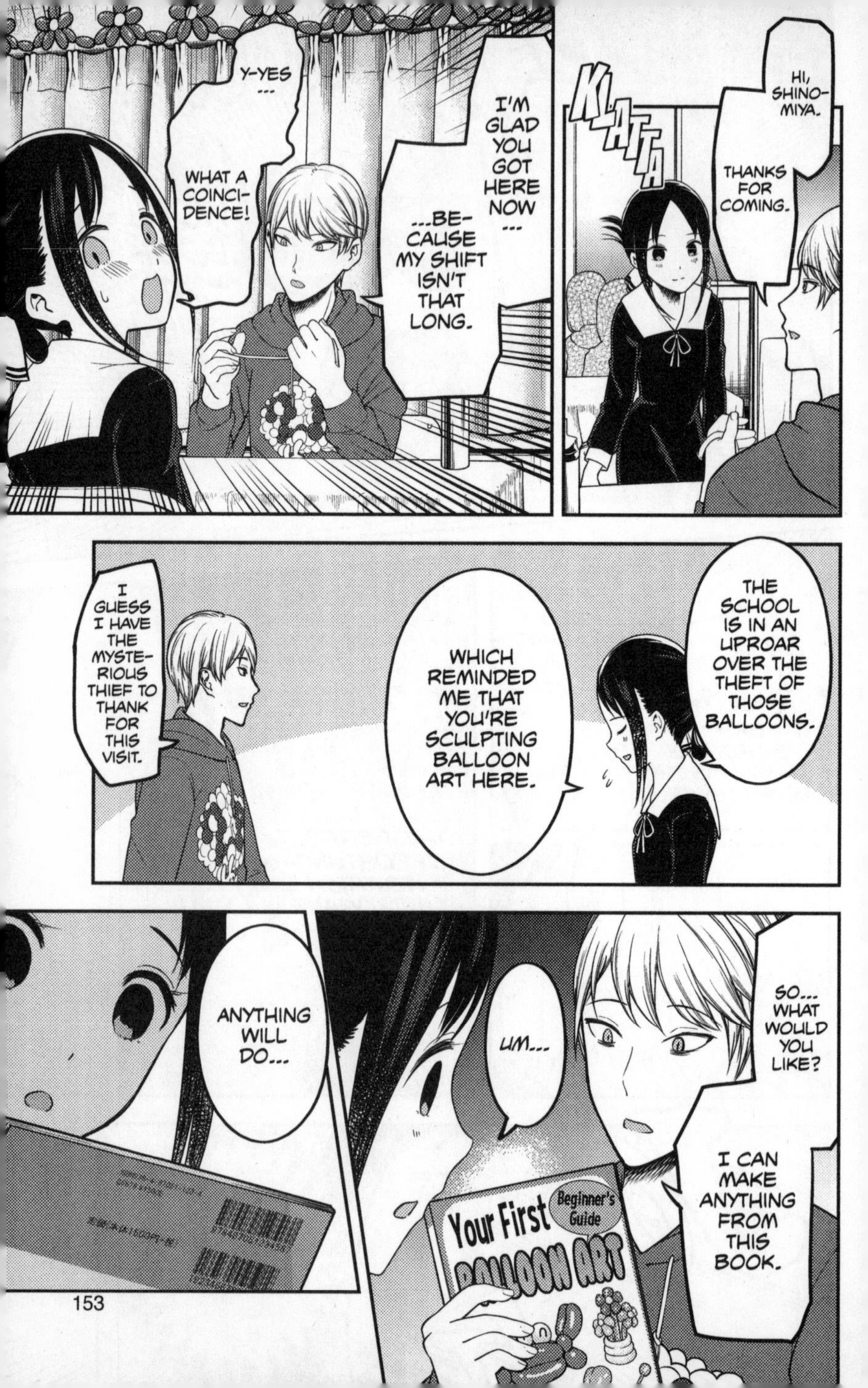
KLATTA
HI, SHINO-MIYA.
THANKS FOR COMING.
I'M GLAD YOU GOT HERE NOW...
...BE-CAUSE MY SHIFT ISN'T THAT LONG.
Y-YES...
WHAT A COINCI-DENCE!
THE SCHOOL IS IN AN UPROAR OVER THE THEFT OF THOSE BALLOONS.
WHICH REMINDED ME THAT YOU'RE SCULPTING BALLOON ART HERE.
I GUESS I HAVE THE MYSTE-RIOUS THIEF TO THANK FOR THIS VISIT.
SO... WHAT WOULD YOU LIKE?
I CAN MAKE ANYTHING FROM THIS BOOK.
Your First
Beginner's Guide
BALLOON ART
UM...
ANYTHING WILL DO...

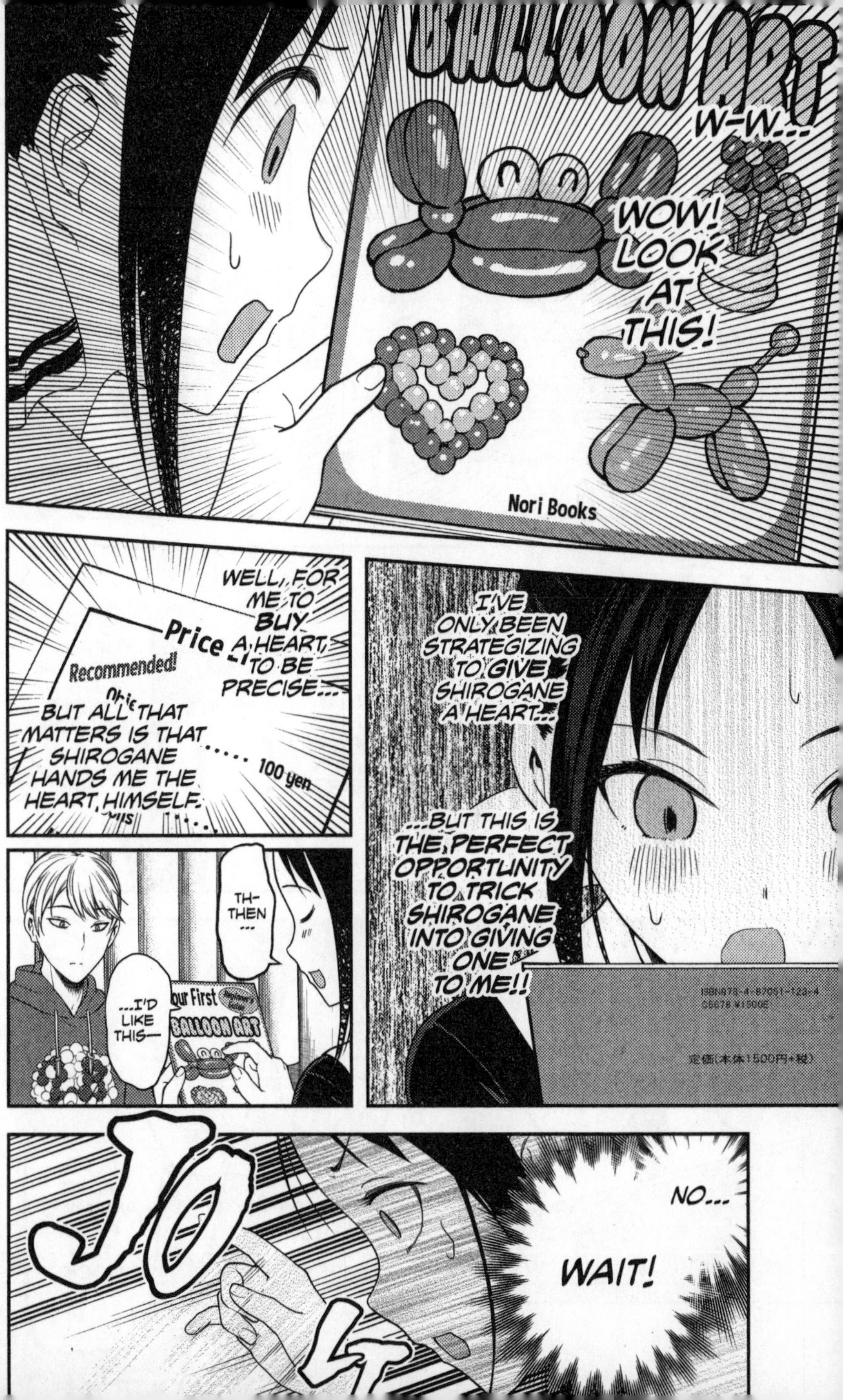
BALLOON ART
W-W...
WOW! LOOK AT THIS!
Nori Books
I'VE ONLY BEEN STRATEGIZING TO GIVE SHIROGANE A HEART...
...BUT THIS IS THE PERFECT OPPORTUNITY TO TRICK SHIROGANE INTO GIVING ONE TO ME!!
ISBN978-4-87051-123-4
C6678 ¥1500E
定価(本体1500円+税)
WELL, FOR ME TO BUY A HEART, TO BE PRECISE...
Price Li
Recommended!
BUT ALL THAT MATTERS IS THAT SHIROGANE HANDS ME THE HEART HIMSELF...
100 yen
TH-THEN...
...I'D LIKE THIS—
BALLOON ART
NO...
WAIT!
JO

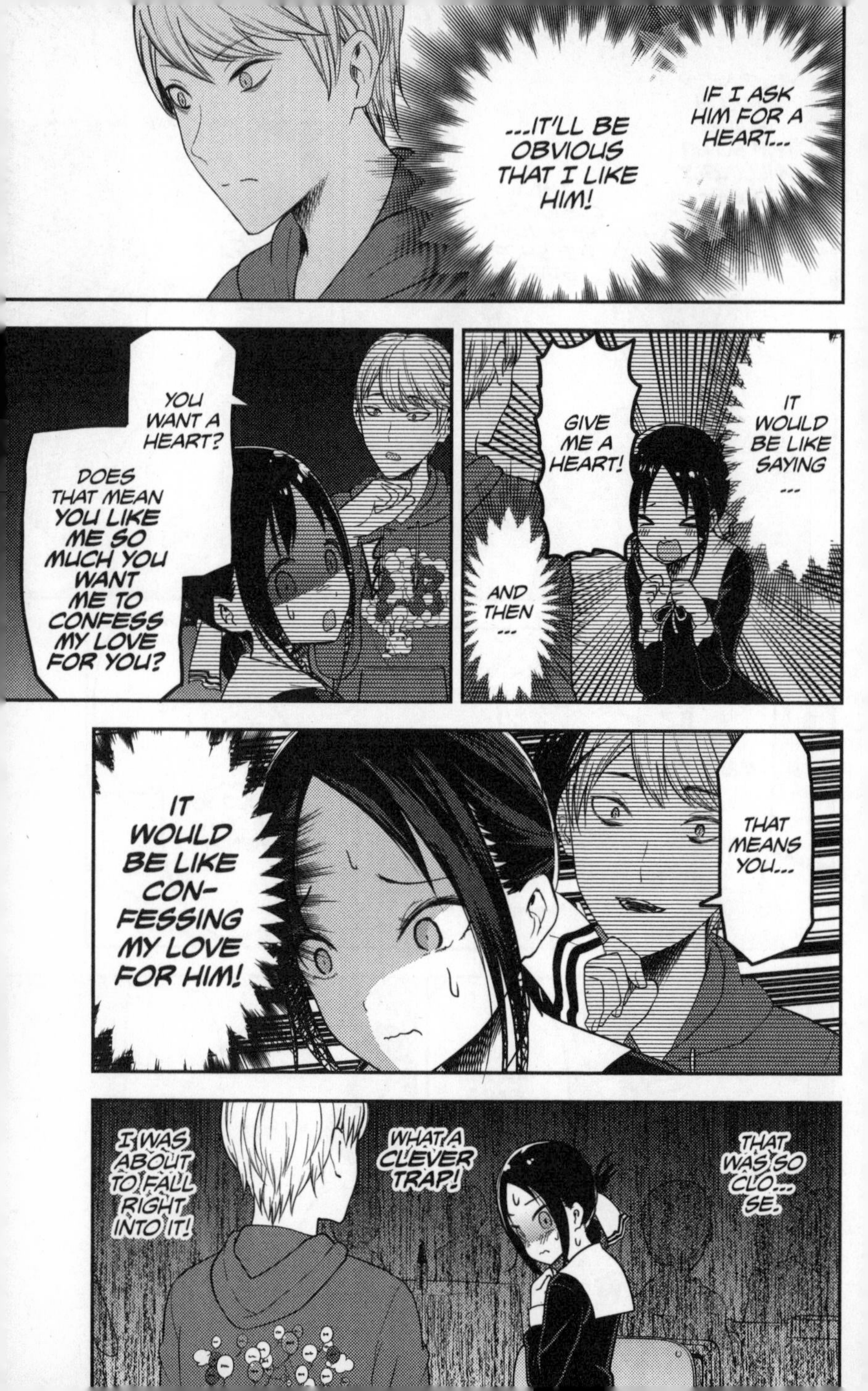
IF I ASK HIM FOR A HEART...
...IT'LL BE OBVIOUS THAT I LIKE HIM!
IT WOULD BE LIKE SAYING ...
GIVE ME A HEART!
AND THEN ...
YOU WANT A HEART?
DOES THAT MEAN YOU LIKE ME SO MUCH YOU WANT ME TO CONFESS MY LOVE FOR YOU?
THAT MEANS YOU...
IT WOULD BE LIKE CON-FESSING MY LOVE FOR HIM!
THAT WAS SO CLO... SE.
WHAT A CLEVER TRAP!
I WAS ABOUT TO FALL RIGHT INTO IT!

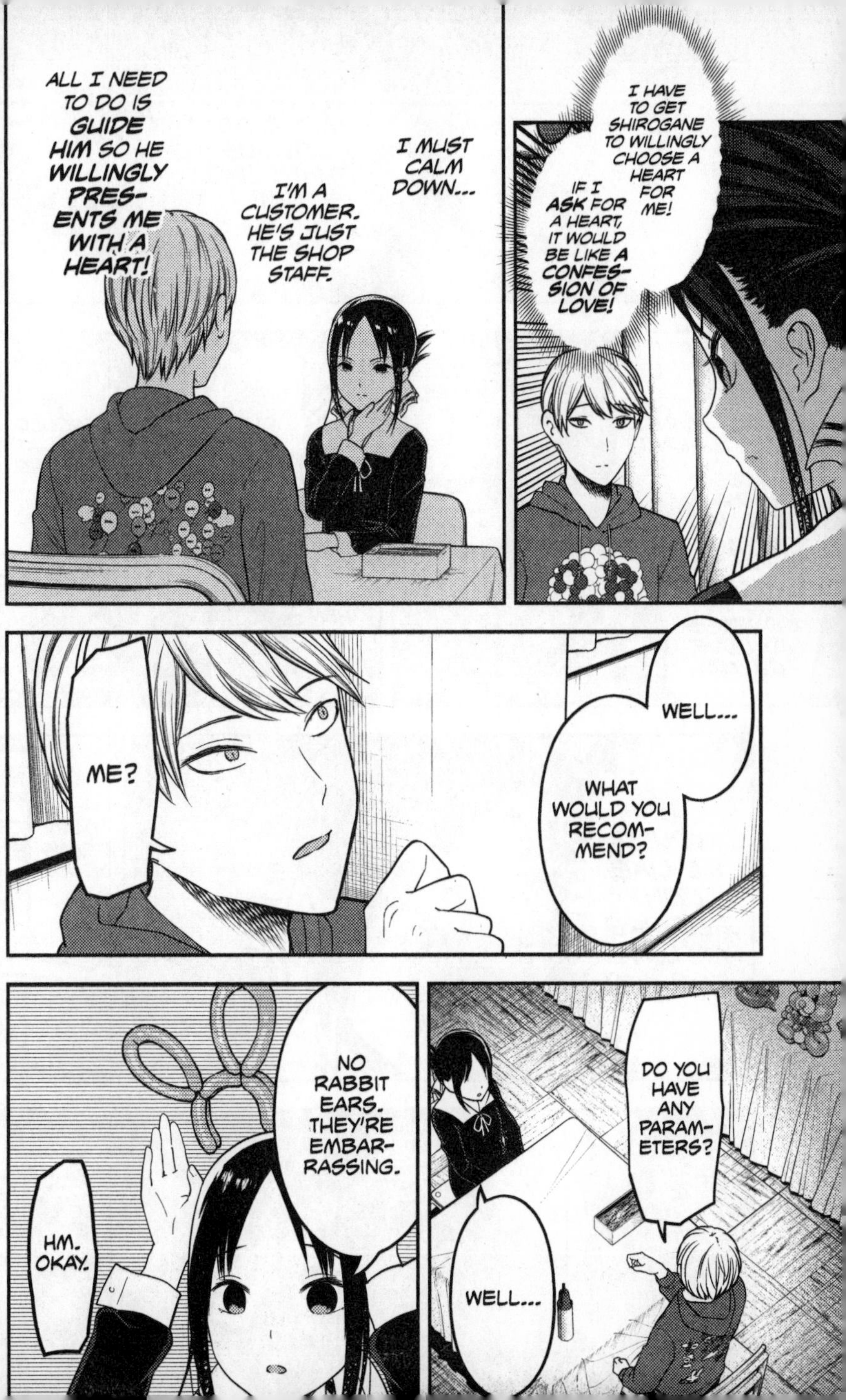
I HAVE TO GET SHIROGANE TO WILLINGLY CHOOSE A HEART FOR ME!
IF I ASK FOR A HEART, IT WOULD BE LIKE A CONFESSION OF LOVE!
I MUST CALM DOWN...
I'M A CUSTOMER. HE'S JUST THE SHOP STAFF.
ALL I NEED TO DO IS GUIDE HIM SO HE WILLINGLY PRESENTS ME WITH A HEART!
WELL...
WHAT WOULD YOU RECOMMEND?
ME?
DO YOU HAVE ANY PARAMETERS?
WELL...
NO RABBIT EARS. THEY'RE EMBARRASSING.
HM. OKAY.

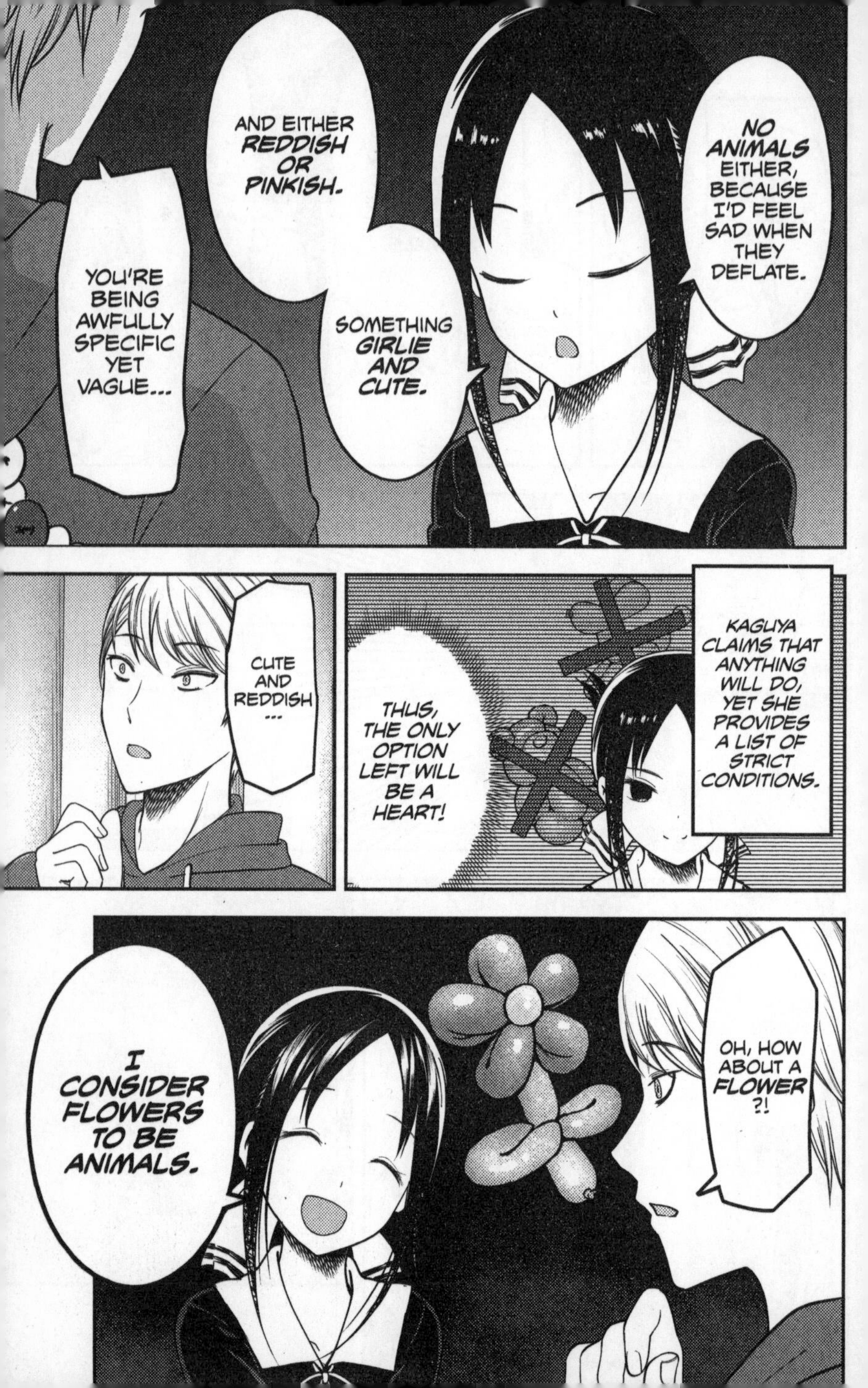
NO ANIMALS EITHER, BECAUSE I'D FEEL SAD WHEN THEY DEFLATE.
AND EITHER REDDISH OR PINKISH.
SOMETHING GIRLIE AND CUTE.
YOU'RE BEING AWFULLY SPECIFIC YET VAGUE...
KAGUYA CLAIMS THAT ANYTHING WILL DO, YET SHE PROVIDES A LIST OF STRICT CONDITIONS.
THUS, THE ONLY OPTION LEFT WILL BE A HEART!
CUTE AND REDDISH...
OH, HOW ABOUT A FLOWER?!
I CONSIDER FLOWERS TO BE ANIMALS.

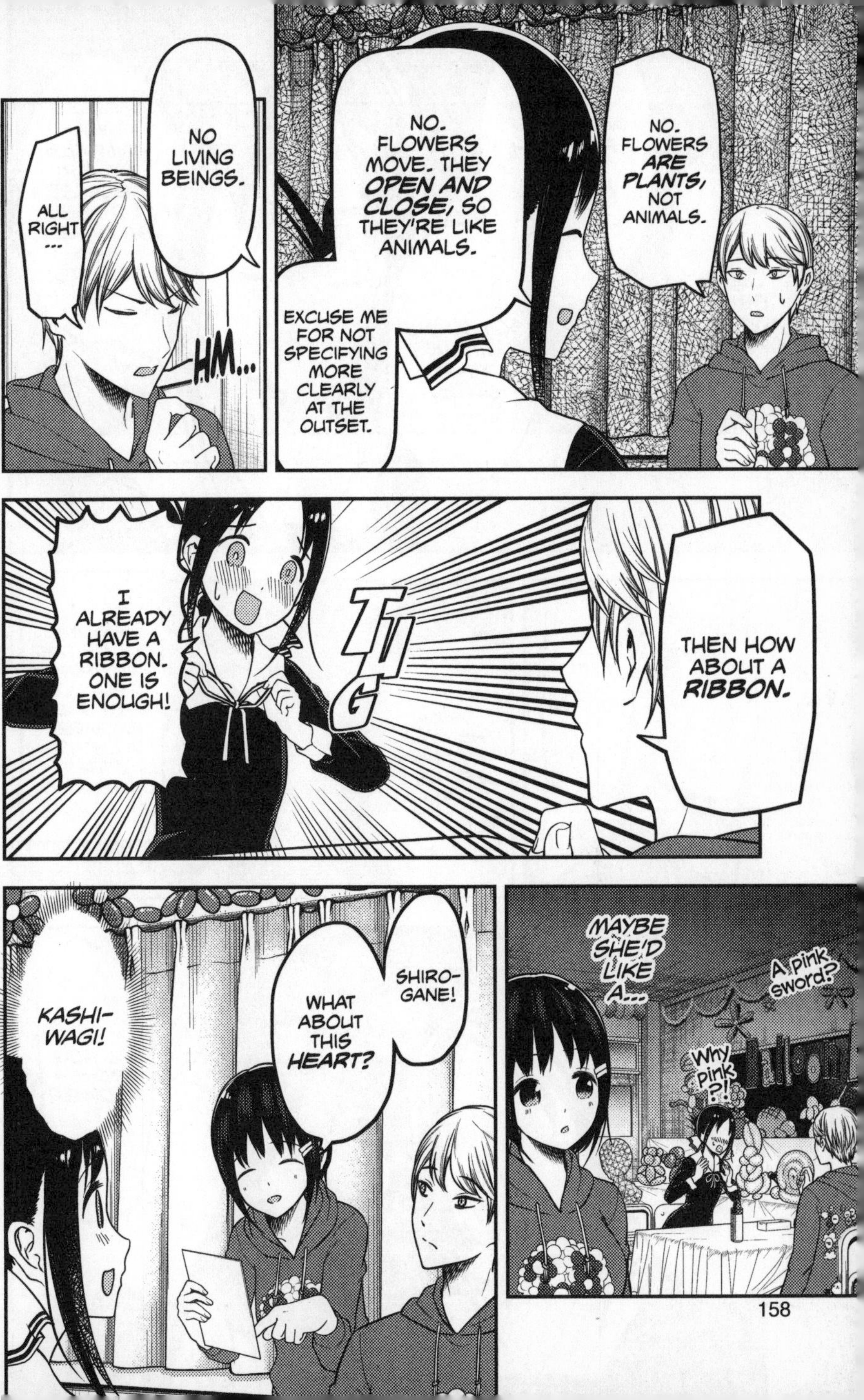
NO. FLOWERS ARE PLANTS, NOT ANIMALS.
NO. FLOWERS MOVE. THEY OPEN AND CLOSE, SO THEY'RE LIKE ANIMALS.
EXCUSE ME FOR NOT SPECIFYING MORE CLEARLY AT THE OUTSET.
NO LIVING BEINGS.
HM...
ALL RIGHT...
THEN HOW ABOUT A RIBBON.
TUG
I ALREADY HAVE A RIBBON. ONE IS ENOUGH!
MAYBE SHE'D LIKE A...
A pink sword?
Why pink?!
SHIRO-GANE!
WHAT ABOUT THIS HEART?
KASHI-WAGI!

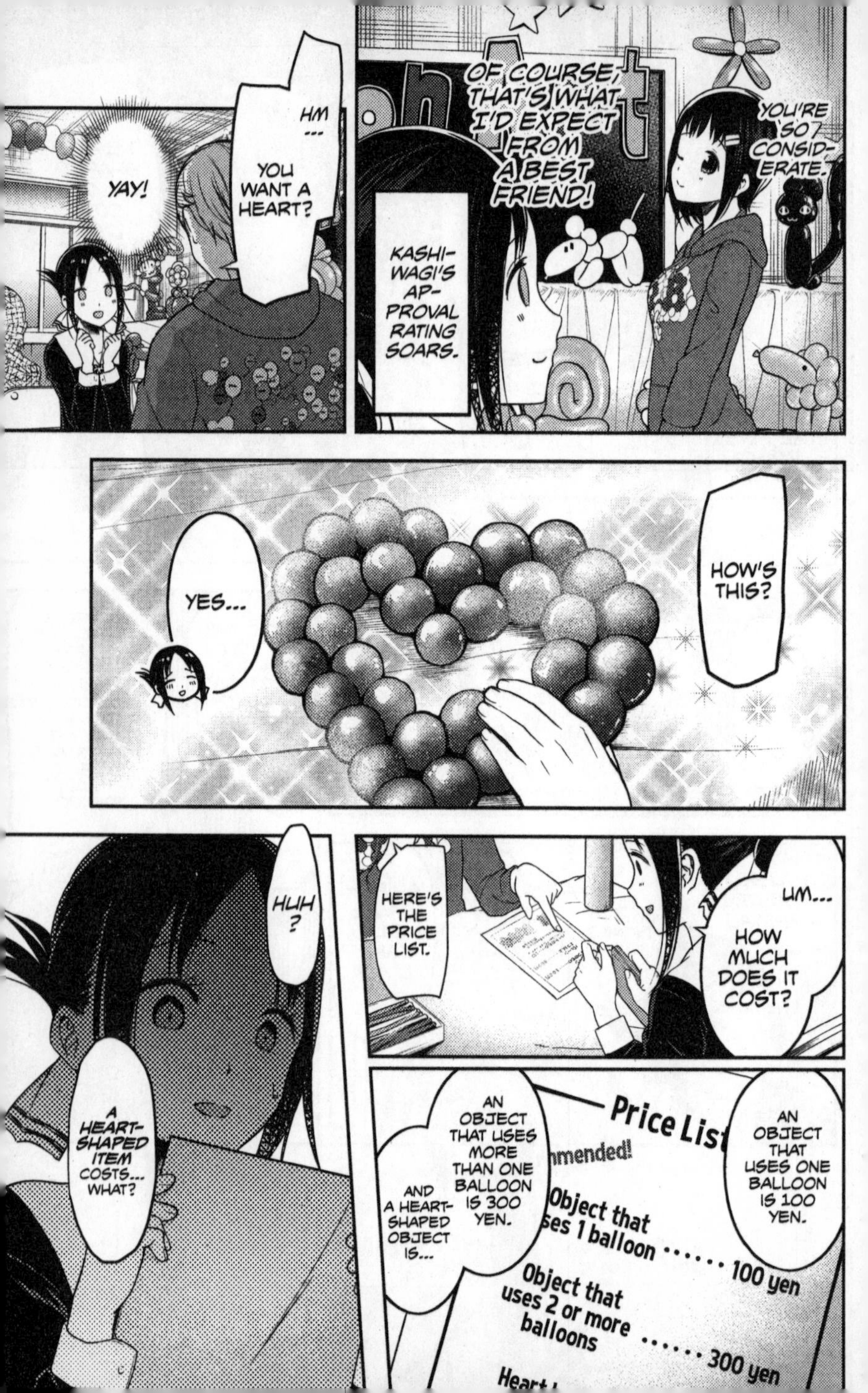
YOU'RE SO CONSIDERATE.
OF COURSE, THAT'S WHAT I'D EXPECT FROM A BEST FRIEND!
KASHIWAGI'S APPROVAL RATING SOARS.
HM... YOU WANT A HEART?
YAY!
HOW'S THIS?
YES...
UM... HOW MUCH DOES IT COST?
HERE'S THE PRICE LIST.
AN OBJECT THAT USES ONE BALLOON IS 100 YEN.
AN OBJECT THAT USES MORE THAN ONE BALLOON IS 300 YEN.
AND A HEART-SHAPED OBJECT IS...
Price List
mmended!
Object that ses 1 balloon ...... 100 yen
Object that uses 2 or more balloons ...... 300 yen
Heart
HUH?
A HEART-SHAPED ITEM COSTS... WHAT?

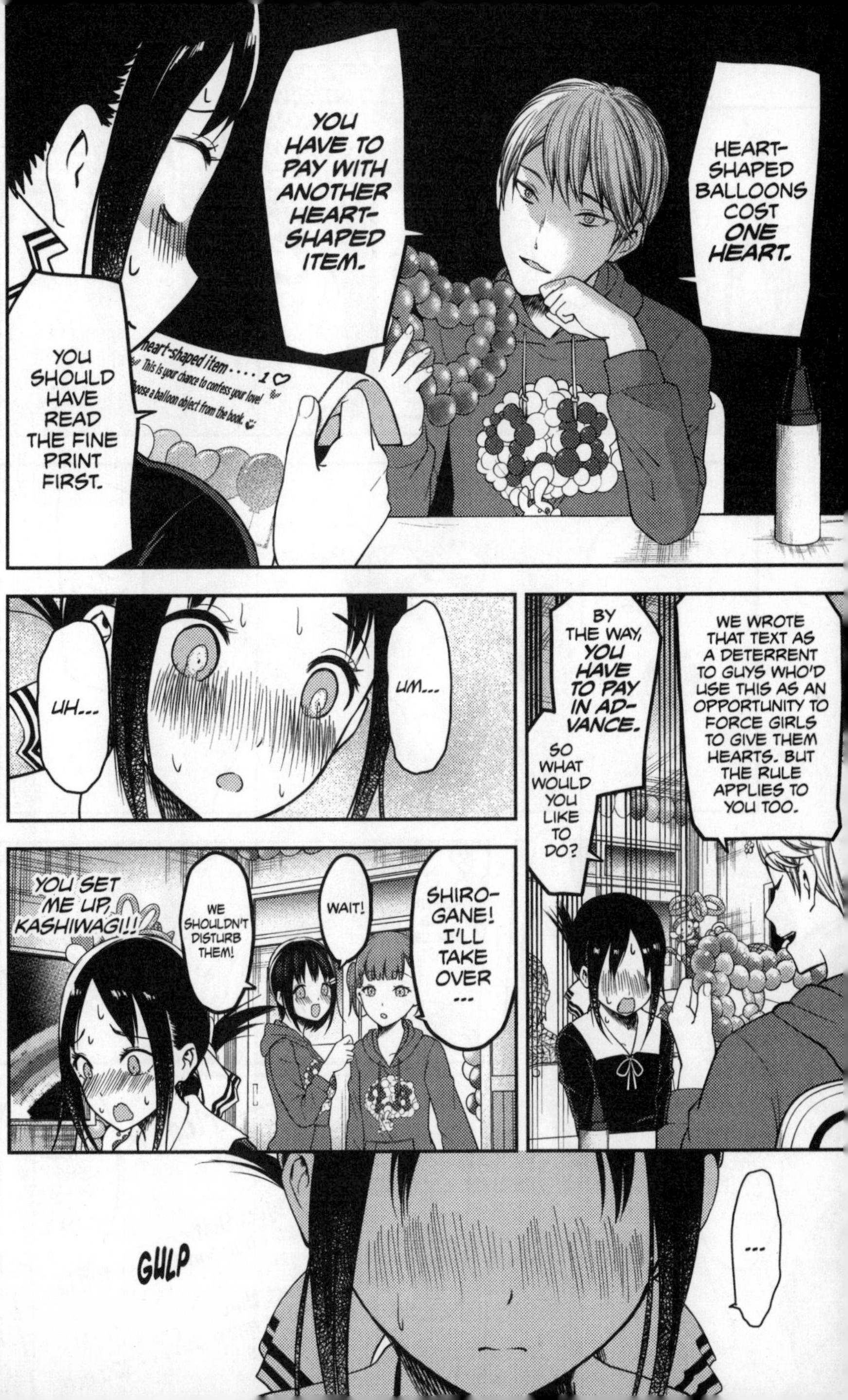
HEART-SHAPED BALLOONS COST ONE HEART.
YOU HAVE TO PAY WITH ANOTHER HEART-SHAPED ITEM.
heart-shaped item ···· 1 ♡
This is your chance to confess your love!
oose a balloon object from the book.
YOU SHOULD HAVE READ THE FINE PRINT FIRST.
WE WROTE THAT TEXT AS A DETERRENT TO GUYS WHO'D USE THIS AS AN OPPORTUNITY TO FORCE GIRLS TO GIVE THEM HEARTS. BUT THE RULE APPLIES TO YOU TOO.
BY THE WAY, YOU HAVE TO PAY IN ADVANCE.
SO WHAT WOULD YOU LIKE TO DO?
UM...
UH...
SHIRO-GANE! I'LL TAKE OVER...
WAIT!
WE SHOULDN'T DISTURB THEM!
YOU SET ME UP, KASHIWAGI!!!
...
GULP

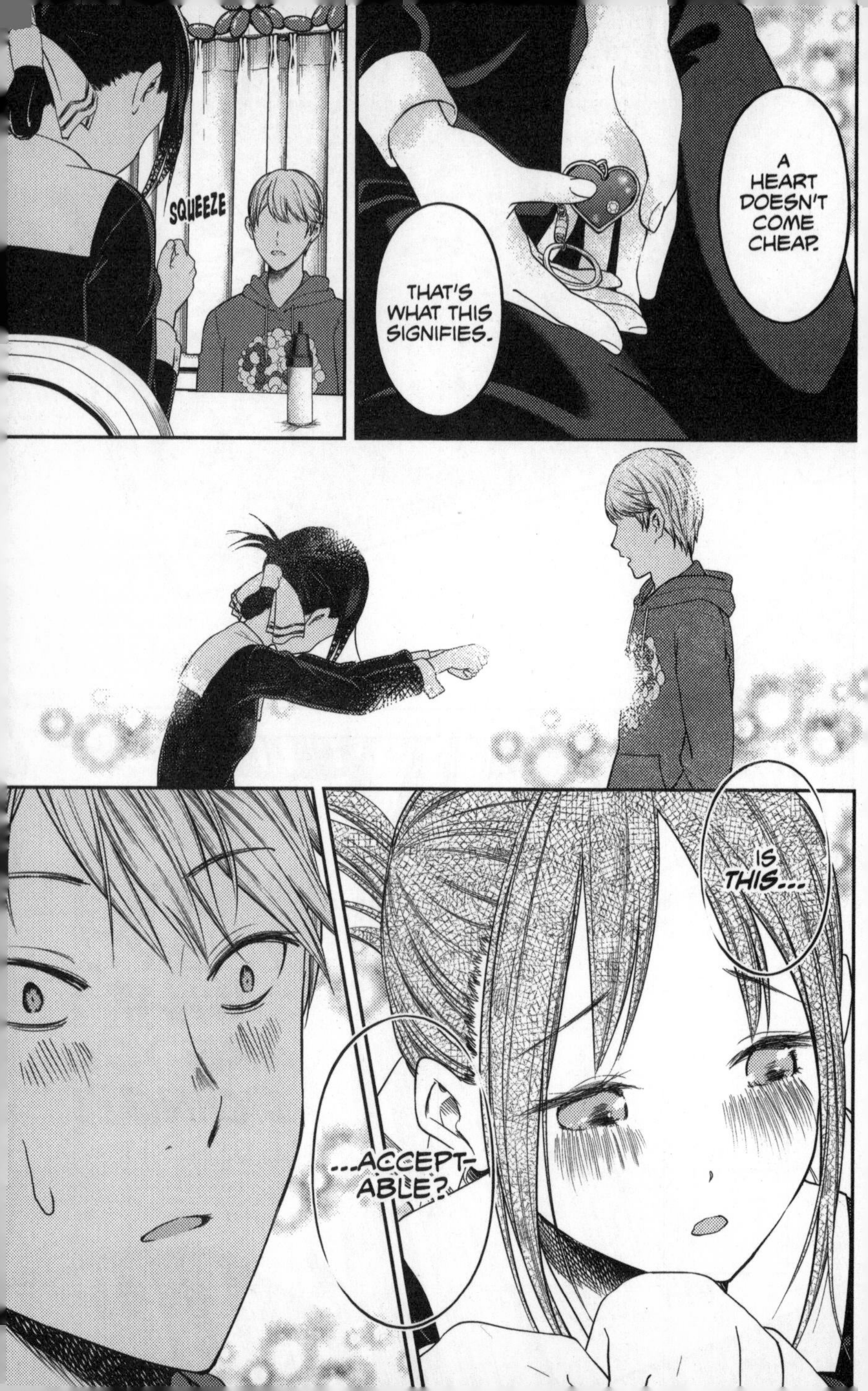
A HEART DOESN'T COME CHEAP.
THAT'S WHAT THIS SIGNIFIES.
SQUEEZE
IS THIS...
...ACCEPT-ABLE?

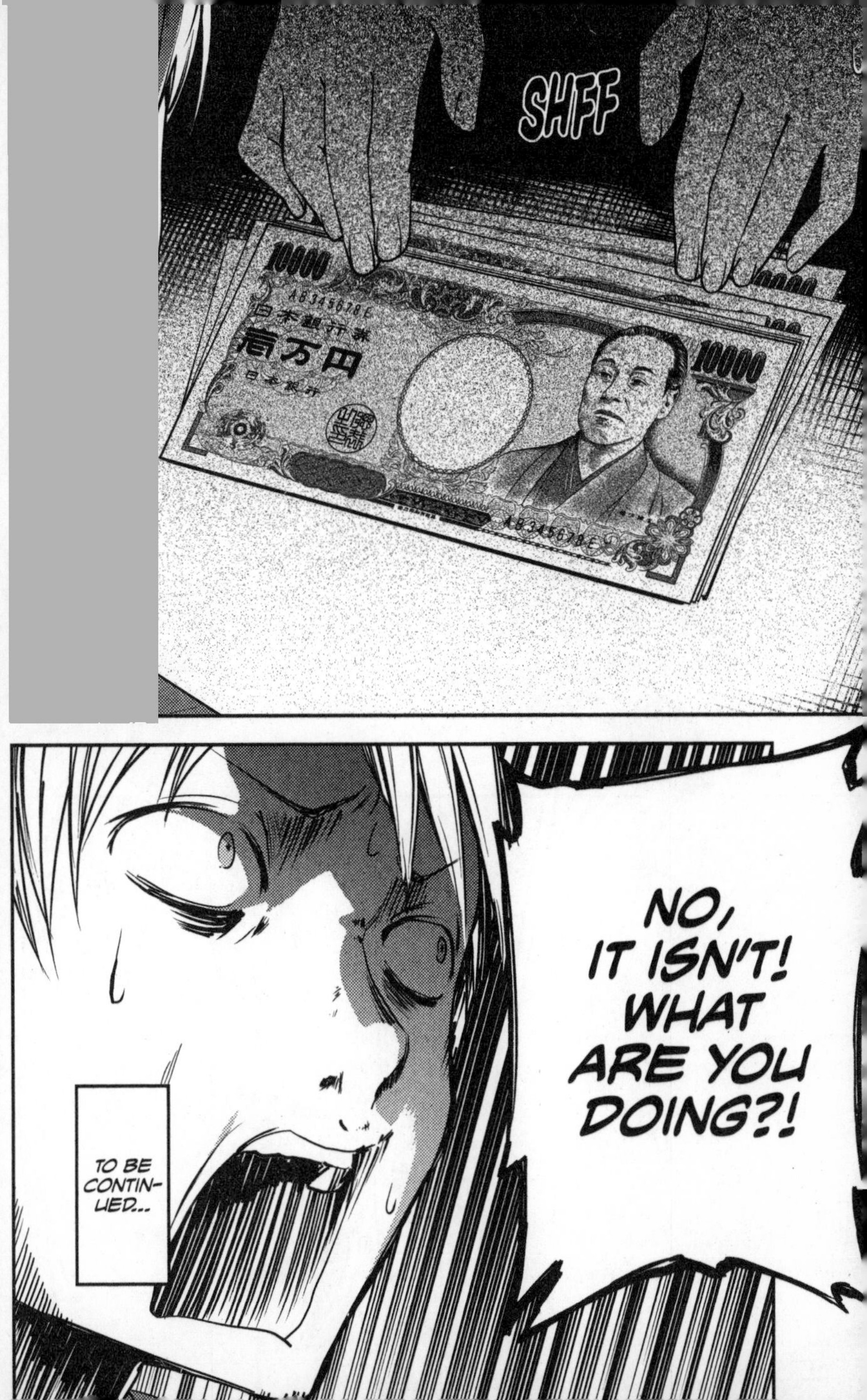
SHFF
10000
日本銀行券
壱万円
日本銀行
NO, IT ISN'T! WHAT ARE YOU DOING?!
TO BE CONTIN-UED...

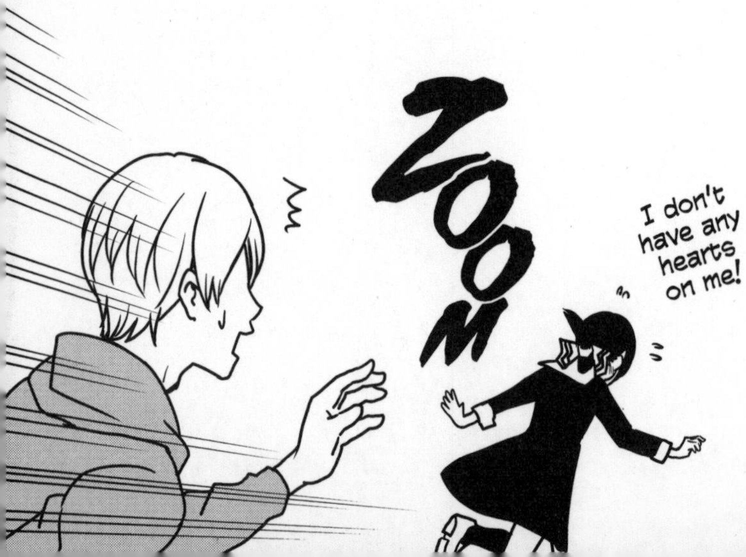
ZOOM
I don't have any hearts on me!

KAGUYA-SAMA

LOVE IS WAR

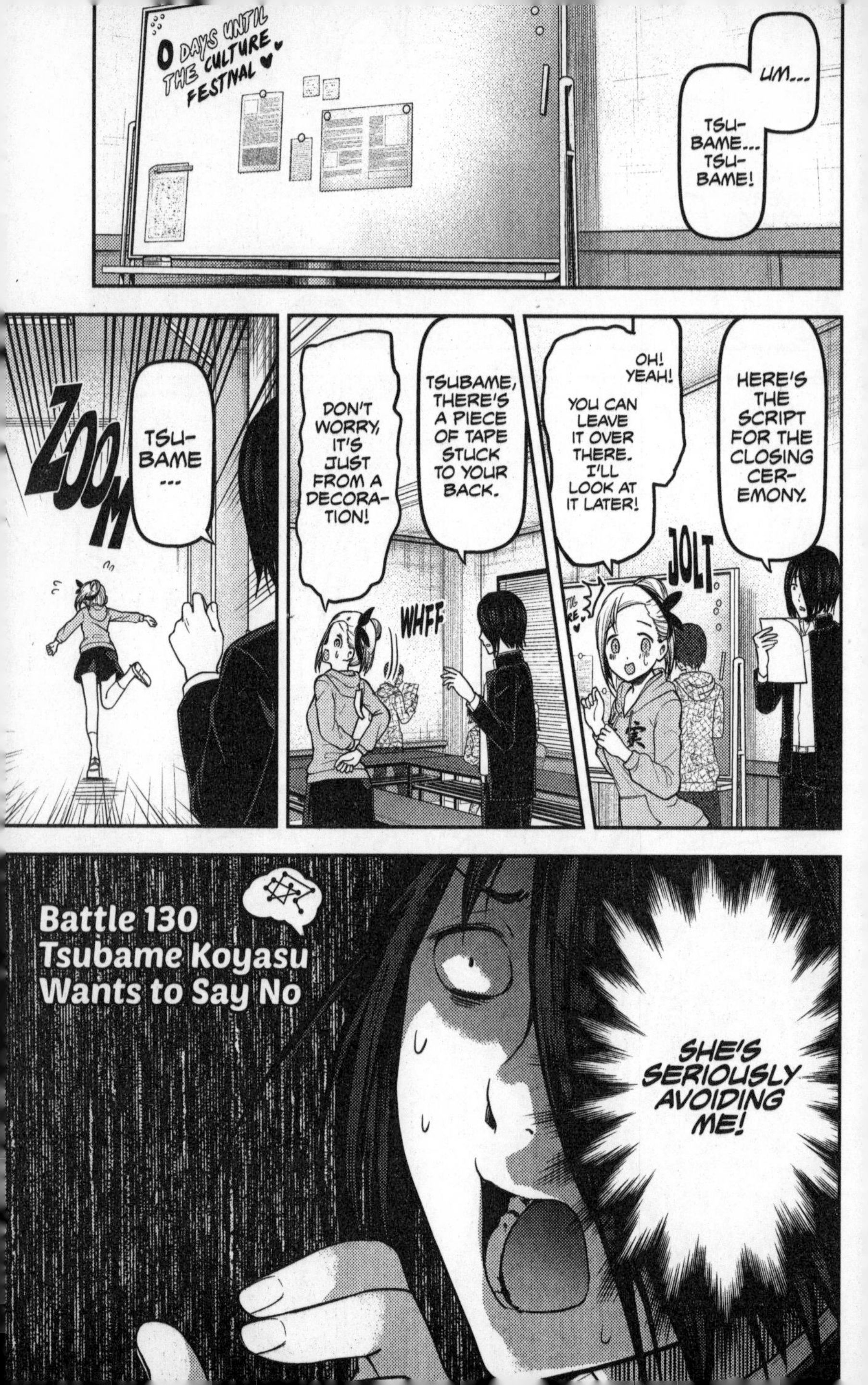
UM...
TSU-BAME... TSU-BAME!
0 DAYS UNTIL THE CULTURE FESTIVAL ♥
HERE'S THE SCRIPT FOR THE CLOSING CER-EMONY.
OH! YEAH!
YOU CAN LEAVE IT OVER THERE. I'LL LOOK AT IT LATER!
JOLT
TSUBAME, THERE'S A PIECE OF TAPE STUCK TO YOUR BACK.
DON'T WORRY, IT'S JUST FROM A DECORA-TION!
WHFF
TSU-BAME...
ZOOM
Battle 130
Tsubame Koyasu
Wants to Say No
SHE'S SERIOUSLY AVOIDING ME!

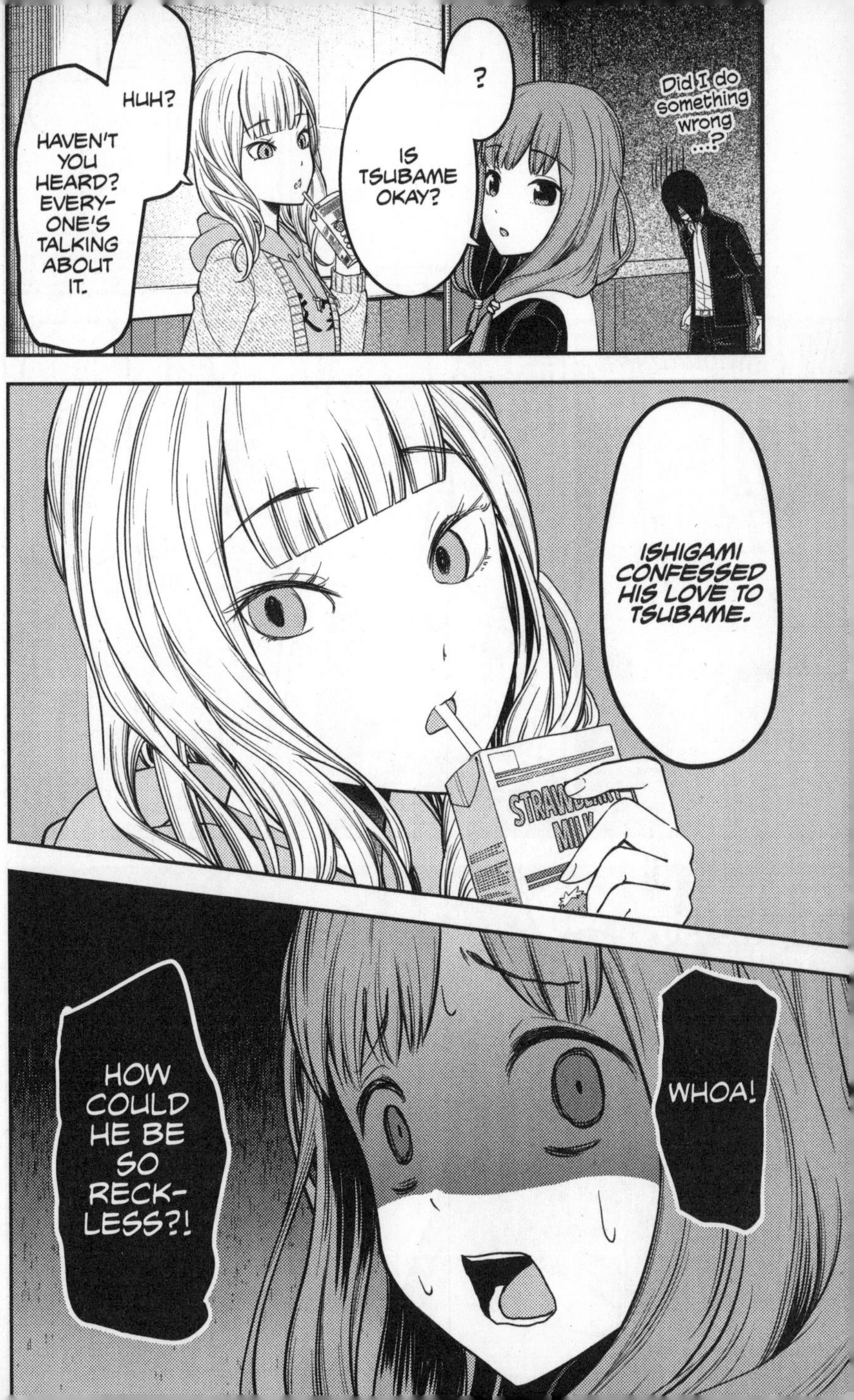
Did I do something wrong ...?
?
IS TSUBAME OKAY?
HUH?
HAVEN'T YOU HEARD? EVERY-ONE'S TALKING ABOUT IT.
ISHIGAMI CONFESSED HIS LOVE TO TSUBAME.
STRAWBERRY MILK
WHOA!
HOW COULD HE BE SO RECK-LESS?!

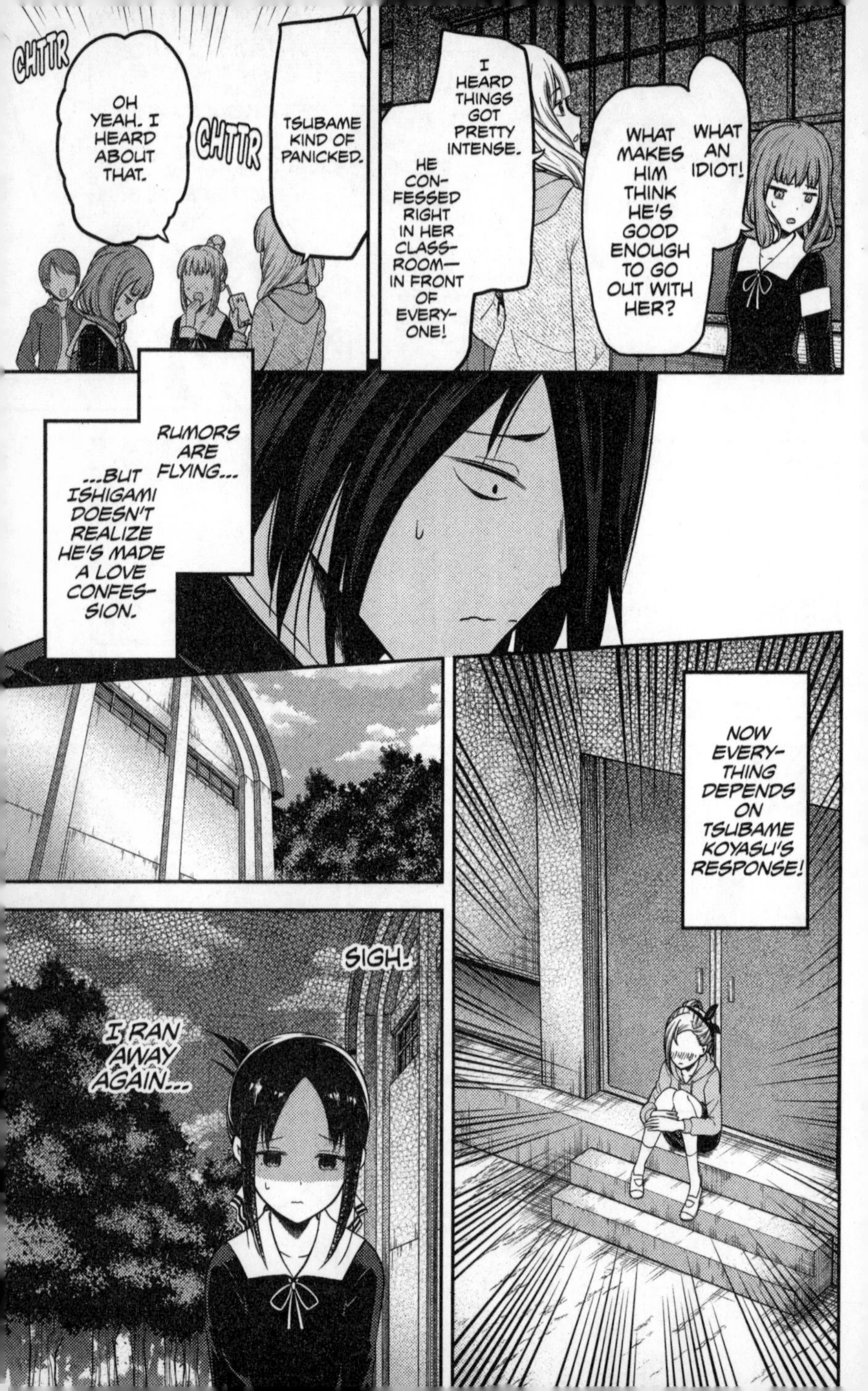
WHAT AN IDIOT!
WHAT MAKES HIM THINK HE'S GOOD ENOUGH TO GO OUT WITH HER?
I HEARD THINGS GOT PRETTY INTENSE.
HE CONFESSED RIGHT IN HER CLASSROOM—IN FRONT OF EVERYONE!
TSUBAME KIND OF PANICKED.
CHTTR
OH YEAH. I HEARD ABOUT THAT.
CHTTR
RUMORS ARE FLYING...
...BUT ISHIGAMI DOESN'T REALIZE HE'S MADE A LOVE CONFESSION.
NOW EVERYTHING DEPENDS ON TSUBAME KOYASU'S RESPONSE!
SIGH.
I RAN AWAY AGAIN...

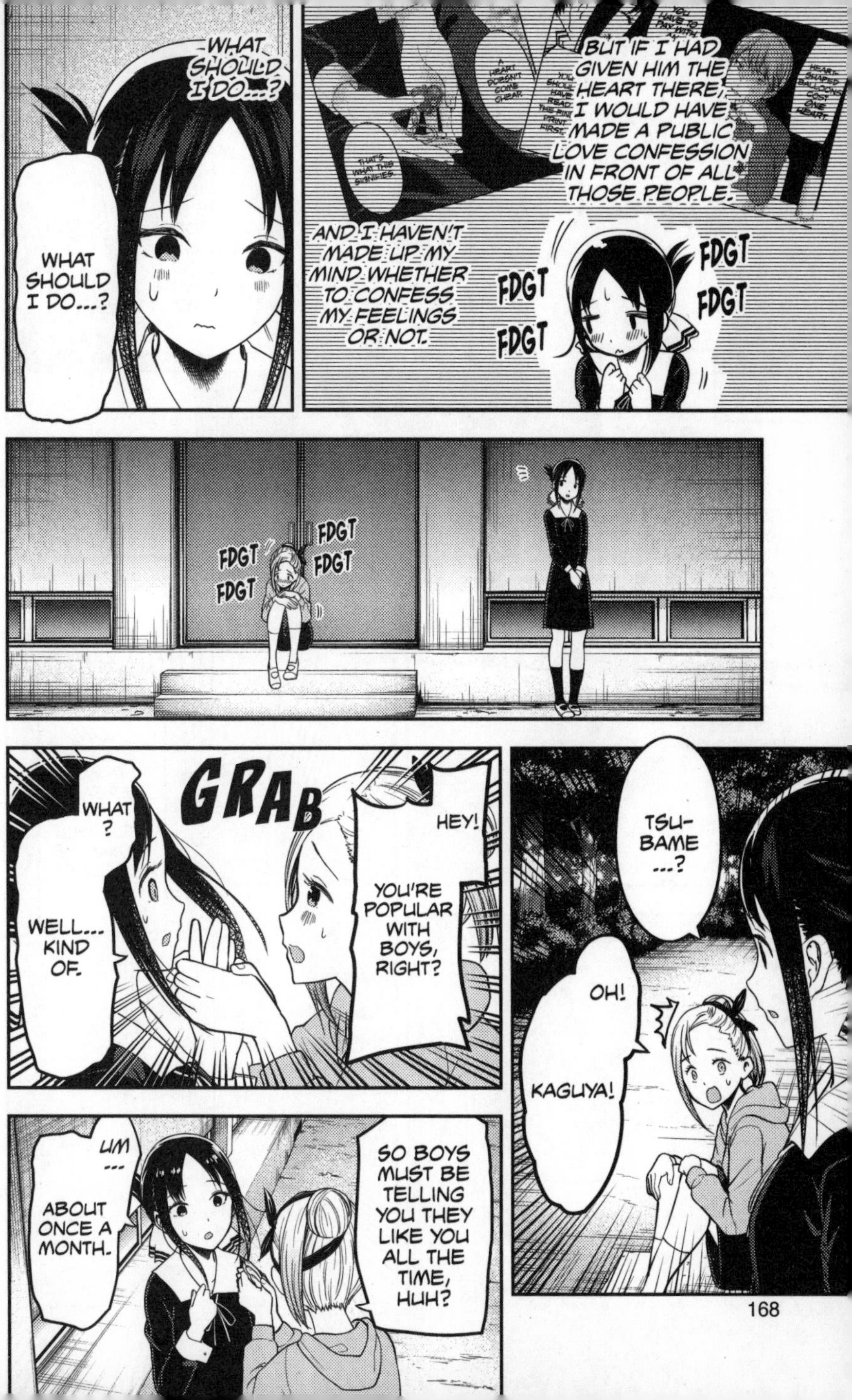
HEART-SHAPED BALLOONS COST ONE HEART.
YOU HAVE TO PAY WITH
A HEART DOESN'T COME CHEAP.
THAT'S WHAT THIS SIGNIFIES
BUT IF I HAD GIVEN HIM THE HEART THERE, I WOULD HAVE MADE A PUBLIC LOVE CONFESSION IN FRONT OF ALL THOSE PEOPLE.
AND I HAVEN'T MADE UP MY MIND WHETHER TO CONFESS MY FEELINGS OR NOT.
FDGT
FDGT
FDGT
FDGT
WHAT SHOULD I DO...?
WHAT SHOULD I DO...?
FDGT
FDGT
FDGT
TSU-BAME...?
OH!
KAGUYA!
GRAB
HEY!
YOU'RE POPULAR WITH BOYS, RIGHT?
WHAT?
WELL... KIND OF.
SO BOYS MUST BE TELLING YOU THEY LIKE YOU ALL THE TIME, HUH?
UM...
ABOUT ONCE A MONTH.

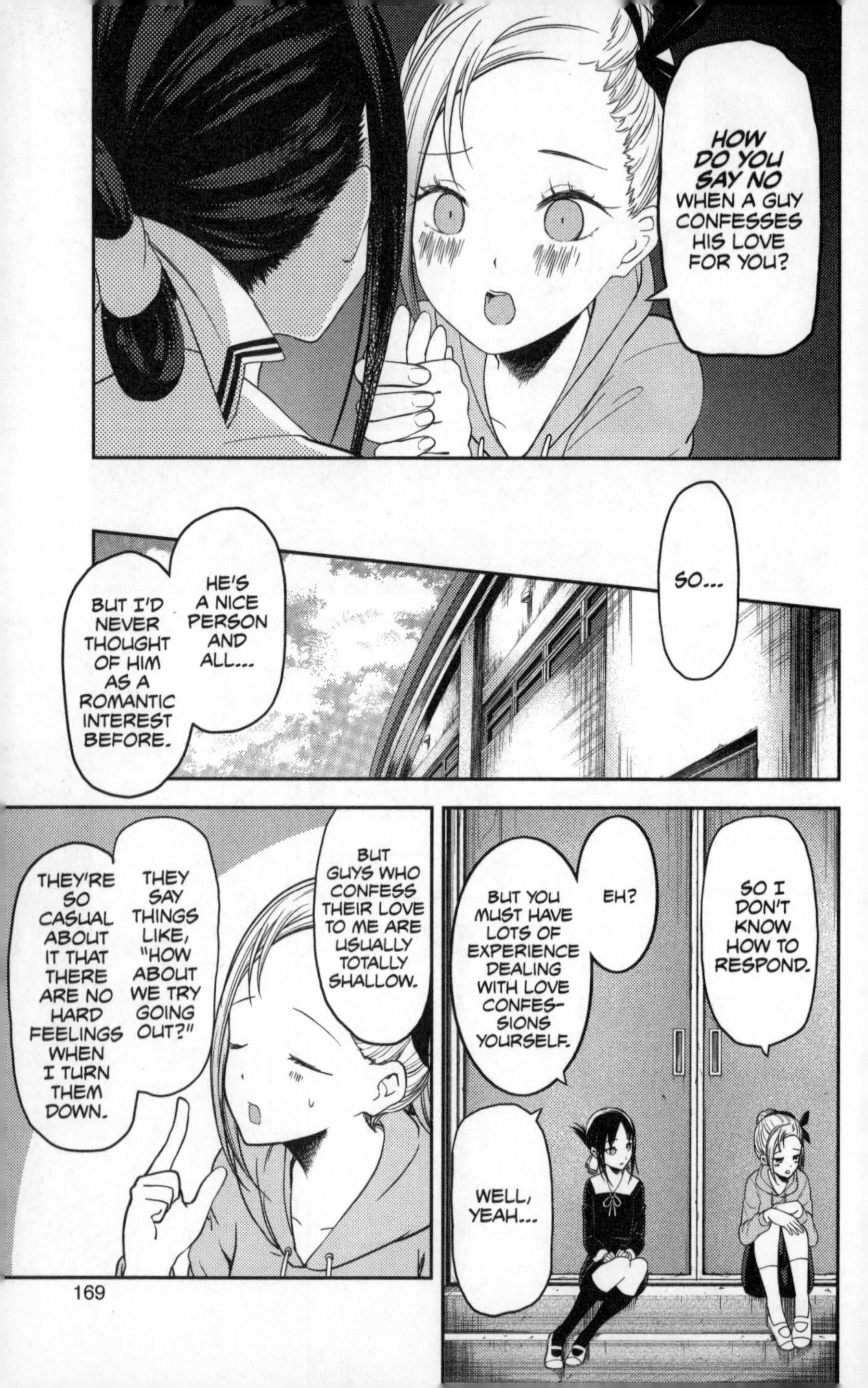
HOW DO YOU SAY NO WHEN A GUY CONFESSES HIS LOVE FOR YOU?
SO...
HE'S A NICE PERSON AND ALL...
BUT I'D NEVER THOUGHT OF HIM AS A ROMANTIC INTEREST BEFORE.
SO I DON'T KNOW HOW TO RESPOND.
EH?
BUT YOU MUST HAVE LOTS OF EXPERIENCE DEALING WITH LOVE CONFES-SIONS YOURSELF.
WELL, YEAH...
BUT GUYS WHO CONFESS THEIR LOVE TO ME ARE USUALLY TOTALLY SHALLOW.
THEY SAY THINGS LIKE, "HOW ABOUT WE TRY GOING OUT?"
THEY'RE SO CASUAL ABOUT IT THAT THERE ARE NO HARD FEELINGS WHEN I TURN THEM DOWN.

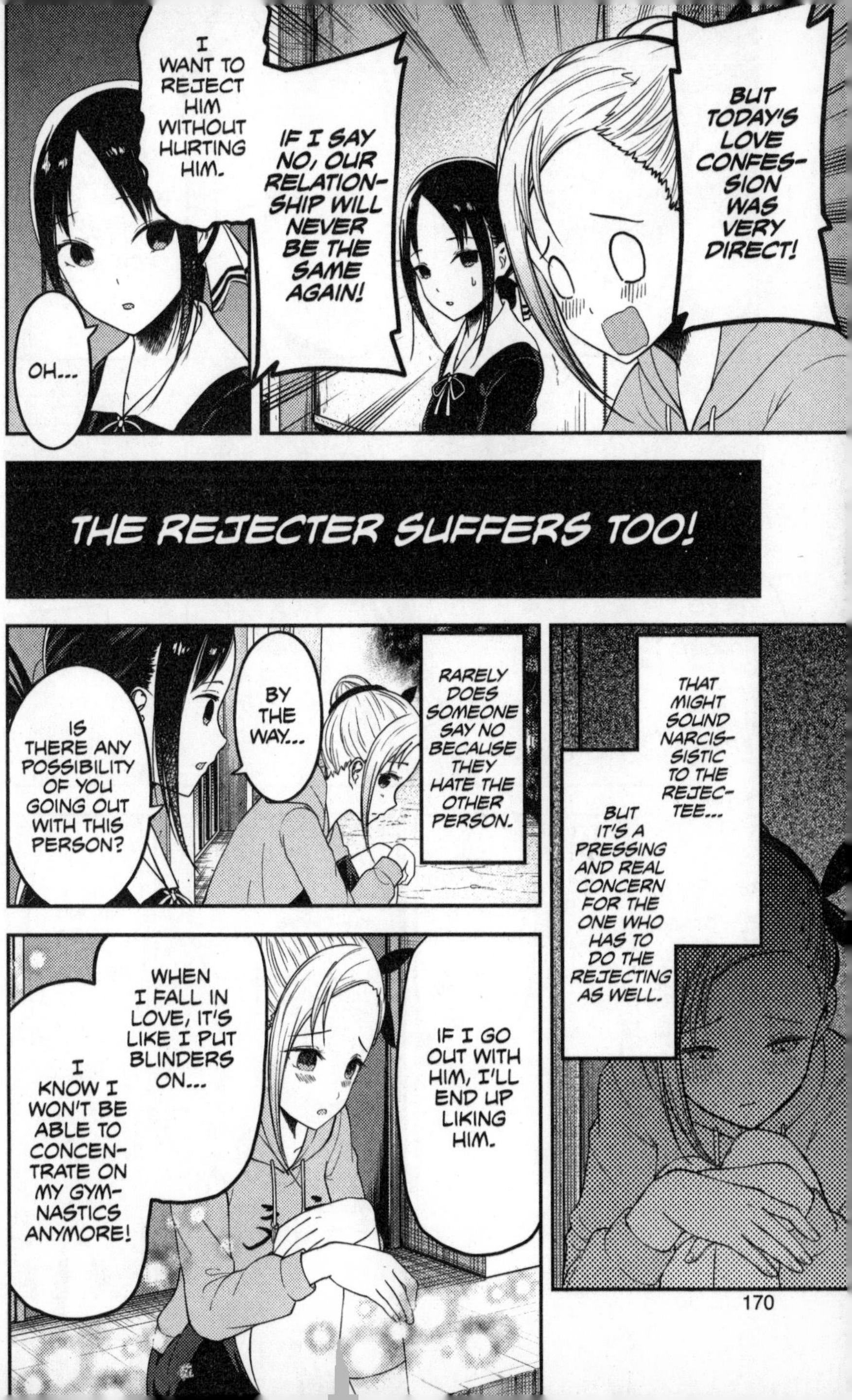
BUT TODAY'S LOVE CONFESSION WAS VERY DIRECT!
IF I SAY NO, OUR RELATIONSHIP WILL NEVER BE THE SAME AGAIN!
I WANT TO REJECT HIM WITHOUT HURTING HIM.
OH...
THE REJECTER SUFFERS TOO!
THAT MIGHT SOUND NARCISSISTIC TO THE REJECTEE...
BUT IT'S A PRESSING AND REAL CONCERN FOR THE ONE WHO HAS TO DO THE REJECTING AS WELL.
RARELY DOES SOMEONE SAY NO BECAUSE THEY HATE THE OTHER PERSON.
BY THE WAY...
IS THERE ANY POSSIBILITY OF YOU GOING OUT WITH THIS PERSON?
IF I GO OUT WITH HIM, I'LL END UP LIKING HIM.
WHEN I FALL IN LOVE, IT'S LIKE I PUT BLINDERS ON...
I KNOW I WON'T BE ABLE TO CONCENTRATE ON MY GYMNASTICS ANYMORE!

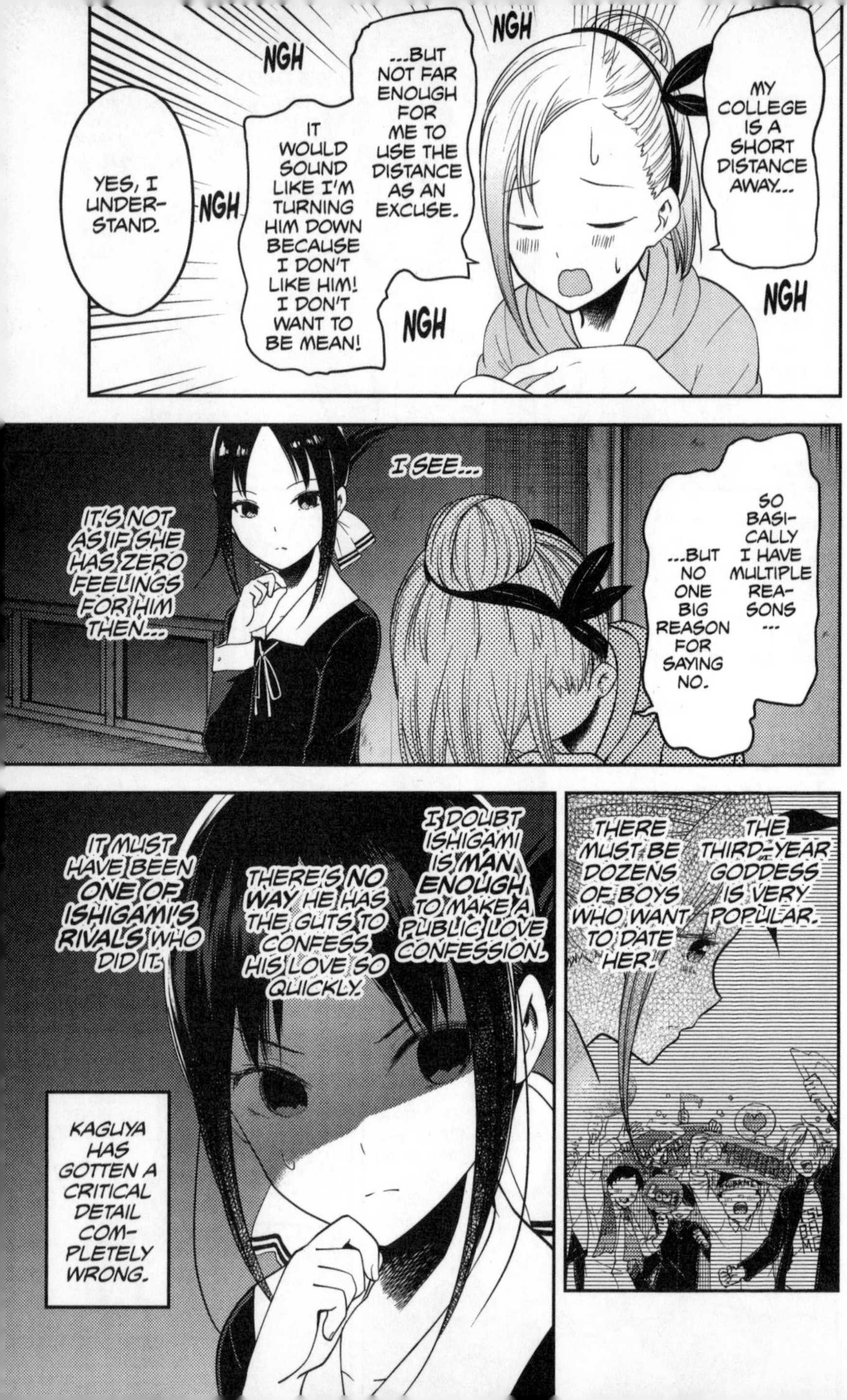
NGH
MY COLLEGE IS A SHORT DISTANCE AWAY...
NGH
...BUT NOT FAR ENOUGH FOR ME TO USE THE DISTANCE AS AN EXCUSE.
IT WOULD SOUND LIKE I'M TURNING HIM DOWN BECAUSE I DON'T LIKE HIM! I DON'T WANT TO BE MEAN!
NGH
NGH
NGH
YES, I UNDER-STAND.
SO BASI-CALLY I HAVE MULTIPLE REA-SONS ...
...BUT NO ONE BIG REASON FOR SAYING NO.
I SEE...
IT'S NOT AS IF SHE HAS ZERO FEELINGS FOR HIM THEN...
THE THIRD-YEAR GODDESS IS VERY POPULAR.
THERE MUST BE DOZENS OF BOYS WHO WANT TO DATE HER.
I DOUBT ISHIGAMI IS MAN ENOUGH TO MAKE A PUBLIC LOVE CONFESSION.
THERE'S NO WAY HE HAS THE GUTS TO CONFESS HIS LOVE SO QUICKLY.
IT MUST HAVE BEEN ONE OF ISHIGAMI'S RIVALS WHO DID IT.
KAGUYA HAS GOTTEN A CRITICAL DETAIL COM-PLETELY WRONG.

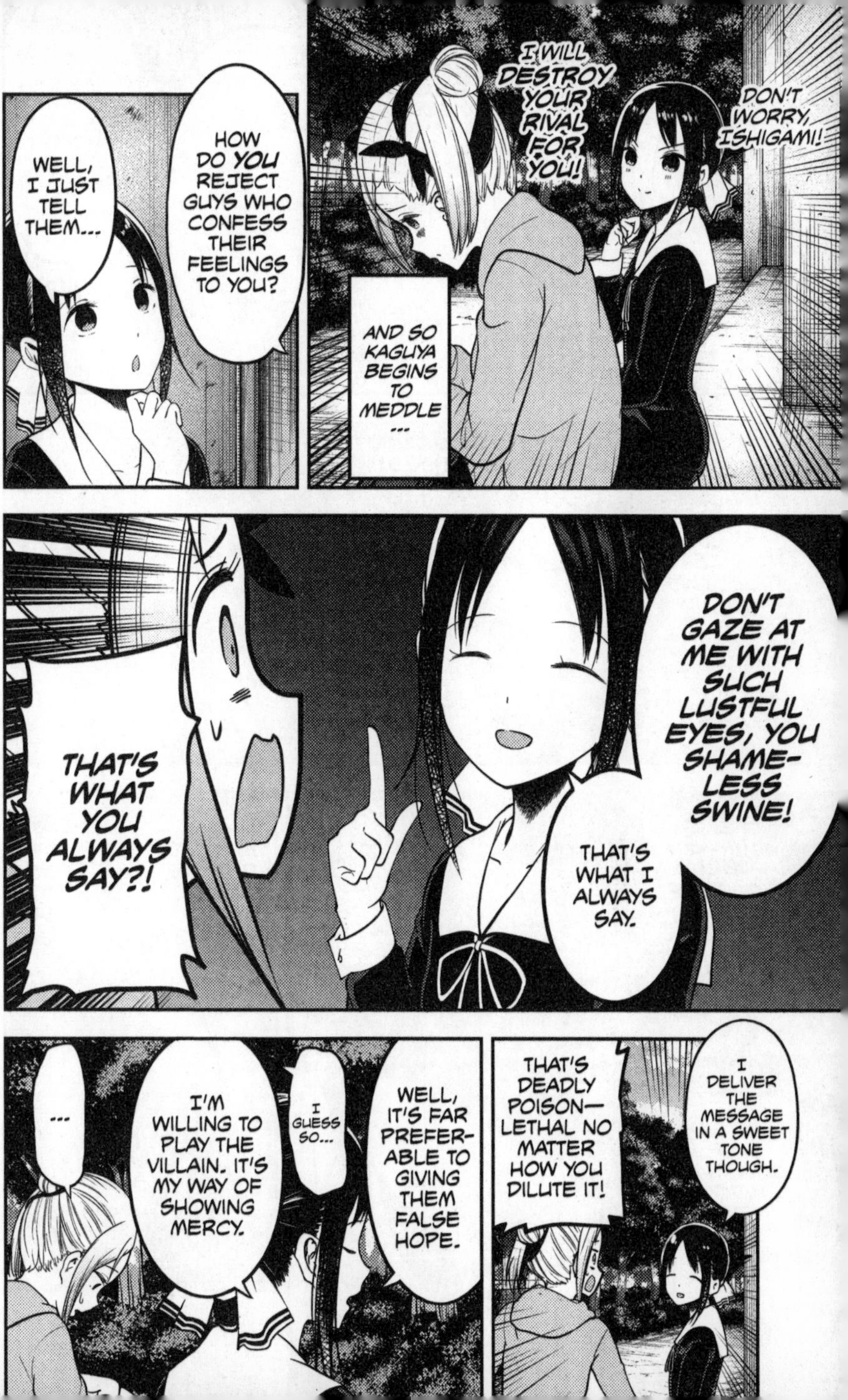
DON'T WORRY, ISHIGAMI!
I WILL DESTROY YOUR RIVAL FOR YOU!
AND SO KAGUYA BEGINS TO MEDDLE...
HOW DO YOU REJECT GUYS WHO CONFESS THEIR FEELINGS TO YOU?
WELL, I JUST TELL THEM...
DON'T GAZE AT ME WITH SUCH LUSTFUL EYES, YOU SHAMELESS SWINE!
THAT'S WHAT I ALWAYS SAY.
THAT'S WHAT YOU ALWAYS SAY?!
I DELIVER THE MESSAGE IN A SWEET TONE THOUGH.
THAT'S DEADLY POISON—LETHAL NO MATTER HOW YOU DILUTE IT!
WELL, IT'S FAR PREFERABLE TO GIVING THEM FALSE HOPE.
I GUESS SO...
I'M WILLING TO PLAY THE VILLAIN. IT'S MY WAY OF SHOWING MERCY.
...

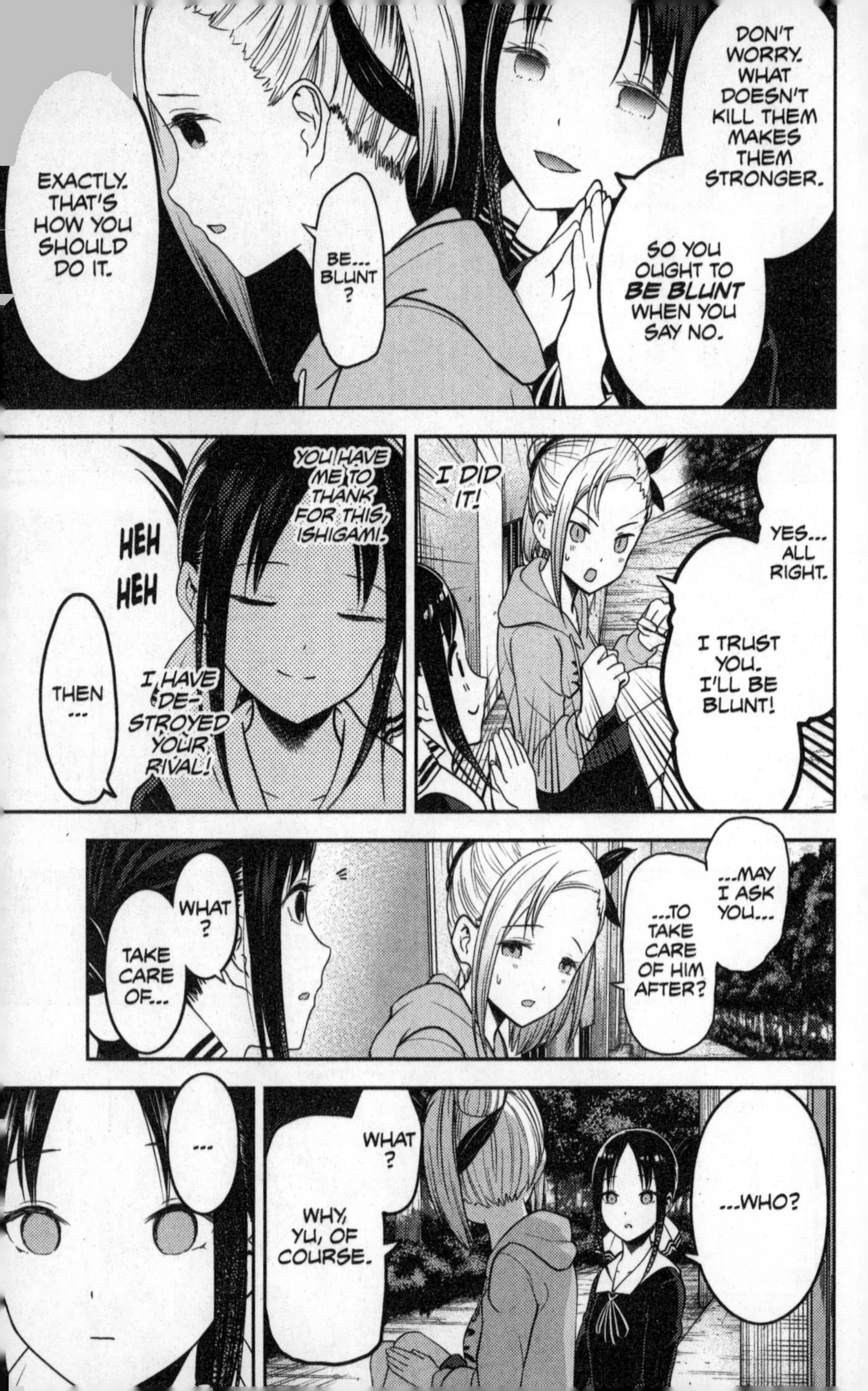
DON'T WORRY. WHAT DOESN'T KILL THEM MAKES THEM STRONGER.
SO YOU OUGHT TO **BE BLUNT** WHEN YOU SAY NO.
BE... BLUNT?
EXACTLY. THAT'S HOW YOU SHOULD DO IT.
YES... ALL RIGHT.
I TRUST YOU. I'LL BE BLUNT!
I DID IT!
YOU HAVE ME TO THANK FOR THIS, ISHIGAMI!
HEH HEH
I HAVE DE-STROYED YOUR RIVAL!
THEN...
...MAY I ASK YOU...
...TO TAKE CARE OF HIM AFTER?
WHAT?
TAKE CARE OF...
...WHO?
WHAT?
WHY, YU, OF COURSE.
...

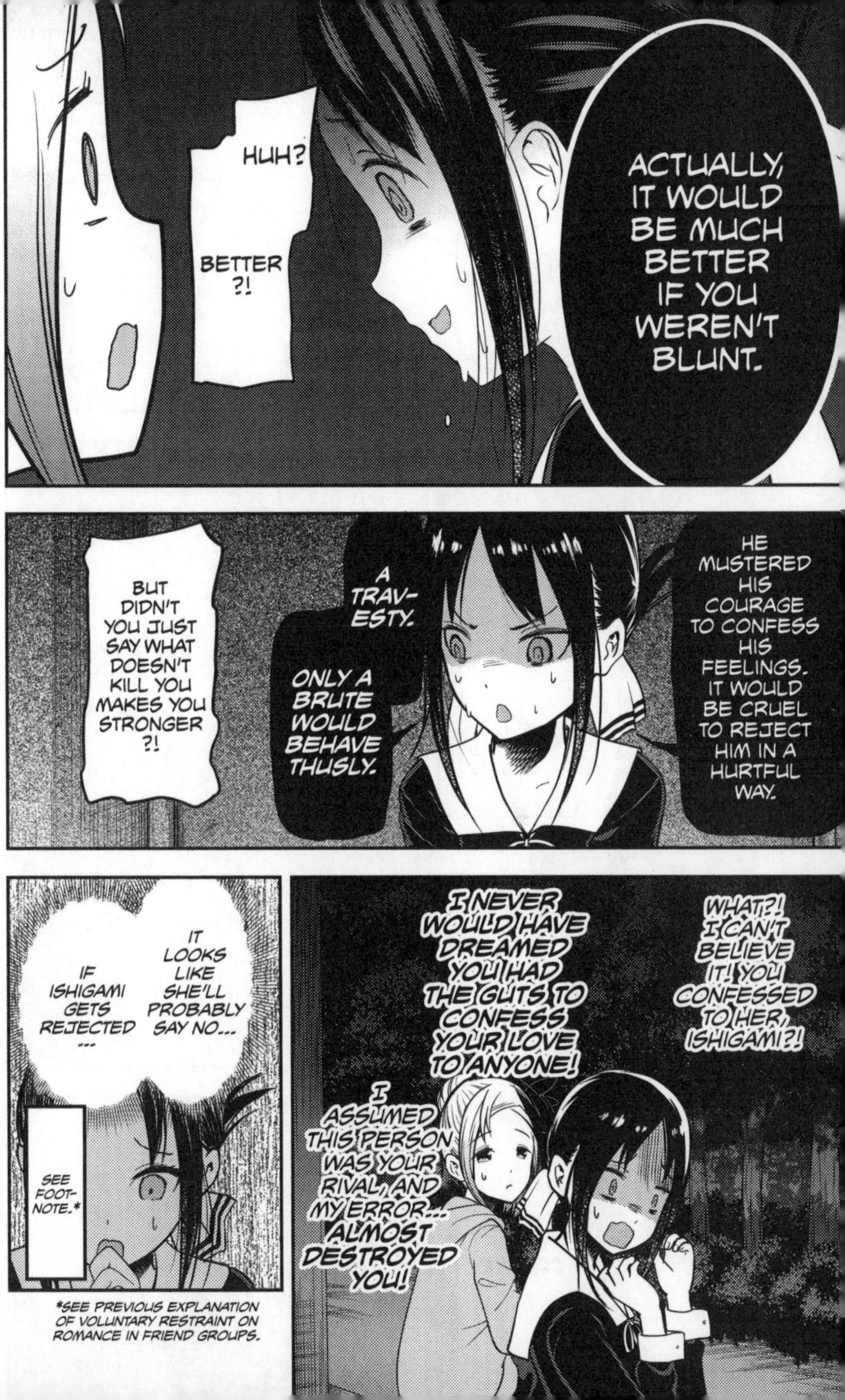
ACTUALLY, IT WOULD BE MUCH BETTER IF YOU WEREN'T BLUNT.
HUH?
BETTER ?!
HE MUSTERED HIS COURAGE TO CONFESS HIS FEELINGS. IT WOULD BE CRUEL TO REJECT HIM IN A HURTFUL WAY.
A TRAV-ESTY.
ONLY A BRUTE WOULD BEHAVE THUSLY.
BUT DIDN'T YOU JUST SAY WHAT DOESN'T KILL YOU MAKES YOU STRONGER ?!
WHAT?! I CAN'T BELIEVE IT! YOU CONFESSED TO HER, ISHIGAMI?!
I NEVER WOULD HAVE DREAMED YOU HAD THE GUTS TO CONFESS YOUR LOVE TO ANYONE!
I ASSUMED THIS PERSON WAS YOUR RIVAL, AND MY ERROR... ALMOST DESTROYED YOU!
IT LOOKS LIKE SHE'LL PROBABLY SAY NO...
IF ISHIGAMI GETS REJECTED ...
SEE FOOT-NOTE.*

*SEE PREVIOUS EXPLANATION OF VOLUNTARY RESTRAINT ON ROMANCE IN FRIEND GROUPS.

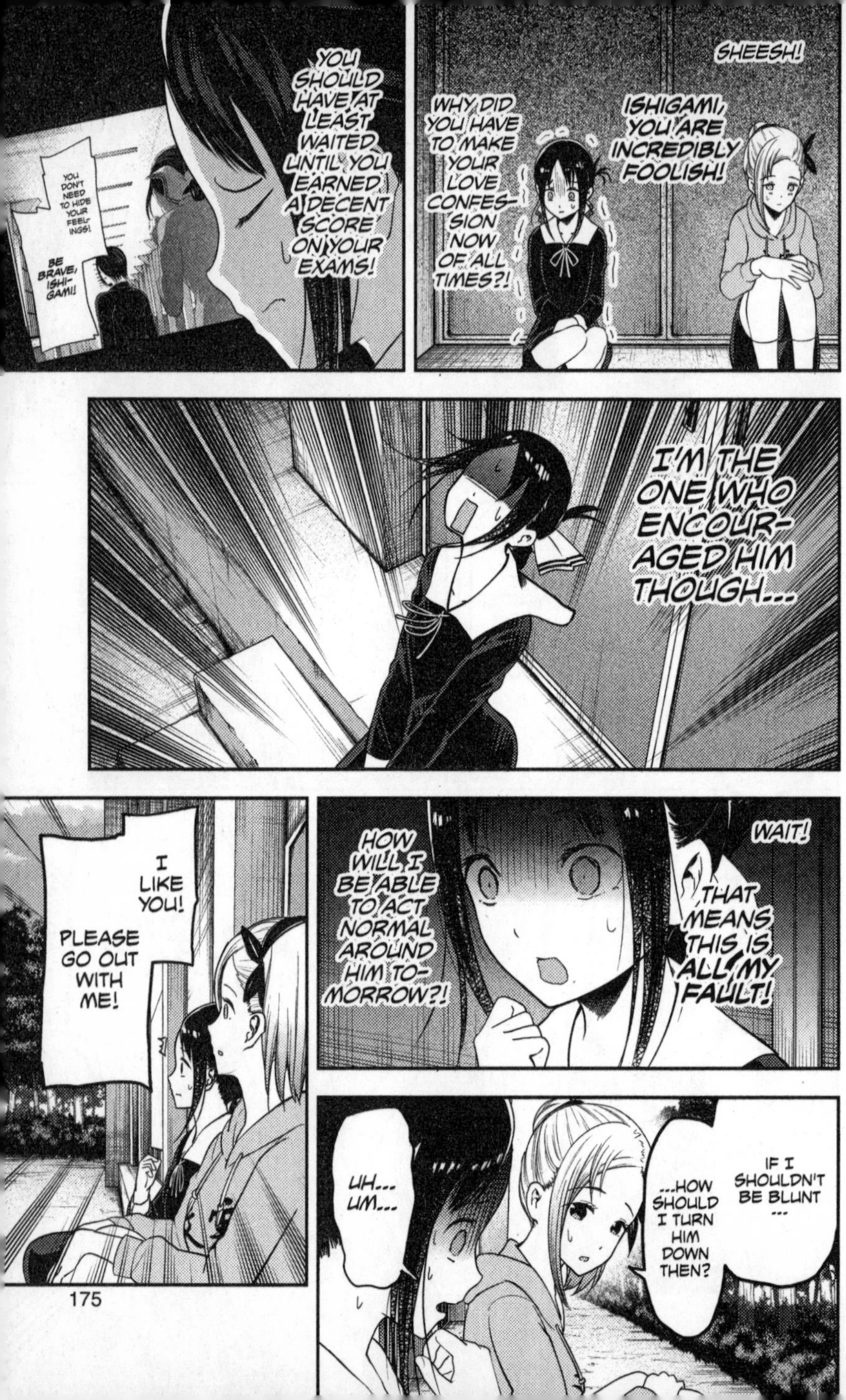
SHEESH!
ISHIGAMI, YOU ARE INCREDIBLY FOOLISH!
WHY DID YOU HAVE TO MAKE YOUR LOVE CONFESSION NOW OF ALL TIMES?!
YOU SHOULD HAVE AT LEAST WAITED UNTIL YOU EARNED A DECENT SCORE ON YOUR EXAMS!
YOU DON'T NEED TO HIDE YOUR FEELINGS!
BE BRAVE, ISHIGAMI!
I'M THE ONE WHO ENCOURAGED HIM THOUGH...
WAIT!
THAT MEANS THIS IS ALL MY FAULT!
HOW WILL I BE ABLE TO ACT NORMAL AROUND HIM TOMORROW?!
IF I SHOULDN'T BE BLUNT...
...HOW SHOULD I TURN HIM DOWN THEN?
UH... UM...
I LIKE YOU!
PLEASE GO OUT WITH ME!

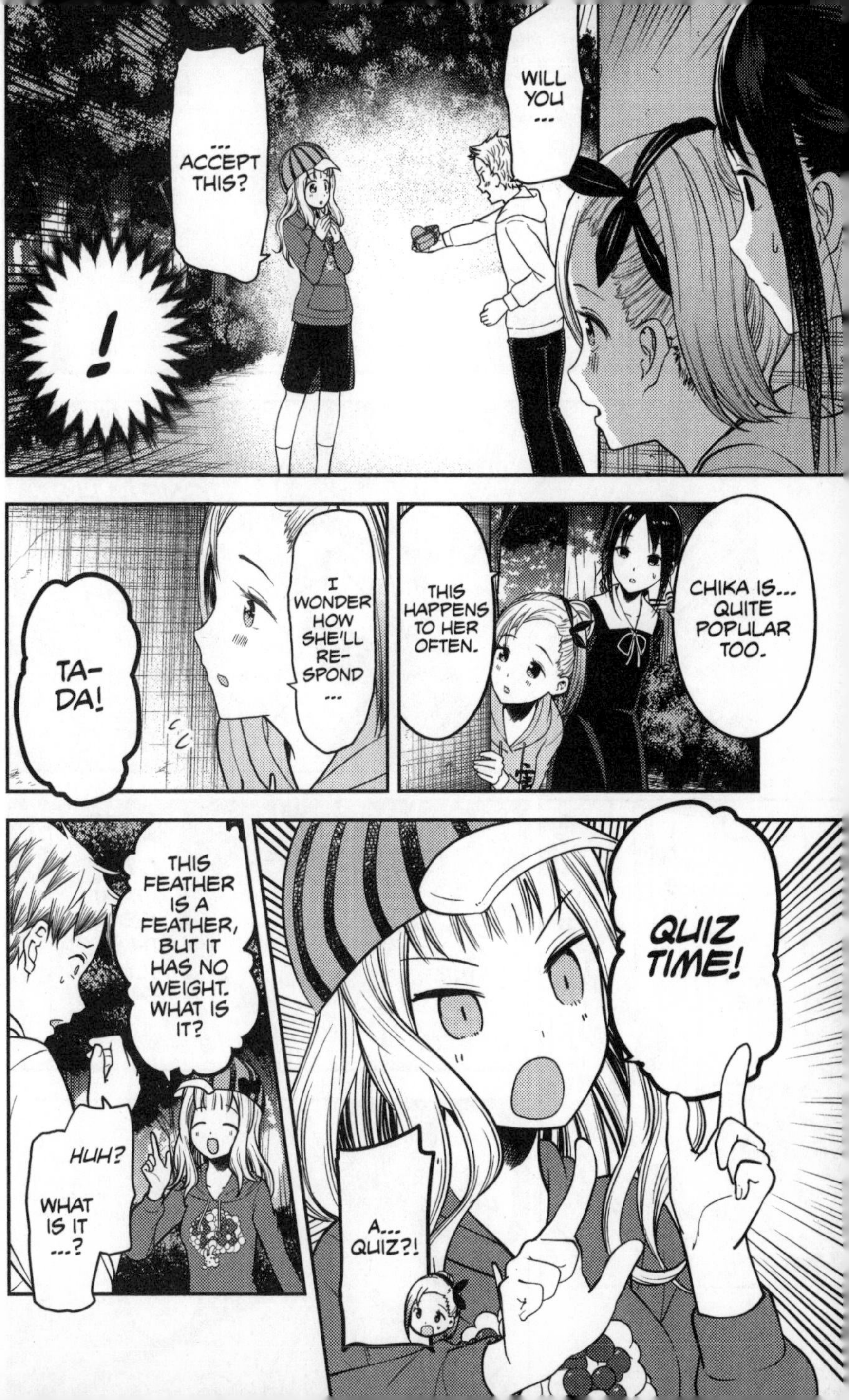
WILL YOU ...
...ACCEPT THIS?
!
CHIKA IS... QUITE POPULAR TOO.
THIS HAPPENS TO HER OFTEN.
I WONDER HOW SHE'LL RE-SPOND ...
TA-DA!
QUIZ TIME!
A... QUIZ?!
THIS FEATHER IS A FEATHER, BUT IT HAS NO WEIGHT. WHAT IS IT?
HUH?
WHAT IS IT ...?

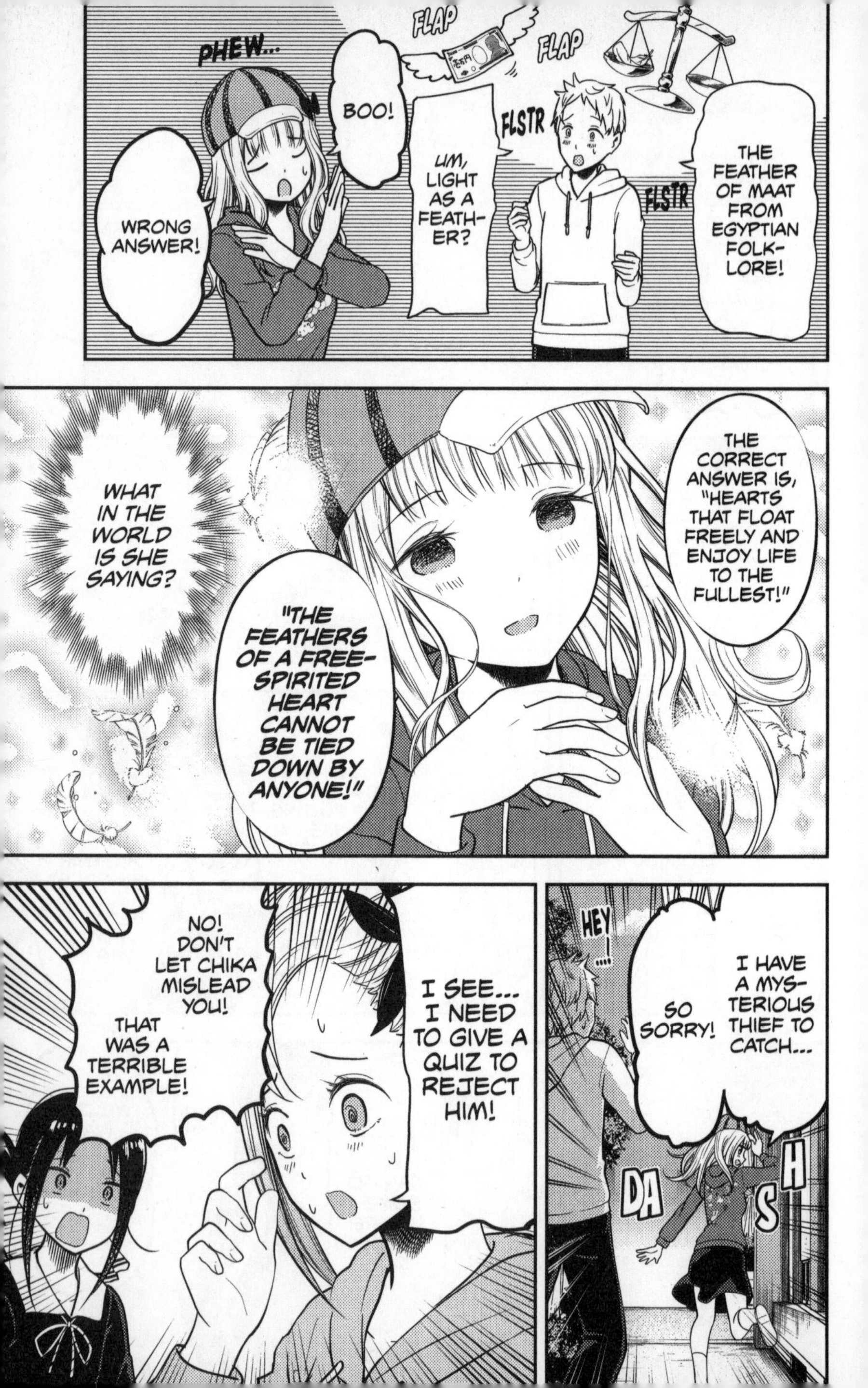
FLAP
FLAP
THE FEATHER OF MAAT FROM EGYPTIAN FOLK-LORE!
FLSTR
FLSTR
UM, LIGHT AS A FEATH-ER?
BOO!
PHEW...
WRONG ANSWER!
THE CORRECT ANSWER IS, "HEARTS THAT FLOAT FREELY AND ENJOY LIFE TO THE FULLEST!"
"THE FEATHERS OF A FREE-SPIRITED HEART CANNOT BE TIED DOWN BY ANYONE!"
WHAT IN THE WORLD IS SHE SAYING?
I HAVE A MYS-TERIOUS THIEF TO CATCH...
SO SORRY!
HEY...!
SH
DA
I SEE... I NEED TO GIVE A QUIZ TO REJECT HIM!
NO! DON'T LET CHIKA MISLEAD YOU!
THAT WAS A TERRIBLE EXAMPLE!

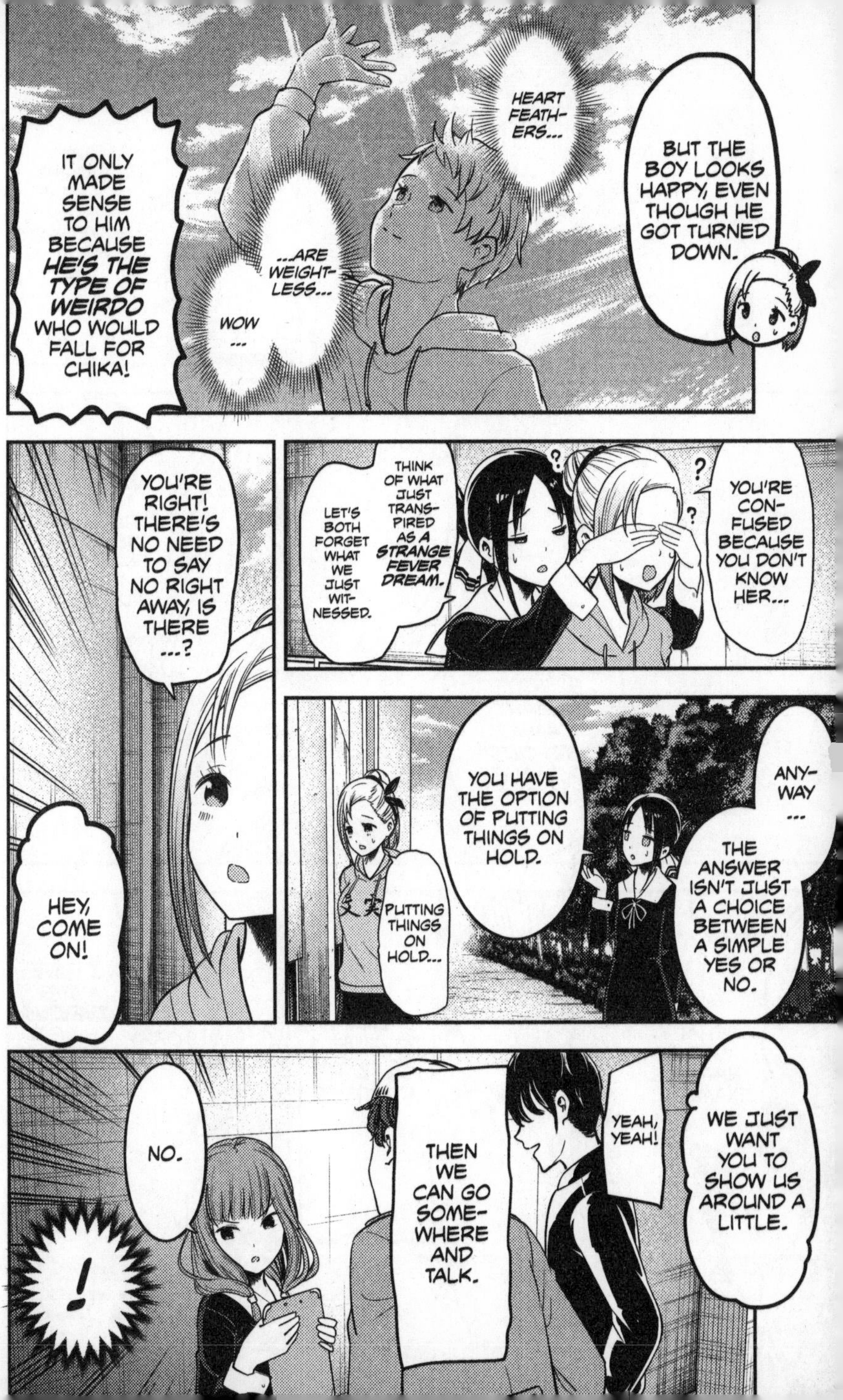
BUT THE BOY LOOKS HAPPY, EVEN THOUGH HE GOT TURNED DOWN.
HEART FEATHERS...
...ARE WEIGHTLESS...
WOW...
IT ONLY MADE SENSE TO HIM BECAUSE ***HE'S THE TYPE OF WEIRDO*** WHO WOULD FALL FOR CHIKA!
?
??
YOU'RE CONFUSED BECAUSE YOU DON'T KNOW HER...
THINK OF WHAT JUST TRANSPIRED AS A ***STRANGE FEVER DREAM.***
LET'S BOTH FORGET WHAT WE JUST WITNESSED.
ANYWAY...
THE ANSWER ISN'T JUST A CHOICE BETWEEN A SIMPLE YES OR NO.
YOU HAVE THE OPTION OF PUTTING THINGS ON HOLD.
PUTTING THINGS ON HOLD...
YOU'RE RIGHT! THERE'S NO NEED TO SAY NO RIGHT AWAY, IS THERE...?
HEY, COME ON!
WE JUST WANT YOU TO SHOW US AROUND A LITTLE.
YEAH, YEAH!
THEN WE CAN GO SOMEWHERE AND TALK.
NO.
!

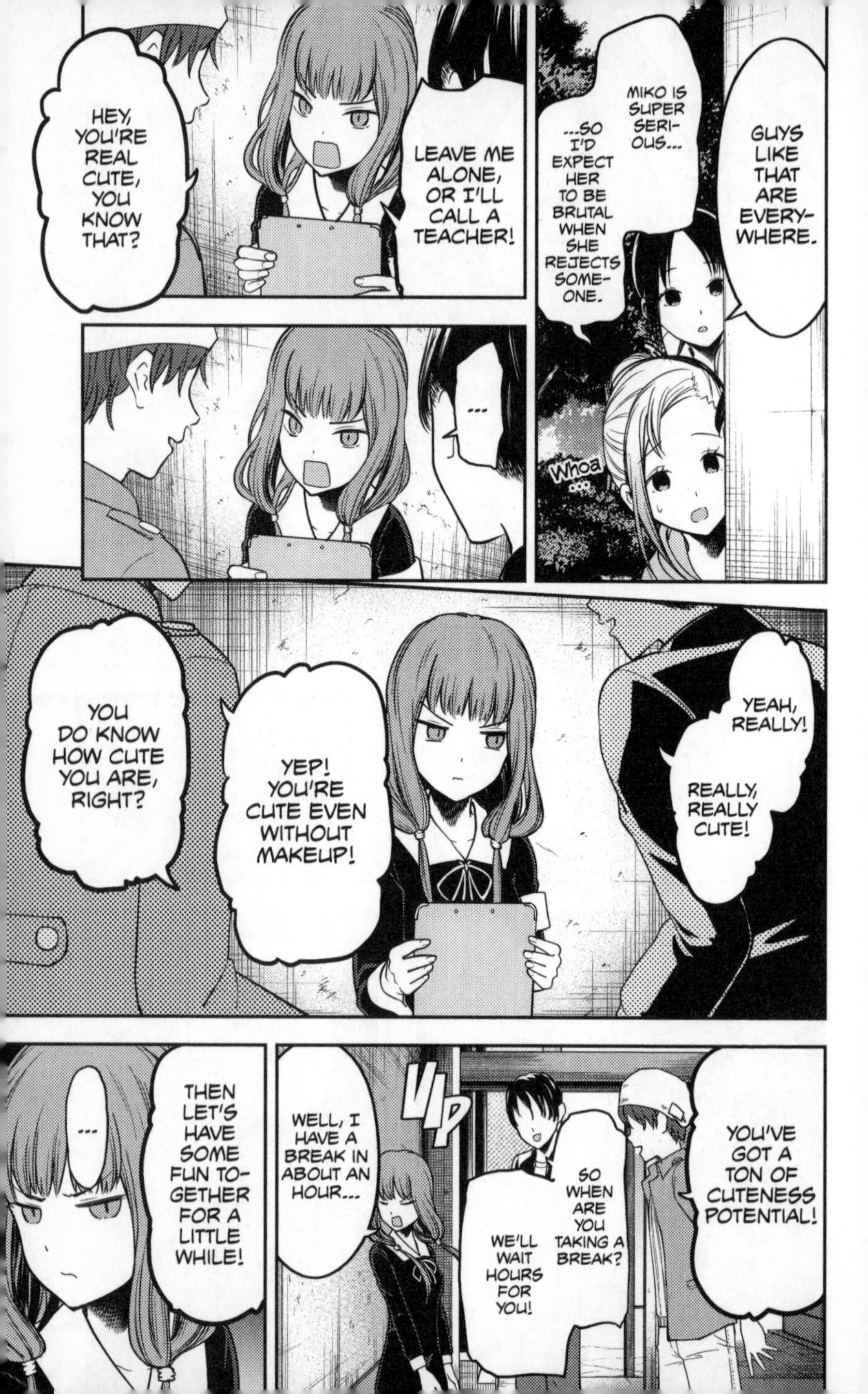
GUYS LIKE THAT ARE EVERY-WHERE.
MIKO IS SUPER SERI-OUS...
...SO I'D EXPECT HER TO BE BRUTAL WHEN SHE REJECTS SOME-ONE.
Whoa...
LEAVE ME ALONE, OR I'LL CALL A TEACHER!
HEY, YOU'RE REAL CUTE, YOU KNOW THAT?
...
YEAH, REALLY!
REALLY, REALLY CUTE!
YEP! YOU'RE CUTE EVEN WITHOUT MAKEUP!
YOU DO KNOW HOW CUTE YOU ARE, RIGHT?
YOU'VE GOT A TON OF CUTENESS POTENTIAL!
SO WHEN ARE YOU TAKING A BREAK?
WE'LL WAIT HOURS FOR YOU!
VIP
WELL, I HAVE A BREAK IN ABOUT AN HOUR...
THEN LET'S HAVE SOME FUN TO-GETHER FOR A LITTLE WHILE!
...

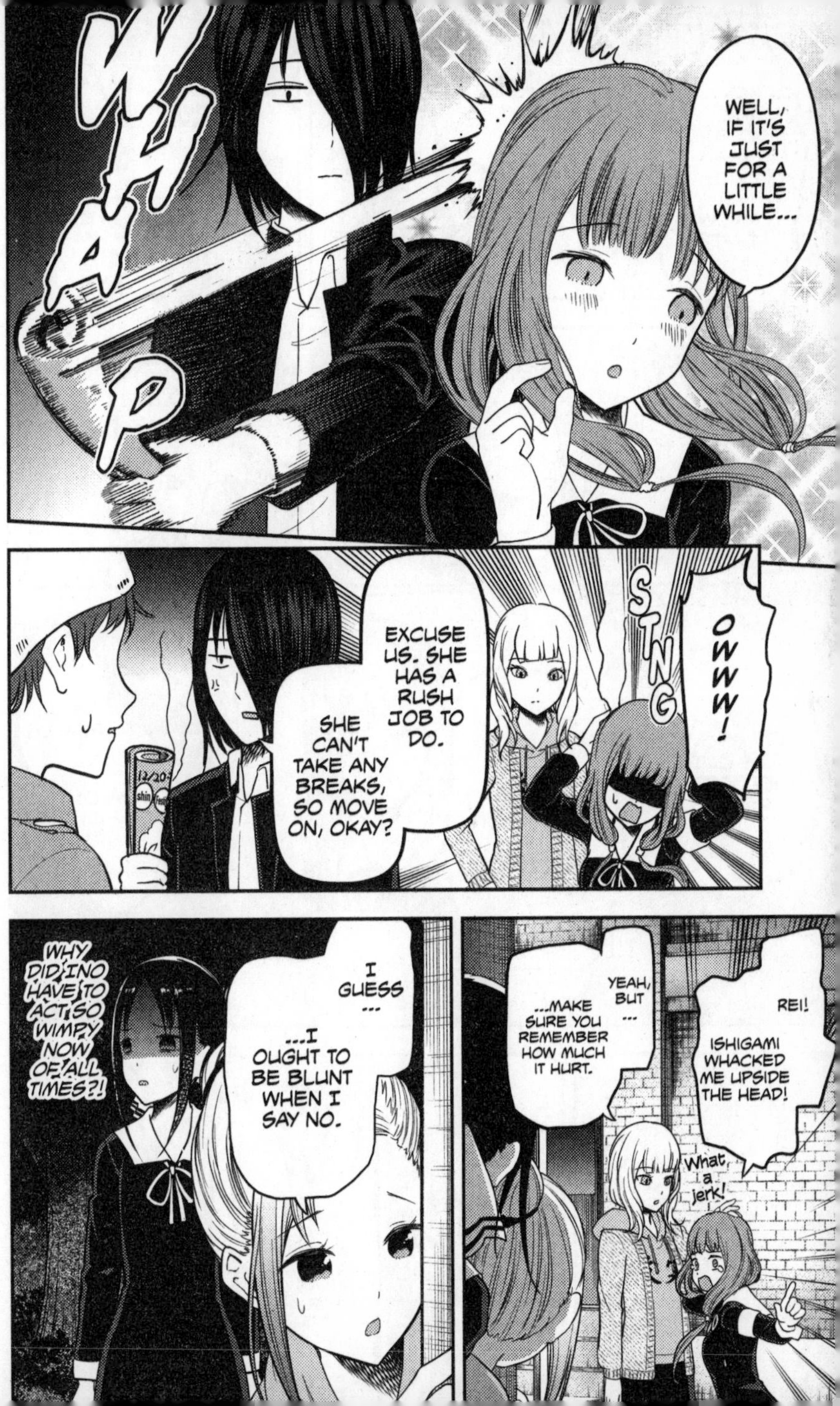
WELL, IF IT'S JUST FOR A LITTLE WHILE...
WHAP
OWWW!
STING
EXCUSE US. SHE HAS A RUSH JOB TO DO.
SHE CAN'T TAKE ANY BREAKS, SO MOVE ON, OKAY?
REI!
ISHIGAMI WHACKED ME UPSIDE THE HEAD!
What a jerk!
YEAH, BUT ...
...MAKE SURE YOU REMEMBER HOW MUCH IT HURT.
I GUESS ...
...I OUGHT TO BE BLUNT WHEN I SAY NO.
WHY DID INO HAVE TO ACT SO WIMPY NOW OF ALL TIMES?!

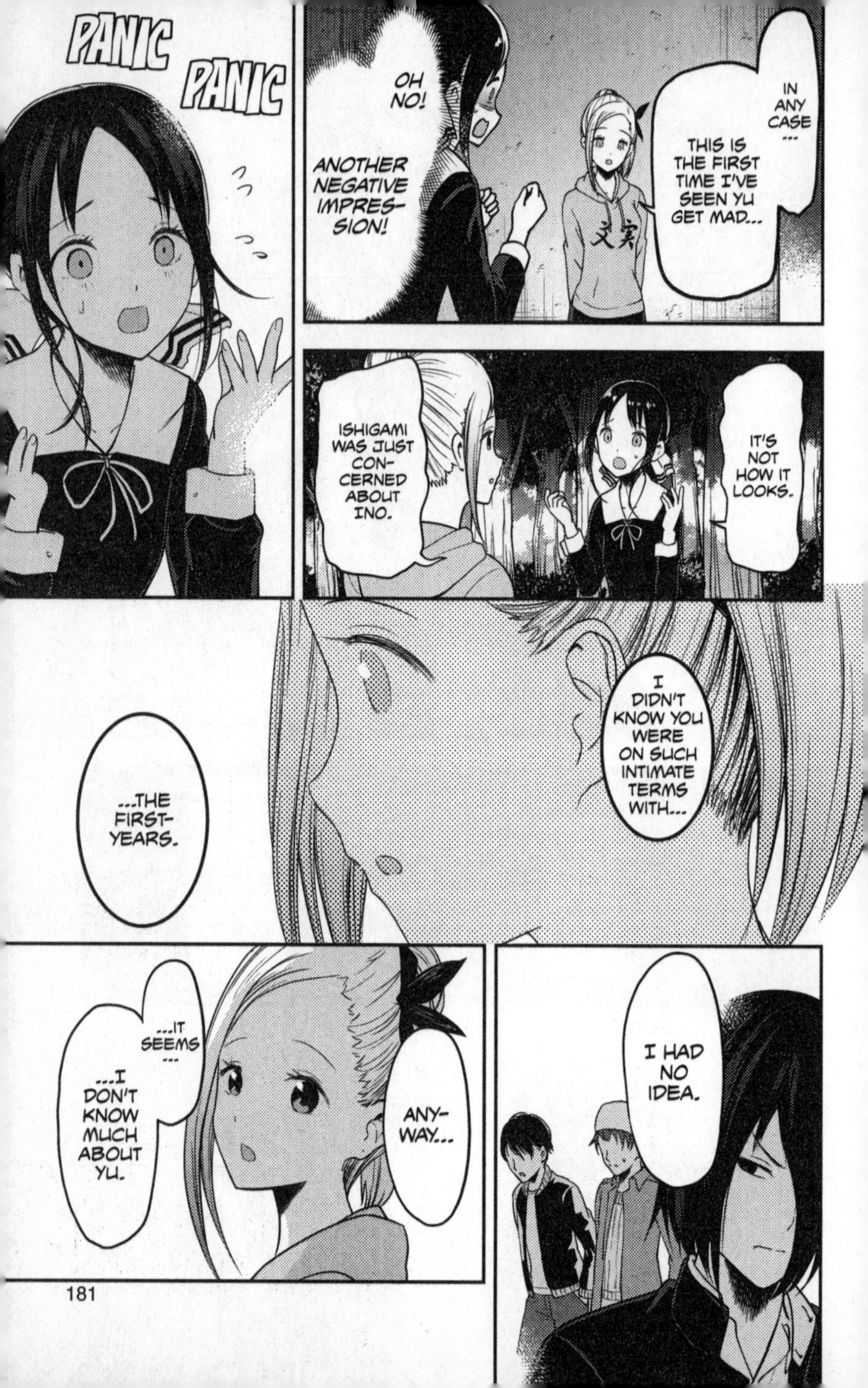
IN ANY CASE...
THIS IS THE FIRST TIME I'VE SEEN YU GET MAD...
OH NO!
ANOTHER NEGATIVE IMPRESSION!
IT'S NOT HOW IT LOOKS.
ISHIGAMI WAS JUST CONCERNED ABOUT INO.
PANIC
PANIC
I DIDN'T KNOW YOU WERE ON SUCH INTIMATE TERMS WITH...
...THE FIRST-YEARS.
I HAD NO IDEA.
ANYWAY...
...IT SEEMS...
...I DON'T KNOW MUCH ABOUT YU.

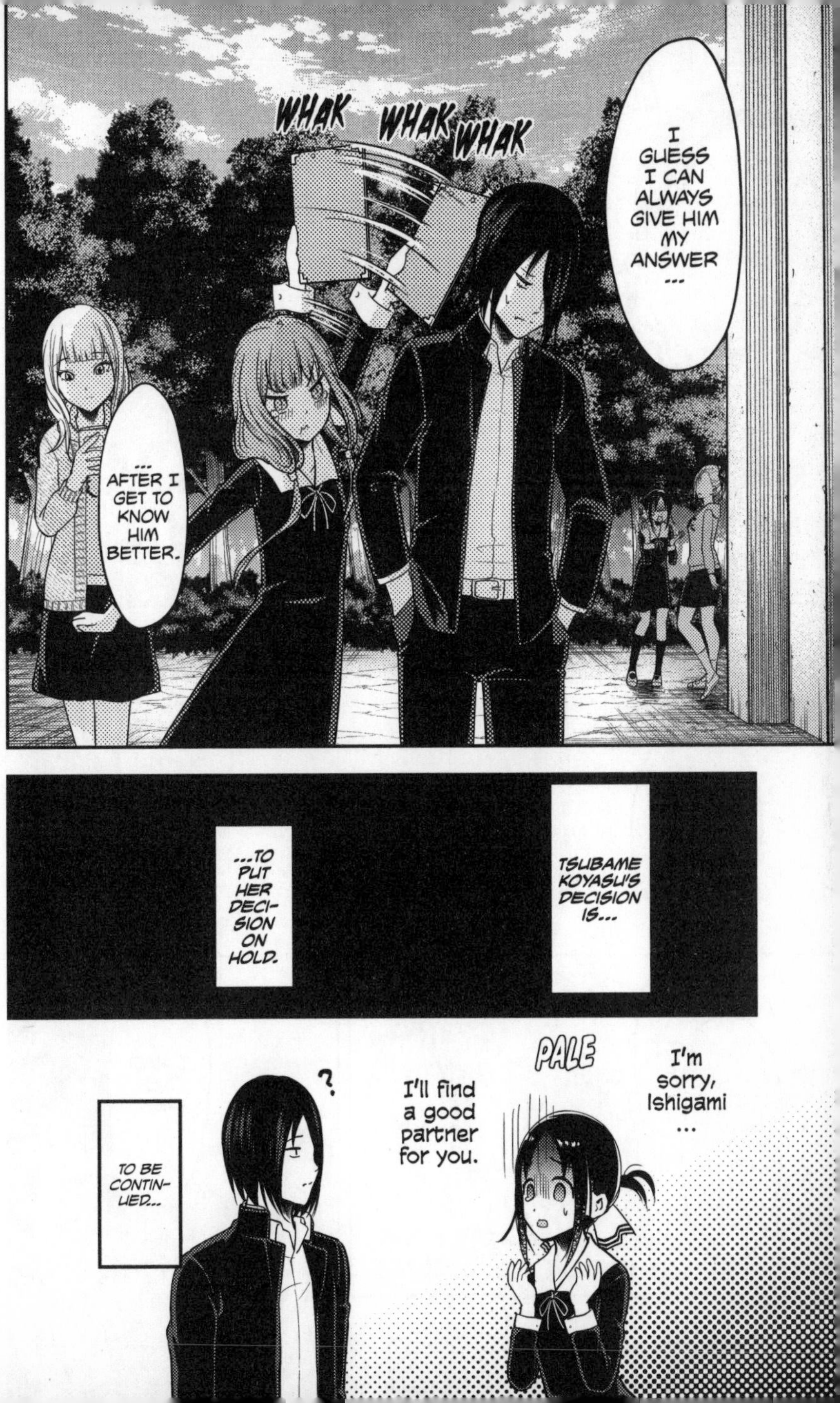
WHAK
WHAK
WHAK
I GUESS I CAN ALWAYS GIVE HIM MY ANSWER ...
... AFTER I GET TO KNOW HIM BETTER.
TSUBAME KOYASU'S DECISION IS...
...TO PUT HER DECI-SION ON HOLD.
PALE
I'm sorry, Ishigami ...
I'll find a good partner for you.
?
TO BE CONTIN-UED...

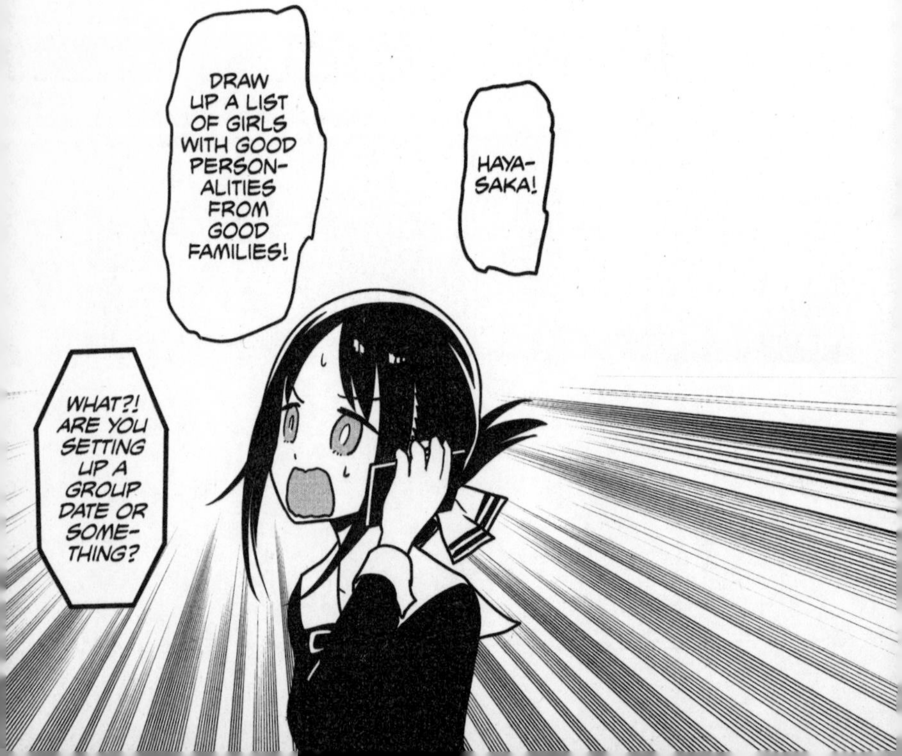
HAYA-SAKA!
DRAW UP A LIST OF GIRLS WITH GOOD PERSON-ALITIES FROM GOOD FAMILIES!
WHAT?! ARE YOU SETTING UP A GROUP DATE OR SOME-THING?

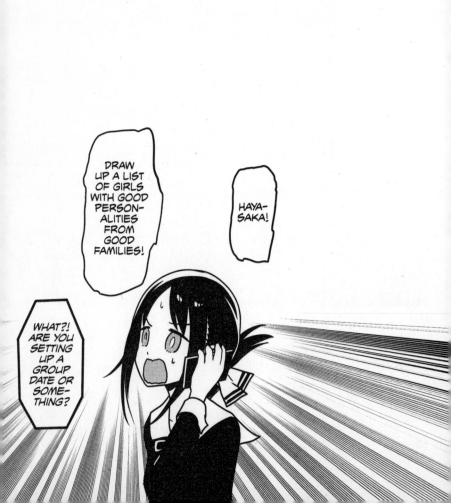

KAGUYA-SAMA
LOVE IS WAR

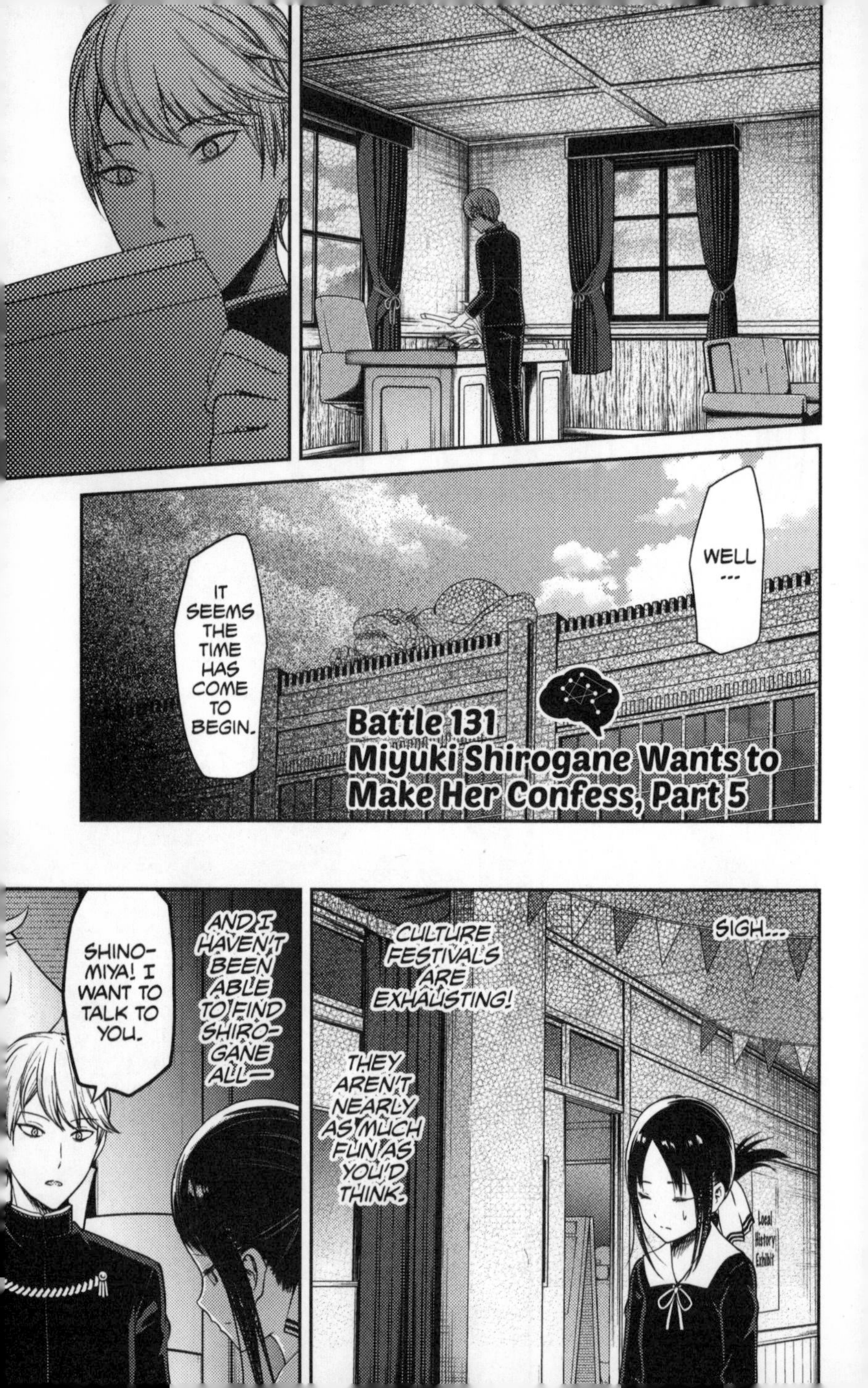
WELL ---
Battle 131
Miyuki Shirogane Wants to Make Her Confess, Part 5
IT SEEMS THE TIME HAS COME TO BEGIN.
SIGH...
CULTURE FESTIVALS ARE EXHAUSTING!
THEY AREN'T NEARLY AS MUCH FUN AS YOU'D THINK.
Local History Exhibit
AND I HAVEN'T BEEN ABLE TO FIND SHIROGANE ALL—
SHINOMIYA! I WANT TO TALK TO YOU.

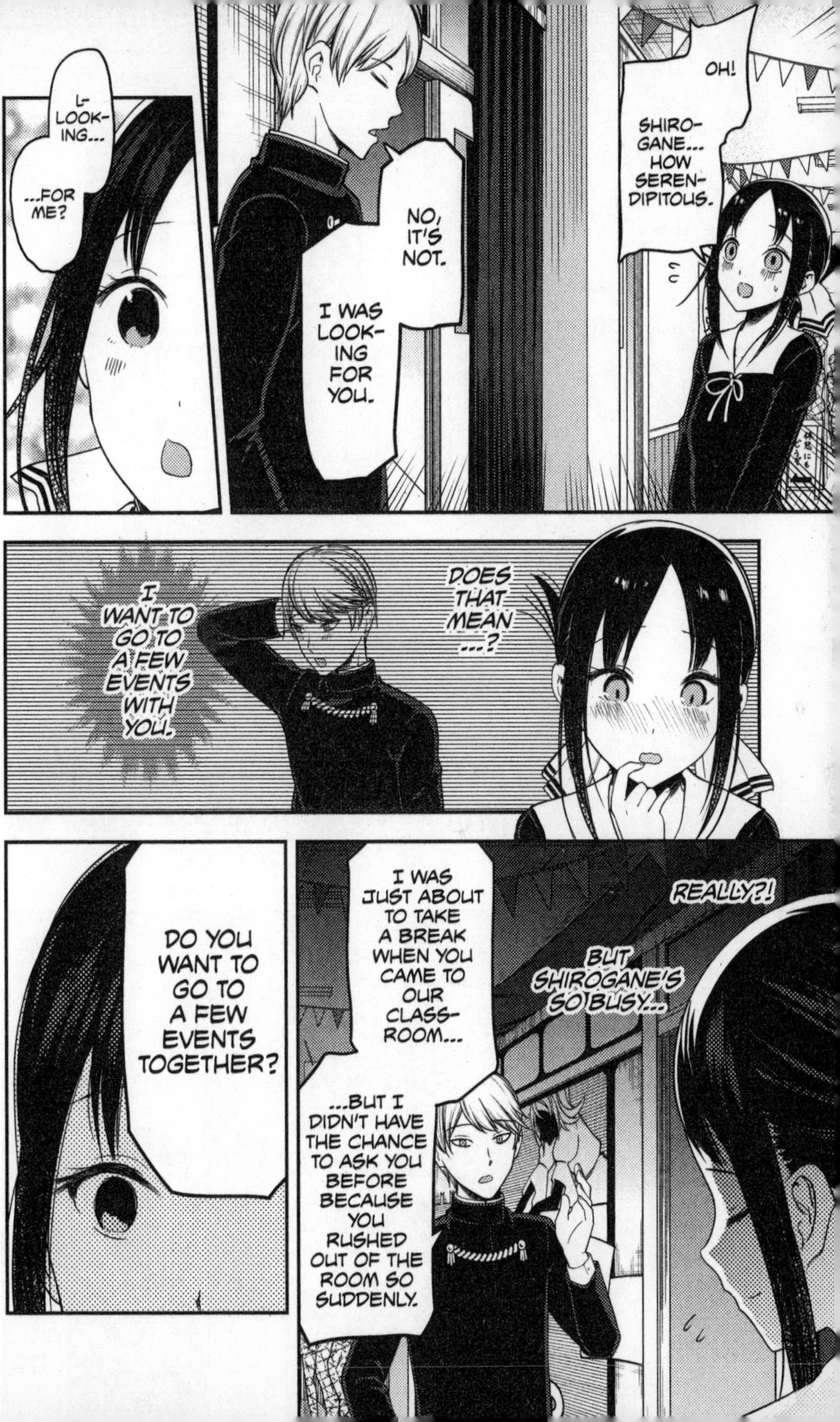
OH!
SHIROGANE... HOW SERENDIPITOUS.
NO, IT'S NOT.
I WAS LOOKING FOR YOU.
L-LOOKING...
...FOR ME?
DOES THAT MEAN...?
I WANT TO GO TO A FEW EVENTS WITH YOU.
REALLY?!
BUT SHIROGANE'S SO BUSY...
I WAS JUST ABOUT TO TAKE A BREAK WHEN YOU CAME TO OUR CLASSROOM...
...BUT I DIDN'T HAVE THE CHANCE TO ASK YOU BEFORE BECAUSE YOU RUSHED OUT OF THE ROOM SO SUDDENLY.
DO YOU WANT TO GO TO A FEW EVENTS TOGETHER?

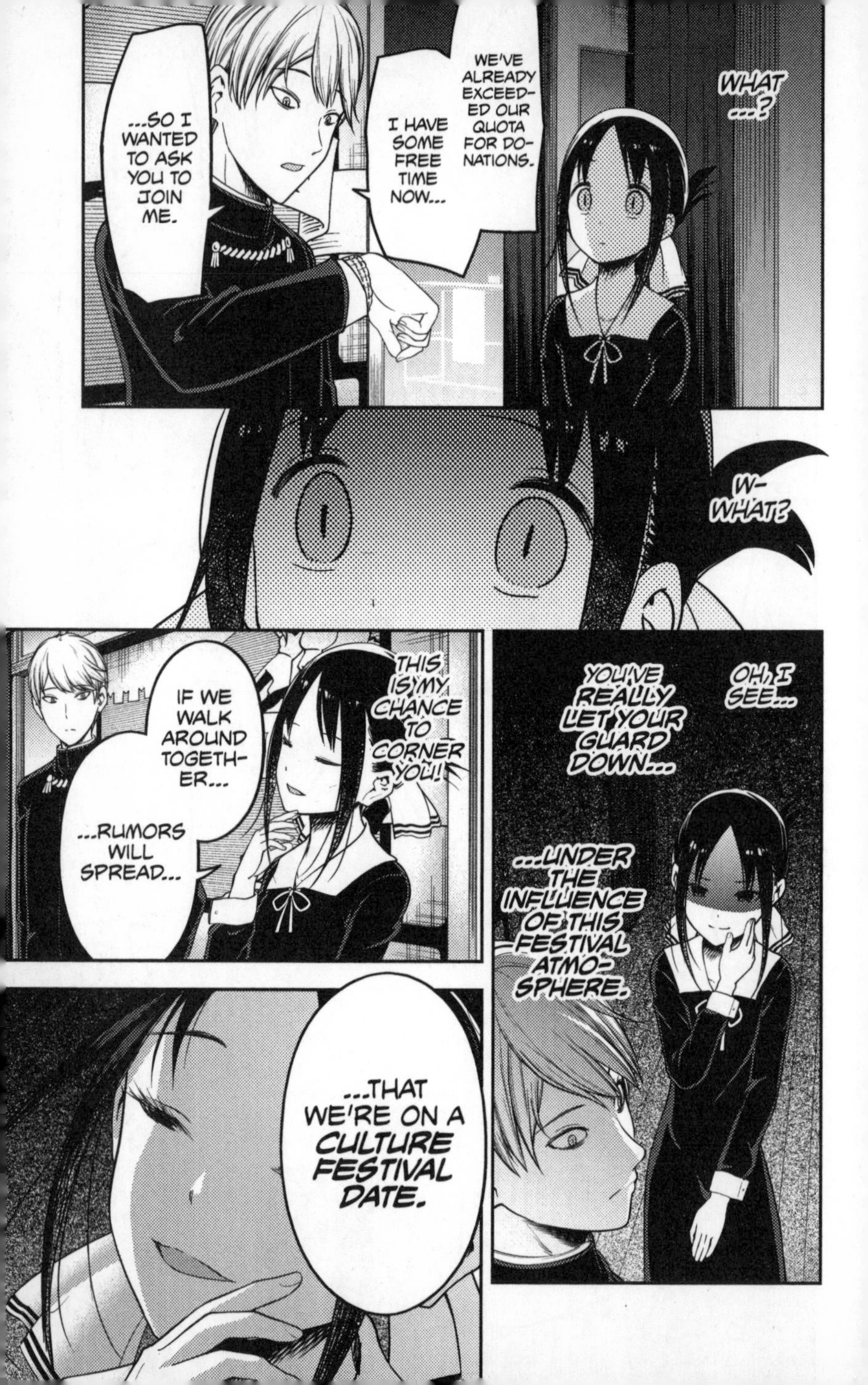
WHAT...?
WE'VE ALREADY EXCEEDED OUR QUOTA FOR DONATIONS.
I HAVE SOME FREE TIME NOW...
...SO I WANTED TO ASK YOU TO JOIN ME.
W-WHAT?
OH, I SEE...
YOU'VE REALLY LET YOUR GUARD DOWN...
...UNDER THE INFLUENCE OF THIS FESTIVAL ATMOSPHERE.
THIS IS MY CHANCE TO CORNER YOU!
IF WE WALK AROUND TOGETHER...
...RUMORS WILL SPREAD...
...THAT WE'RE ON A CULTURE FESTIVAL DATE.

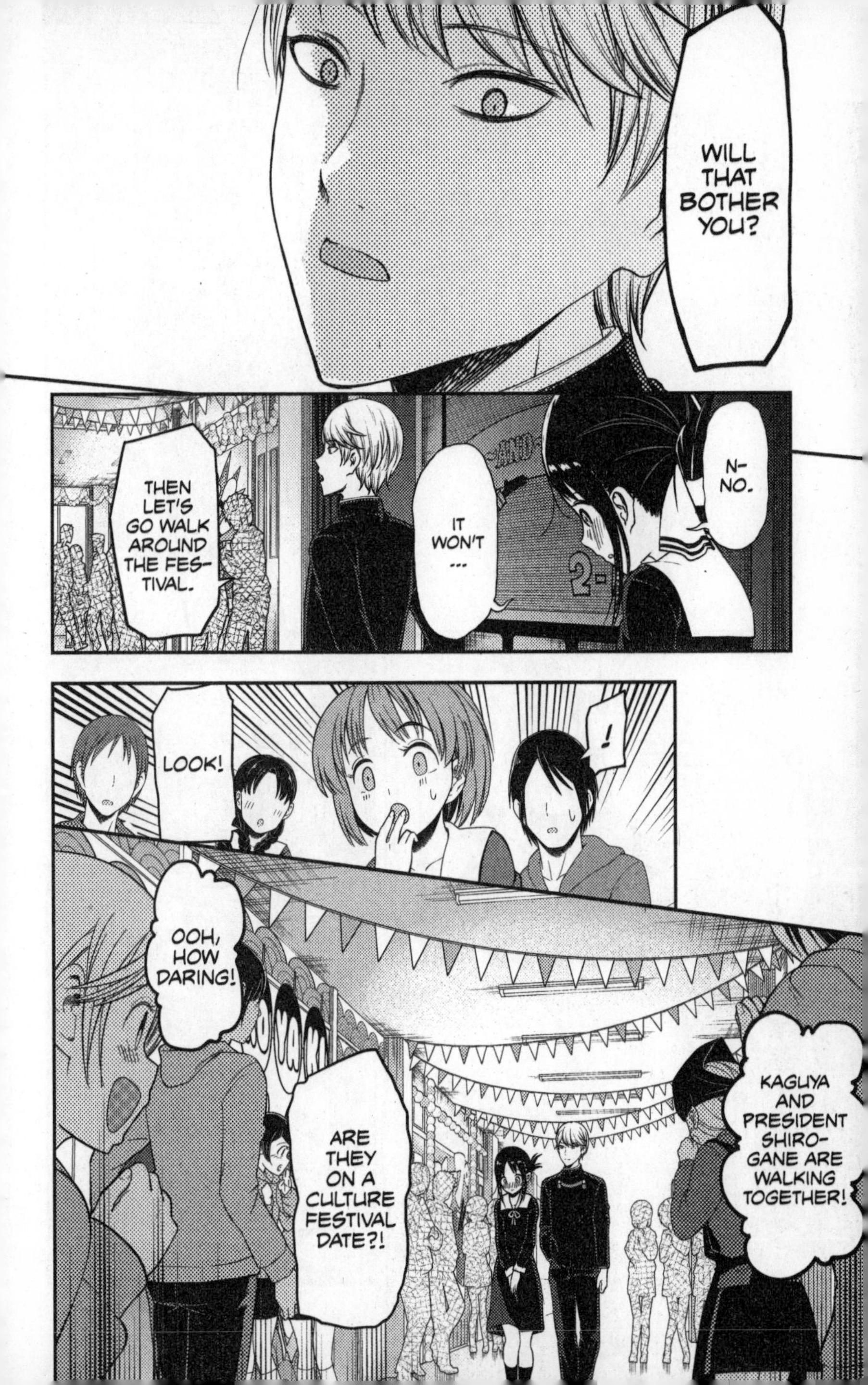
WILL THAT BOTHER YOU?
N-NO.
IT WON'T...
THEN LET'S GO WALK AROUND THE FES-TIVAL.
!
LOOK!
KAGUYA AND PRESIDENT SHIRO-GANE ARE WALKING TOGETHER!
ARE THEY ON A CULTURE FESTIVAL DATE?!
OOH, HOW DARING!

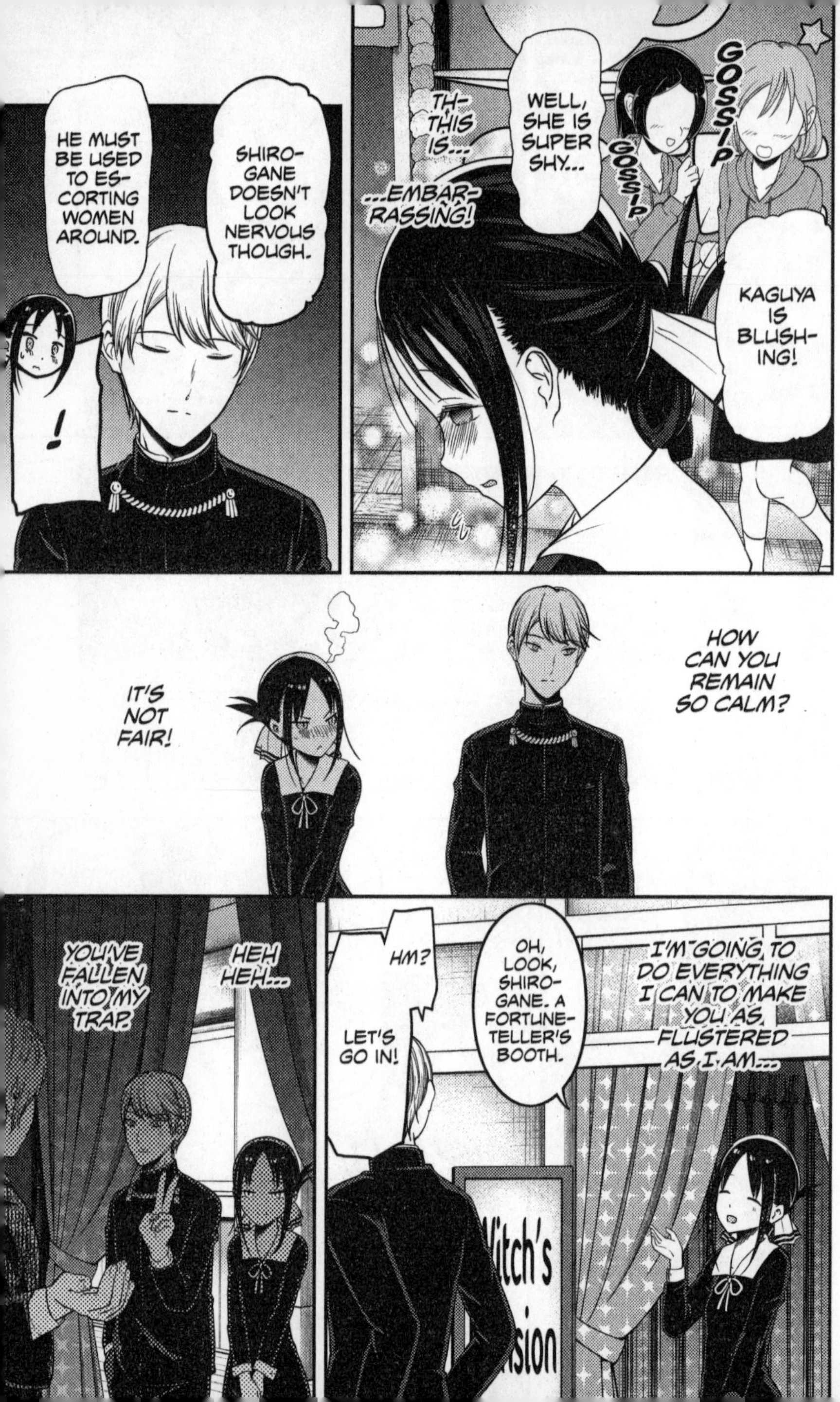
GOSSIP
GOSSIP
WELL, SHE IS SUPER SHY...
KAGUYA IS BLUSHING!
TH-THIS IS...
...EMBARRASSING!
SHIROGANE DOESN'T LOOK NERVOUS THOUGH.
HE MUST BE USED TO ESCORTING WOMEN AROUND.
!
HOW CAN YOU REMAIN SO CALM?
IT'S NOT FAIR!
I'M GOING TO DO EVERYTHING I CAN TO MAKE YOU AS FLUSTERED AS I AM...
OH, LOOK, SHIROGANE. A FORTUNE-TELLER'S BOOTH.
HM?
LET'S GO IN!
HEH HEH...
YOU'VE FALLEN INTO MY TRAP.

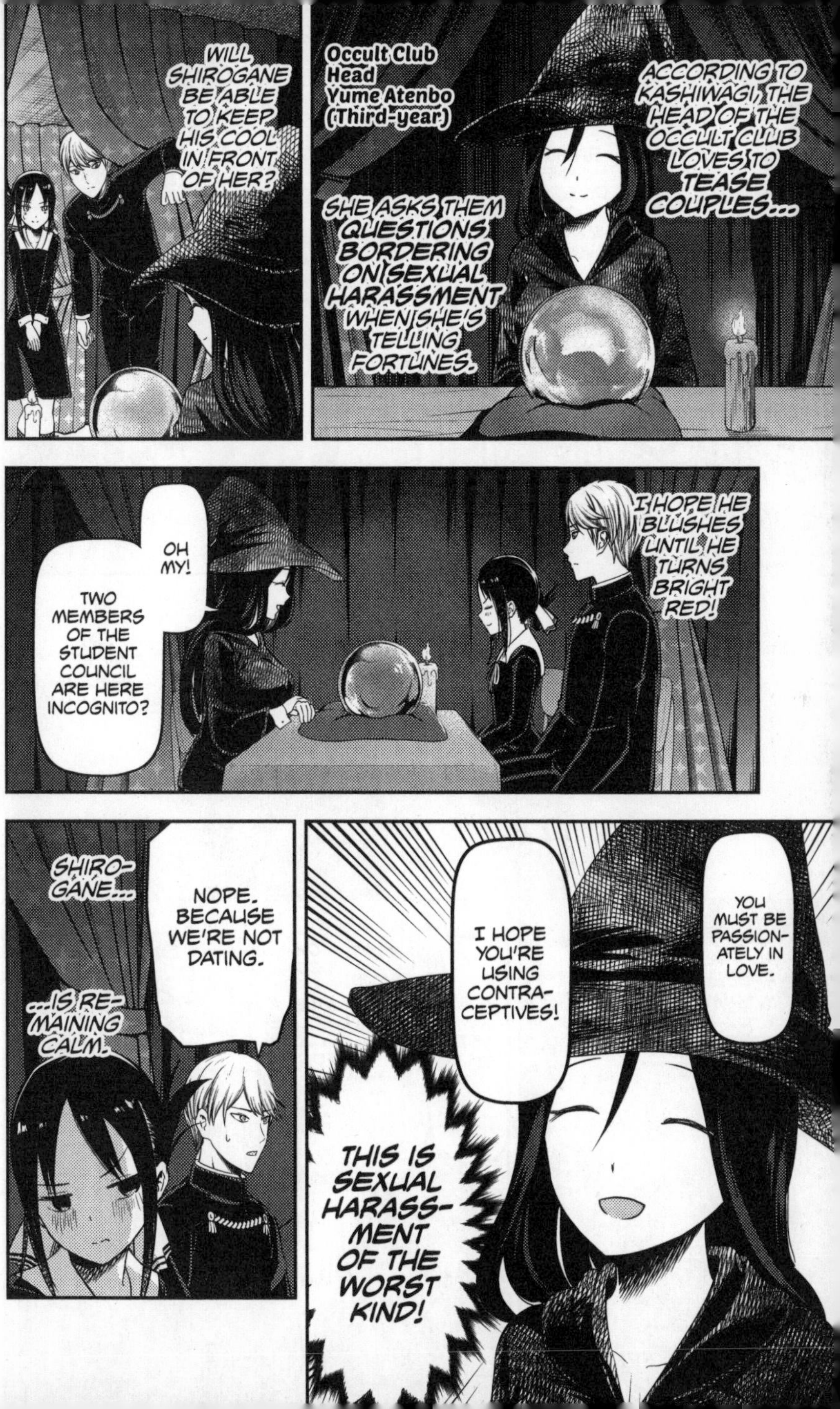
ACCORDING TO KASHIWAGI, THE HEAD OF THE OCCULT CLUB LOVES TO TEASE COUPLES...
Occult Club Head Yume Atenbo (Third-year)
SHE ASKS THEM QUESTIONS BORDERING ON SEXUAL HARASSMENT WHEN SHE'S TELLING FORTUNES.
WILL SHIROGANE BE ABLE TO KEEP HIS COOL IN FRONT OF HER?
I HOPE HE BLUSHES UNTIL HE TURNS BRIGHT RED!
OH MY!
TWO MEMBERS OF THE STUDENT COUNCIL ARE HERE INCOGNITO?
YOU MUST BE PASSIONATELY IN LOVE.
I HOPE YOU'RE USING CONTRACEPTIVES!
THIS IS SEXUAL HARASSMENT OF THE WORST KIND!
SHIROGANE...
NOPE. BECAUSE WE'RE NOT DATING.
...IS REMAINING CALM.

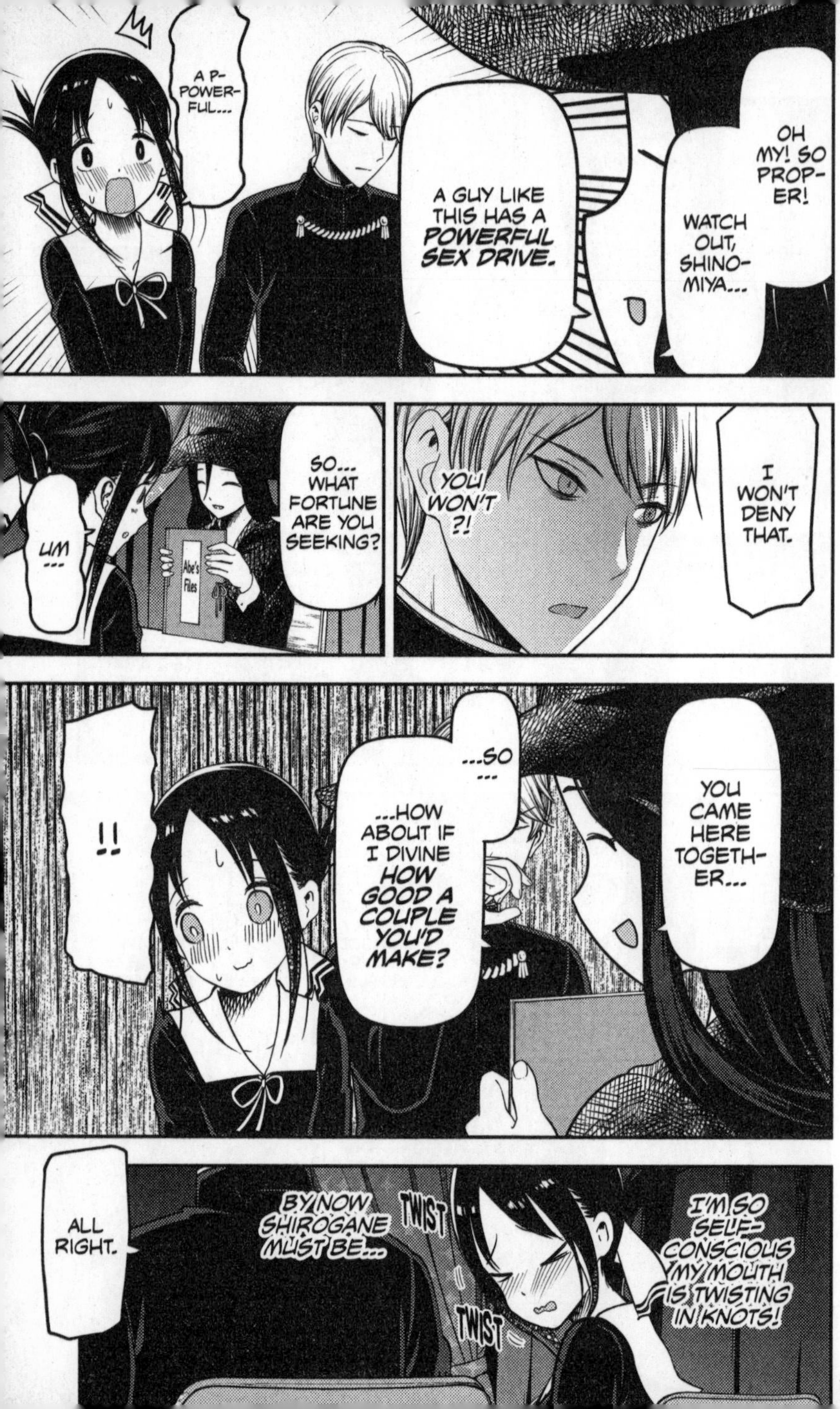
OH MY! SO PROPER!
WATCH OUT, SHINOMIYA...
A GUY LIKE THIS HAS A POWERFUL SEX DRIVE.
A P-POWERFUL...
I WON'T DENY THAT.
YOU WON'T?!
SO... WHAT FORTUNE ARE YOU SEEKING?
UM...
YOU CAME HERE TOGETHER...
...SO...
...HOW ABOUT IF I DIVINE HOW GOOD A COUPLE YOU'D MAKE?
!!
I'M SO SELF-CONSCIOUS MY MOUTH IS TWISTING IN KNOTS!
TWIST
TWIST
BY NOW SHIROGANE MUST BE...
ALL RIGHT.

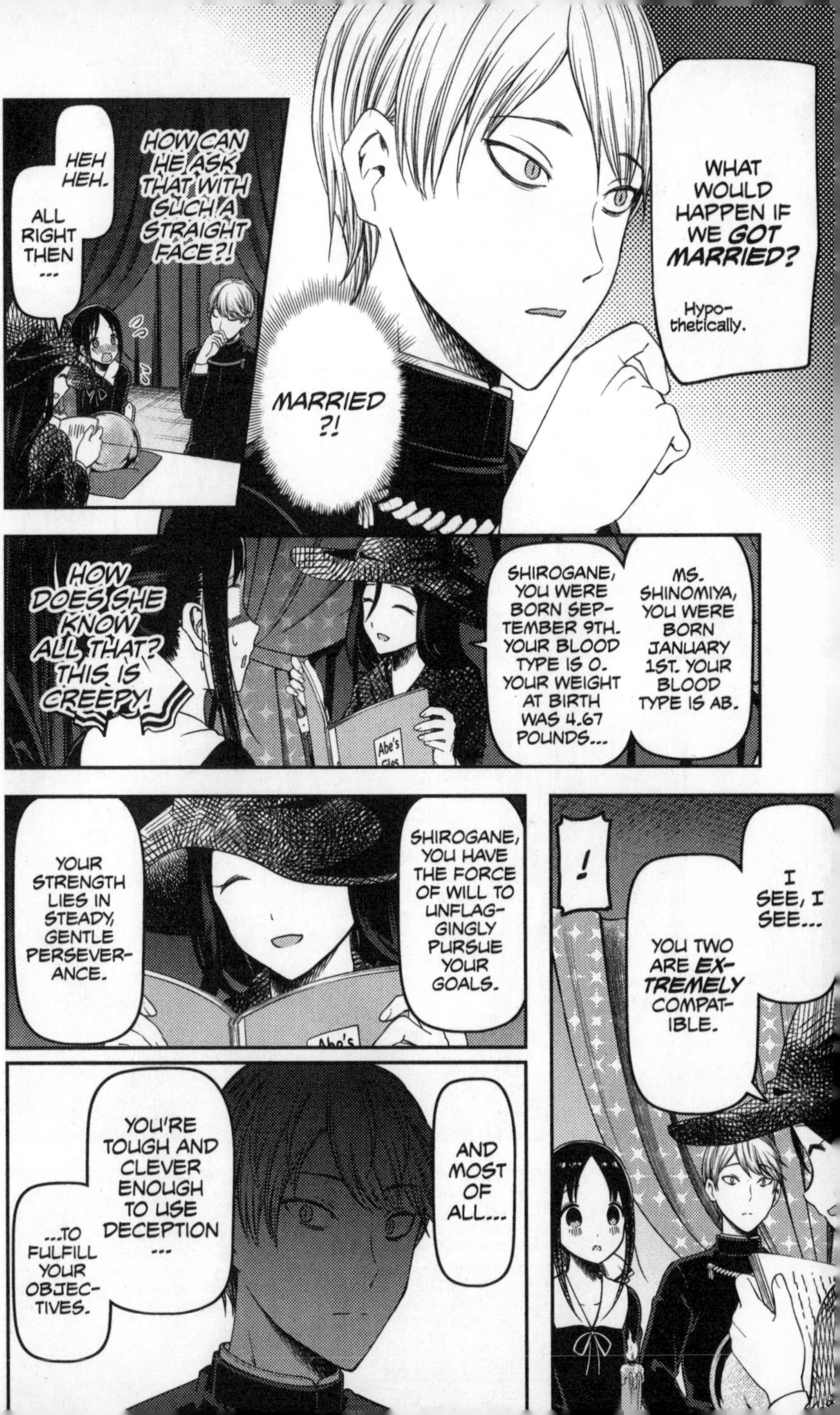
WHAT WOULD HAPPEN IF WE GOT MARRIED?
Hypo-thetically.
MARRIED?!
HOW CAN HE ASK THAT WITH SUCH A STRAIGHT FACE?!
HEH HEH.
ALL RIGHT THEN ...
MS. SHINOMIYA, YOU WERE BORN JANUARY 1ST. YOUR BLOOD TYPE IS AB.
SHIROGANE, YOU WERE BORN SEP-TEMBER 9TH. YOUR BLOOD TYPE IS O. YOUR WEIGHT AT BIRTH WAS 4.67 POUNDS...
HOW DOES SHE KNOW ALL THAT? THIS IS CREEPY!
!
I SEE, I SEE...
YOU TWO ARE EXTREMELY COMPAT-IBLE.
SHIROGANE, YOU HAVE THE FORCE OF WILL TO UNFLAG-GINGLY PURSUE YOUR GOALS.
YOUR STRENGTH LIES IN STEADY, GENTLE PERSEVER-ANCE.
AND MOST OF ALL...
YOU'RE TOUGH AND CLEVER ENOUGH TO USE DECEPTION ...
...TO FULFILL YOUR OBJEC-TIVES.

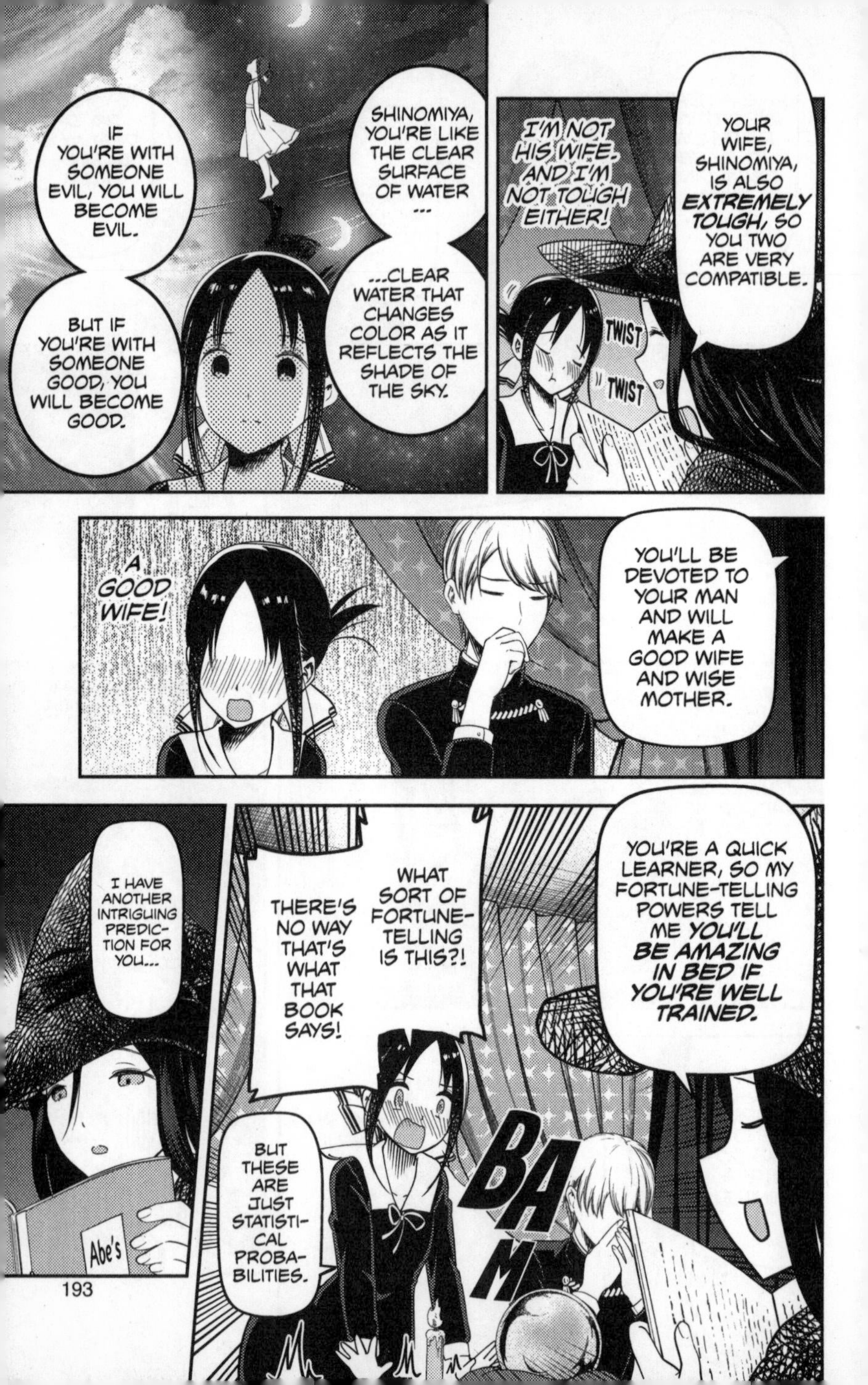

YOUR WIFE, SHINOMIYA, IS ALSO EXTREMELY TOUGH, SO YOU TWO ARE VERY COMPATIBLE.
I'M NOT HIS WIFE. AND I'M NOT TOUGH EITHER!
TWIST
TWIST
SHINOMIYA, YOU'RE LIKE THE CLEAR SURFACE OF WATER...
...CLEAR WATER THAT CHANGES COLOR AS IT REFLECTS THE SHADE OF THE SKY.
IF YOU'RE WITH SOMEONE EVIL, YOU WILL BECOME EVIL.
BUT IF YOU'RE WITH SOMEONE GOOD, YOU WILL BECOME GOOD.
YOU'LL BE DEVOTED TO YOUR MAN AND WILL MAKE A GOOD WIFE AND WISE MOTHER.
A GOOD WIFE!
YOU'RE A QUICK LEARNER, SO MY FORTUNE-TELLING POWERS TELL ME YOU'LL BE AMAZING IN BED IF YOU'RE WELL TRAINED.
BAM
WHAT SORT OF FORTUNE-TELLING IS THIS?!
THERE'S NO WAY THAT'S WHAT THAT BOOK SAYS!
BUT THESE ARE JUST STATISTICAL PROBABILITIES.
I HAVE ANOTHER INTRIGUING PREDICTION FOR YOU...
Abe's

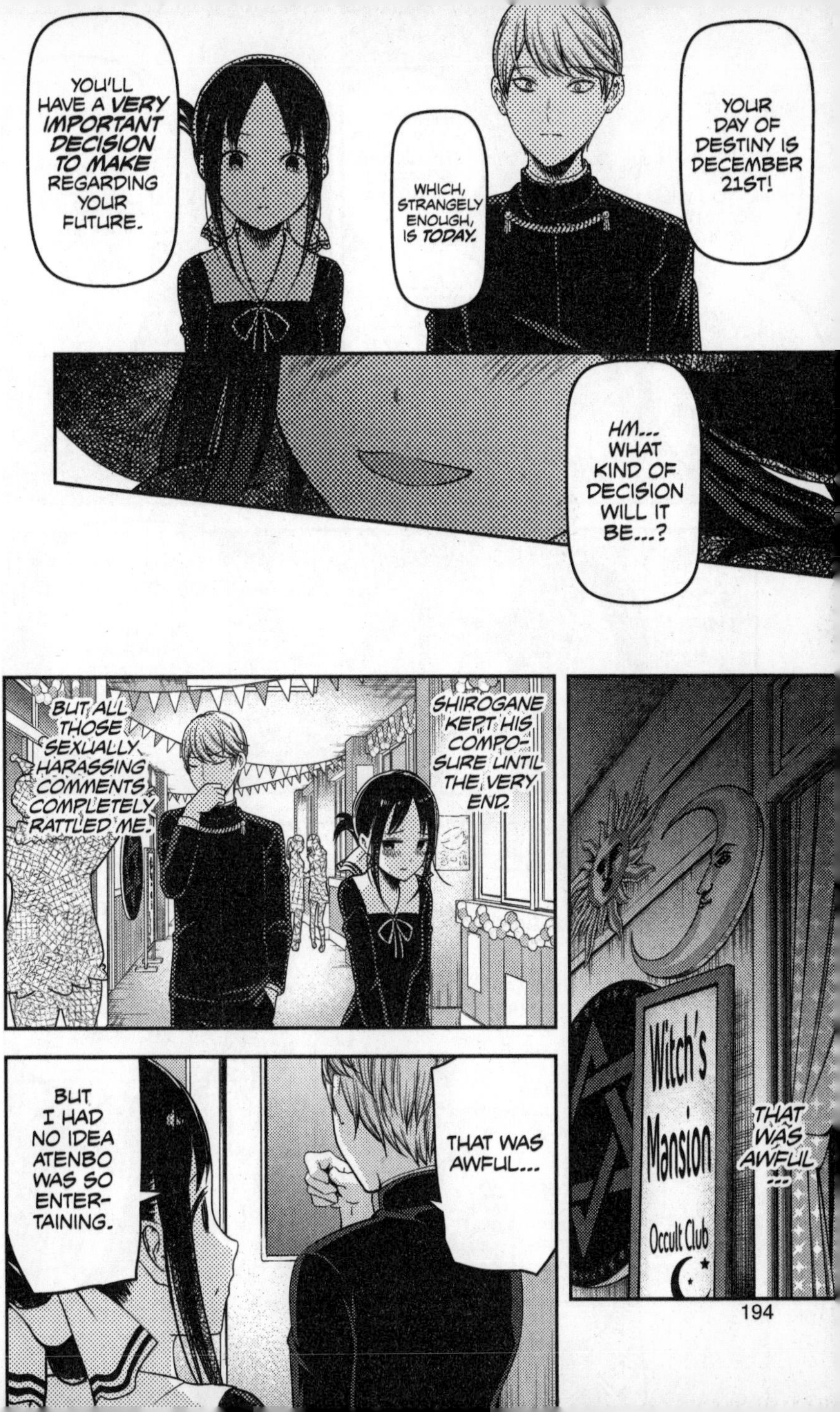

YOUR DAY OF DESTINY IS DECEMBER 21ST!
WHICH, STRANGELY ENOUGH, IS *TODAY.*
YOU'LL HAVE A ***VERY IMPORTANT DECISION TO MAKE*** REGARDING YOUR FUTURE.
HM... WHAT KIND OF DECISION WILL IT BE...?
Witch's Mansion
Occult Club
THAT WAS AWFUL...
SHIROGANE KEPT HIS COMPO-SURE UNTIL THE VERY END.
BUT ALL THOSE SEXUALLY HARASSING COMMENTS COMPLETELY RATTLED ME.
THAT WAS AWFUL...
BUT I HAD NO IDEA ATENBO WAS SO ENTER-TAINING.

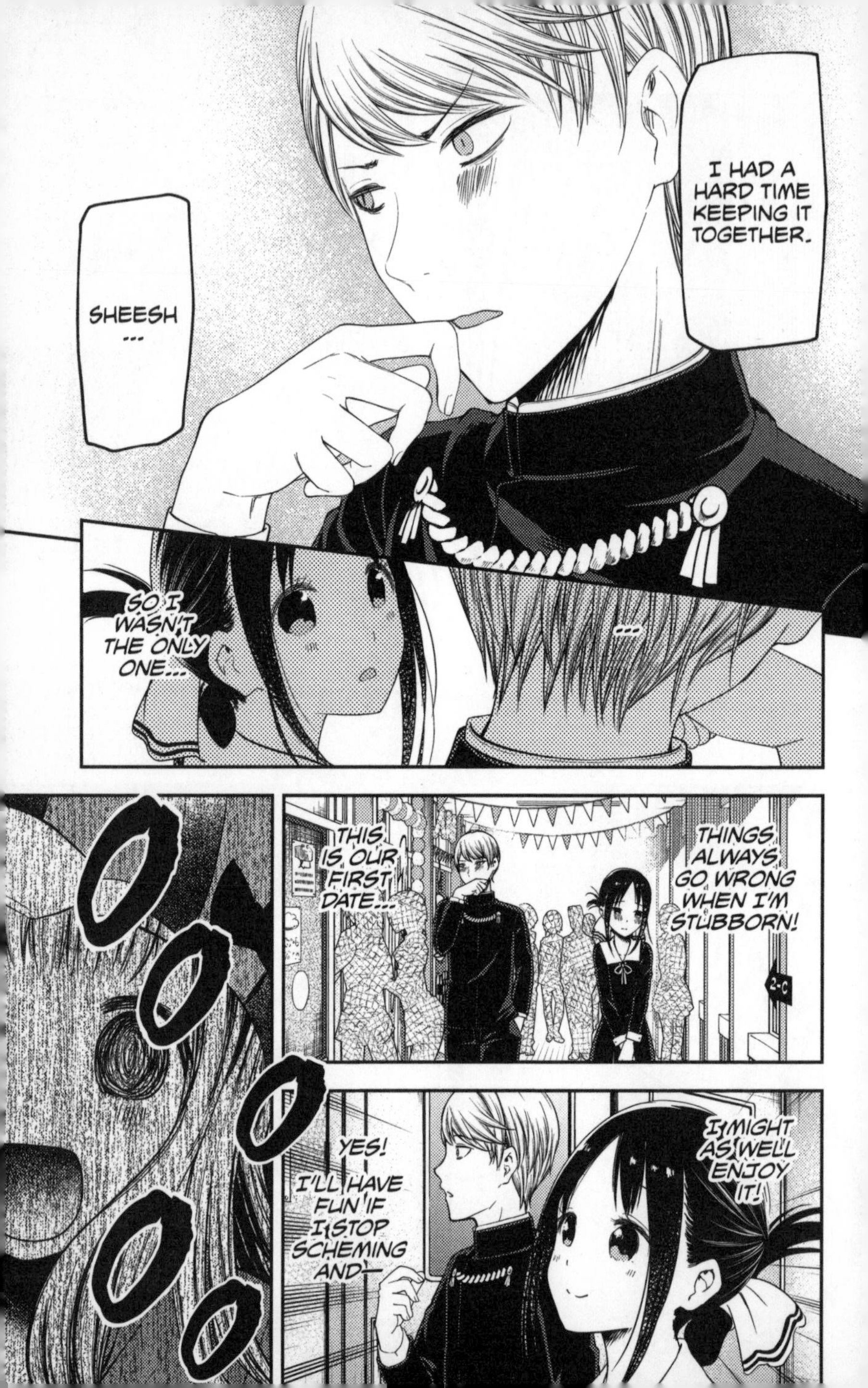
I HAD A HARD TIME KEEPING IT TOGETHER.
SHEESH ...
...
SO I WASN'T THE ONLY ONE...
THINGS ALWAYS GO WRONG WHEN I'M STUBBORN!
2-C
THIS IS OUR FIRST DATE...
I MIGHT AS WELL ENJOY IT!
YES! I'LL HAVE FUN IF I STOP SCHEMING AND—

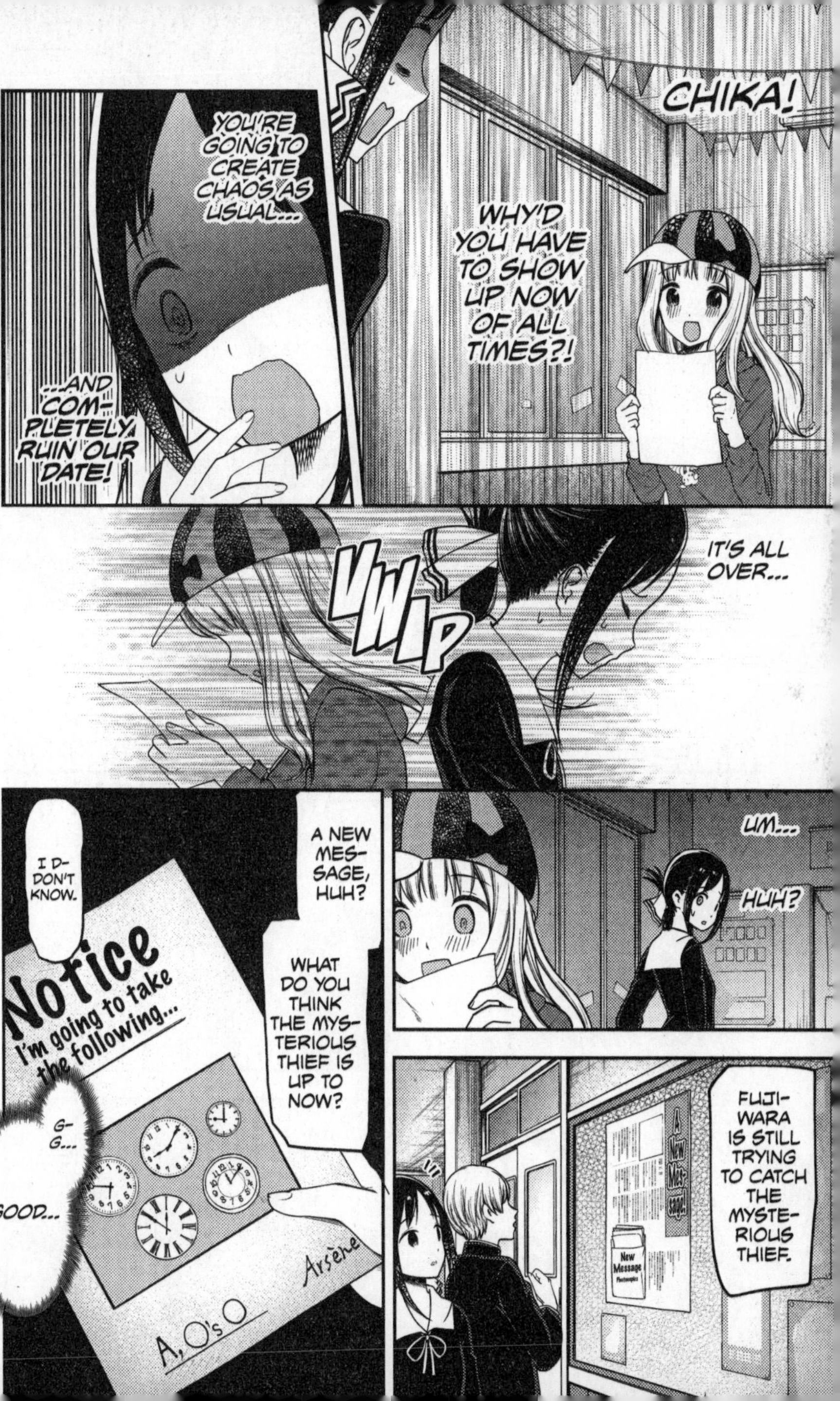
CHIKA!
WHY'D YOU HAVE TO SHOW UP NOW OF ALL TIMES?!
YOU'RE GOING TO CREATE CHAOS AS USUAL...
...AND COMPLETELY RUIN OUR DATE!
IT'S ALL OVER...
VWIP
UM...
HUH?
FUJIWARA IS STILL TRYING TO CATCH THE MYSTERIOUS THIEF.
A New Message!
New Message
A NEW MESSAGE, HUH?
WHAT DO YOU THINK THE MYSTERIOUS THIEF IS UP TO NOW?
I D-DON'T KNOW.
Notice
I'm going to take the following...
Arsène
A, ◯'s ◯
G-G...
GOOD...

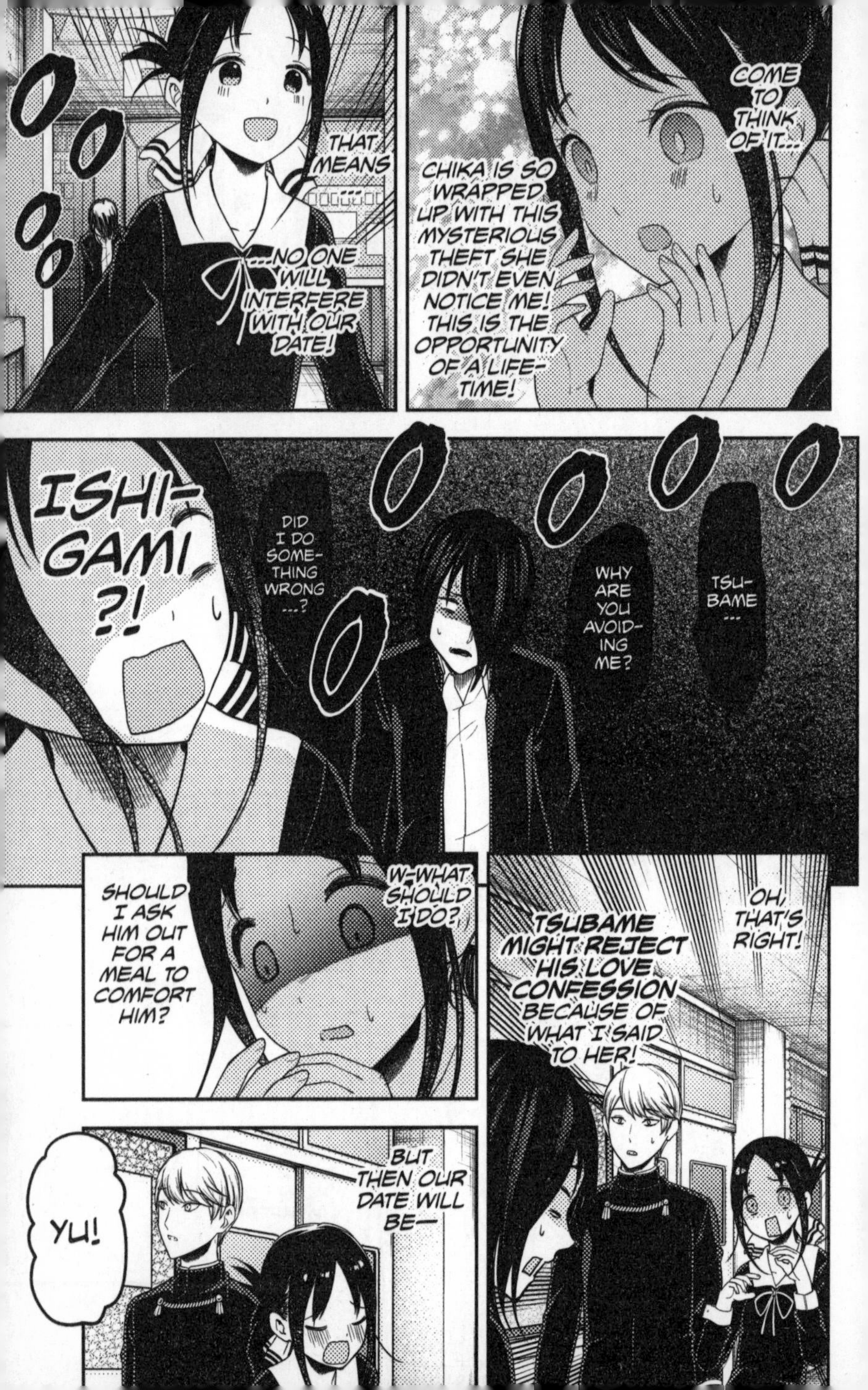
COME TO THINK OF IT...
CHIKA IS SO WRAPPED UP WITH THIS MYSTERIOUS THEFT SHE DIDN'T EVEN NOTICE ME! THIS IS THE OPPORTUNITY OF A LIFE-TIME!
THAT MEANS...
...NO ONE WILL INTERFERE WITH OUR DATE!
TSU-BAME...
WHY ARE YOU AVOID-ING ME?
DID I DO SOME-THING WRONG...?
ISHI-GAMI?!
OH, THAT'S RIGHT!
TSUBAME MIGHT REJECT HIS LOVE CONFESSION BECAUSE OF WHAT I SAID TO HER!
W-WHAT SHOULD I DO?
SHOULD I ASK HIM OUT FOR A MEAL TO COMFORT HIM?
BUT THEN OUR DATE WILL BE—
YU!

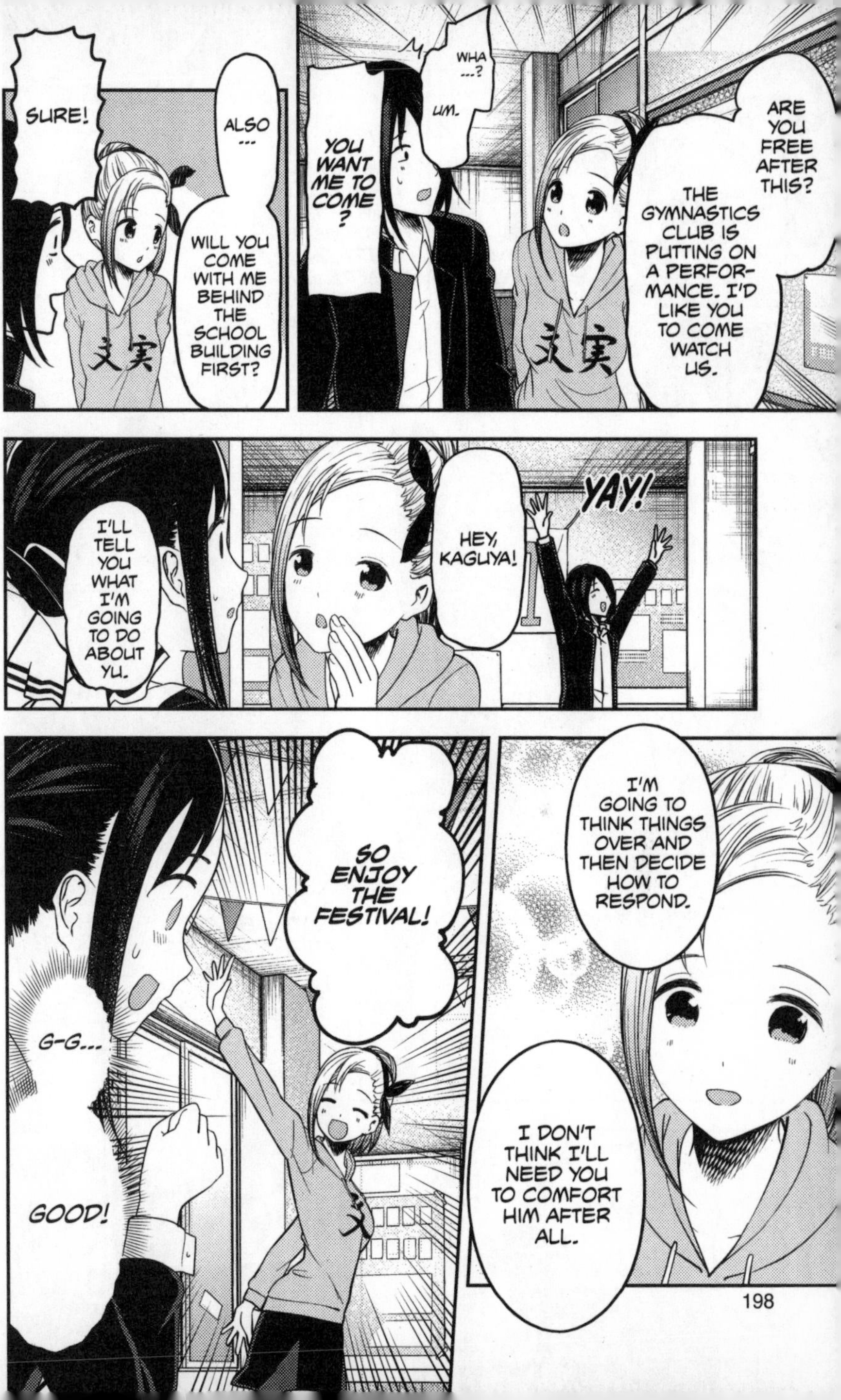
ARE YOU FREE AFTER THIS?
THE GYMNASTICS CLUB IS PUTTING ON A PERFORMANCE. I'D LIKE YOU TO COME WATCH US.
WHA ...?
UM.
YOU WANT ME TO COME?
ALSO ...
WILL YOU COME WITH ME BEHIND THE SCHOOL BUILDING FIRST?
SURE!
YAY!
HEY, KAGUYA!
I'LL TELL YOU WHAT I'M GOING TO DO ABOUT YU.
I'M GOING TO THINK THINGS OVER AND THEN DECIDE HOW TO RESPOND.
I DON'T THINK I'LL NEED YOU TO COMFORT HIM AFTER ALL.
SO ENJOY THE FESTIVAL!
G-G...
GOOD!

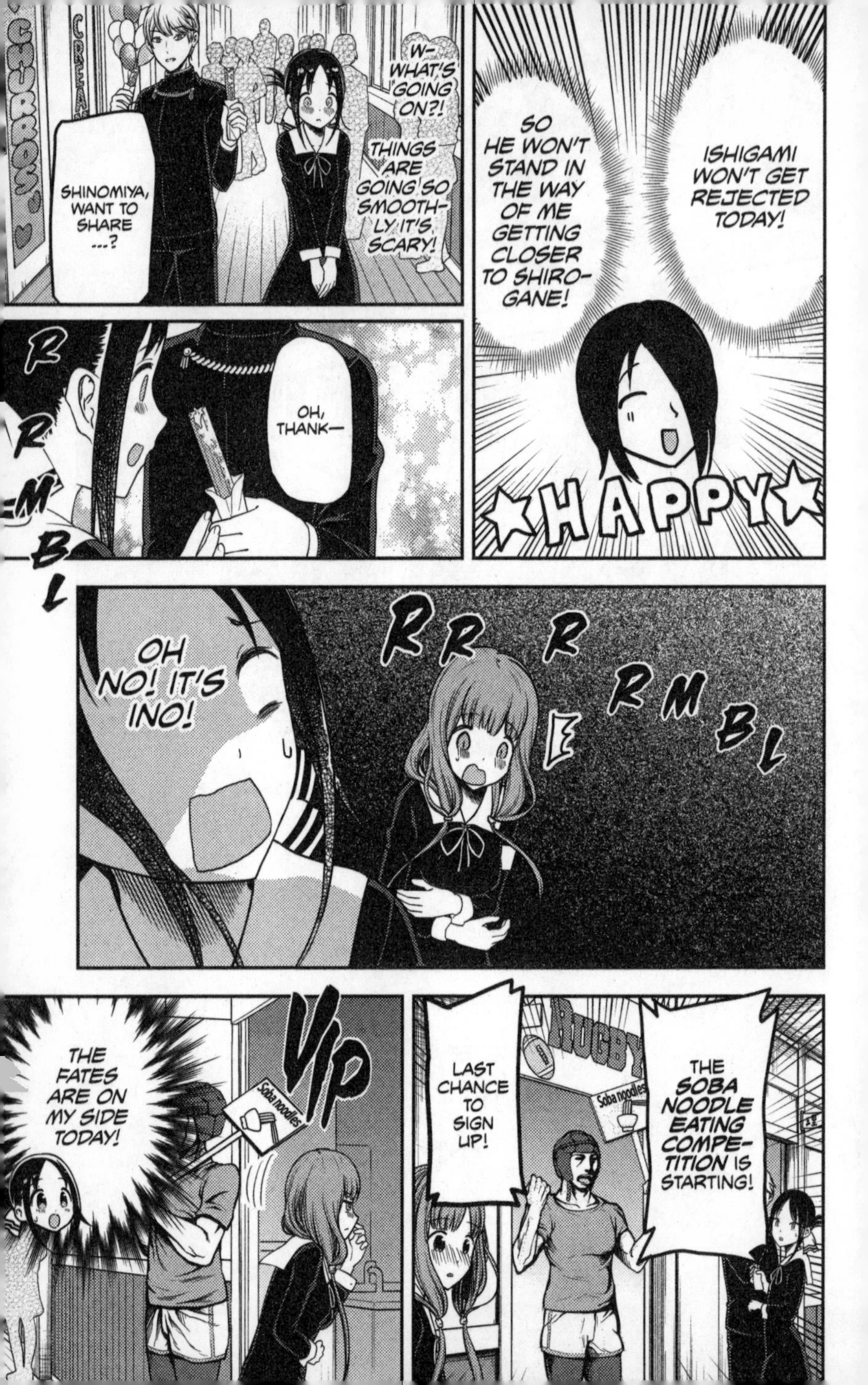
ISHIGAMI WON'T GET REJECTED TODAY!
SO HE WON'T STAND IN THE WAY OF ME GETTING CLOSER TO SHIRO-GANE!
★HAPPY★
CHURROS
W-WHAT'S GOING ON?!
THINGS ARE GOING SO SMOOTH-LY IT'S SCARY!
SHINOMIYA, WANT TO SHARE ---?
OH, THANK—
RRMBL
OH NO! IT'S INO!
RRRRMBLE
RUGBY
Soba noodles
THE SOBA NOODLE EATING COMPE-TITION IS STARTING!
LAST CHANCE TO SIGN UP!
THE FATES ARE ON MY SIDE TODAY!
Soba noodles

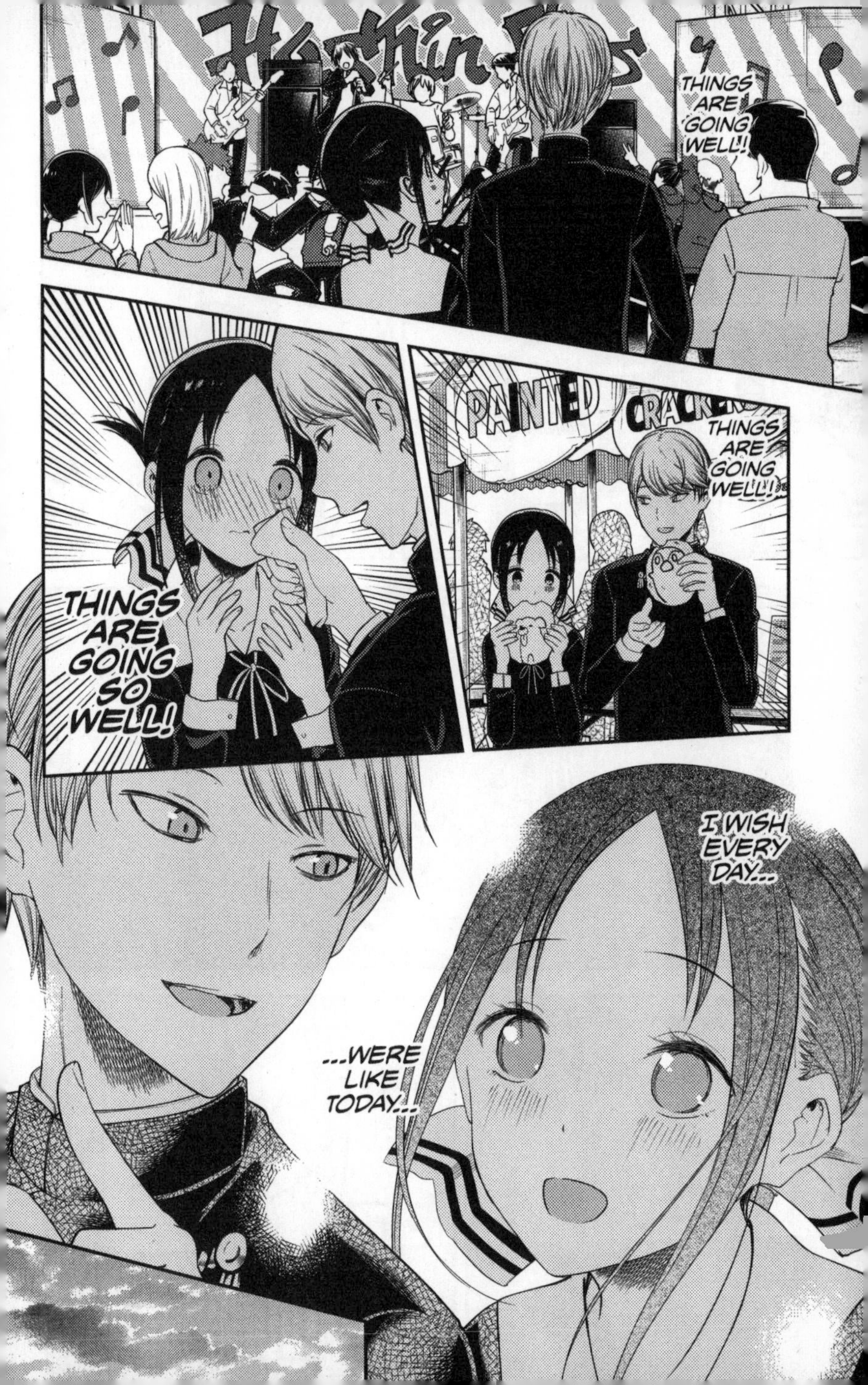
THINGS ARE GOING WELL!!
PAINTED
CRACKERS
THINGS ARE GOING WELL!!
THINGS ARE GOING SO WELL!
I WISH EVERY DAY...
...WERE LIKE TODAY...

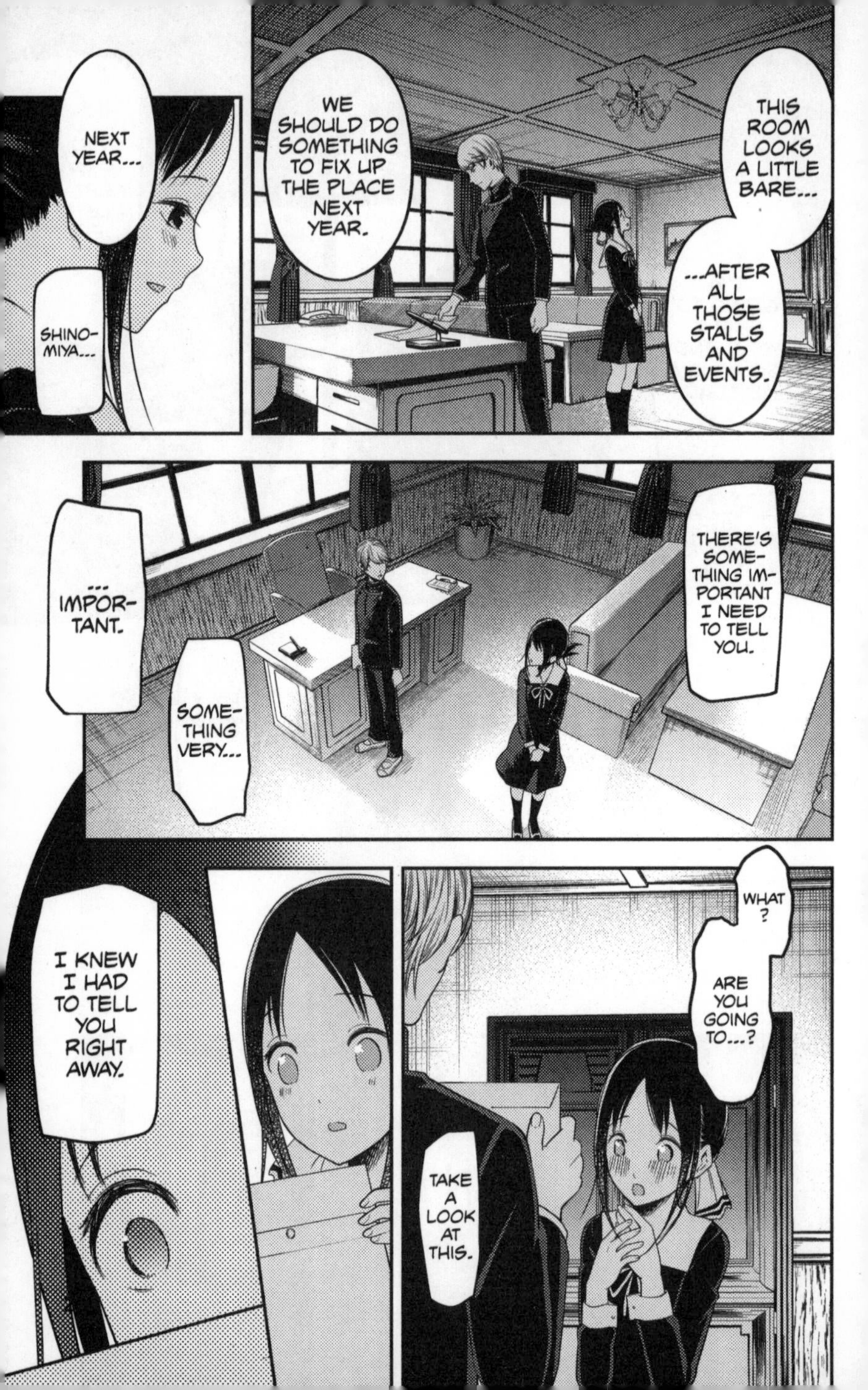
THIS ROOM LOOKS A LITTLE BARE...
...AFTER ALL THOSE STALLS AND EVENTS.
WE SHOULD DO SOMETHING TO FIX UP THE PLACE NEXT YEAR.
NEXT YEAR...
SHINOMIYA...
THERE'S SOMETHING IMPORTANT I NEED TO TELL YOU.
SOMETHING VERY...
...IMPORTANT.
WHAT?
ARE YOU GOING TO...?
TAKE A LOOK AT THIS.
I KNEW I HAD TO TELL YOU RIGHT AWAY.

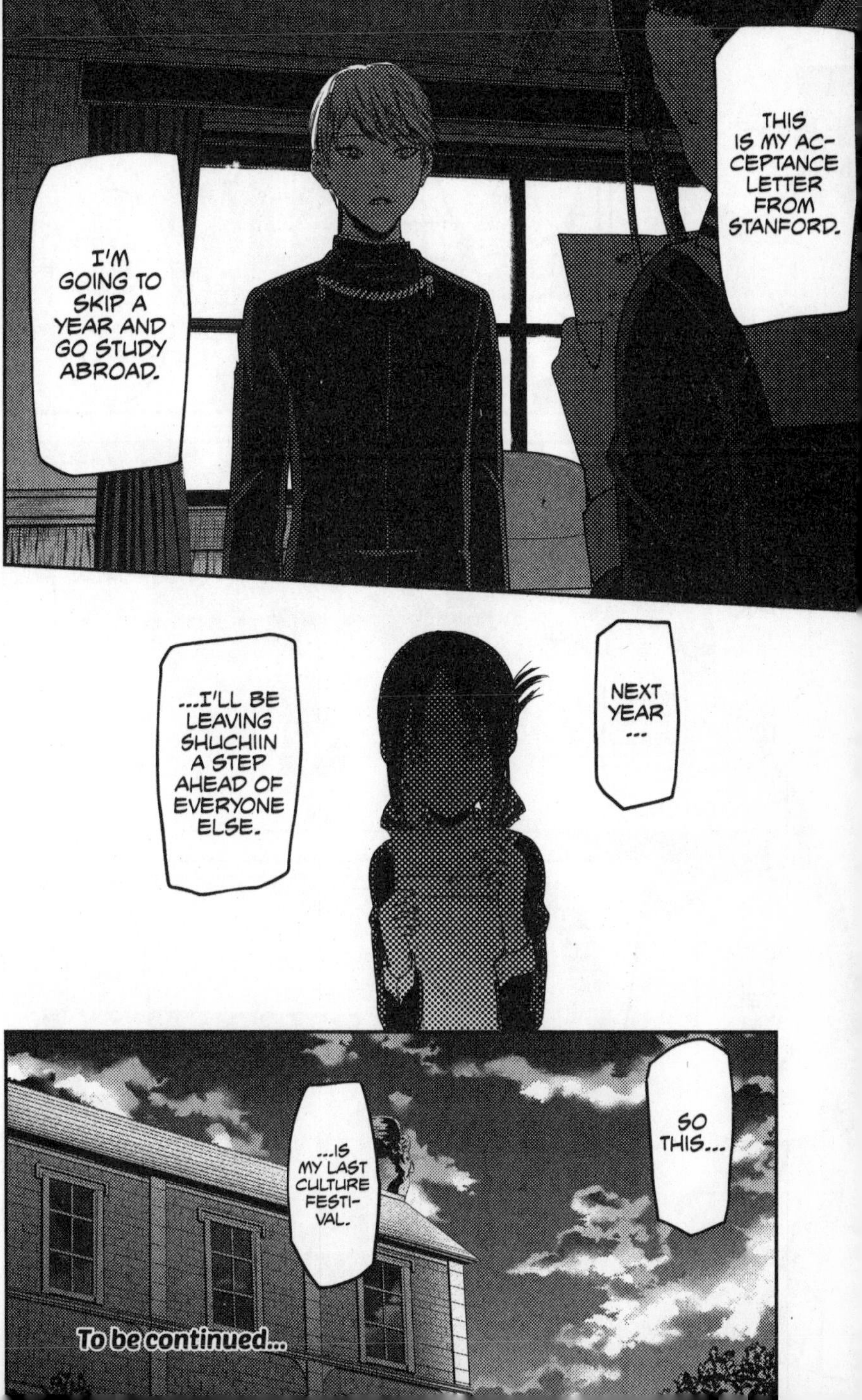
THIS IS MY ACCEPTANCE LETTER FROM STANFORD.
I'M GOING TO SKIP A YEAR AND GO STUDY ABROAD.
NEXT YEAR...
...I'LL BE LEAVING SHUCHIIN A STEP AHEAD OF EVERYONE ELSE.
SO THIS...
...IS MY LAST CULTURE FESTIVAL.
To be continued...

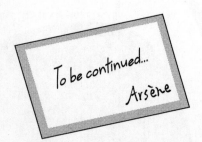

To be continued...

Arsène

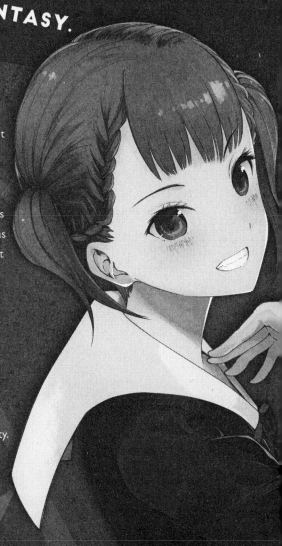

"PURE LOVE" IS A FANTASY.

AKA AKASAKA

Aka Akasaka got his start as an assistant to Jinsei Kataoka and Kazuma Kondou, the creators of *Deadman Wonderland*. His first serialized manga was an adaptation of the light novel series *Sayonara Piano Sonata*, published by Kadokawa in 2011. *Kaguya-sama: Love Is War* began serialization in *Miracle Jump* in 2015 but was later moved to *Weekly Young Jump* in 2016 due to its popularity.

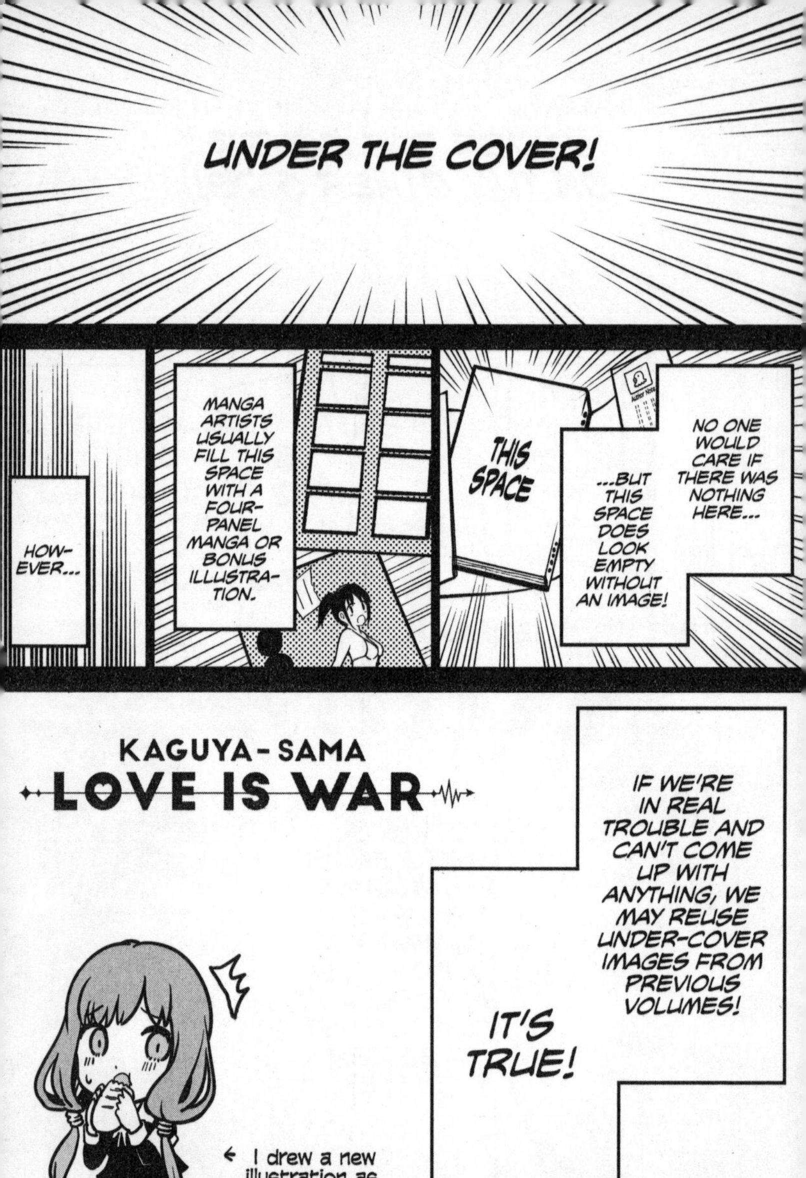
UNDER THE COVER!
NO ONE WOULD CARE IF THERE WAS NOTHING HERE...
...BUT THIS SPACE DOES LOOK EMPTY WITHOUT AN IMAGE!
THIS SPACE
MANGA ARTISTS USUALLY FILL THIS SPACE WITH A FOUR-PANEL MANGA OR BONUS ILLUSTRATION.
HOW-EVER...
IF WE'RE IN REAL TROUBLE AND CAN'T COME UP WITH ANYTHING, WE MAY REUSE UNDER-COVER IMAGES FROM PREVIOUS VOLUMES!
IT'S TRUE!
KAGUYA-SAMA
LOVE IS WAR
← I drew a new illustration as an apology.

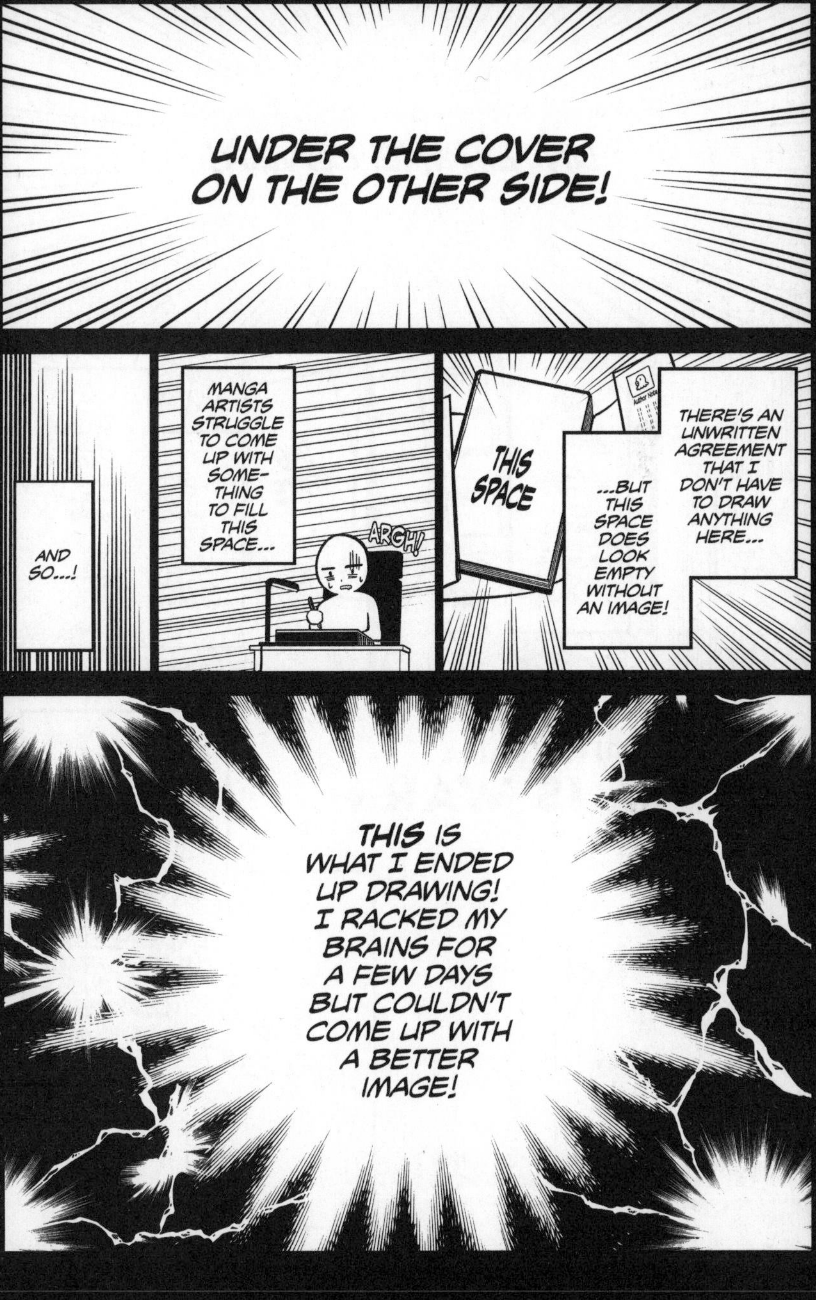
UNDER THE COVER ON THE OTHER SIDE!
THERE'S AN UNWRITTEN AGREEMENT THAT I DON'T HAVE TO DRAW ANYTHING HERE...
...BUT THIS SPACE DOES LOOK EMPTY WITHOUT AN IMAGE!
THIS SPACE
MANGA ARTISTS STRUGGLE TO COME UP WITH SOME-THING TO FILL THIS SPACE...
ARGH!
AND SO...!
THIS IS WHAT I ENDED UP DRAWING! I RACKED MY BRAINS FOR A FEW DAYS BUT COULDN'T COME UP WITH A BETTER IMAGE!

KAGUYA-SAMA
LOVE IS WAR

SHONEN JUMP MANGA EDITION

13

STORY AND ART BY
Aka Akasaka

Translation/Tomoko Kimura
English Adaptation/Annette Roman
Touch-Up Art & Lettering/Stephen Dutro
Cover & Interior Design/Alice Lewis
Editor/Annette Roman

KAGUYA-SAMA WA KOKURASETAI~TENSAITACHI NO REN'AI ZUNO SEN~
© 2015 by Aka Akasaka
All rights reserved.
First published in Japan in 2015 by SHUEISHA Inc., Tokyo.
English translation rights arranged by SHUEISHA Inc.

Printed in Italy

Published by VIZ Media, LLC
P.O. Box 77010
San Francisco, CA 94107

10 9 8 7 6 5 4 3 2
First printing, March 2020
Second printing, June 2021

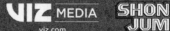

VIZ MEDIA
viz.com

SHONEN JUMP

COMING NEXT VOLUME

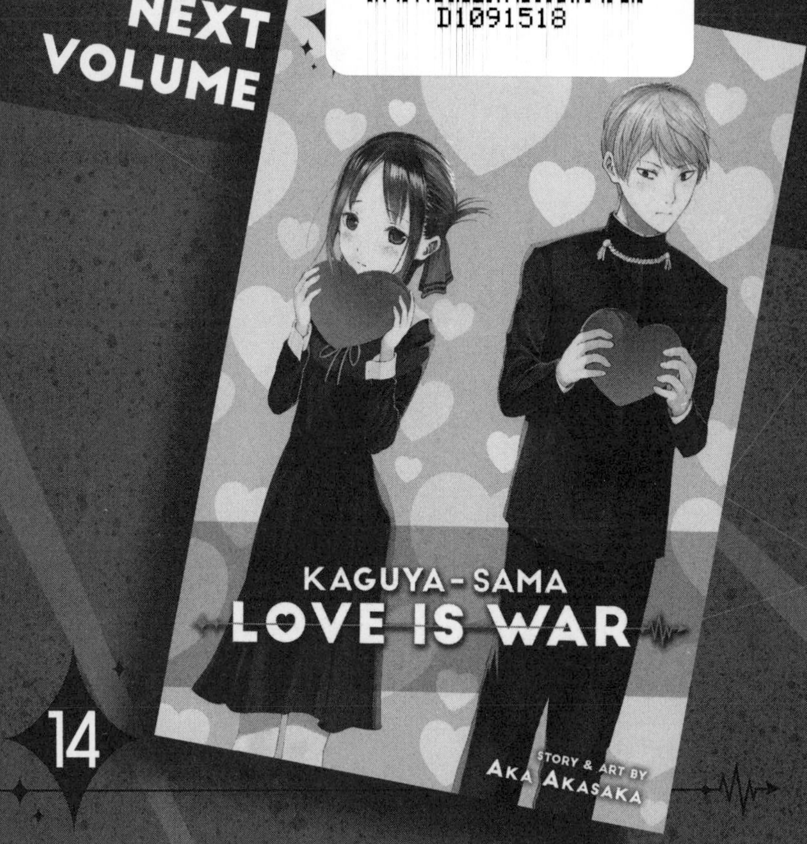
KAGUYA-SAMA
LOVE IS WAR
14
STORY & ART BY
AKA AKASAKA

Will it be Miyuki or Kaguya who finally breaks down and confesses their love for the other? Will the love confession be terribly bungled or epically orchestrated? And will the recipient respond appropriately, insanely, or in kind? While these questions will have answers, the romantic quandaries of the rest of the members of the student council will raise a whole new set of questions...

Three months is a long time.